PINAKOTHEK DER MODERNE MUNICH

MODERN ART COLLECTION

Deutscher
Kunstverlag

Deutscher
Kunstverlag

PINAKOTHEK DER MODERNE MUNICH
MODERN ART COLLECTION

Edited by Bernhard Maaz

With contributions by
Judith Csiki, Nadine Engel, Simone Förster, Inka Graeve Ingelmann, Verena Hein, Oliver Kase, Bernhard Maaz, Bernhart Schwenk, Benjamin Sommer, Franziska Stöhr, Corinna Thierolf and Anna Volz

PINAKOTHEK
DER MODERNE

CONTENTS

7 The Modern Art Collection – Facets of Its History
29 Beginnings – The Avant-garde(s) after 1900
41 Expressionism – *Brücke* and *Der Blaue Reiter*
57 Fragmentation and Re-Formation – From Cubism to Futurism
69 Apocalypse – Artists and the First World War
85 Abstraction and Construction – The Bauhaus and Its Circle
99 The Golden Twenties? – *Neue Sachlichkeit* and Neoclassicism
119 *Neues Sehen* – Photography in the 1920s and 1930s
133 Visions – Surrealism and Magic Realism
147 Propaganda, Conformism, Withdrawal, Criticism, Exclusion, and Exile – The Nazi Period
163 Pain and Hope – After the Second World War
175 'The Global Language of Abstraction' – Gestures and Constructions
193 The Infinite and the Tangible – The Unbounding of the Image
211 Unease – The Post-War Generation
233 New Documents – The Photography of the 1960s and 1970s
251 Installations – In Space and Time
261 Emotion and Hardness – Painting after 1970
277 Objectively Subjective – A Paradigm Shift in Photography
297 Close-Up – Video and Media Art
313 Starting Line – Art in the 21st Century
340 Index of Persons
343 Credits

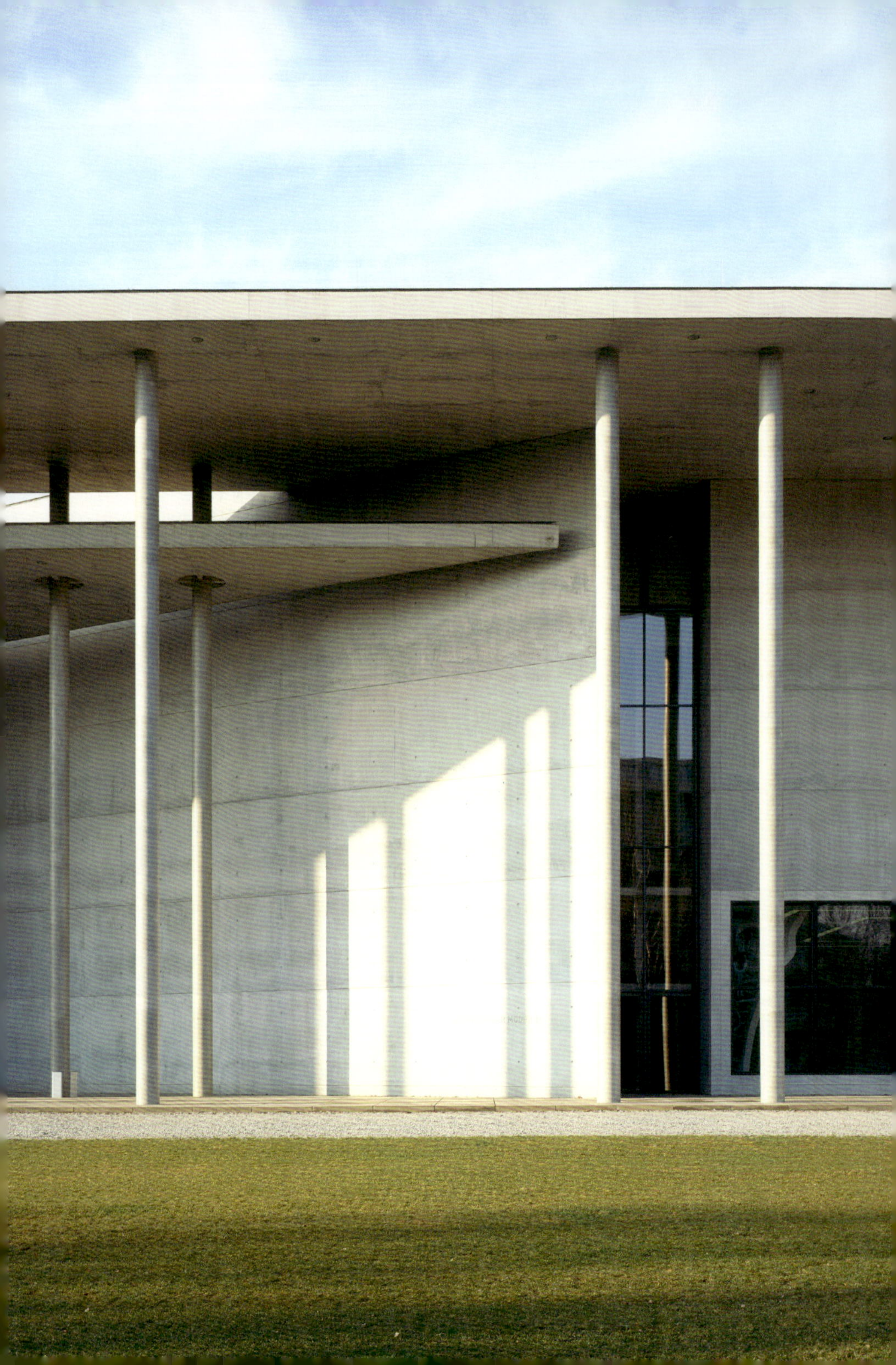

THE MODERN ART COLLECTION
FACETS OF ITS HISTORY

Modern(ism)

With its name and own separate site, the Pinakothek der Moderne arguably follows in the tradition established by the Alte Pinakothek and the Neue Pinakothek buildings, designed respectively by Leo von Klenze and Alexander von Branca. However, the task facing the building's architect, Stephan Braunfels, was different to that of his predecessors. Characterized primarily by concrete and glass, and its signature interplay between clear open spaces and a shading wall (fig. 1), the building was intended from the very outset to house a number of collections: the Architekturmuseum der TU München, the Staatliche Graphische Sammlung Munich, Die Neue Sammlung – The Design Museum Munich, and (the subject of the present book) the Sammlung Moderne Kunst (Modern Art Collection). Visitors heading to these treasures walk through outdoor spaces used for displaying sculptures, which together with the area surrounding the Alte Pinakothek and Neue Pinakothek is known as the nucleus of Munich's Kunstareal. Eduardo Chillida's *Buscando la Luz* (fig. 2) here provides a welcome soft-edged contrast to the delicate grey of the building's exposed concrete and its alternately transparent or mirrored, albeit hard, glass surfaces. The vivid shade of the rust patina on steel creates an appealing interplay with the surrounding colours and materials, while the marks left by rain running over the surfaces of the sculpture lend the work a sense of transformability, dynamism, and charm. Furthermore, the way the space is defined resembles a gesture inviting people to approach, like an introduction leading up to the museum in which the theme of sculpture both continues and mixes with other art forms.

The name 'Pinakothek der Moderne' is well established, yet where does 'the modern' actually begin? Is it in Dürer's work, because modern men and women appear as individuals? Caspar David Friedrich, because his work thematizes the isolation of modern man? Monet or Manet, because they create summary, fluid, impressionistic visions in place of a contoured view of the world? Or with Vincent van Gogh, because the productive artistic life he

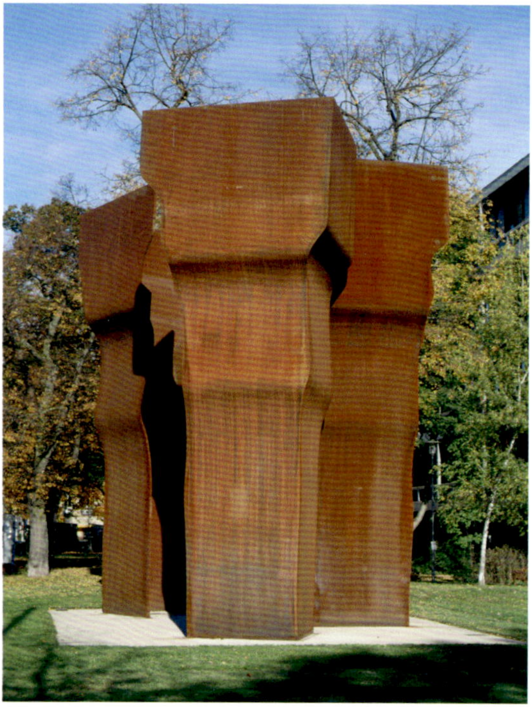

1 (Page 6) The Pinakothek der Moderne, view from the north.

2 Eduardo Chillida, Buscando la Luz (Looking for the Light), 1997, in three parts, rolled steel, each 798 cm in height, each occupying space measuring approx. 150 × 140 × 150 cm, inv. no. B 900; acquired 2002 with funding for *Kunst am Bau* and a donation of a private benefactor.

led was of a radicalism and individuality practically never seen before in any other artist? One might also tentatively entertain the notion that modern art began with Pablo Picasso and Georges Braque. Following in direct succession to them, or so William Boyd would have readers of the novel *Nat Tate* believe (published in 1998, shortly before the opening of the Pinakothek der Moderne) was a great but unknown figure, the legendary artist 'Nat Tate'. Tate is portrayed as a shy loner: 'and he is barely remembered by any of the school's more celebrated alumni. He dressed soberly, almost old-fashionedly, in jackets and ties (a habit he was never fully to abandon), worked hard and, out of classroom hours, kept himself largely to himself'.[1] The dandy, the beau, the loner, the intellectual combatant *par excellence*? Who is a modern artist, or rather, what is he (or she) like? The account proceeds to give more about Tate's fortunes and other facts, with the biographer then resuming: 'My own feeling is that the meeting with Braque and the opportunity to see some of Braque's great final paintings removed the last supports from a person and a personality that was, by all accounts, a fragile one, however charming and easy on the eye.'[2] Crushed by the superiority of the great names of art history, this fictional artist takes his own life: 'There was in his suicide a great unhappy massing of symbols – of art, of blissful escape, of despair.'[3] Much to the reader's relief, the author reveals at the end of the book that Nat Tate is a sophisticated, humorous fiction, whose apparent biography draws together details, facts, and clichés of the modern artist as a particular character type. Regardless of Tate's fictional status, the text is enormously relevant. Work and counterfeiting, value and reputation, desire and the market – all are subject to ironic scrutiny in a book which appeared long before the name of the master counterfeiter Wolfgang Beltracchi gained widespread notoriety: a man exposed as a diabolically shrewd operator, who had freeloaded off modern art and the modern art market, an imitator unburdened by conscience and a legendary charlatan. Ultimately, the question remains: where in art is the essence of 'the modern' to be found? Where is it to be observed as something insurmountable – *unhintergehbar*, to employ the philosophical term – and ineluctable, or at the very least, unchanging? The greatest achievements of modernism are in its defence of creativity, the individual, and the freedom of art, which draws life from social relevance and topicality.

Modern art(ists) in Munich

Modern art had its geographic centres. Paris! Berlin! Dresden. And Munich. After Dresden became, in 1905, the birthplace of *Brücke* artist community, and by extension, German Expressionism, the group soon relocated to Berlin (only for half the members then to disband). Then, with Russian artists acting as a significant catalyst, Munich gave rise to *Der Blaue Reiter*. Nevertheless, overall Berlin continued to set the standard. After being effectively 'banished' by the Kaiser from his post as head of the Nationalgalerie in Berlin, Hugo von Tschudi worked as a museum director in Bavaria between 1909 and 1911. In the short period Tschudi spent here before his early death, he proved destined never to fulfil the goal already denied to him in Berlin: to bring together and establish a modern gallery collection that would serve as an international benchmark. In the years up to 1914, Heinz Braune continued to pursue the course set by these innovative plans thanks to the 'Tschudi Fund', to which its namesake had made a commendable bequest. Braune worked with finely honed instincts towards bringing works to Munich by such artists as Vincent van Gogh, who, although deceased, were nonetheless still a palpable force in art. Their works could now be secured using donated money.

However, things then went quiet again. Writing in 1919 to Walter Kaesbach about the Berlin Kronprinzenpalais – which not long after would serve, along with the Bauhaus in Dessau, as the inspiration for the Museum of Modern Art in New York, the now legendary MoMA[4] – Erich Hauer noted: 'We visited the new gallery together. The overall impact is rather favourable, particularly in comparison with the modern German section in Munich and Hamburg. Unfortunately, there are still some anomalies. For example, the absence of Mueller, the single solitary drawing by Schmidt-Rottluff, the absence of Rohlfs and Munch. But this can of course still be remedied.'[5] The absence of Rohlfs was not 'remedied' until 2017. However, the Bayerische Staatsgemäldesammlungen (Bavarian State Painting Collections) continued to rise in ranks in the late 20th century to become one of the most important museum organizations of modern art. The commitment to acquisitions after Tschudi's death – which he had himself been unable to accomplish in his lifetime – laid an unmistakable cornerstone in a collection which, in the period after 1945, was to enjoy similarly integral contributions from collectors, patrons, and benefactors. Tschudi, the freethinker from Switzerland, was a friend to art and artists, and maintained contact with the painters of *Der Blaue Reiter*. When in 1917, a year after Franz Marc was killed in the First World War, the artist's painting *Red Deer II* (p. 48) entered the Munich collections, the acquisition was the act of

3 Franz Marc, Cows I, 1913, oil on canvas, 92 × 130.8 cm, inv. no. 10987; acquired 1949.

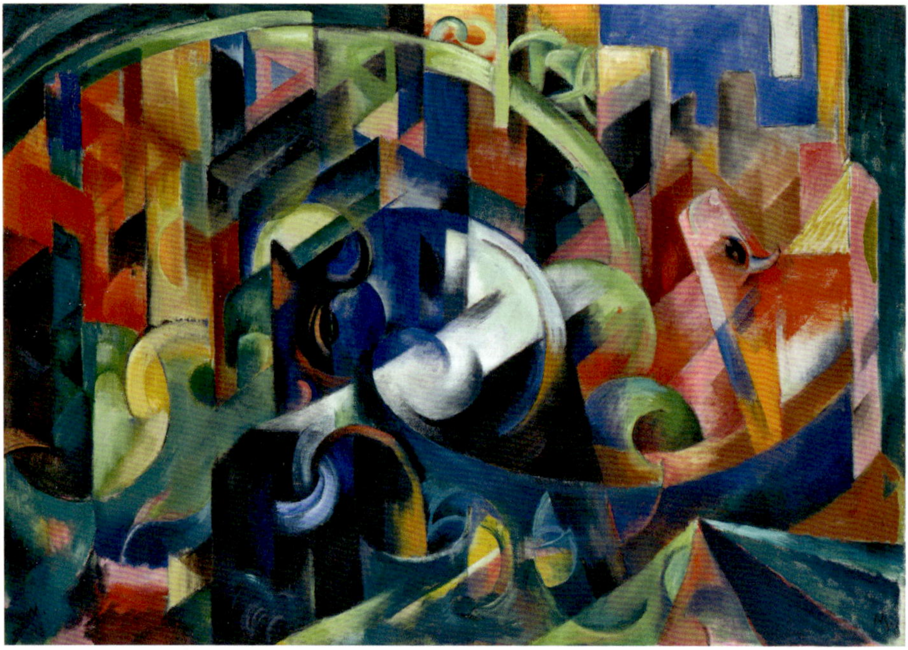

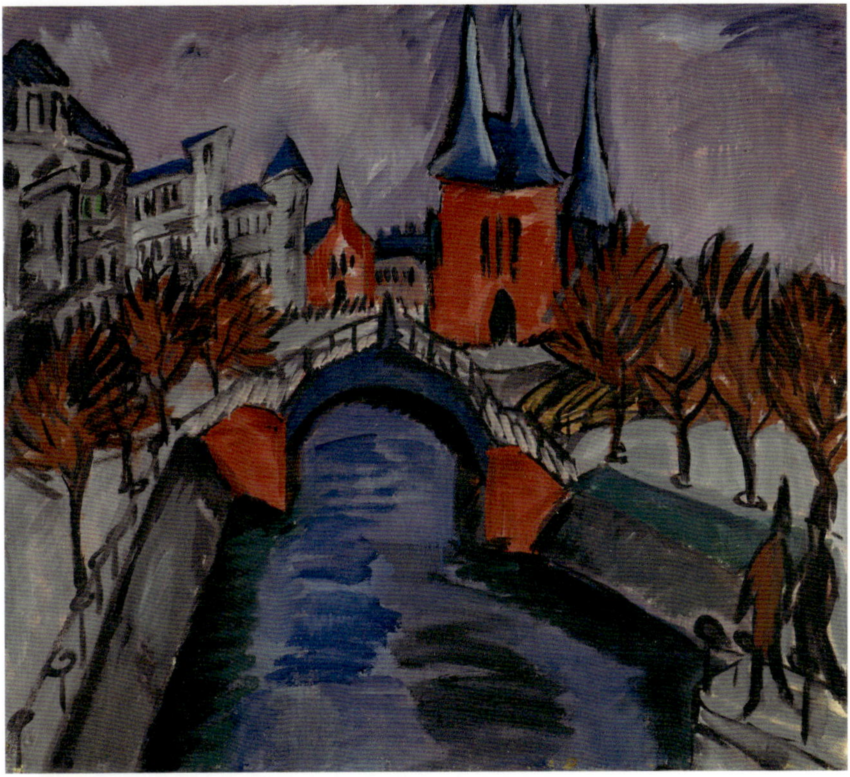

4 Ernst Ludwig Kirchner, Elisabethufer, 1913, oil on canvas, 83.5 × 94 cm, inv. no. 14530; bequest of Martha and Markus Kruss, 1977.

an individual, but at the same time it served as a monument and keystone to pre-war modern art in the city – a memento, a final cadence. As the war raged, this work by Franz Marc became an emblem of lives cut short, modern art brought low, and creativity forever silenced.

Marc's *Red Deer II* cut a lonely figure at the museum. Prior to the First World War, then-director general Friedrich Dörnhöffer founded the Neue Staatsgalerie in the exhibition building at Königsplatz, but his notion of 'modern' was different to our own. Works such as Franz Marc's *Cows I* would not appear until a generation later in the period after the Second World War (fig. 3). Such works' consistent potential for innovation, their neo-Romantic energy, and relentless questioning of nature and human experience were to remain unappreciated for many years. During the entire period of the Weimar Republic, there was no attempt to seize upon the opportunity to create a

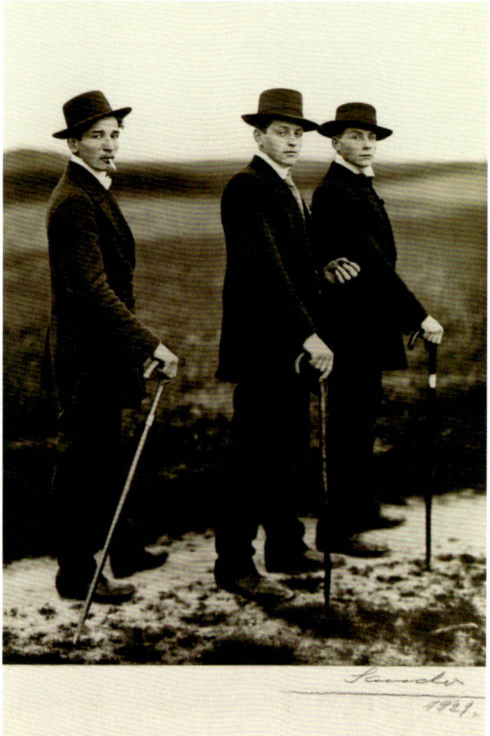

5 August Sander, Young Farmers, 1914, gelatin silver print on paper, 22.8 × 17 cm, inv. no. AJW 364; Ann and Jürgen Wilde Foundation.

groundbreaking museum of modern art. What had occurred before the First World War was forgotten and duly faded. Munich did not produce pictures of the modern city comparable to those by Berlin artists, such as Ernst Ludwig Kirchner's *Elisabethufer* (fig. 4). Marc and Macke were killed in action, Kandinsky emigrated, while other artists moved to the countryside or remained entrenched in the war. As for other styles in art, it is worth noting the example of August Sander, who created a photographic work in 1914 that only entered the museum's collection one hundred years later (fig. 5).

Munich without modernism?

The Bayerische Staatsgemäldesammlungen enjoyed constant growth from the 16th century, its richest gains after the decades around 1800 being achieved by dynastic factors. During the reign of Ludwig I of Bavaria in the first half of the 19th century, the king ordered the construction of the Alte Pinakothek and provided artists with a variety of commissions for his building projects and became a keen buyer of their works. This lent the collection a new sense of purpose, followed by an acquisitions policy that was international in scope in the years before and after 1900. However, an examination of the inventory published in 1920 of exhibited modern artworks reveals how thin the pickings were in terms of items of lasting value.[6] Numerous conventional works had accumulated. Who today knows Hugo von Habermann, Karl Hagemeister, Theodor Hagen? Experts know about the one-time significance of Lovis Corinth, Franz von Stuck, Hans Thoma and Wilhelm Trübner: they were the epitome of modernizing forces that went beyond salon art. The truly groundbreaking figures of this time were internationally successfully painters like Cézanne, Denis, Gauguin, Van Gogh, Manet, Monet, Pissarro, Renoir, and Vuillard. The Neue Pinakothek at this stage still stood on the site later occupied by Branca's successor building, with works that were a century ago considered 'modern' crystallizing into the core component held in the collection's home. However, '[the] separation of the modern art section from the main collection proved inevitable, as the Neue Pinakothek building possessed neither sufficient nor

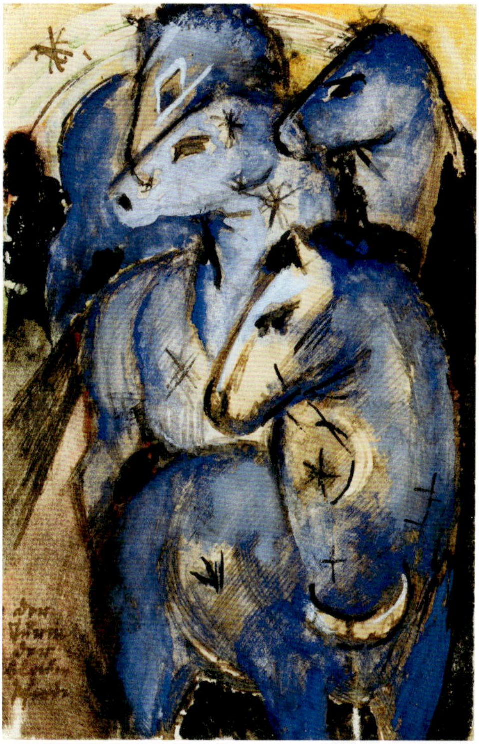

6 Franz Marc, The Tower of Blue Horses, 1912, ink and gouache on card, 14.1 × 9.4 cm, inv. no. 13550; donation of Sofie and Emmanuel Fohn, 1964.

appropriate space to display the group judiciously'.[7] Tellingly, the third edition of the inventory published in 1925 was substantially expanded to include (in particular) drawing, and hence a new art form for the collection. Some of these drawings came to the collection as loans, others as donations, and included the work of such artists as Cézanne, Corot, Van Gogh, Manet, and Rodin. The German Expressionists were still absent, although of course visitors would still have expected to see works by deceased Munich-based artists, for example Franz Marc's postcard with *The Tower of Blue Horses* (fig. 6). Yet this work would have to wait another four decades to join the collection, and then only thanks to Sofie and Emanuel Fohn's donation, which in conjunction with other works of modern art was intended (and has proven) to be a belated enhancement to the collection. Nevertheless in the years up to 1925, new acquisitions included Alexander Kanoldt's *Still Life with Mask* (1920), Edvard Munch's *Peasant with White Horse* and *Young Lady on a Veranda* – works, that is, with considerable innovative power. The reason these works would then have to leave the museum again, however, becomes clear from the historical context of 1937: they were considered 'degenerate'.

Missed, ostracized, persecuted

The Neue Staatsgalerie headed by Friedrich Dörnhöffer was expanded in 1932 to include a new wing through the creation of a 'Living Artist Section' housed in the still-unfinished (!) new library building of the Deutsches Museum abutting the River Isar.[8] However, the location and historical context meant this was a branch destined never to blossom, effectively relegating modern art to an architectural stopgap in a cut-off location. After the Nazis came to power in 1933, developing the project was no longer a realistic prospect. Munich was therefore left behind for want of buildings, budget, and courage.

With Dörnhöffer's advancing age resulting in his replacement as director-general by Ernst Buchner, an individual loyal to the Nazi regime (the Berlin Nationalgalerie with its significant collection of modern works lost a number of directors during the 1930s following targeted dismissals), there followed a period of constant political manoeuvring. That same year, the new director-general was obliged to create space in the Neue Pinakothek for the *Great Munich Art Exhibition*, transforming the museum into an expedient exposition venue, after Adolf Hitler yielded to the lobbying of the respective heads of the project and exhibition. Consequently, what little there was of modern art from the late 19th century onwards – which already lacked any examples of Expressionism, Futurism, Cubism, Orphism, Dadaism, Critical Realism, Bauhaus, Surrealism, not to mention a number of other artistic movements – was, as it were, banished to a location alien to its purpose: visitors who wished to see modern art had to go to the Deutsches Museum, where it was displayed in the context of the history of technology, and to the library building extension, where the Neue Staatsgalerie at Königsplatz was exhibiting major works from the Neue Pinakothek.

The absences in the collection described above were striking, but they did mean that the campaign raging throughout Germany against 'degenerate art' was unable to create many more gaps: the absences were, after all, already there. Nonetheless, the *Degenerate Art* exhibition at the Munich Hofgarten, which began just one day after the opening of the Haus der Kunst, was a seminal moment in art history. Among the approximately 130 works from the Staatsgemäldesammlungen confiscated on the grounds of 'degeneracy' included Günther Graßmann's perfectly harmless winter landscape *Farms in the Chiemgau*[9] (p. 154) and Franz Marc's *Red Deer II*. The latter work, though soon returned to the collection, was effectively neutered, or rather made invisible, after it became the subject of an exhibition ban. The once legendary lights of Munich as a 'city of art' had dimmed, although in reality they had only glimmered in the period after the First World War, with Berlin having taken the lead in modern at from the 1920s at the very latest.

After the Second World War

The first two decades after the Second World War witnessed the revitalization of modern art in Munich, producing figures like art critic Franz Roh, art dealer Günther Franke, and a number of artists such as Rupprecht Geiger. However, in the city's public museums, modern art lived a shadowy existence. Buchner's Nazi past led to his dismissal as director-general in 1945; he was succeeded by Eberhard Hanfstaengl. Having in 1933 replaced Ludwig Justis as director-general of the Berlin Nationalgalerie, Hanfstaengl had gained a reputation as a pliable figure close to the Nazi regime. However, he was subsequently dismissed from that role on account of his unwillingness to pursue National Socialist cultural-political doctrine with sufficient rigour. By his own reckoning, Hanfstaengl argued in 1945 that in hindsight, the benefits of his cautious approach to modern art outweighed his proximity to the political system in 1933. It was incumbent on him to reconstruct the museums, and looking back at the years post-1945 he wrote: 'The four public art museums: the Alte and Neue Pinakothek, the Staatsgalerie, and the Schack-Galerie were more or less destroyed or badly damaged.'[10] The American military government therefore assigned the west wing of the Haus der Kunst as the only usable area. The following decades were put to reconstructing the build-

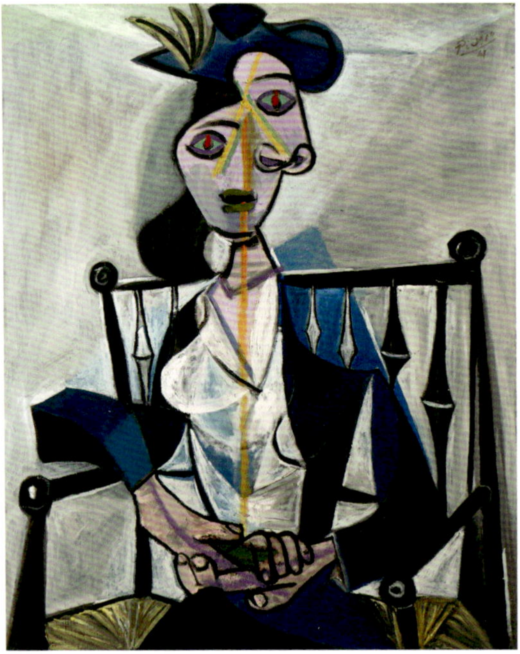

7 Pablo Picasso, Femme assise au fauteuil: Dora Maar (Seated Woman: Dora Maar), 1941, oil on canvas, 99.8 × 80.5 cm, inv. no. 14240; bequest of Theodor and Woty Werner, 1971.

ings cited above, while a parallel programme was pursued to compensate 'the losses brought about by an ignorant art policy'.[11] Here the term 'ignorant' takes on a downright euphemistic quality, applied as it was to the confiscation and destruction of 'degenerate' art. Without sufficient funds available for acquisitions, Hanfstaengl entertained the idea – or possibly presented it as threat in order to ensure funding – of resorting to the 'dubious method of exchange'[12]. By this he meant that he would be forced to fall back on the Alte Pinakothek's (storeroom) collection, as had been the practice in some places up to the 1920s. However, Hanfstaengl also pointed the way to a longer-sighted alternative by lobbying for 'a generous taxation policy'[13] that would benefit, and so generate, private donations.

The modern art collection, headed by Hanfstaengl from 1945, put Lovis Corinth's *The Knight* and *Walchensee*, and Oskar Kokoschka's *Venice* on display, and so featured three relatively recent artworks acquired in the 1920s. In addition to these was a work by Franz Marc, whose *Red Deer II* (mentioned earlier in the chapter) represented a key work of modern art, plus Henri Matisse's *Still Life with Geraniums* (p. 38) and his sculpture *The Slave*, two pieces acquired in the spirit of Hugo von Tschudi from the period before the First World War. Looking back at the first decade after the war, Hanfstaengl could appraise what had been achieved with pride: newly incorporated into what could now be rightly termed a 'modern art' collection were numerous illustrious names: Willi Baumeister, Max Beckmann, Edgar Ende, Werner Gilles, Erich Heckel, Karl Hofer, Wassily Kandinsky, Ernst Ludwig Kirchner, August Macke, Otto Mueller, Gabriele Münter, Emil Nolde, Hans Purrmann, Oskar Schlemmer, Karl Schmidt-Rottluff, and Fritz Winter. Furthermore, in addition to paintings there were now also drawings by figures such as Josef Scharl, Fritz Winter, and other artists mentioned above, while prints were represented at the Staatliche Graphische Sammlung.[14] The foundations for a veritable Sammlung der Moderne had been laid which, moreover, adopted a collection strategy that embraced multiple genres, thereby taking into account the increasingly blurred boundaries between the various art forms in modern art.

Donations, bequests, acquisitions

These efforts to establish a collection of modern art gained new impetus from the mid-1960s thanks (for example) to Sofie and Emanuel Fohn's donation of works by Jankel Adler, Max Beckmann, Otto Dix, Karl Hofer, Alexei Jawlensky,

8 Max Beckmann, Woman with Mandolin in Yellow and Red, 1950, oil on canvas, 92 × 140 cm, inv. no. 15253; acquired 1991.

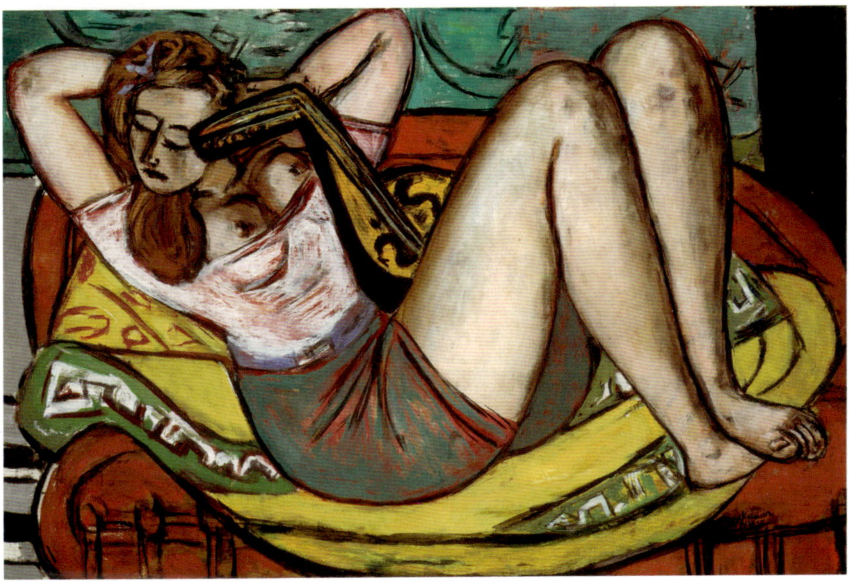

Oskar Kokoschka, August Macke, Franz Marc, and Paula Modersohn-Becker. A similarly radical accession was provided by the legacy of Theodor and Woty Werner, who bequeathed works by Paul Klee, Juan Gris, and Pablo Picasso (fig. 7). Equally significant was the Günther Franke Endowment in 1974, featuring numerous works by Max Beckmann, and the acquisition of artworks from the estate of Etta and Otto Stangl, which allowed the collection to grow into what it is today: the largest collection of Max Beckmann's art in Europe (fig. 8). Moreover, significant suites of works joined the collection by virtue of the legacy of Klaus Gebhard, which boasted art by Willi Baumeister, Max Ernst, Jasper Johns, Ernst Ludwig Kirchner, Paul Klee, Giorgio Morandi, and Robert Rauschenberg, and items bequeathed by Martha and Markus Kruss encompassing works by artists of *Brücke* through to Ernst Wilhelm Nay. The Theo Wormland Foundation first presented the museums with loans in the early 1980s before its complete endowment in 2013 gave rise to a collection practically without peer in Germany, specializing in Surrealism and the New Figuration, and ranging from works by Werner Heldt via Max Ernst and René Magritte through to Pablo Picasso.

9 Henry Moore, Reclining Figure, 1969/70, 220 × 364 cm, inv. no. B 776; acquired in 1981 with the transfer of the new building of the Neue Pinakothek.

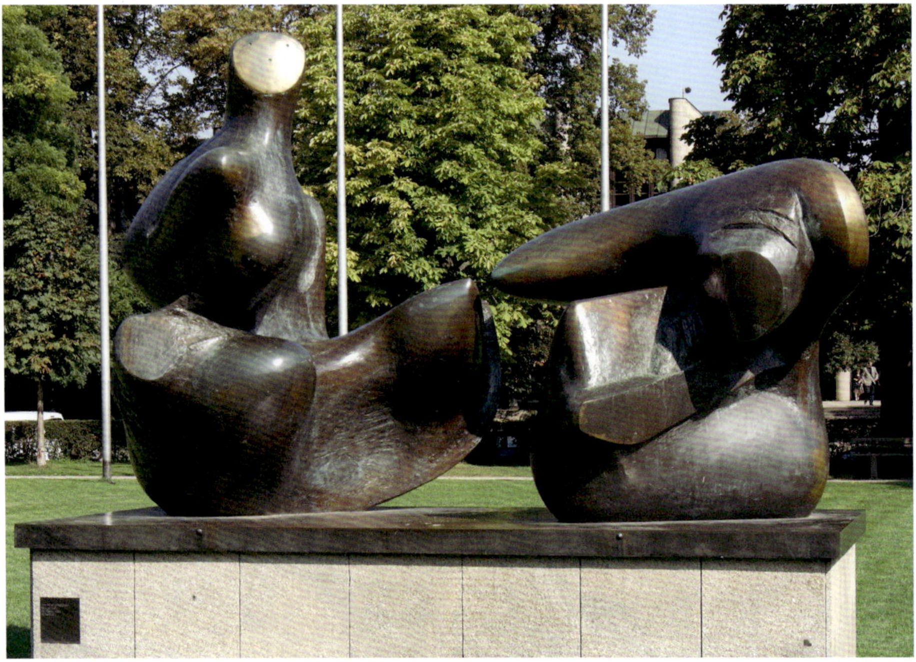

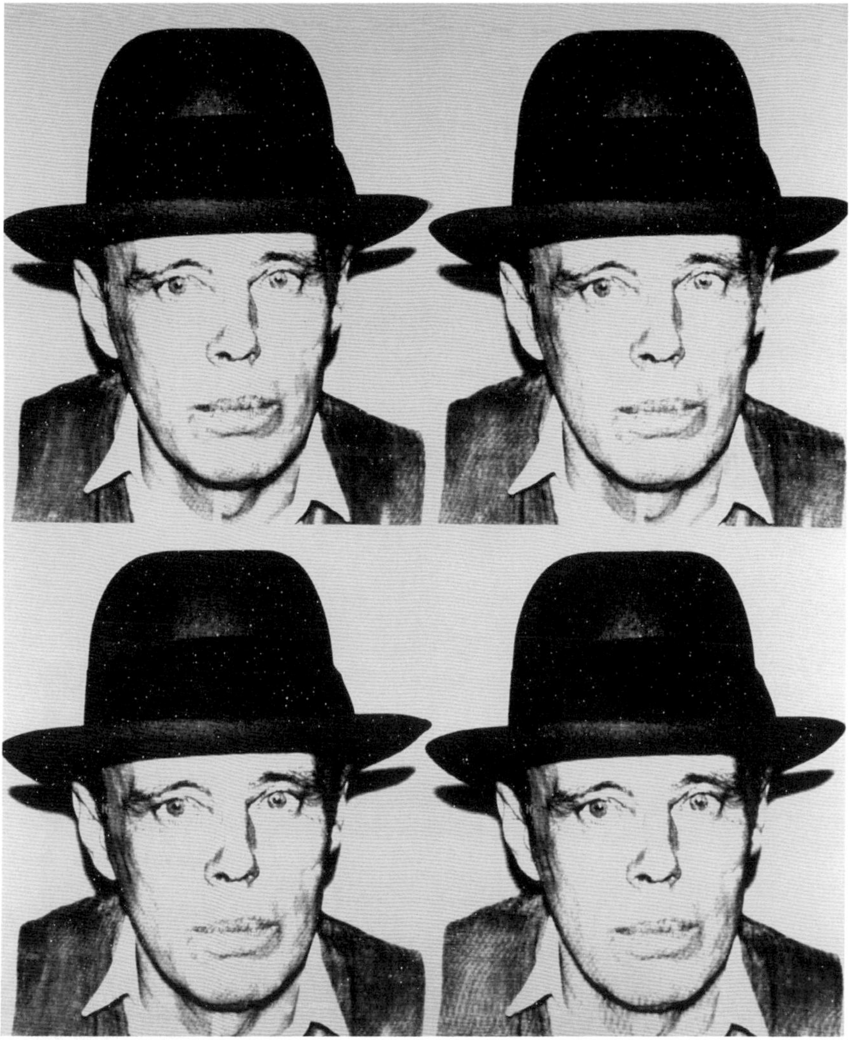

10 Andy Warhol, Joseph Beuys, 1980, screen print, synthetic resin and diamond dust on canvas, 213.5 × 178 cm, inv. no. GV 126; acquired 2001 by PIN. Freunde der Pinakothek der Moderne for the Modern Art Collection.

There were of course also standard acquisitions, such as Henry Moore's *Reclining Figure* (fig. 9), characterized by its carefully struck balance between traditional figurative representation and modern art's transcendence of form, on display in the outdoor space between the different Pinakothek museums. This sculpture has subsequently become as much a part of the canon of post-war modern art as Francis Bacon's *Crucifixion* (pp. 166–167). The Galerie-Verein acquired this triptych just one year after its foundation in 1966, effectively signalling the direction the organization intended to take. Works by Joseph Beuys also numbered among its formative acquisitions (p. 172, 191, 202, pp. 254–255). Known today as 'PIN. Freunde der Pinakothek der Moderne', an organization working on behalf of the four museum collections housed in the building (its remit expanding in recent years to also include the Museum Brandhorst), the patrons society brought together a group of actively engaged art-lovers. Alongside collector-donors (as well as collector couples) and the state, the organization constitutes the third pillar maintaining the collection. Recent works acquired by this organization were accorded considerable recognition in a major exhibition and an accompanying catalogue, featuring yet more major artists: Georges Braque, Heinrich Maria Davringhausen, Wassily Kandinsky, Paul Klee, Fernand Léger.[15] American artists, who today occupy an important place in Munich and lend a lustre to the city's art collections for which it is known far and wide, number among those names, including Carl Andre, Dan Flavin, Franz Kline, Willem de Kooning, Donald Judd, Sol LeWitt, Fred Sandback, Richard Serra, and Andy Warhol (fig. 10), as well as Canadian artists such as Jeff Wall (fig. 11). The pioneering efforts behind these acquisitions are perhaps not immediately obvious from our modern-day perspective; their boldness can only be

11 Jeff Wall, An Eviction, 1988/2004, large picture slide in lightbox, 229 × 414 cm, inv. no. 15319; acquired 1992.

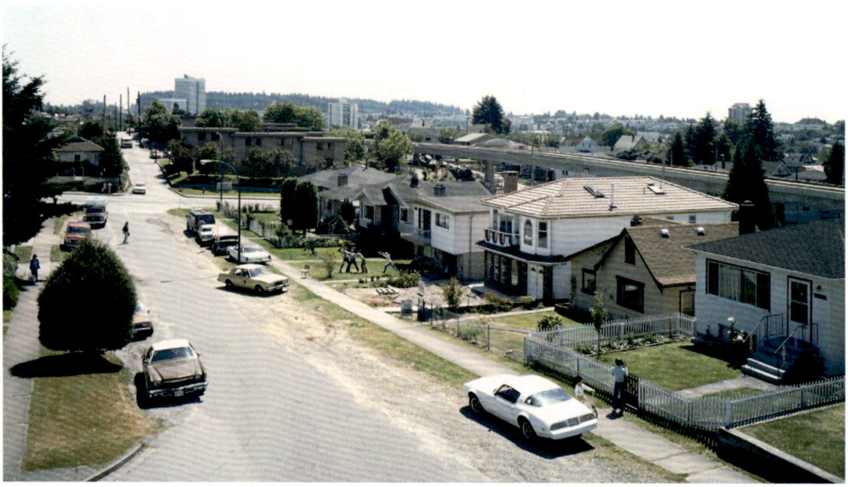

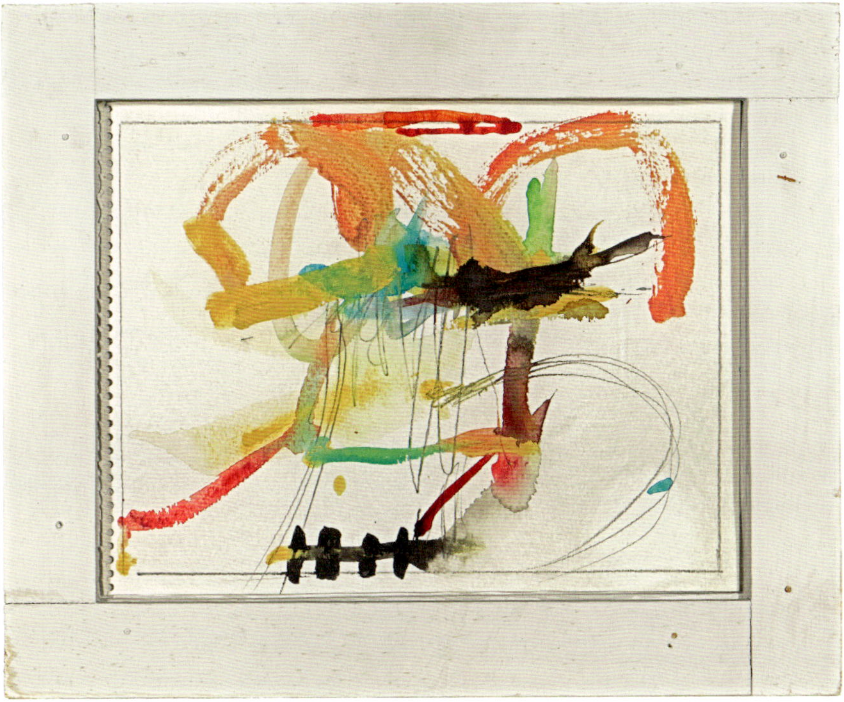

12 Richard Tuttle, False Nexus, 1991, watercolour and pencil on paper, 22.5 × 30.5 cm, inv. no. 16415; donation of Christof and Ursula Engelhorn, Art Mentor Foundation, Lucerne, 2015.

gauged when understood in the context of the reticence and rejection that characterized attitudes to modern art in that period.

Mention should also be made of works by Baselitz, Immendorf, Kiefer, Lüpertz, Palermo, Penck, Polke, Rainer, Richter, and Soulages, transferred by Duke (formerly Prince) Franz of Bavaria to the collection via the Wittelsbacher Ausgleichsfond. Similarly, Otto van de Loos' donation of Antonio Saura's *Crucifixion* (p. 170), and most recently, the donation by the Art Mentor Foundation of works from Albers via Morandi through to Richard Tuttle (fig. 12) and Dan Flavin (p. 256). Permanent loans such as the Klüser Beuys Collection, the funds invested in perpetuity by the Michael & Eleonore Stoffel Foundation (fig. 13, 14), and works from Hartwig Garnerus' collection, lay the groundwork for future developments. The interplay of these forces gave rise to what the Modern Art Collection has become today: a rich kaleidoscope of modern art.

There was, however, one bitter note. In 1968, the Galerie-Verein explored an idea proposed by the then director-general Halldor Sohner to secure the Karl

Ströher Collection for Munich. This collection contained an extraordinary array of American art from Pop Art through to the abstracts and Dan Flavin, in addition to works by Joseph Beuys. There was even the option for the collection to be given as a donation, on condition that the deal included the acquisition for $3 million of the Scull Collection, with its array of work by artists including Willem de Kooning, Barnett Newman, and Mark Rothko. The sudden death of the director-general and the reluctance of his successor to put up this significant sum effectively put a stop to an accession that would have lent Munich tremendous appeal at a relatively early stage of the collection's history.[16]

A building for the Modern Art Collection

Even long before the start of the new millennium, it was clear that there was insufficient room at the Haus der Kunst for all the artworks held by the Modern Art Collection that should ideally be on display.[17] The fruits of four decades of collecting had brought together such a vibrant abundance of artworks that

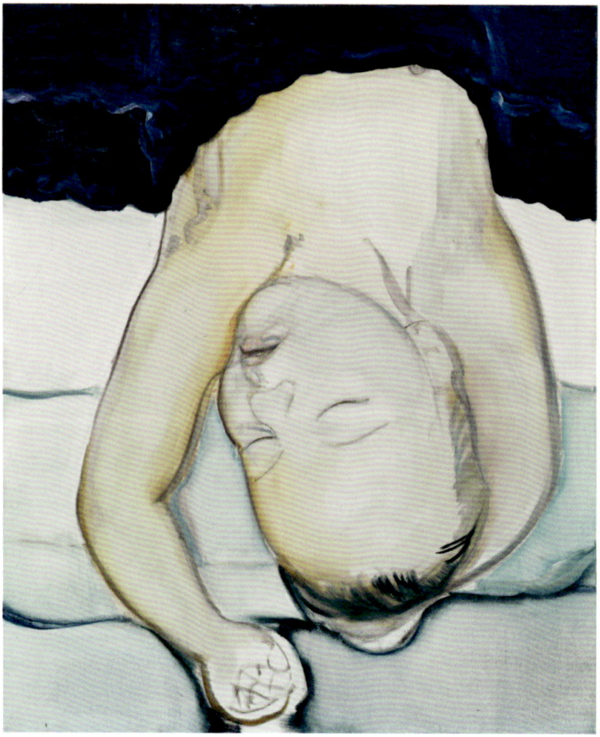

13 Marlene Dumas, Cupid, 1994, oil on canvas, 180 × 140 cm, inv. no. MES 45; Michael & Eleonore Stoffel Foundation in the Bayerische Staatsgemäldesammlungen, 2008.

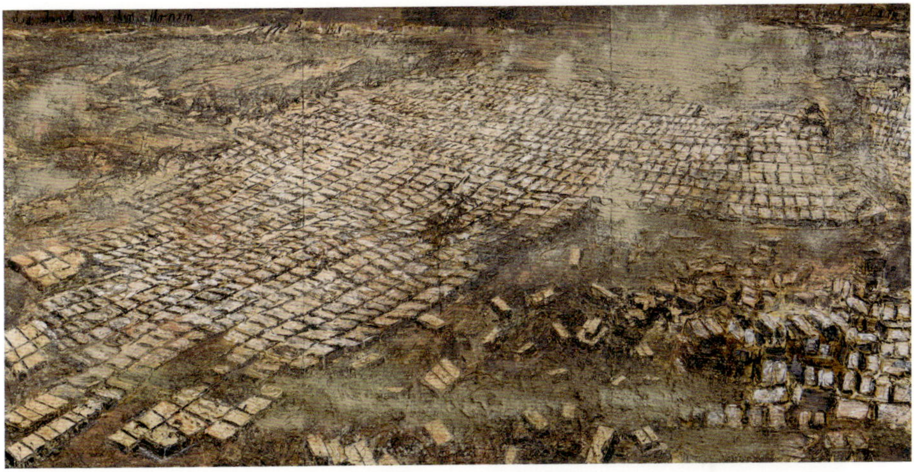

14 Anselm Kiefer, Der Sand aus den Urnen (The Sand from the Urns), 2009, acrylic, oil, shellac, sand and charcoal on canvas, 280 × 570 cm, inv. no. MES 295; Michael & Eleonore Stoffel Foundation in the Bayerische Staatsgemäldesammlungen, 2017.

the collection put in a formal request for a new home. In 1990, the plot on the western side of Türkenstrasse was duly made available, having for a long time been seen as having development potential for the Technische Universität. Just two years later, the winner of the ensuing architectural competition was announced. Two years after that, the Stiftung Pinakothek der Moderne was founded with the aim of raising ten percent of the calculated construction costs, as demanded by the Free State of Bavaria on condition that it would pay for the rest. Construction work began two years later, although the topping out would not take place for another two years, and the official opening was finally held some four years later, in 2002. The building, the collections it houses, and the exhibitions it hosts have subsequently become a firm fixture in the public consciousness. Visitors experience the variety of rooms and their array of visual perspectives. They become immersed in the quietly poetic quality of the various encounters (fig. 15) and contents the rooms offer, the way these enter into dialogue with the surroundings, as witnessed in the interaction between the Türkentor gatehouse and Walter de Maria's artwork (fig. 16). Visitors appreciate the sense of drama created by the views unravelling before their eyes (fig. 17).

This is a good place to learn more about modern art and modernism in all its facets. After over a century of widespread scepticism towards modern art, its limited accessibility, its sometimes astronomical market values, there has emerged a rich body of literature characterized by the critical scrutiny and ironic refraction of the subject – William Boyd, mentioned earlier in this

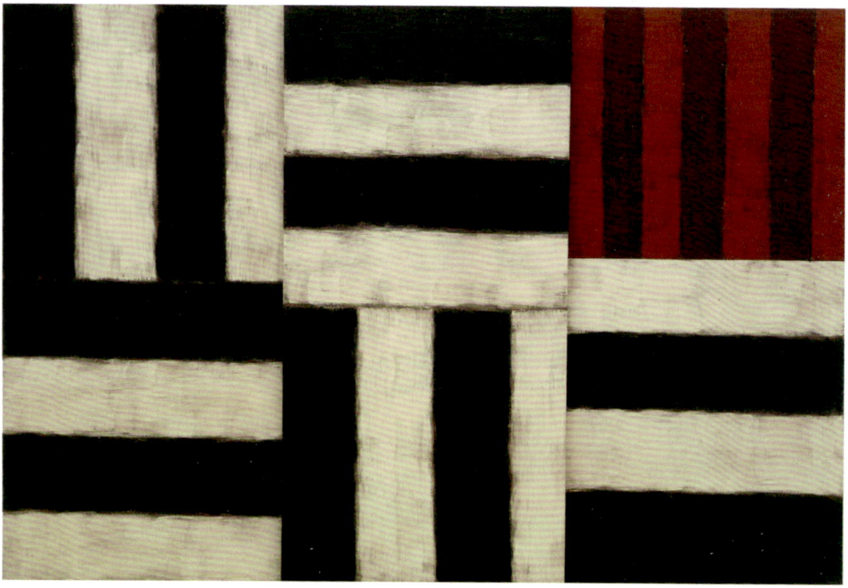

15 Sean Scully, Stone Light, 1992, oil on canvas, 280 × 419 × 15.5 cm, inv. no. 15384; acquired 1994.

introduction, is one such example. One of the most ingenious, humorous, and brilliant texts comes from the pen of Joost Zwagerman: *Duel* is a book about the implacably central role that the great masters of post-war modern art occupy on the market, the disconcerting changes made to the seemingly steadfast criteria used for valuing modern art, the market mechanisms and players (be they collectors, artists, and museums), and the instability of its financial values. This turns the focus of the book to the actual values of art, and those values' engagement with questions relating to humanity. Zwagerman first evokes the sacrosanct masters – not by chance, the same names cited by Boyd: 'Are these our new sacred images, the complete oeuvre of Picasso, Braque [...]?'[18] Yes, the reader wants to reply, these are the icons of modern art – which is why a museum considers itself lucky to boast one of them in its collection. The text then makes an allusion – though without mentioning him by name – to Jeff Koons: 'An inflatable bunny is art.'[19] A young female artist, who oscillates between subversion and courting the establishment as she searches for her place in art, reflects in the book on modern art and poses the question: 'Why does everything have to begin in the studio and end in our latter-day cathedrals, the museum? Why must we be driven, half-slavishly, to museums to look at the art there like good boys and girls?'[20] The answer is obvious: because it is precisely here that encounters can be staged, bringing together public discourse with the principal works of art and masterpieces as originals: this is the privilege and duty of the museum.

It is noteworthy that in this case an author raises questions about the relationship between art production, the market, collectors, and other interested parties, while sharpening (or exaggerating) his thesis. If, then, you return to the question of who art is for, you reach the conclusion that museums are not only noble cathedrals of art, but also democratic arenas for discussing *why* people should go to see these artworks. The present book sets out to make small but incisive contributions to the debate about what people can find in and around museums. It does not give readers an in-depth study of the collection, instead drawing attention to a number of focal points. Furthermore, its subjective proximity to works results in something approaching aphoristic brevity. The nature of this book means that artists who are represented in the collection with perhaps three or four dozen works cannot be accorded the sort of attention they deserve, and that it is not possible to present in comprehen-

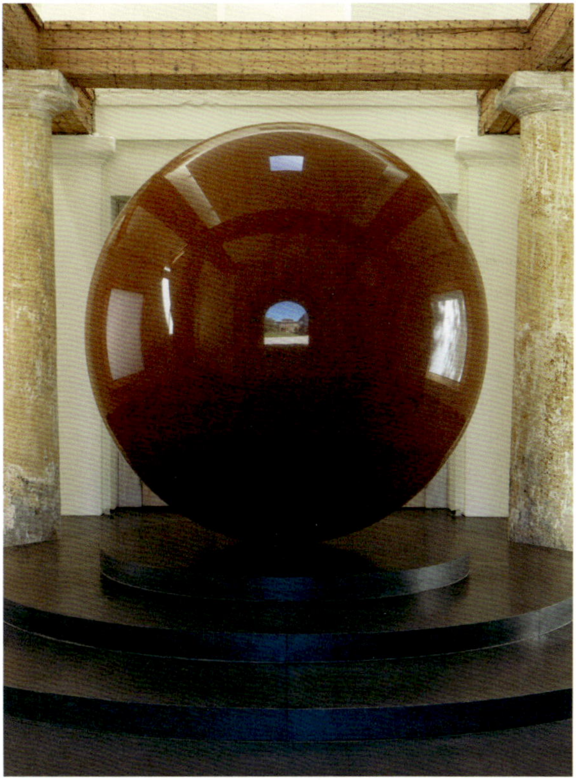

16 Walter de Maria, Large Red Sphere, 2010, granite, diameter 260 cm, inv. no. UAB 666; Udo and Anette Brandhorst Foundation, 2010.

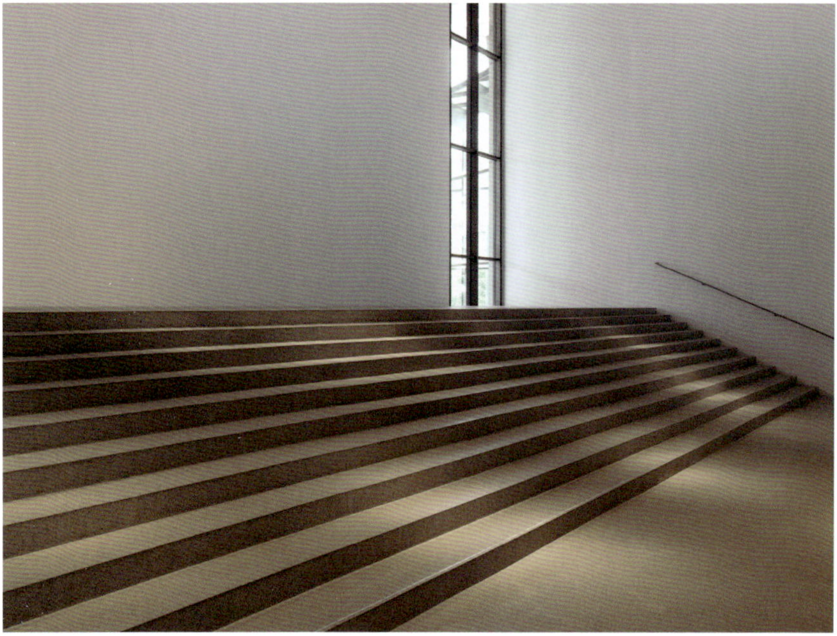

17 Stairway in the Pinakothek der Moderne.

sive detail some of the international connectedness at play (by which is meant the significant presence of American artists in the collection). These shortfalls leave room for more publications in the future. Ultimately, any such book is about the act of visiting the museum, a place that is constantly changing itself and the presentation of its contents in the steadfast hope of remaining a dependable institution. Furthermore, it is a place that can turn around the arguments sometimes levelled against modern art into a positive experience, as visitors can experience the art's radiant power and vitality. Art acts as a stimulus for reflecting on the world and life, inspiring us to discuss questions about humanity. In modern art, these questions are no longer defined by religious themes, but instead find a whole variety of different forms of expression, whether in representational or abstract depictions, photography, painting, sculpture, installations, and video art.

Work continues apace in this gigantic edifice of modernism. The hubbub of voices has over the years come to resemble a Babel-like mix of languages, but the work that goes on here has not changed. Being home to the Haus der Kunst, the Sammlung Brandhorst and the Sammlung Goetz, the Lenbachhaus, and the Villa Stuck, Munich does not lack in locations where modern art is on display and explored as a theme. That the Pinakothek der Moderne enjoys a special role in the city, providing the broadest and most solid documentation of modern art in its European and North American contexts, is obvious: visitors to the Pinakothek museums not only expect to see Dürer and Rubens, Raphael and Rembrandt, Turner and Marées, but also Marc and Kirchner, Beckmann and Beuys, Baselitz and Warhol. The richness of these collections is a cause for discussion and reflection, but also for gratitude to all those who have helped put them together, and offered their protection and support.

Bernhard Maaz

1 William Boyd, *Nat Tate: An American Artist 1928–1960*, London 2011, p. 21.
2 Ibid, p. 65
3 Ibid, p. 66.
4 Peter-Klaus Schuster (ed.), *Die Nationalgalerie*, Berlin/Cologne 2001, p. 314.
5 Quoted from Karlheinz Gabler, *Erich Heckel und sein Kreis. Dokumente, Fotos, Briefe, Schriften*, Stuttgart/Zürich 1983, p. 150.
6 Friedrich Dörnhöffer (ed.), *Verzeichnis der in der Neuen Staatsgalerie ausgestellten Gemälde und Bildwerke*. Official edition, Munich 1920.
7 Ibid, p. 3.
8 Dagmar Lott, 'Münchens Neue Staatsgalerie im Dritten Reich', in: *Nationalsozialismus und 'Entartete Kunst'. Die "Kunststadt" München 1937*, ed. by Peter-Klaus Schuster, Munich 1987, pp. 289–300, here p. 290.
9 Bernhard Maaz, 'Angepasst, aufrecht oder entartet. Geschichte (in) der Kunst in der Pinakothek der Moderne', in: *Aviso* 2016, 3rd ed., pp. 38–43, here p. 39, 42.
10 Eberhard Hanfstaengl, *Bayerische Staatsgemäldesammlungen. Neuerwerbungen zeitgenössischer Malerei und Plastik 1945–1950*, Munich 1951, p. 3.
11 Ibid.
12 Ibid, p. 4.
13 Ibid.
14 Ibid, pp. 7–39.
15 *PIN. Freunde der Pinakothek der Moderne e. V., vertreten durch den Vorstand Katharina von Perfall u. a. (ed.), PIN. A Perfect match, Munich* 2015.
16 Ibid, pp. 212–214.
17 Carla Schulz-Hoffmann et. al., *Staatsgalerie moderner Kunst*, Munich 1995, p. 5.
18 Joost Zwagerman, *Duell*, 3rd ed., Bonn 2016, p. 48.
19 Ibid.
20 Ibid, p. 51.

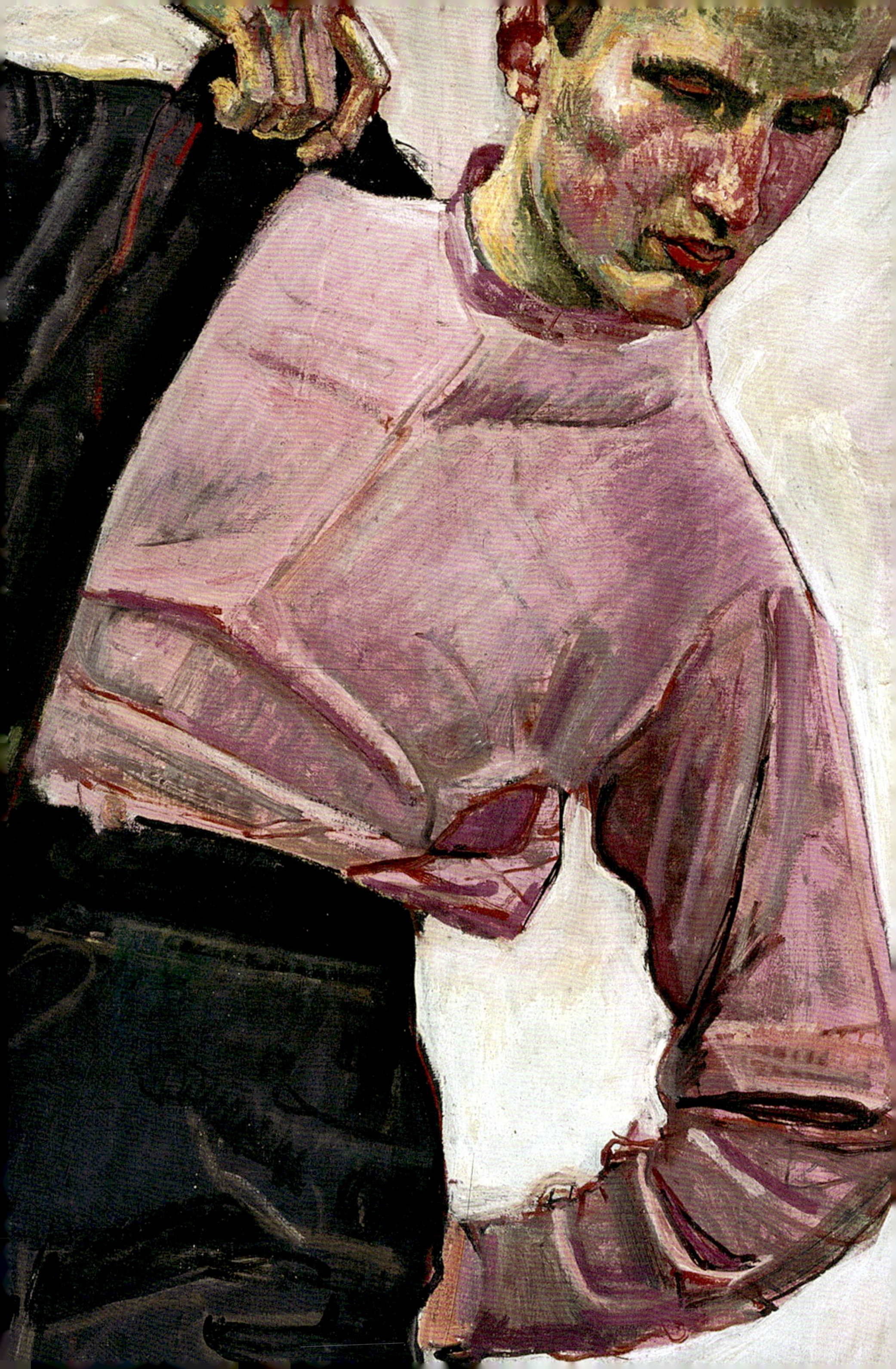

BEGINNINGS
THE AVANT-GARDE(S) AFTER 1900

In his foreword to the second book planned by *Der Blaue Reiter* group of artists, Franz Marc wrote in 1914: 'The world is crammed to suffocation. On every stone man has put the token of his cleverness. Every word is leased or invested. What can you do [...] but give up everything and flee? What but draw a dividing line between yesterday and today? That is the great task of our time.' As a representative of his generation and conscious of standing on the threshold of a new epoch, Marc formulated a critique of tradition and convention. The way forward was to be brought about by effecting a deliberate break with the past, which equated in short with the academic, realistic, and illusionary art of the 19th century. Of key significance for this departure towards new artistic territory was the term 'avant-garde', suggestive of an overriding attitude shared by the nascent movement of European modern art, despite its regional and stylistic variations. The term 'avant-garde' is cognate to the English 'vanguard', military terminology for the unit first sent out towards enemy lines to scout the lay of the land. Advancing, as it were, courageously into *terra incognita*, Franz Marc and the Expressionists were inspired by the pathos of discovery. 'Therefore we venture forth into new fields and we are shocked to find that everything is still untrodden, unspoken, uncultivated, unexplored.' The starting point for this voyage of discovery was the conviction that it was no longer sufficient to depict outward appearance, but rather that the subjective, inner experience of reality is integral to the perception process and should be included in the work. In place of reality emerge the perceptions of the artist; in lieu of the object is the relationship between subject and object. This therefore posed a challenge both to the classical genres of painting and formal media and painting techniques, such as the importance hitherto accorded to one-point perspective, studies and preliminary drawings, local colours, natural light effects, and the imperative for the picture surface to be completely painted and sealed with varnish.

The onset of this break can be traced to the late 19th century, when Paul Cézanne, George Seurat, Paul Gauguin, Vincent van Gogh, and Edvard Munch broke new ground in painting. Accompanying these revolutionary individual approaches in the last two decades of the 19th century was a movement away from the illusionistic painted surface.

For a range of different objectives, such approaches were replaced by open pictures with gaps, featuring incomplete or sketch-like passages, rough surfaces, and flatly applied paint lacking any illusion of space or recession into depth. With the faithful imitation of nature in retreat, the focus shifted to the artistic medium, and the processes involved in perception and production. By breaking down the painted surface into points and marks, Cézanne and Seurat established a systematic and constructive picture composition that would be continued in the work of Cubist artists. Conversely, the subjective and spontaneous expressive force of Gauguin and Van Gogh were succeeded by Expressionism.

The earliest works at the Modern Art Collection provide some examples of the diverse routes taken by modern art after 1900, the beginnings of which can be seen in the collection of the Bayerische Staatsgemäldesammlungen at the Neue Pinakothek. Thus the Pinakothek der Moderne opens with a late work painted in 1908 by Ferdinand Hodler (born 1853), the *Jena Student*. In the Swiss Symbolist's fully worked-up figure study for the patriotic wall painting *Departure of German Students for the War of Liberation of 1813*, it is not only the theme of artists and war (which was subsequently to have such fatal resonance for the 20th century) that rings out for the first time. Hodler's work is also testament to the crisis and revitalization of classical history painting. The student reaching his decision to enlist voluntarily for the war becomes the artist's theme. Instead of the triumphant collective, we see the reflective and cautious gesture of the individual. The German painter Paula Modersohn-Becker's *Nude Child with Goldfish Bowl* alludes indirectly to the French pioneers of modern art and the influence of Paul Gauguin. The unrefined painting style, the construction of the figure, and the flat, unmodelled application of paint embody (both in subject and rendering) an Expressionistic passion for the simple, childlike, and 'primitive'. The year 1905 marked the most significant collective foundational events for both the French and German avant-garde movements, witnessing the first appearance of works by Fauvist artists at the Salon d'Automne in Paris, and the creation of the *Brücke* artist community in Dresden. The dramatic intensification of expression in paintings by Henri Matisse, André Derain, and Maurice de Vlaminck led the art critic Louis de Vauxcelles to describe the painters as 'les fauves', or 'wild animals'. The application of pure, uninterrupted colour, without modelling of light or shadow, the simplification of form, and the luxuriant brushstrokes, whose texture are no longer bound to correspond to the object they depict, produced a triumph of colour that would set the standard for the 20th century. Among the works to be seen in Munich, Georges Braque's *La Calanque – Temps gris* from 1907 represents a superlative example of this sort of work. Around 1907–08, the German artists of *Brücke* drew considerable inspiration and encouragement from the *Fauves*. However, clear differences between the Expressionists and the *Fauves* can be seen in such landscape paintings as Karl Schmidt-Rottluff's *Park Corner in Dangast*. Inspired by woodcuts, the angular brushstrokes denote a desire for expressive concision and violent gestures that deviates from the soft and more elegant French culture of painting.

Encounters with works by the Norwegian painter Edvard Munch would also prove decisive in the way colours were used to intensify expressive power. A clear example of this is evident in *Woman in Red Dress*, which enters into direct dialogue with the Fauvists and the Expressionists of *Brücke*. The dazzling and evocative use of colour transforms the landscape into an echo chamber of different moods, shifting between fear, desire, and unease, with the sketch-like quality of the forms and figures leaving them open to further interpretation. This psychological quality of colour is equally a feature of the early paintings of *Brücke*. Characteristic features of Kirchner's artworks are the speed and variation of the brushwork, and the intense luminosity of colour in yellow, orange, and red tones. Where Kirchner's portrait of his girlfriend *Dodo* is characterized by inner turbulence and agitation, Matisse created in *Still Life with Geraniums* a masterpiece of 'decorative surface style' that transcends the approaches adopted by the other *Fauves*. Characterized by its careful balance between still life and interior painting, between space and surface, the composition is a perfect illustrative example of Matisse's quest for the 'art of balance, purity, and calm'. Commissioned by the museum director Hugo von Tschudi, Matisse's painting for decades set the benchmark for quality at Munich's Modern Art Collection. It was only after more than 40 years after the commission in 1909 that the collection could once again boast similarly substantial new accessions of modern art.

Oliver Kase

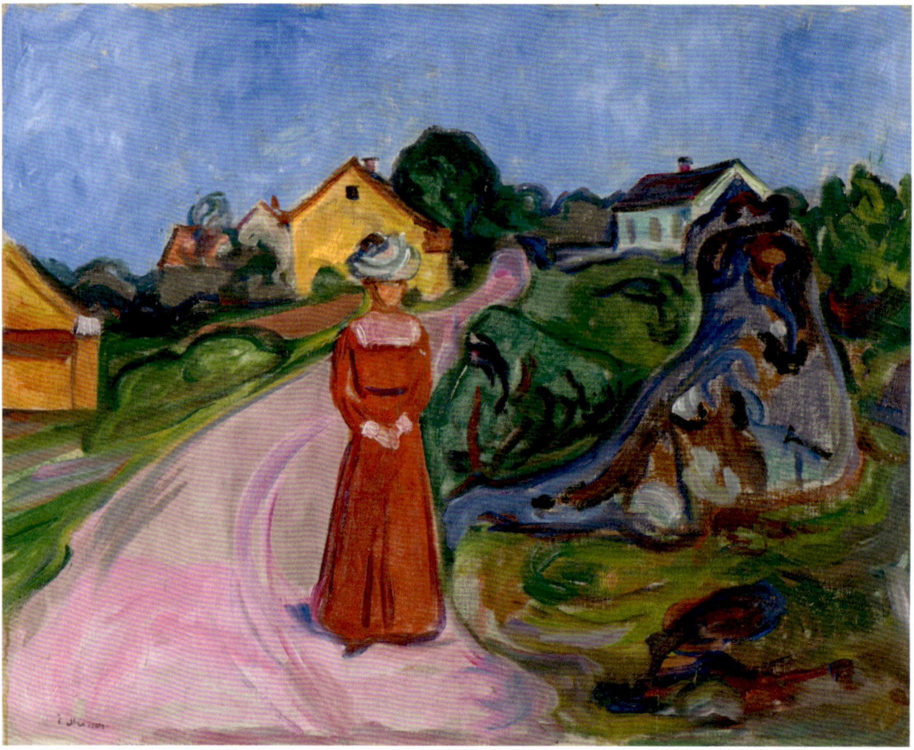

Edvard Munch | Woman in Red Dress (Road in Åsgårdstrand) | c. 1902–03
Oil on canvas, 59.7 × 75.5 cm, inv. no. 11709
Acquired 1953

Seen in the wake of Munch's picture spaces and the power of his colours, even a real place such as Åsgårdstrand, where from 1889 the artist spent his summers, takes on an unnerving quality. With the clear outline of the houses in the background, the painting seems like a typical village landscape. Only on taking a second look does the unusual formation of the landscape in the right-hand half of the picture become apparent, its contours pouring out into a blue current at the feet of a faceless woman in a red dress. Thus Munch gives visual form to something that Sigmund Freud would subsequently formulate in 1919: it is proximity to the familiar that gives rise to the uncanny. NE

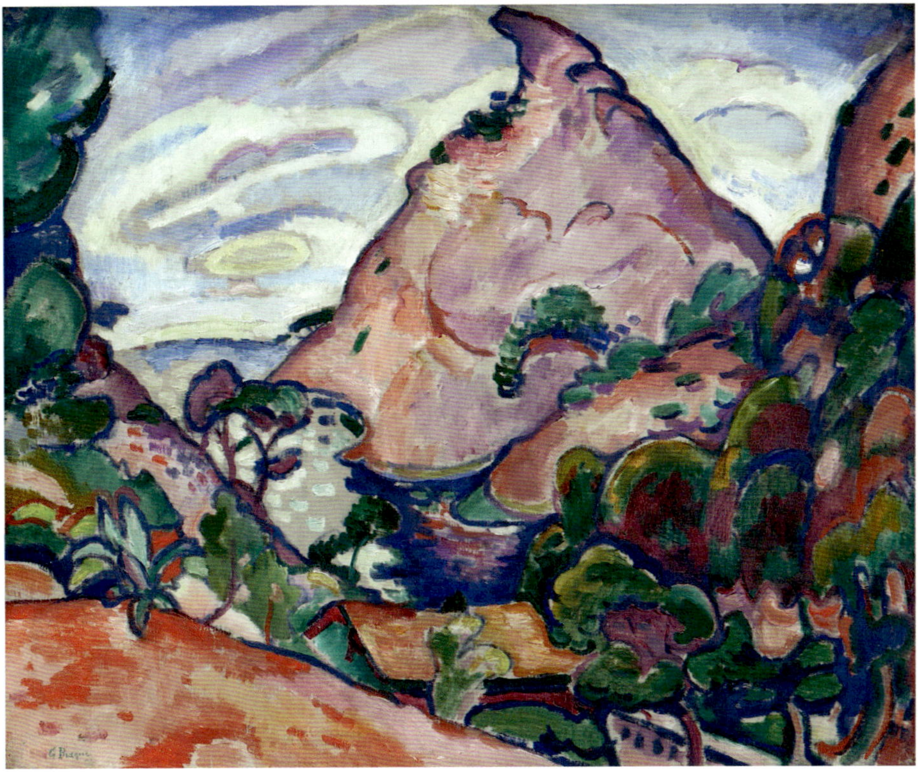

Georges Braque | La Calanque – Temps gris (Bay near La Ciotat) | 1907
Oil on canvas, 60 × 73 cm, inv. no. 13426
Acquired 1964

Following in the footsteps of Paul Cézanne, after the turn of the 20th century many artists made the pilgrimage to the coast east of Marseille. In 1906–07, Georges Braque spent a large portion of his time near La Ciotat, the location of the rocky bay depicted in *La Calanque – Temps gris*. In critical response to his great artistic role model, Braque, the youngest member of the Fauvist group, painted here alongside Henri Matisse and André Derain. Beginning with an impressionistic visual concept, within a few months he had shifted towards expressive colour compositions that would in September 1907 eventually result in the first Cubist oil paintings. NE

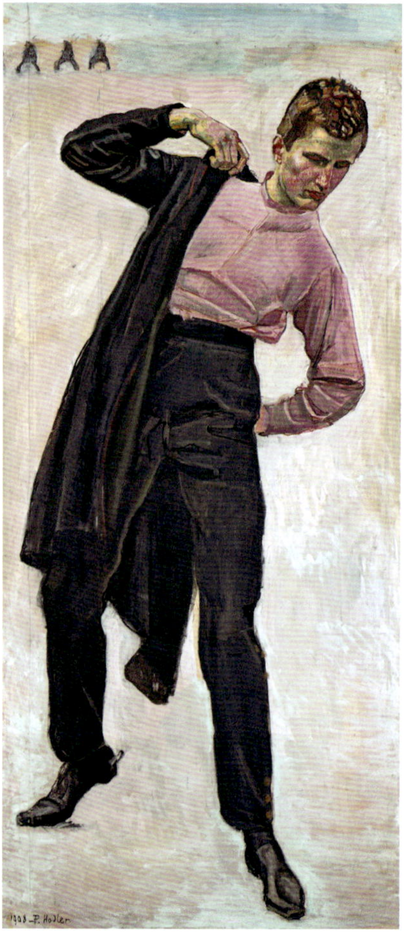

Ferdinand Hodler | Jenenser Student (Jena Student) | 1908
Oil on canvas, 212 × 92 cm, inv. no. 8643
Donation of Friedrich Wilhelm Freiherr von Bissing as part of the 'Tschudi Fund', 1912

The Swiss painter Ferdinand Hodler was commissioned in 1907 to create a wall painting for the University of Jena, entitled *German Students Departing for the War of Liberation of 1813*. The Lützow volunteer corps had enlisted large numbers of students from Jena in the struggle against the Napoleonic occupation of Prussia. Created in Munich, this preliminary study shows the central figure of the painting as he is spurred into action: the moment is depicted as an individual decision, with the student seen slipping on his soldier's tunic. Shortly afterwards, the First World War would reveal the falsehood of the heroic significance of the individual's decision to enlist voluntarily. OK

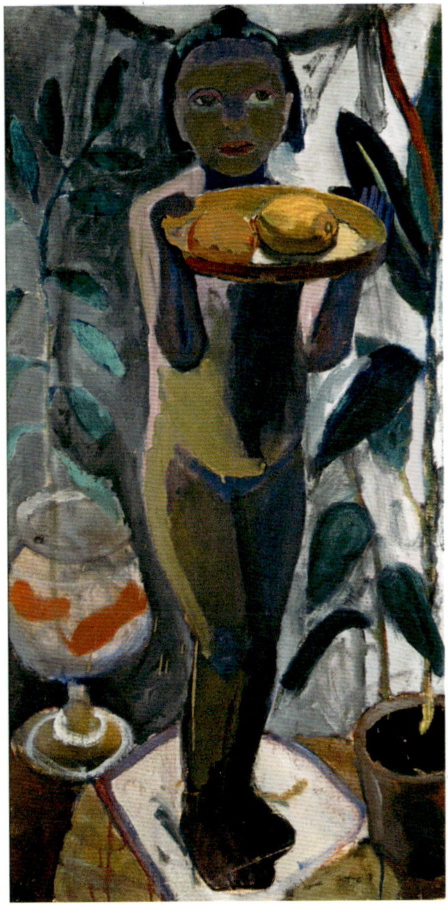

Paula Modersohn-Becker | Kinderakt mit Goldfischglas (Nude Child with Goldfish Bowl) | c. 1906–07
Oil on canvas, 105.5 × 54.5 cm, inv. no. 13468

Paula Modersohn-Becker was active in a male-dominated world as a female artist who, of all things, took the female nude as her subject. Having made her home in the landscape around Worpswede, the artist drew creative energy from the seething life of Paris, where shortly before her death she painted *Nude Child with Goldfish Bowl*. The artistic influences of Vincent van Gogh and Paul Gauguin are in clear evidence, and yet Modersohn-Becker uses the ambivalence of her nude figure, which wavers between person and sculpture, child and woman, concealment and performance, to subvert the fascination for the exotic and indeterminate that had taken hold of Paris at that time. NE

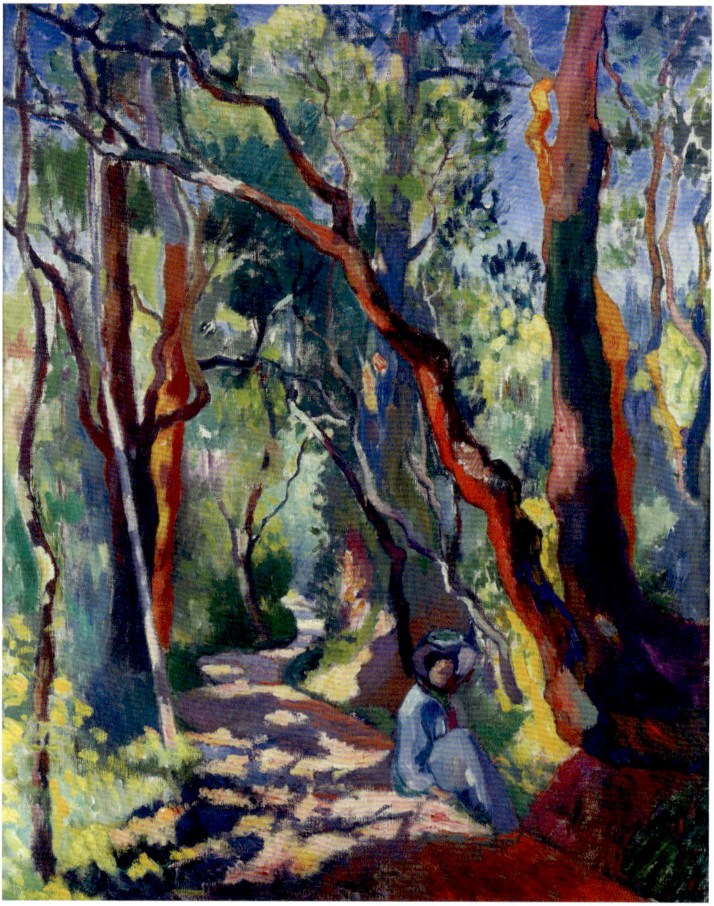

Henri Manguin | Die Allee (The Allée –The Park Path) | 1905
Oil on canvas, 92 × 73.1 cm, inv. no. 14218
Bequest of Elly Köhler, Gauting, 1971

Manguin enrollen at the École des Beaux-Arts in 1894 and was one of the arists described as 'fauves' ('savages') by one critic in response to their group exhibition at the 190 Salon d'Automne in Paris. Probably painted in Saint-Tropez, *The Allée* also dates from 1905. The depiction of the Mediterranean park or forest path winding its way into the distance is infused by bright, warm colours conveying southern *joie de vivre*. The free and impasto brushwork of the dappled sunlight on the footpath and in the foliage creates a vibrating rhythm, bringing humankind and nature into chromatic harmony. In this work we see the melding of a Neo-Impressionist painting technique and the Fauvist expression of colour. OK

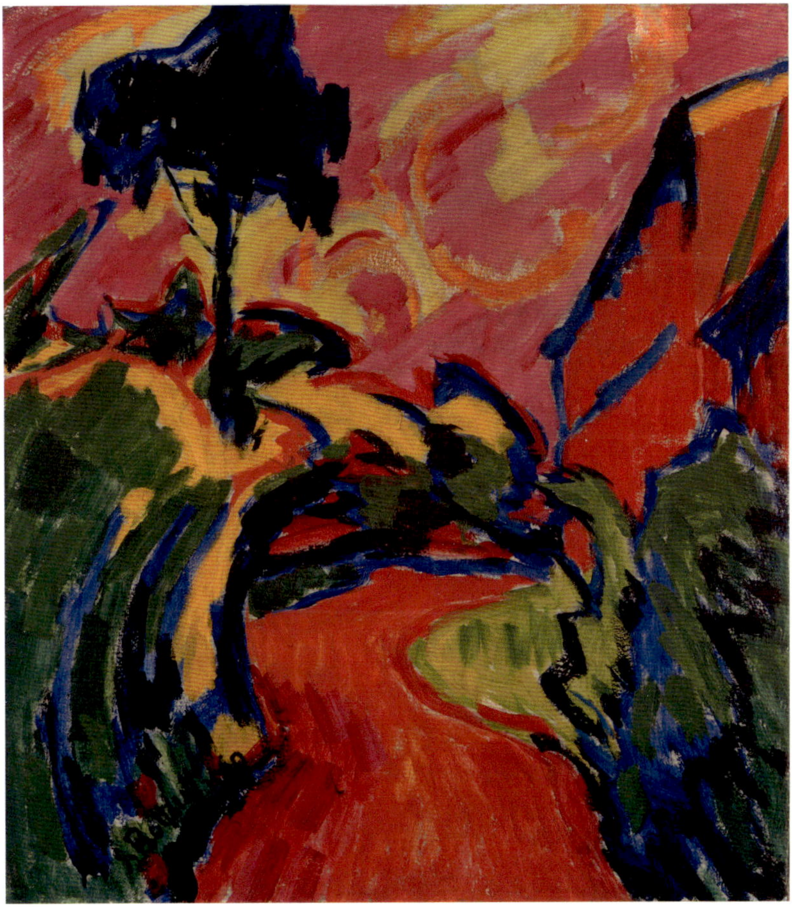

Karl Schmidt Rottluff | Parkweg (Parkecke in Dangast) (Park Path – Park Corner in Dangast) | 1910
Oil on canvas, 83.5 × 75.5 cm, inv. no. 14523
Bequest of Martha and Markus Kruss, 1977

Schmidt-Rottluff spent the summer months of 1907 and 1912 at Dangast, a North Sea resort on the Jade Bay. The impressions he gained of the area's wide landscape and pristine natural environment provided the catalyst for his Expressionist landscape painting. Schmidt-Rottluff inscribes the artificially laid park path and guesthouse with the experience of unadulterated nature. The artist uses forceful brushstrokes to bring together the shimmering sunlight, the hedges moving in the wind, and the lush abundance of nature to create a landscape of flaming intensity and pulsating colour. OK

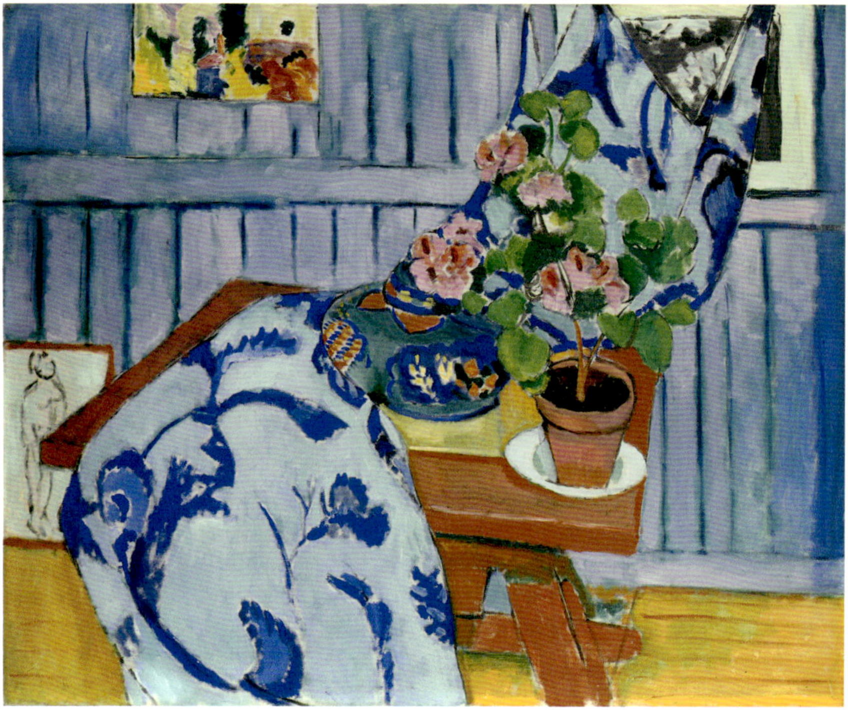

Henri Matisse | Intérieur avec pot de fleurs (Still Life with Geraniums) | 1910
Oil on canvas, 93 × 115 cm, inv. no. 8669
Donation of Marcus Kappel as part of the 'Tschudi Fund', 1912

The still life by Matisse was painted following a commission by Hugo von Tschudi, the visionary director of the Staatliche Galerien of Bavaria, and acquired in 1912. It was the first of Matisse's paintings to be shown in a German public museum. As much an interior painting as a still life, it is a mature work by the artist in the 'decorative surface style'. The blue drapery stretched across the picture forms a bold sweep of energy that unifies the geraniums and the Chinese porcelain vase on the table. It emerges in contrast to the three-dimensional interior and so is transformed into an ornamental, self-luminous field of colour.
OK

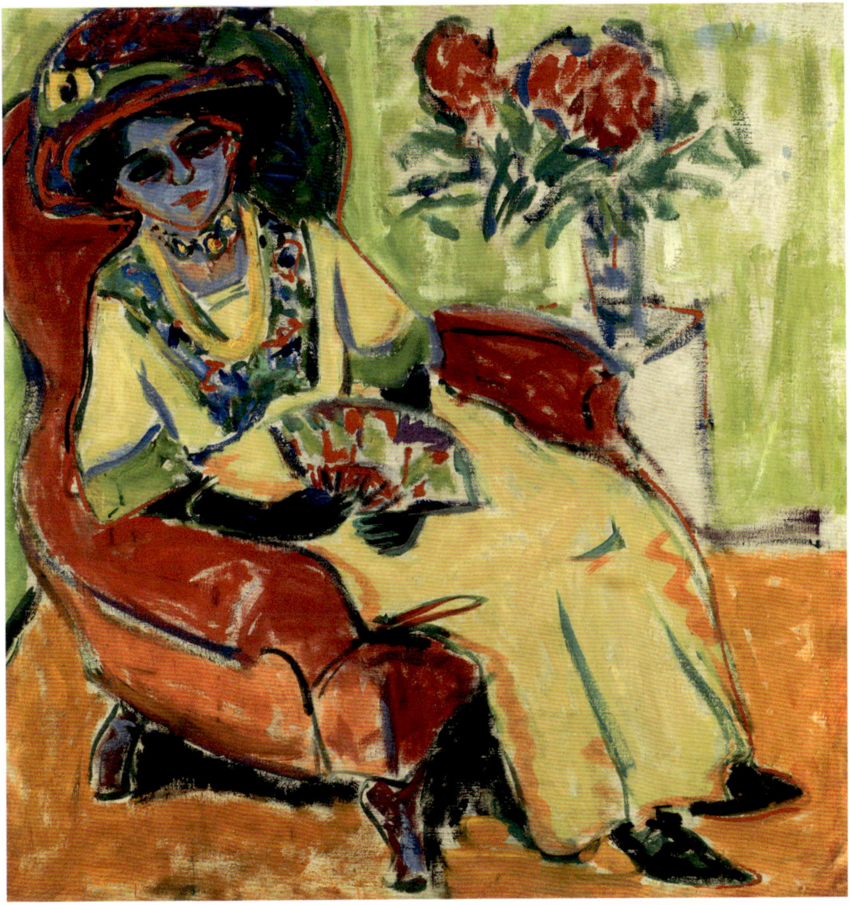

Ernst Ludwig Kirchner | Bildnis Dodo (Portrait of Dodo) | 1909
(on the verso of *Masks on the Road* | 1910)
Oil on canvas, 112 × 114.5 cm, inv no. 13061
Acquired 1960

From 1909 in Dresden, the milliner Doris Große (known as 'Dodo') was Kirchner's model and lover. The *Portrait of Dodo* is an early masterpiece by the artist that bears testimony to his productive interaction with the Fauve artists centred around Henri Matisse. However, at the same time it also reveals Kirchner's propensity for self-contained, psychologically charged expressive force. Drawing upon the aesthetics of sketches and colour pastel drawings, Kirchner uses the light ground as a stylistic device, while creating spontaneity and drama through the playful alternation in the application of paint, switching between fluid and broad brushstrokes and daubed patches of impasto. OK

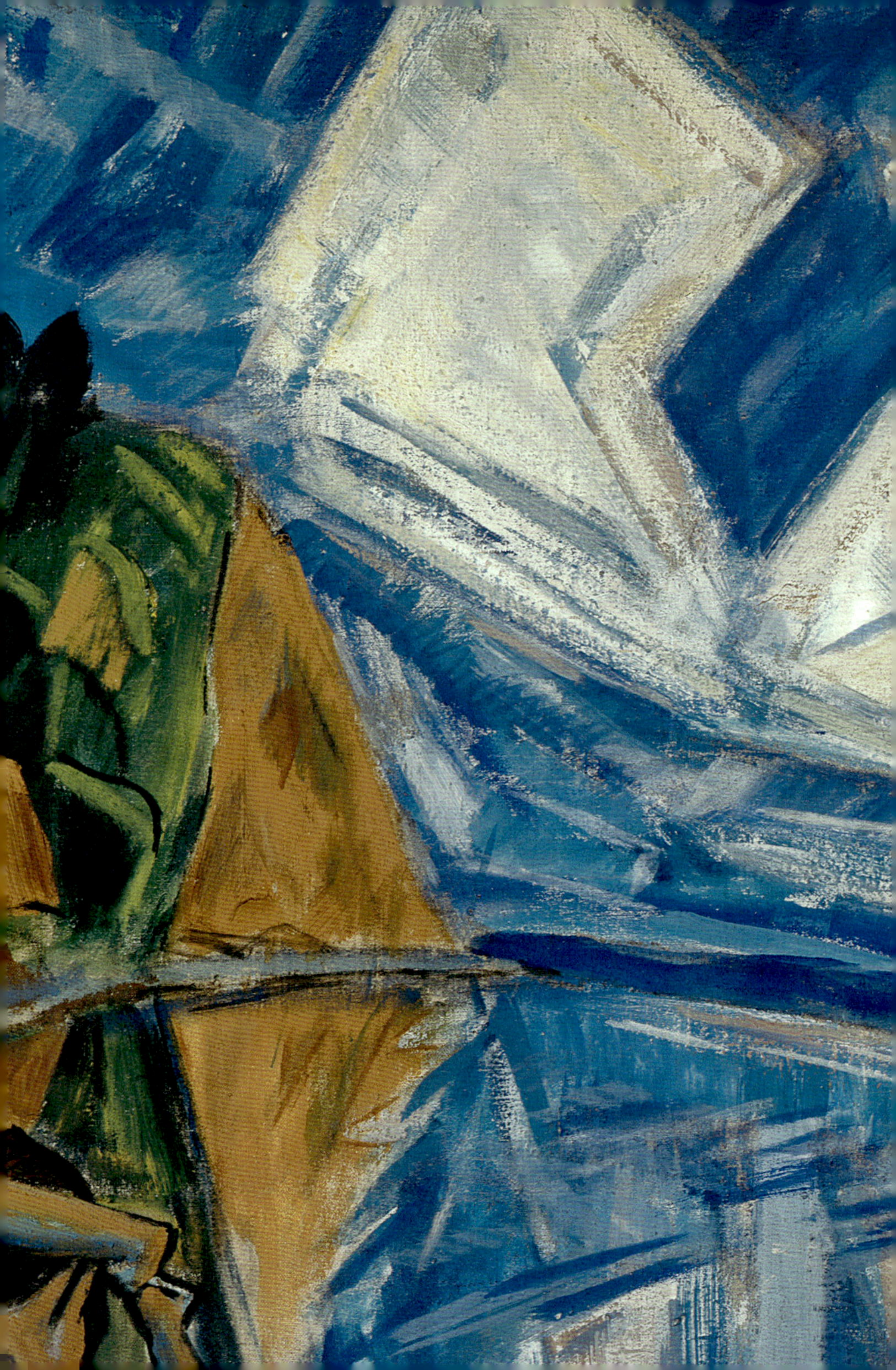

EXPRESSIONISM
BRÜCKE AND *DER BLAUE REITER*

'In this time of the great struggle for a new art we fight like disorganized "savages" against an old, established power. [...] The dreaded weapons of the "savages" are their *new ideas*.' These provocative words written by Franz Marc in 1911 proclaimed an intellectual rebirth of the arts, which Marc associated with the French *Fauves* ('wild beasts'), as well as the Russian and German Expressionists. Marc called on young artists to revolt against the academic establishment. Adopting Nietzsche's pathos of denial, Franz Marc's generation rejected the centuries-old traditions and established education models that were upheld by the art academies. They no longer aspired to be mere epigones of the 19th century: 'Today art is moving in a direction, of which our fathers would never even have dreamed,' Marc wrote in 1912. This artistic patricide targeted the rigidly formulaic and long-prevailing doctrine of faithfully rendering nature through art. Marc's sense of an imminent awakening, of living 'in a time of immense radical change in all things, all ideas' was shared by the founders of *Brücke* ('Bridge').

The architecture students Fritz Bleyl, Erich Heckel, Ernst Ludwig Kirchner, and Karl Schmidt-Rottluff, just 20 to 25 years of age, founded *Brücke* in Dresden in 1905. The aim of its programme, which Kirchner formulated in 1906, was to bring together 'a new generation of those artists and connoisseurs' who 'want to achieve freedom of life and action against the well-established older forces'. The group did not adhere to a particular style but shared a common belief in spontaneity and authenticity: 'Everyone is with us who, directly and without falsification, conveys what drives him to create.' The *Brücke* collective had little similarity with the inward-looking, Nazarene movement that preceded it, but was rather a business-minded interest group with a specific mission. It used original prints to recruit well-off 'passive members' to support the group, and additionally organized and participated in exhibitions throughout the country. Emil Nolde joined the group for just a short time in 1906–07, Max Pechstein became a member in 1906, and Otto Mueller in 1910. The subject matter taken up by *Brücke* artists reflects an underlying creative tension between city life and the countryside that intensified after their move from Dresden to Berlin in 1911: the contrast between an Arcadian yearning for true harmony between man and nature, expressed through the subject of the nude and outdoor bathers, and the nonstop action of the big city in depictions of circus acts, variety shows, dance performances, and the never-ending hustle and bustle of the streets. The *Brücke* group disbanded in 1913, following a dispute during work on their own *Chronicle* in which Kirchner claimed the innovative ideas of the group as his own – as personal ambition prevailed over the ideal of developing a common style.

Brücke and *Der Blaue Reiter* ('The Blue Rider') shared an enthusiasm for non-European cultures, especially Oceanic and African woodcarvings which they believed would enable them to rediscover how to create original and authentic works. While the name *Brücke*, probably proposed by Heckel, plays on Nietzsche's metaphor of mankind as a bridge, Wassily Kandinsky first considered the semantically similar term 'Die Kette', 'the chain', for *Der Blaue Reiter* collective, explaining his suggestion as representing a 'link to the past and a ray to the future'. According to Kandinsky, they ultimately chose *Der Blaue Reiter* due to his and Marc's penchant for the colour blue, horses, and horsemen. That it also invokes Christian and Romantic associations was certainly deliberate and fitted with the group's programme, too. In contrast to *Brücke*, *Der Blaue Reiter* drew up an official manifesto that was published as an almanac in May 1912. It contained texts by numerous contemporary artists of the avant-garde movement, as well as illustrations of a wide variety of European and non-European artworks from antiquity to the modern day, as well as folk art and musical accompaniments. The uncannily topical idea behind this combinative approach aimed at encouraging the reader to link artworks and texts through playful association rather than hierarchical or geographical criteria. The publication of the almanac was preceded by two exhibitions, which also featured works by the artists August Macke and Paul Klee, who were friends with Kandinsky and Marc: *The First Exhibition of the Editorial Board of Der Blaue Reiter* in 1911–12 at Galerie Thannhauser and *The Second Exhibition of the Editorial Board of Der Blaue Reiter: Black and White* held in 1912 at the bookshop and gallery of Hans Goltz, which was dedicated to works on paper. Although there were some overlaps and areas of common interest between *Brücke* and *Der Blaue Reiter*, the intentions of each group were different. *Brücke* was dedicated to the depiction of people in their living environment, prioritizing sensuality and vitality. Furthermore, especially while still in Dresden, the group strove to develop a legitimate, collective style. *Der Blaue Reiter*, on the other hand, put great emphasis on artistic individuality and internationality, and was driven by the religiously motivated aim for greater spiritualization and internalization of art, which ultimately led to abstraction.

The Pinakothek der Moderne only began to collect works from both artist groups at quite a late stage, but has since managed to build up significant holdings in these areas through regular acquisitions. An active and direct connection between *Der Blaue Reiter* and the Bayerische Staatsgemäldesammlungen was in fact established early on through the museum's director Hugo von Tschudi, who is mentioned as a patron of the artist group in the almanac and to whose memory the book was even dedicated. But this link was abruptly severed in 1911 when Tschudi died unexpectedly. The museum only turned its attention again to *Der Blaue Reiter* much later after the Second World War, when modern art, well into its second generation, had gained acceptance, and efforts were initiated to destigmatize Franz Marc, who had been defamed by the Nazis as a 'degenerate' artist. The donation of *Red Deer II* by Annette von Eckardt in 1917 strangely had little impact and it was not until 1948–49 that the Bayerische Staatsgemäldesammlungen acquired further works from the widow of the artist, Maria Marc: *Cows I* (p. 10) and the two late masterpieces from 1914, *Tyrol* and *Fighting Forms*. In 1964, Sofie and Emanuel Fohn donated *The Mandrill*, one of Marc's most important animal works, and the illustrated postcards addressed to Else Lasker-Schüler. Of no less importance are the two *Improvisations* by Wassily Kandinsky. His early *Improvisation 12* with the subject of the horseman, a gift from Kandinsky to Marc, was also bought from Maria Marc in 1951, and *Dreamy Improvisation* from 1913, with its dissolution of painterly and graphic notation into pure abstraction, was acquired in 1969.

The collection's holdings of *Der Blaue Reiter* comprises a select handful of some of its most iconic works and is complemented by the *Brücke* collection of fifty paintings, including nineteen by Ernst Ludwig Kirchner alone. The range of Kirchner's works in Munich spans from his early critical response to Henri Matisse in *Portrait of Dodo* (p. 39) to major works from the period of Berlin Expressionism, such as the 'first' street scene *Masks on the Street*, as well as *Circus* and *Dance School*, and on to the programmatic *Self-Portrait as an Invalid* and large-scale works from the early Davos period, such as *The Two Brothers M.* Meanwhile, the *Glass Day* by Erich Heckel and the *Dance around the Golden Calf* by Emil Nolde represent two further iconic works by *Brücke* artists, which illustrate the broad spectrum of German Expressionism and the overarching goal of liberating the spirit, albeit in opposing ways – through calm reflection or frenzied ecstasy, through the cool depths of the sea or the fire of dance.

Oliver Kase

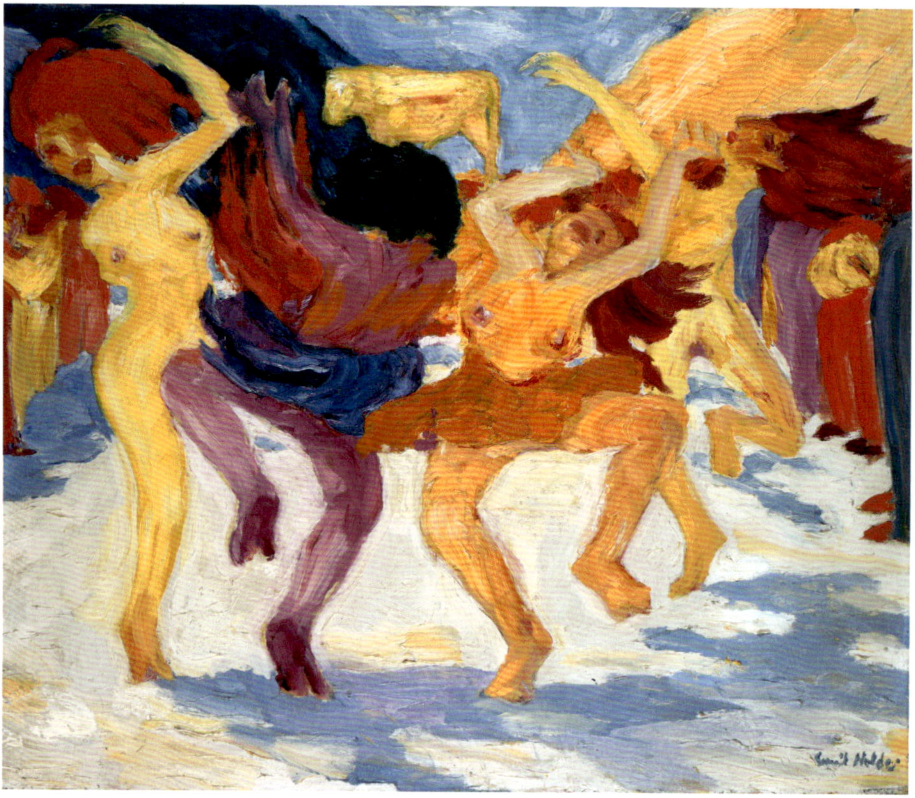

Emil Nolde | Tanz um das Goldene Kalb (Dance around the Golden Calf) | 1910
Oil on canvas, 88 × 105 cm, inv. no. 13351
Acquired 1963

In the early 20th century, a novel synthesis of painting and dance emerged that is also reflected in Nolde's work. *Dance around the Golden Calf* belongs to a group of six religious pictures from the year 1910, the subject of which is transformed by Nolde's brush into studies of expressions of ecstasy combined with fantastical visions of an exotic world. The bodies of the dancers are subsumed in a frenzy of movement and gesticulation by the intensity of the palette and the brushwork. Instead of a moralistic depiction of greed as described in the Bible, Nolde captures a moment of sheer joy, of self-abandonment, and thus absolute freedom.

NE

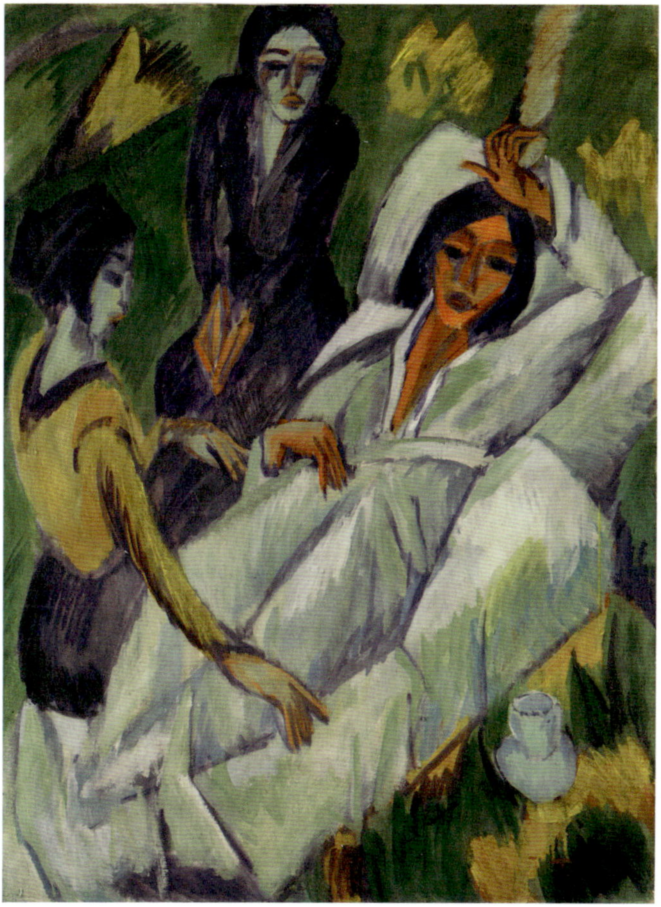

Ernst Ludwig Kirchner | Frauen beim Tee (Women at Teatime) | 1914
Oil on canvas, 100.5 × 76 cm, inv. no. 14525
Bequest of Martha and Markus Kruss, 1977

The painting, which Kirchner also described as a 'sickbed' scene, shows the dialogue between three women at a bed placed diagonally in the picture space. Rendered from a noticeably raised viewpoint, the main figure reclines in a white dressing gown, in an elegantly relaxed pose with her hand positioned above her head. The surrounding space completely dissolves into an ornamental pattern of green and yellow jagged forms. The scene with Erna Schilling, Kirchner's partner and muse, posing in bed is set in his studio, where the artist would deploy exotic fabrics and furniture to conjure up a subjective, alternative world, outside of everyday life. The psychologically charged scene of the three women remains enigmatic thanks to Kirchner's nervous handling of the brush with starkly angular forms. OK

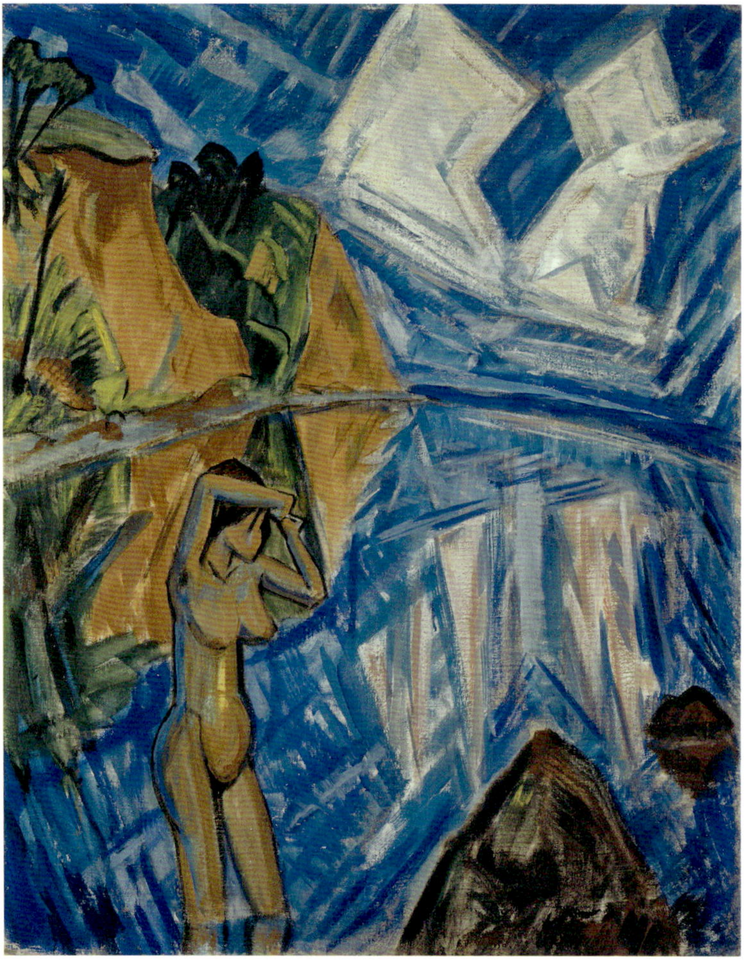

Erich Heckel | Gläserner Tag (Glass Day) | 1913
Oil on canvas, 117 × 92 cm, inv. no. 14534
Bequest of Martha and Markus Kruss, 1977

Like the other artists from *Brücke*, Heckel was also very interested in painting nudes in natural settings, but rather than depicting joyful scenes of people bathing, he preferred to focus on the contemplative dialogue between a single figure and nature. The Baltic coast near Osterholz is depicted as a starkly composed landscape of crystalline forms. The blue tones and the interlinked, mirrored images of heaven and earth invoke a sense of Romantic yearning for nature in a vision of cosmic harmony. Here the philosophical leanings of *Der Blaue Reiter* supplants the vitalism of *Brücke*. OK

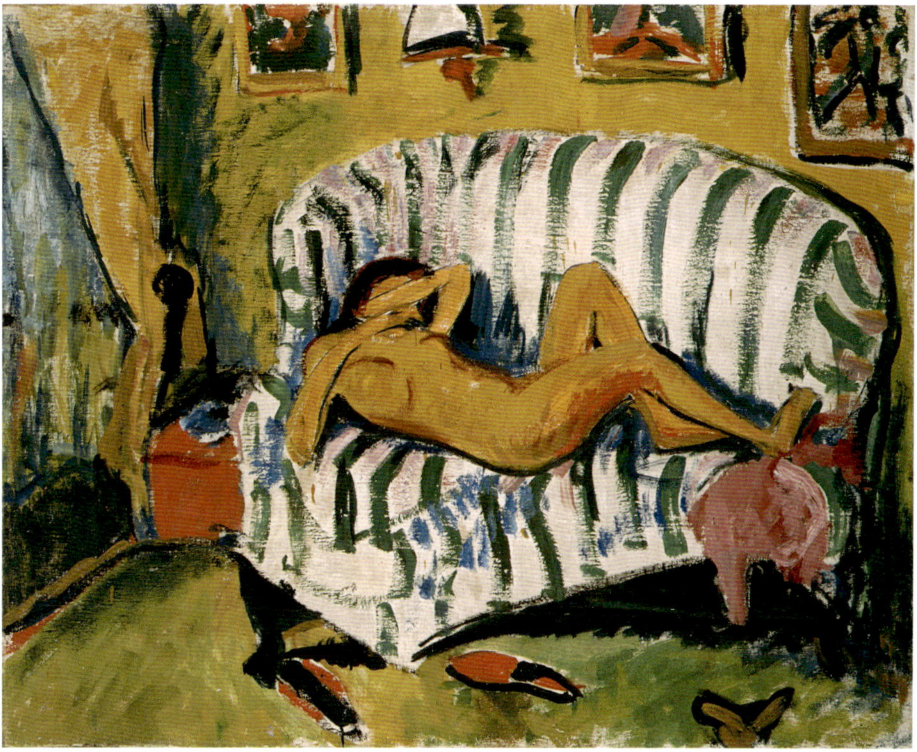

Erich Heckel | Liegendes Mädchen (Reclining Girl) | 1909
Oil on canvas, 96.5 × 121.2 cm, inv. no. 11341
Acquired 1952

Few other works by Erich Heckel embody the radical rejuvenation of the medium of painting through an uninhibited lust for life as emphatically as *Reclining Girl*. Although it is set indoors, the room glows in intense yellow and green tones – nature even makes its way into the parlour. The variation and openness of the brushstrokes is particularly well mastered in the strong, green stripes of the sofa and the flowing forms of the red pillow. Just as the artist's painting technique conveys vitality, the outstretched nude is an expression of a spontaneous study of movement that rejects academic constraints. OK

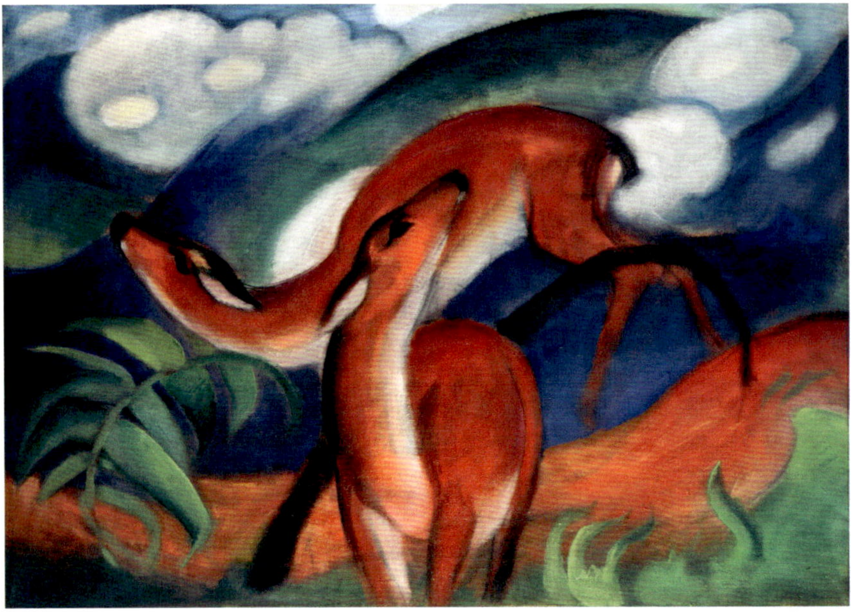

Franz Marc | Rote Rehe II (Red Deer II) | 1912
Oil on canvas, 70 × 100 cm, inv. no.8923
Donation of Annette von Eckardt, 1917

Creating the desired unity of creature and cosmos was the main focus of Marc's animal pictures. In *Red Deer II*, a gentle, swelling wave, painted in a style reminiscent of *Jugendstil*, serves to unite animal and landscape. Donated by Marc's lover and patron Annette von Eckardt, *Red Deer II* was the first notable painting from the period of German Expressionism acquired by the Pinakotheken. The later defamation of Marc as a 'degenerate' artist in 1937, and the confiscation and eventual return (in 1940) of *Red Deer II* also makes it a perfect example of the Nazi Party's ambivalent attitude towards Franz Marc. OK

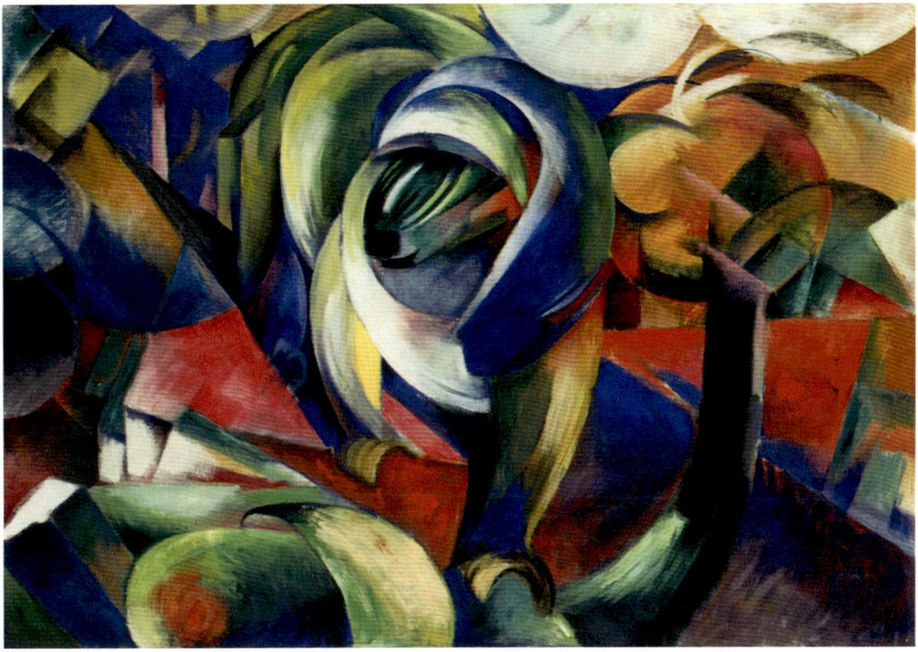

Franz Marc | Der Mandrill (The Mandrill) | 1913
Oil on canvas, 91 × 131 cm, inv. no. 13467
Donation of Sofie and Emanuel Fohn, 1964

After *The Mandrill* was purchased by the Hamburg Kunsthalle in 1918, a glass pane had to be installed to protect the painting from protestors. Today it is an established masterpiece among Franz Marc's animal paintings. Emanating outwards from the brilliant red-blue colour of the large primate, his mane and body are formed of concentric circles that identify him as the central force within the image and simultaneously mark a further step towards abstraction. Marc is indebted to Delaunay's circle paintings and his theory of spectral colours, which inspired him to take the merger of animal and cosmos to new heights in this work.
OK

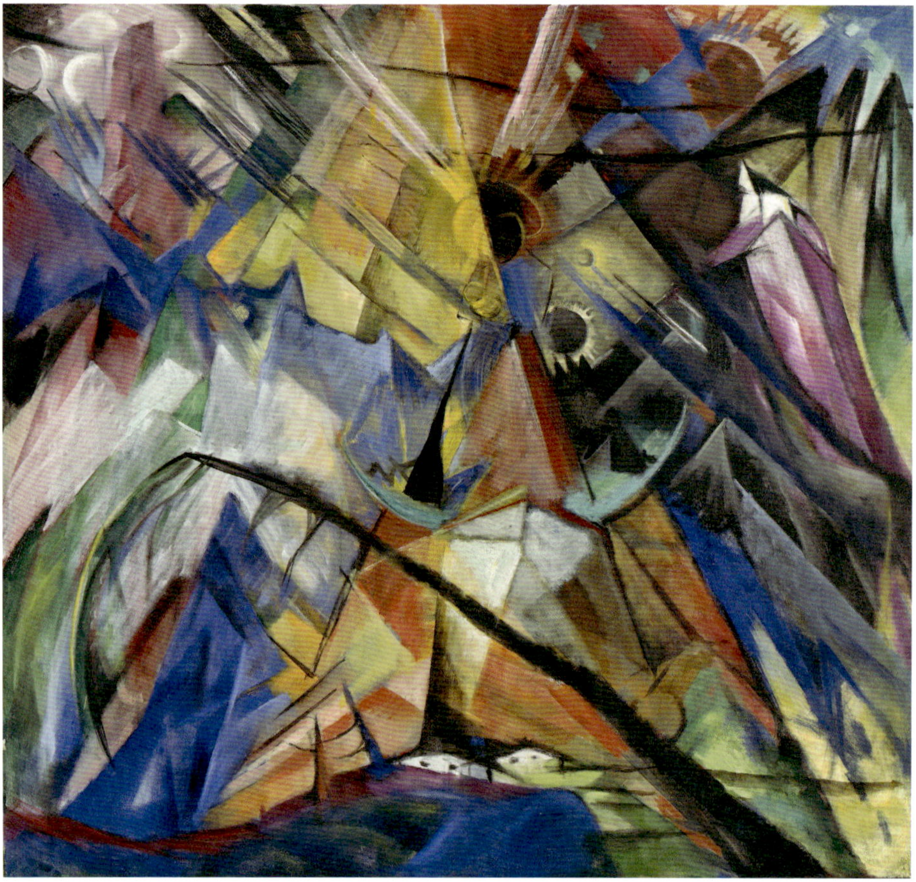

Franz Marc | Tirol (Tyrol) | 1913–14
Oil on canvas, 135.7 × 144.5 cm, inv. no. 10973
Acquired 1949

Inspired by his impressions of a trip to South Tyrol with Maria Franck, Franz Marc completed the painting *Tyrol* in 1913. In the place of animals, the artist depicts a landscape of tall mountain peaks composed of abstract crystalline shapes glowing in luminous colours. In 1914, Marc added a Madonna figure to the cosmic landscape, placed on the crescent moon. By doing so, he transformed the Tyrolean landscape into the setting of an apocalyptic vision, where sun and moon, light and dark are in conflict. Marc thus anticipates the catastrophe of the First World War in this work and articulates his hope for the renewal of Europe.
OK

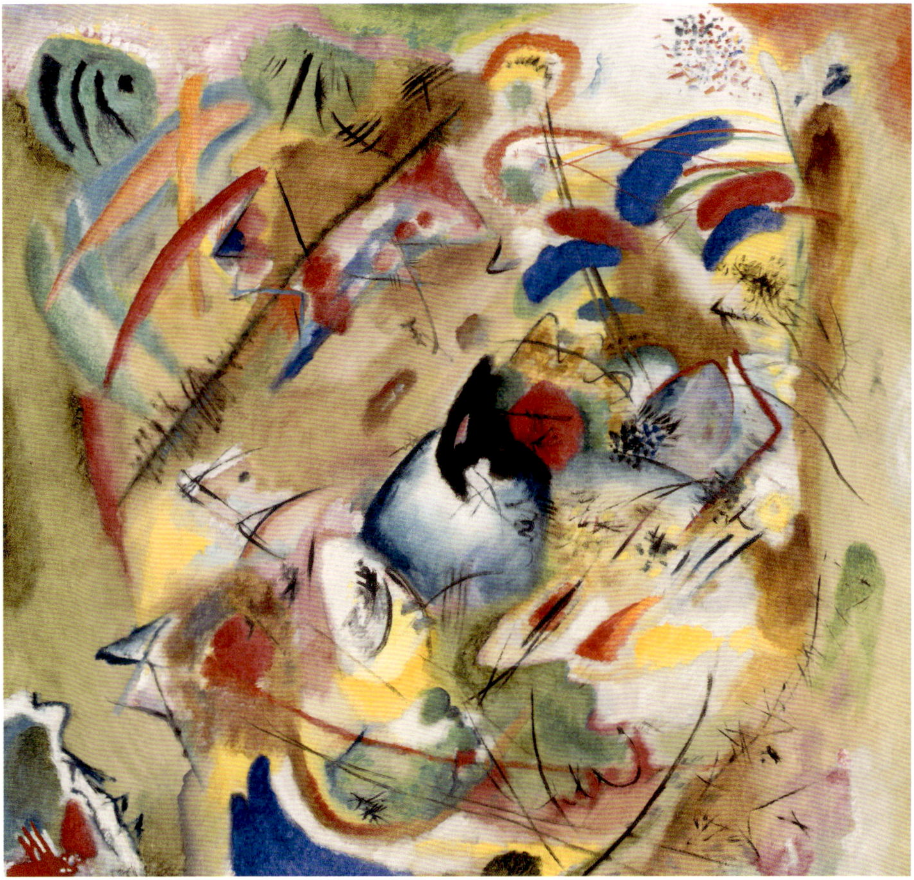

Wassily Kandinsky | Träumerische Improvisation (Dreamy Improvisation) | 1913
Oil on canvas, 130.5 × 130.5 cm, inv. no. 14091
Acquired 1969 with support of PIN. Freunde der Pinakothek der Moderne

Wassily Kandinsky described his 'improvisations' as unconscious, primarily sudden impressions of an 'inner nature'. The artist created over 35 improvisations between 1909 and 1914 that each has an associative subtitle. The series of works successively distance themselves from figuration in order to allow their 'inner sound' to resonate ever more clearly. *Dreamy Improvisation* is a pure abstract masterpiece, free of any concrete references. The grey-brown ochre tones and white passages of the painting create a light, airy atmosphere that begins to reverberate with movement and sound through the skilful use of delicate lines and daubs of colour. OK

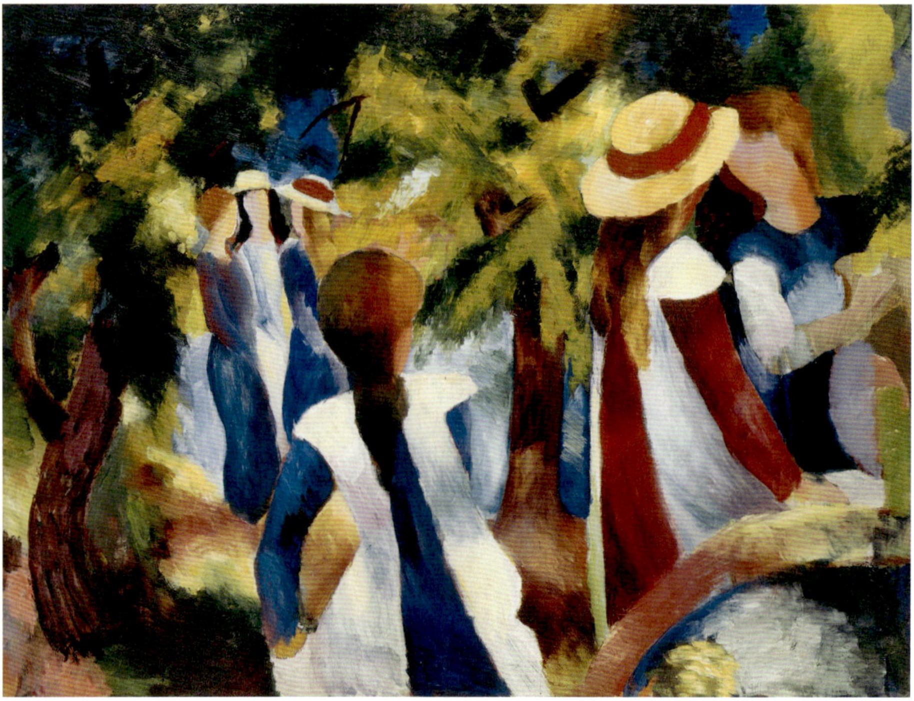

August Macke | Mädchen unter Bäumen (Girls under Trees) | 1914
Oil on canvas, 119.5 × 159 cm, inv. no. 13466
Donation of Sofie and Emanuel Fohn, 1964

Two groups of girls resting under trees in a park on a summer's day – the painting exudes the serene, leisurely atmosphere of a Sunday in an array of brilliant colours. The subject of visiting a park or garden derives from French Impressionism and the work similarly incorporates Robert Delaunay's groundbreaking ideas on simultaneous contrast. Macke began the painting before he left for Tunisia with Klee, finishing it after his return to Bonn during a frenzied period of creativity that was very much influenced by perceptions of colour. Macke was conscripted six weeks later and died on the West Front in France on 26 September 1914.
OK

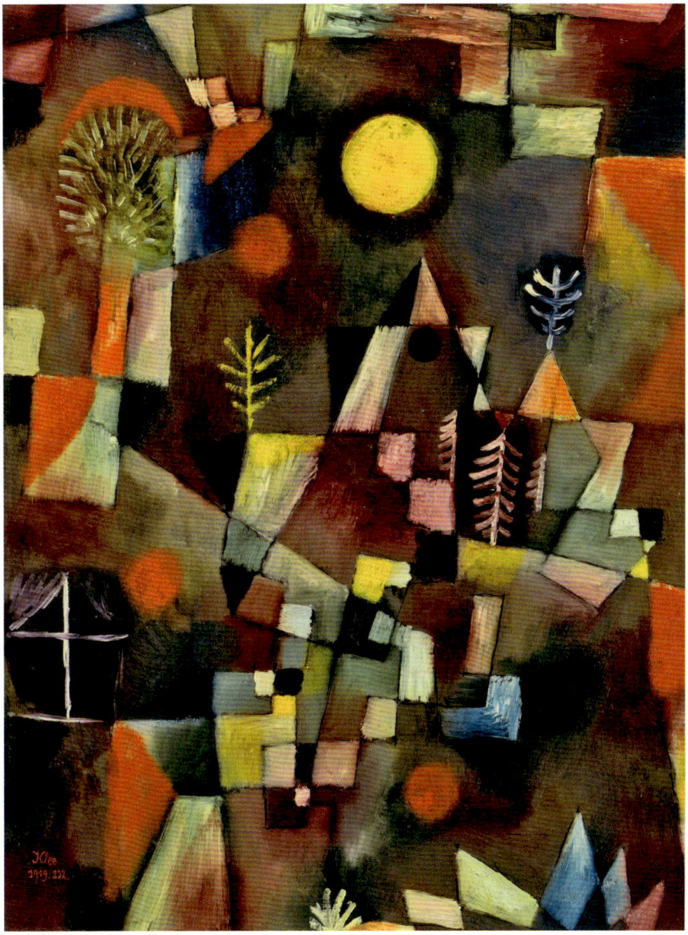

Paul Klee | Der Vollmond (Full Moon) | 1919
Oil on paper and card, 49.8 × 38 cm, inv. no. 15249
Acquired 1991

Following on from his early works on paper, Paul Klee first took up oil painting in 1919. His *Full Moon* is one of the most significant works from this phase, in which the artist systematized his pictorial architecture and combined it with landscape views. The composition comprises colourful rectangular and triangular shapes rising up towards a yellow full moon that bathes the night in a silvery, mystical light. The window frame, the moon, the trees, and mountain peaks are references to Romantic symbols of the longing for transcendence, to which Klee adds a contemporary measure of abstraction resulting in a 'cool Romanticism [...] without pathos'. OK

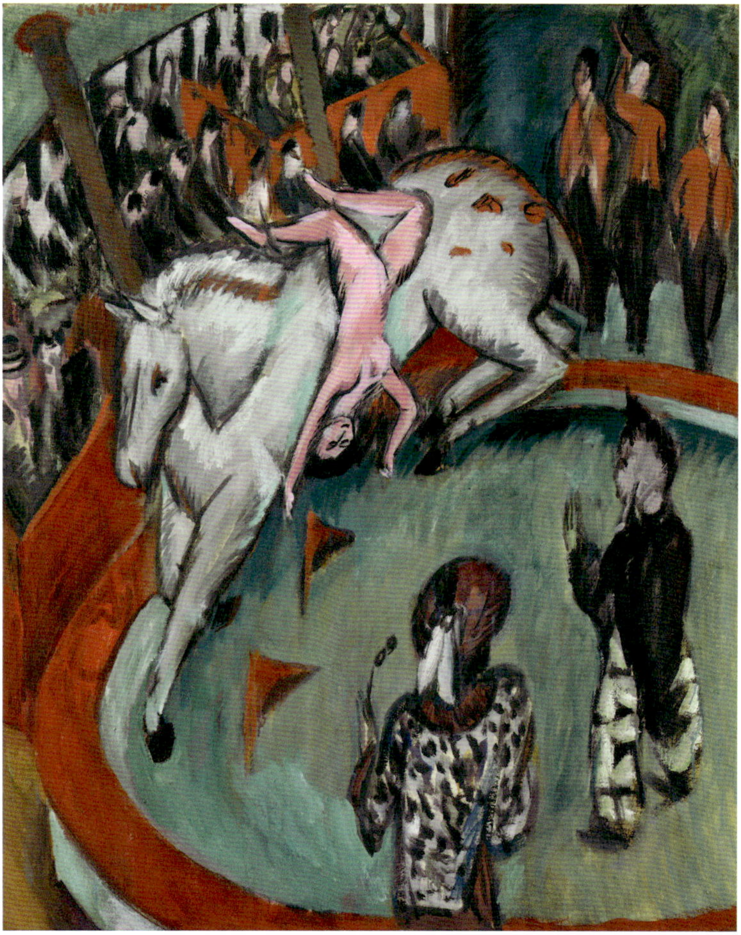

Ernst Ludwig Kirchner | Cirkus (Circus) | 1913
Oil on canvas, 119.8 × 99.8 cm, inv. no. 14715
Acquired 1982

Kirchner hones in on the highlight of a circus act – a woman hanging upside down from the back of a horse as it canters around the arena. The circus rider served as the artist's alter ego in several of his paintings. Here he unites the two competing perspectives of the performer and the audience in a paradoxical manner and combines a view at eye-level with a view from above, invoking a sense of identification and voyeurism respectively. The circus tent as the location of thrills and magic, the distorted perspective, the nervous and dashed brushwork, the luminosity of the complimentary colours – all of these aspects combined make this a truly iconic example of Expressionism during the Berlin period of *Brücke*. OK

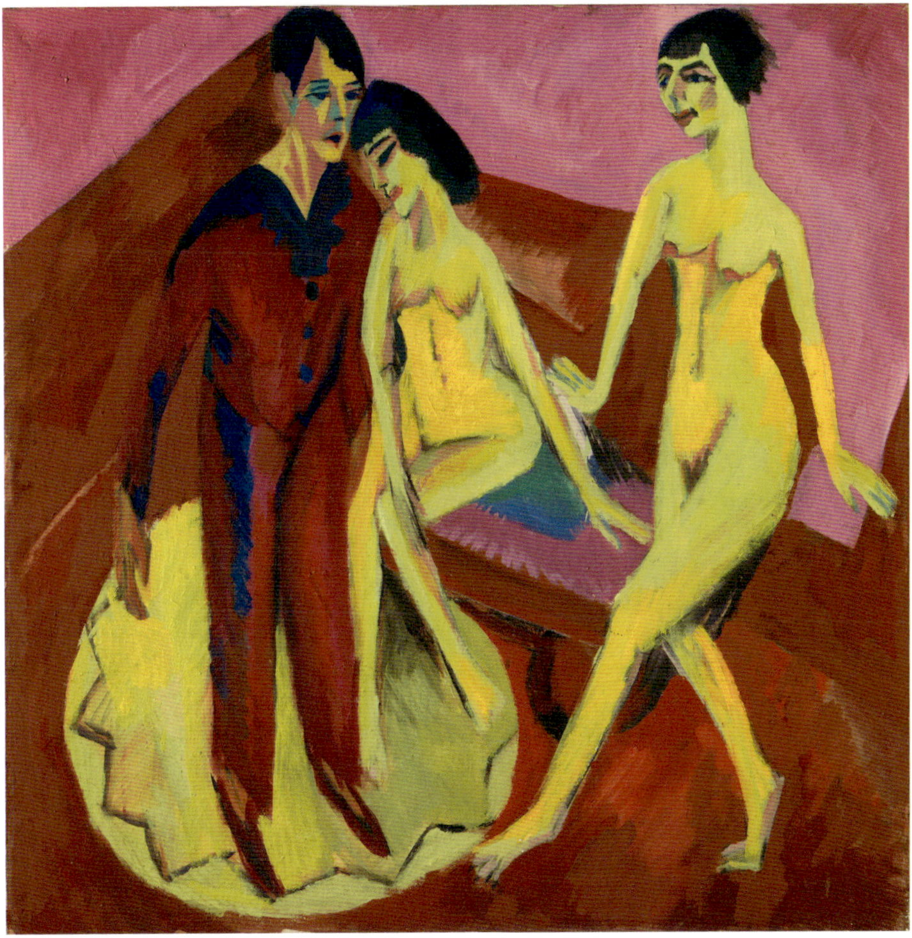

Ernst Ludwig Kirchner | Tanzschule (Dance School) | 1914/25
Oil on canvas, 114.5 × 115.5 cm, inv. no. 13350
Acquired 1963

This monumental composition, which remained in Kirchner's possession during his lifetime, depicts a stiff, upright man dressed in a Pierrot costume and two naked women; the woman sitting on the left nestles up to him, while the one on the right vies for his attention by performing a few steps on tiptoe. It is a self-portrait of the artist and the sisters Gerda (left) and Erna Schilling, who Kirchner met at a Berlin nightclub where they were working as dancers. The tense three-way relationship is underlined by the use of a vivid yellow and pink that were later retouched and intensified. OK

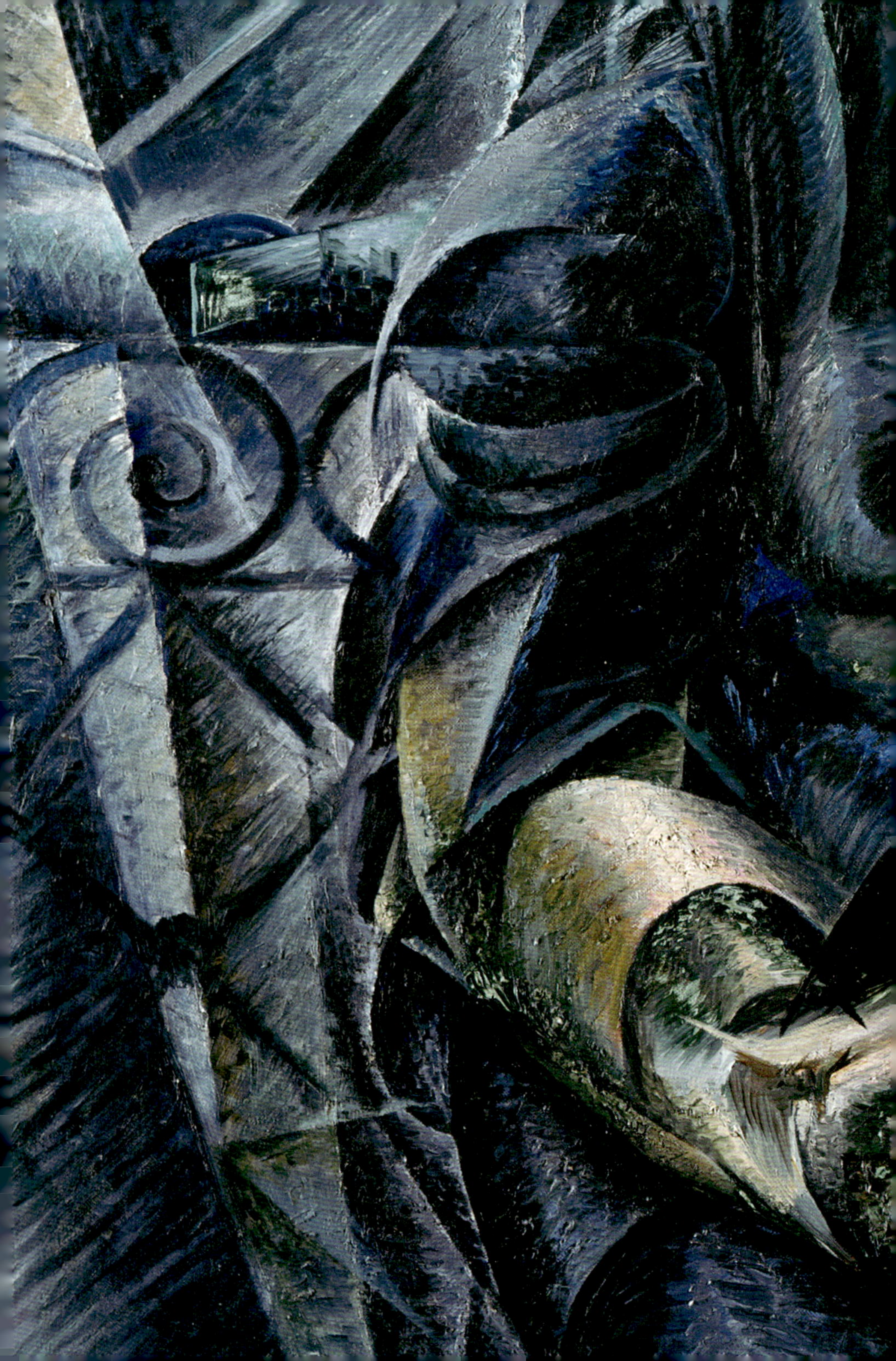

FRAGMENTATION AND RE-FORMATION
FROM CUBISM TO FUTURISM

In the early 20th century, traditional forms of expression were called into question in the visual arts, in music, and in literature. Of the various avant-gardes of that period, Cubism put forward an answer to the crisis of representation which was both the most radical and the most intellectual. Doubts about the possibility of directly reproducing the visible led the Cubists to separate art from nature, and to analyse painting's internal rules and structures. Cubism's innovative power is located in this move away from the imitation of nature, and in the search for painting's essential principles of form.

The beginning of Cubism in France is marked by Pablo Picasso's *Les Demoiselles d'Avignon*: the picture, painted in 1906–07, is characterized by an archaic reduction of the figure into block-like forms. In the following years, Picasso and Georges Braque developed the Cubist style in a close dialogue of mutual influence. As Braque put it: the two artists were linked 'like mountain-climbers roped together'. As well as African masks, the work of Cézanne – who was given a commemorative exhibition in Paris in 1907 – provided the decisive impulse for Picasso and Braque. Cézanne had reduced the image to a tectonic layering of patches; he had abandoned local colours, emphasizing basic formal elements, like the sphere, the cone, and the cylinder. Braque and Picasso radicalized Cézanne's approach, breaking with the illusion of three-dimensional space and with the self-contained figure. They wanted to liberate the visible world from the contingencies of external form: reality was broken down into fragments and facets, with objects decomposed into sections, presented simultaneously from a variety of points of view, intermeshed with the surrounding space. Unlike the *Fauves*, the Cubists' focus was not on the emancipation of colour, but on the essence of form: natural colours were replaced by a monochrome, grey-brown background. In 1908, Braque wrote: 'I must [...] create a new kind of beauty, a beauty that appears to me as volume, line, mass, and weight.' For the Cubists, the specific subject of their paintings was of lesser importance. However, their conscious decision to limit themselves to still lifes and figures holding string instruments is testimony to their always penetrating analysis of the object.

Cubist paintings by Picasso and Braque were on show at Munich's Galerie Thannhauser as early as 1910; the world's first ever Picasso retrospective took place in the same gallery in 1913. All the more remarkable, then, that the Bayerische Staatsgemäldesammlungen only acquired their first Cubist work in 1967. Funding for the purchase of Braque's *Femme à la mandoline* came largely from the proceeds of the sale of Old Master paintings from the collection of Hermann Göring, linking the acquisition to the problematic attempt at 'reparation' for art confiscated by the Nazis from the Bayerische Staatsgemäldesammlungen during the 1937 *Degenerate Art* action. Nonetheless, *Femme à la mandoline* represents a highly significant acquisition. A masterpiece of fully-developed 'Analytical Cubism', it is the first Cubist picture in Braque's oeuvre to have an oval format. The painting, completed early in 1910, was followed by a significant number of oval-shaped works by both Braque and Picasso. The oval shape increased the tension between form and picture surface, thanks to the intensified concentration on horizontal lines and the vertically-tiered blocks of figures. With its abstract decomposition of the figure, Picasso's *Femme au violon*, completed one year later, represents a high-point of Analytical Cubism, but also its end-point. Beginning in 1912, the Cubists began to collage fragments of reality, like newspaper cuttings, into their works, in an attempt to recreate a recognizable connection to the real world. This was the starting point for Cubism's second phase, 'Synthetic Cubism', which gathered together fragmented forms into larger ensembles, more multifaceted and colourful, which also included some graphic elements. Alongside Picasso and Braque, the Spanish painter Juan Gris was also among the protagonists of this phase. *Bouteille de Bordeaux* is among the works by Gris held at the Pinakothek der Moderne. In a 'synthetic' manner, Gris combined a wide variety of object-fragments and material forms, creating his own pictorial reality and a new sense of the 'objectness' of the objects depicted. Only in 1971 did Cubism become a substantial area of the collection, thanks to the bequest of Woty and Theodor Werner. This artist-couple lived in Paris in the 1930s, where they were friends with Georges Braque and Christian Zervos. Their collection included Cubist works by Gris, Picasso, and Braque.

The Cubists' influence was felt by all other avant-garde movements, most acutely, however, by the Italian Futurists. Umberto Boccioni may have criticized the static quality of Cubist pictures, and their scientific, rational analysis, but Cubism was nonetheless the starting point for the Futurists' exaltation of modernity, speed, technology, and the modern metropolis. In the famous sentence in the 1909 *First Futurist Manifesto* – 'A racing car [...] a roaring car [...] is more beautiful than the Victory of Samothrace' – the writer Filippo Tommaso Marinetti announced a new concept of beauty, refuting past traditions and norms, and declaring museums to be 'cemeteries'. In his 1912 painting *Volumi orizzontali*, Boccioni experimented with the Futurist idea of simultaneous representation of motion, but used a traditional subject: a portrait of his mother. Within the figure itself, Boccioni deploys an innovative dynamism, visible in the structure of the body and the head's dissolution into swirls and facets. By contrast, Gino Severini's *Sculptural Synthesis of the Idea of War*, painted in 1915 (p. 74) uses Synthetic Cubism to illustrate the Futurists' emphatic relationship to war and technology.

The art of Robert Delaunay, although critical of Futurism, nonetheless also emphasized similar principles of simultaneity and dynamism – the permanent, simultaneous movement of modern life. In *L'Équipe de Cardiff* Delaunay brings together metropolitan motifs, including advertisements, rugby players, aeroplanes, and a Ferris wheel, into a Futurist-Cubist assemblage. Here, air and movement are suggested by magically luminous, shimmering colours, rather than by fragmented individual forms. With scientific ambition, Delaunay aimed at a pure, abstract style of painting, which would express the optical perception of the world through a prismatic splitting of light, while enriching impressions of movement with simultaneous, contrasting colours. Referring to the mythical singer Orpheus, the poet Guillaume Apollinaire gave the name 'Orphism' to Delaunay's colour spaces and their lyrical and musical effects. In addition to Delaunay's integration of colour and the Futurists' addition of movement, Cubism also evolved through the application of its principles to sculpture. Two key works of this trend – sculptures by Alexander Archipenko and Rudolf Belling – can be seen in the Modern Art Collection. Archipenko's *The Boxers* is testimony to the reduction of sculpture to Cubism's basic, stereometric forms. As in painting, here the incorporation of empty space breaks up the outline of the figure, creating an impression of movement and archaic power. Rudolf Belling's *Triad* is a masterpiece by German modernism's only prominent sculptor: with an expansive, dancer-like gesture, the piece continues the drive to incorporate movement within representation and reaches a utopian, late-Expressionist form of Cubism. With its analytical purism and aesthetic radicalism, Cubism's influence continued long into the second half of the 20th century, more so than any other avant-garde style.

Oliver Kase

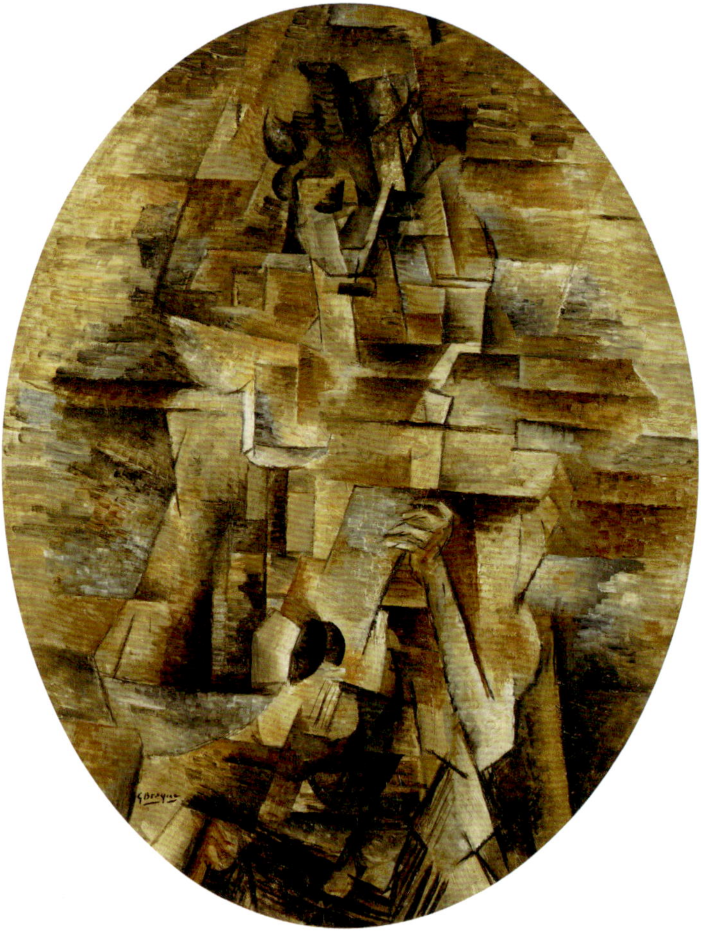

Georges Braque | **Femme à la mandoline** (Woman with a Mandolin) | 1910
Oil on canvas, 91.5 × 72.5 cm, inv. no. 13824
Acquired 1967 for the Modern Art Collection with support of PIN. Freunde der Pinakothek der Moderne

Figures playing string instruments were among Braque's and Picasso's favourite subjects to express their ideas about Cubist painting. This choice of subject was influenced by Picasso's visit to a retrospective of the work of Camille Corot at the Autumn Salon of 1909, which also featured paintings with figures playing music. But while Corot still believed in the basic idea of art imitating nature, the Cubists insisted on the autonomy of artistic reality. In place of imitation came geometric dissection. BSO

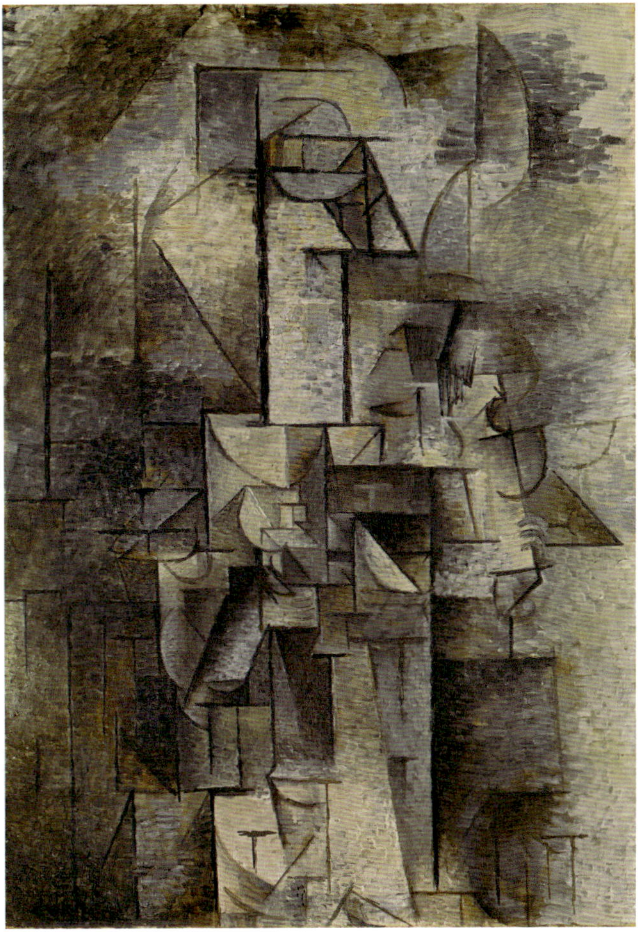

Pablo Picasso | La Femme au violon (La Violiniste) (Woman with a Violin) | 1911
Oil on canvas, 92 × 65 cm, inv. no. 16819
2022–2024 acquited together with the Ernst von Siemens Kunststiftung and with the support of the Federal Government Commissioner for Culture and the Media, the Kulturstiftung der Länder, the Würth Group and Fritz Schäfer, Schweinfurt

Compared with Braque's 1910 painting *Femme à la mandoline*, Picasso's *Femme au violon* marks a new stage in analytical decomposition. The two artists worked in a relationship of friendly competition. In Picasso's picture, the human body, the instrument, and the surrounding space all interpenetrate: the spectator can no longer easily distinguish between them. They form an abstract yet sensuous pattern of resonance, with finely dashed lines that seem almost to vibrate. The *Femme au violon* formed part of Picasso's first ever solo exhibition, held in his honour in Munich in 1913. BSO

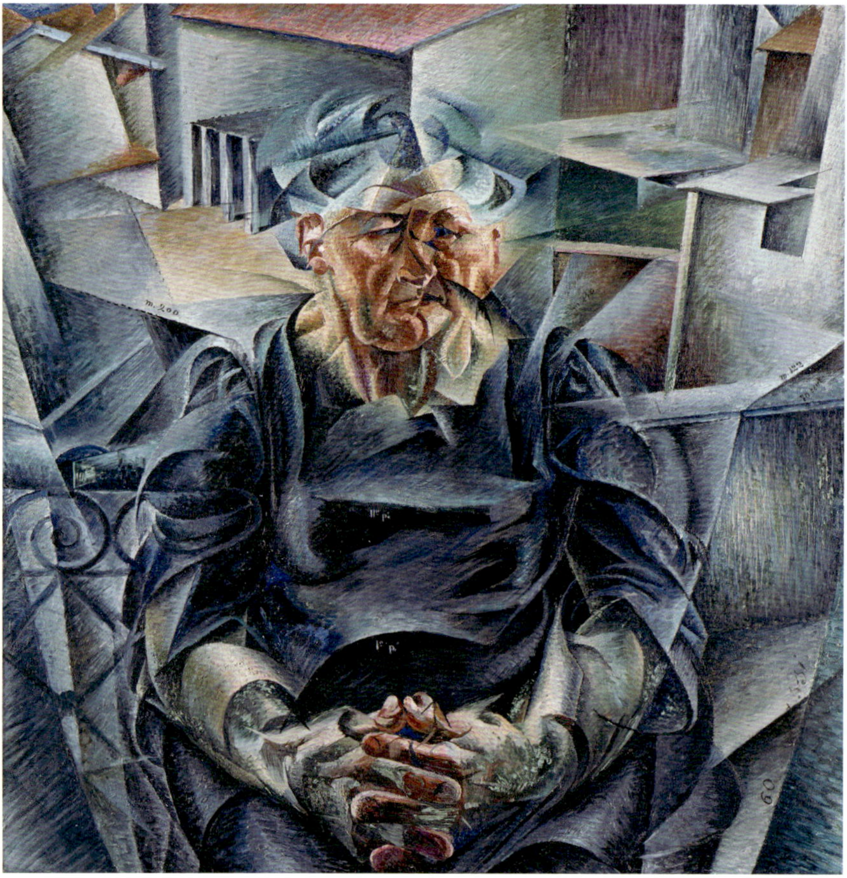

Umberto Boccioni | Volumi orizzontali (Horizontal Volumes) | 1912
Oil on canvas, 95 × 95.5 cm, inv. no. 14611
Acquired 1979

Volumi orizzontali shows Cecilia Forlani Boccioni, the mother of the artist. She is sitting on the balcony of her Milan apartment, while the surrounding sea of geometrically-formed houses seems to revolve around her. Her head has been drawn into the maelstrom outside, and is reproduced from three simultaneous points of view. Boccioni was a leading Futurist, sharing their principal preoccupation – the representation of movement as the fundamental principle of modern life. Here, the quiet, seated posture and interlaced hands form a stark contrast with this dynamism. Clearly the mother embodies her son's longing for peace and stability in the turbulent city. BSO

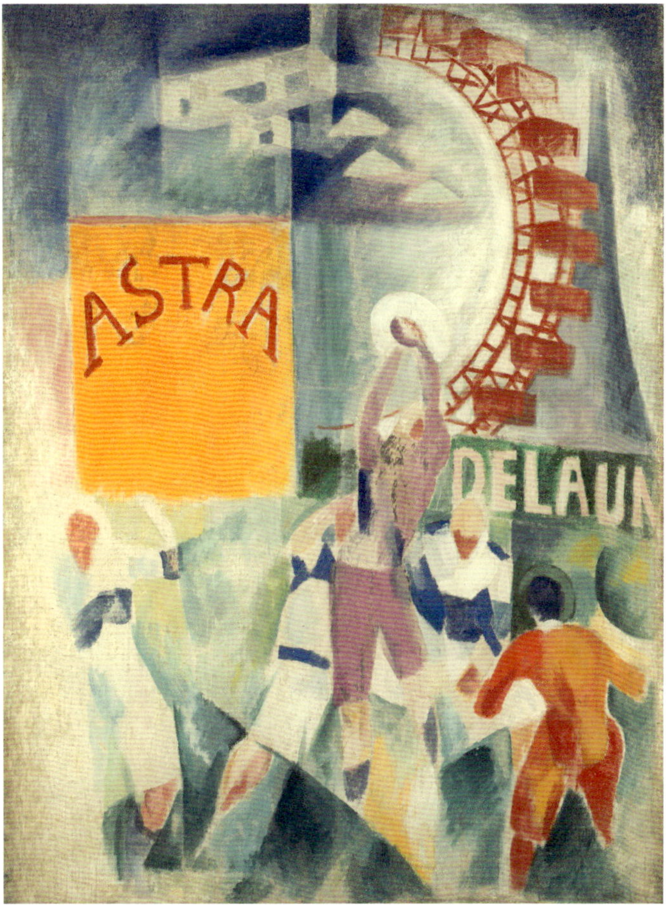

Robert Delaunay | **L'Équipe de Cardiff** (The Cardiff Team) | 1913
Oil on canvas, 129.8 × 96.6 cm, inv. no. 13340
Acquired 1963

Delaunay's art emerges from an intensive engagement with the theory of simultaneous contrasts. As a painter, Delaunay was fascinated by how colours could have different effects under changing light conditions, at times even seeming to be 'in motion'. His works occupy an opposite pole to Braque's and Picasso's almost monochromatic Cubist pictures. Here Delaunay illustrates the play of colours within rugby, a game of movement. In addition, he makes reference to the dynamism of the great city, in the form of the big wheel, the Eiffel Tower, the double-decker buses. The inscription 'ASTRA' refers to an aeroplane manufacturer. In this way, the picture resembles an advertising poster capturing the feel of modern life in 1913.
BSO

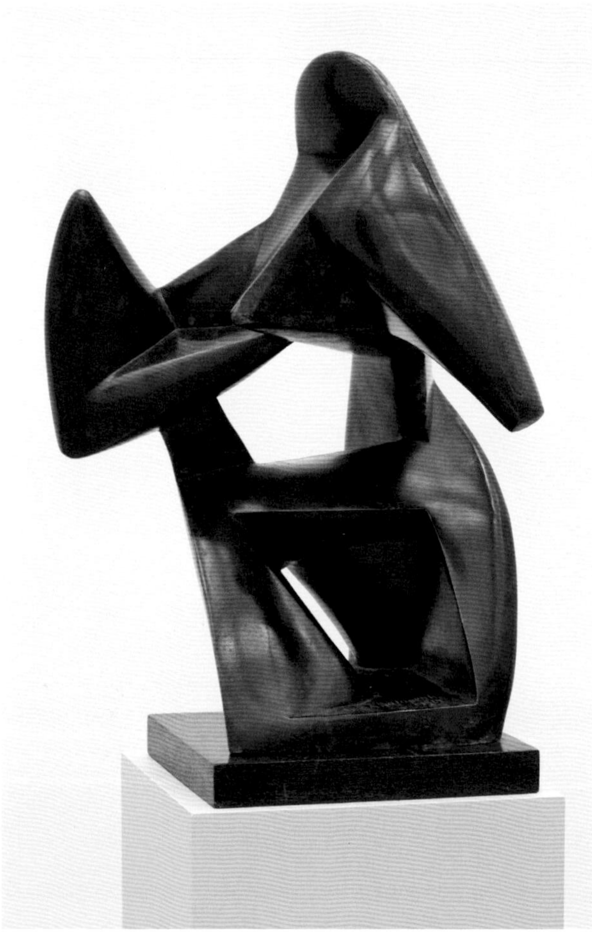

Alexander Archipenko | La Lutte (The Boxers) | 1914
Bronze, 63.7 × 42 × 41 cm (with plinth), inv. no. B 411
Acquired 1964

Alexander Archipenko's *The Boxers* illustrates the power of continuous movement. The two fighters, caught up in an exchange of blows, seem reduced to geometric forms, dynamically reacting to each other. The work forms part of a series of earlier sculptures, made in Paris, in which the Ukrainian-born Archipenko took up ideas from Cubism and Futurism so as to rethink the relation of bodies and space in sculpture. *The Boxers* is among Archipenko's most abstract creations, but in the Paris of the early 20th century, boxing matches were enormously popular with the public. BSO

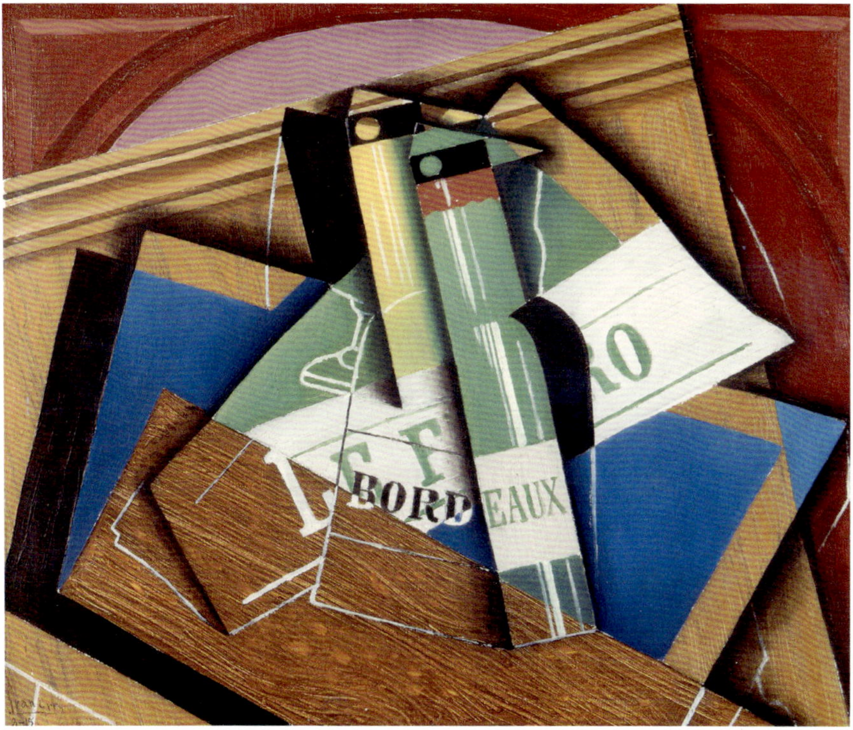

Juan Gris | La Bouteille de Bordeaux (The Bordeaux Bottle) | 1915
Oil on canvas, 50 × 61 cm, inv. no. 14237
Bequest of Theodor and Woty Werner, 1971

In a 1924 lecture, Juan Gris summed up his aesthetic position: 'Up until now, painters have always turned an object into a picture. However, my working method is precisely the opposite [...] Mathematics as a pictorial means leads me to the representation of an object [...] Only as my own viewer can I extract the object from of my picture.' This deductive approach can be traced in the painting *The Bordeaux Bottle*. Here, a variety of forms interpenetrate, setting off associations – a labelled bottle, the grainy wood of a table or a barrel, the front page of a newspaper, a glass, the arch of a cellar. BSO

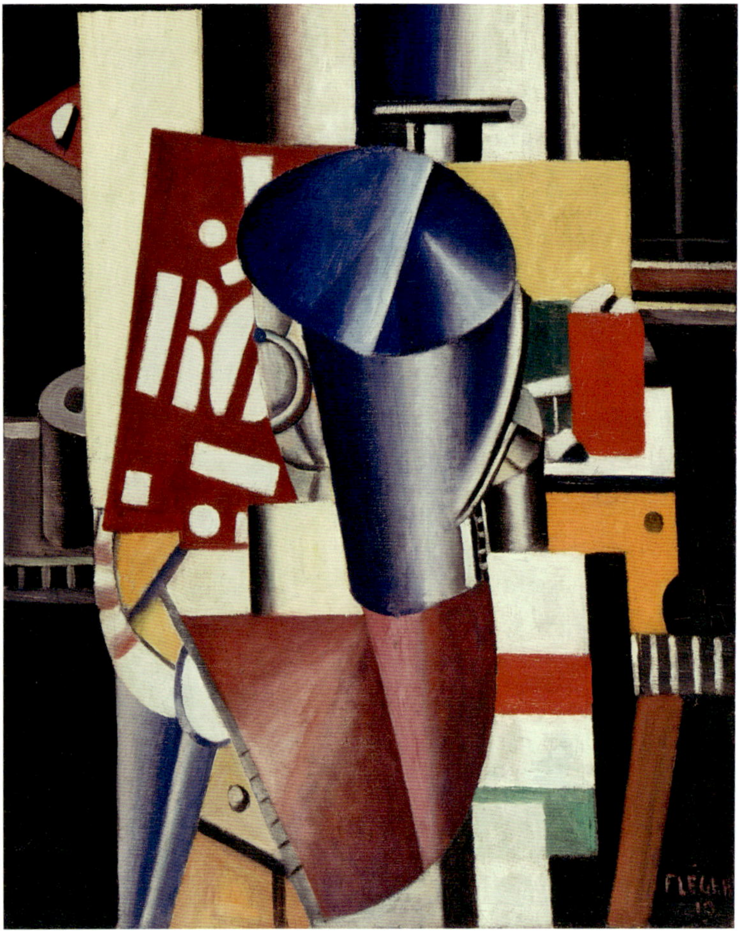

Fernand Léger | **Le Typographe** (The Typographer) | 1919
Oil on canvas, 81 × 65 cm, inv. no. GV 16
Acquired 1971 by PIN. Freunde der Pinakothek der Moderne for the Modern Art Collection

A shiny metallic cylinder, parts of a gearbox, alphabetic templates, and poster-like colour fields fill Fernand Léger's composition, which oscillates between abstraction and figuration. Rather than an actual typographic machine, we see mechanical elements and coded references to production. Léger's enthusiasm for technical devices had begun with a visit to the Paris Air Show in 1912: he was fascinated, he later wrote, by the 'the beautiful metal objects, hard, solid, and usable, shiny steel in a thousand varieties, next to pure blue and unadulterated cinnabar'. BSO

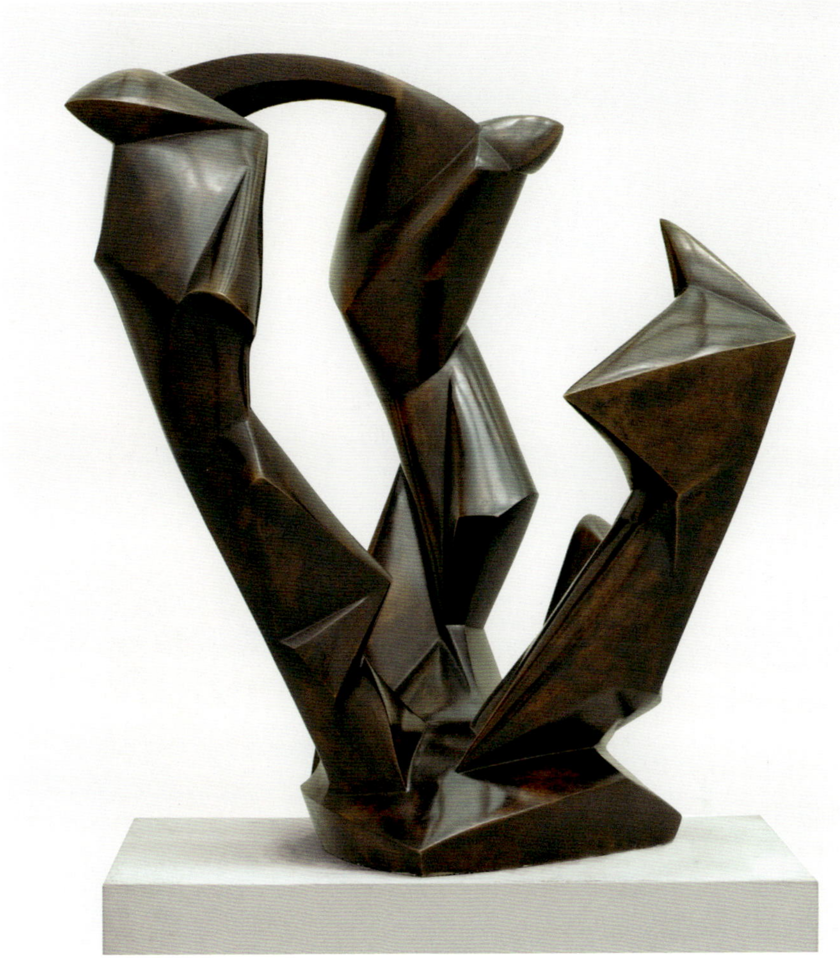

Rudolf Belling | Dreiklang (Triad) | 1918–19
Bronze, patinized, approx. 90 × 85 × 75 cm, inv. no. B 388
Acquired 1963

Rudolf Belling was the first German sculptor to move in the direction of an abstract, Cubist-Expressionist visual idiom, taking his first steps in this direction while working in Berlin around 1918. His sculpture *Triad* bears witness to this. This masterpiece, which launches into and penetrates the surrounding space, is made to be viewed in the round. It thus expresses Belling's rejection of the ideal of a picture-like form of sculpture only to be viewed frontally, as advocated around this time by Adolf von Hildebrand. On another level, the title's musical allusion can be understood to refer to the idea of unifying all the arts. BSO

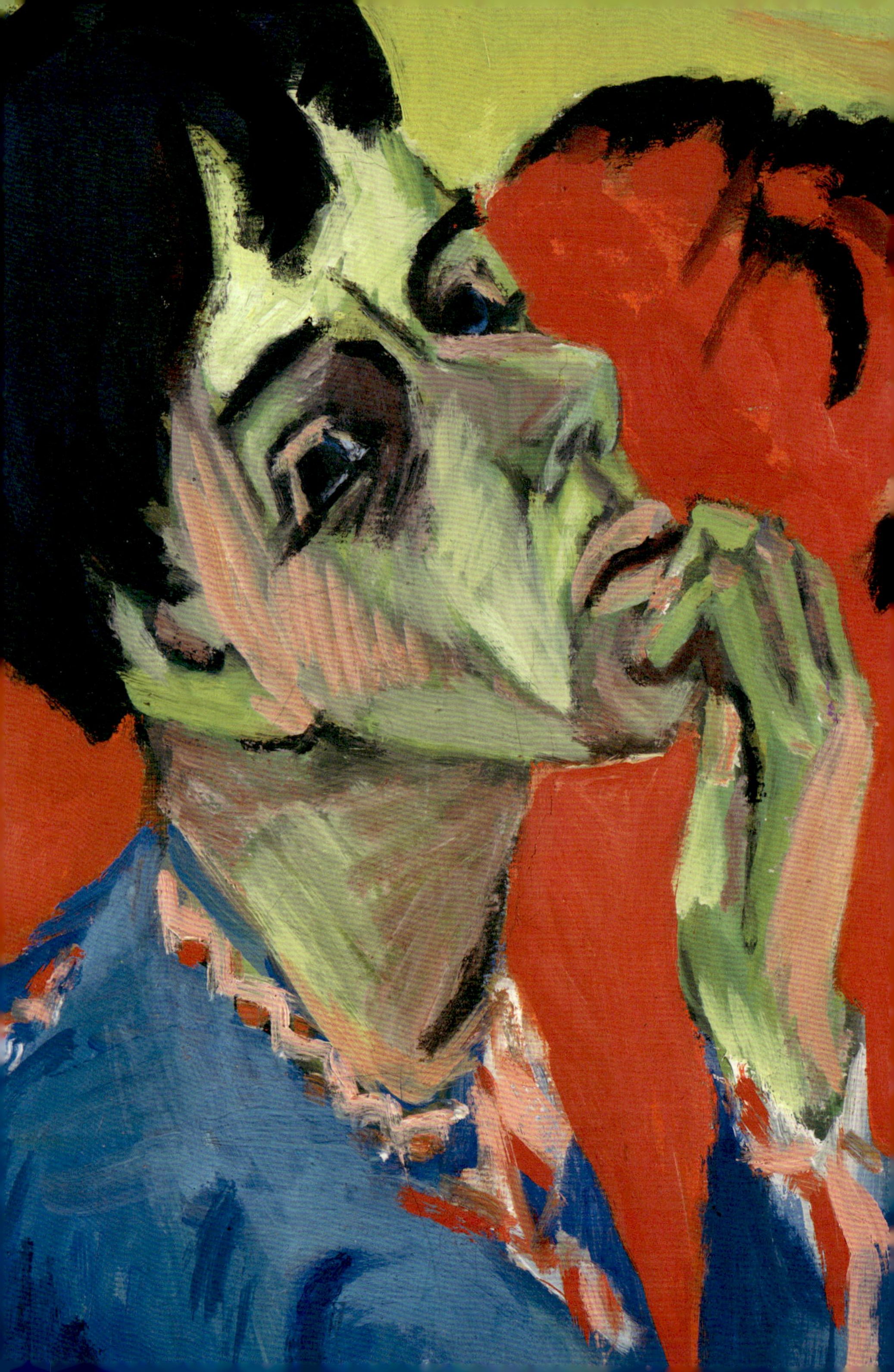

APOCALYPSE
ARTISTS AND THE FIRST WORLD WAR

'We want to glorify the war – the world's only hygiene,' demanded Filippo Tommaso Marinetti in the 1909 *Manifesto of Futurism*. The Italian Futurists were not alone in harbouring this provocative enthusiasm for war. Before 1914, numerous artists and intellectuals paid homage to an idea of war that just a few years later would be overtaken by the reality of the First World War. The demoralizing trench warfare and mass killing of the industrialized war resulted in the loss for many of their initial euphoria. As Franz Marc wrote on 25 October 1914 in his obituary for his friend August Macke, who had died in the war: 'How numerous and dreadful might the mutilations be that this terrible war has wrought upon our future?' One and half years later, the author of those lines would himself number among the First World War's victims. By 1914, *Der Blaue Reiter* was already history: the Russians Wassily Kandinsky, Marianne von Werefkin, and Alexei Jawlensky were forced to leave Germany as 'enemy aliens'. Like *Der Blaue Reiter*, many networks of the new art movements were broken up by the First World War. In the years leading up to 1914, internationalism had been the defining symbol of the avant-garde; the reciprocal exchange of ideas and cross-national artistic influence became characteristic features of the era, as were pioneering exhibitions such as those of *The Editorial Board of Der Blaue Reiter* in 1911–12 at the Galerie Thannhauser in Munich, the 1912 *Sonderbund* in Cologne, the *First German Autumn Salon* by Herwarth Walden in 1913 in Berlin, and the 1913 *Armory Show* in New York.

Given the terrible consequences of the First World War for the avant-garde, it seems strange how enthusiastically many artists and intellectuals had initially welcomed the conflict. After more than four decades of peace, war had become associated with the idea of a powerful force that would bring with it freedom from moribund bourgeois structures and prevailing hierarchies, tearing asunder the shackles of the long 19th century. Even before 1914, art vocabulary had become militaristic. 'Avant-garde', 'Phalanx', and 'Der Sturm' ('The Charge') were names given to groups and publications, while the talk everywhere was of mental weapons and battles. The war brought together people's yearning for a short, intense course of events. The hope was that the war would break over Europe like a brief cooling storm. In Germany, Franz Marc was one of the most vociferous supporters of the war as, like Marinetti, he felt the event would produce the long-awaited 'purification' or 'cleansing'. A range of anti-bourgeois or explicitly patriotic motivations were evident among artists who volunteered for military service, some of whom (such as Otto Dix and Max Beckmann) also saw the war as a way of satisfying their artistic hunger for an intensified reality and new subjects.

As early as 1915, disillusionment and war fatigue had already become widespread, with artists lamenting losses in the ranks of their peers and among families and friends, as the war's brutal and barbarous contempt for human life grew abundantly clear.

The works featured in this chapter shed light on some of the exhibits exploring the 'primal catastrophe' of the First World War. How did artists see war before the outbreak of hostilities? How did the First World War change artists and their work? Even before the outbreak of war, Ludwig Meidner and Franz Marc created between 1912 and 1914 apocalyptic or prophetic pictures of the catastrophe. Painting in dialogue with literary Expressionism, the philosophy of Friedrich Nietzsche, and Futurism, Meidner created *Apocalyptic Landscapes* in 1912 – visionary premonitions of the war and natural catastrophes, for which real events such as the 1908 Messina earthquake and the Balkan War of 1912–13 also provided inspiration. Franz Marc's *Tyrol* (p. 50) and *Fighting Forms* from 1914 were works that became iconic prefigurations of the war. Colours erupt in crystalline storms and an unravelling spiral, revealing the hidden forces of a world order turned upside down. A completely contrasting work, albeit one with a similarly affirmative nature, is Gino Severini's *War*, which employs Cubo-Futurist montage techniques to pay homage to new military technology. Severini considered depictions of battlefields and war scenes to be antiquated and wanted to create 'physical symbols' for the 'idea of war'. A lung complaint, however, meant that the artist himself was spared from the front and could instead make do with the distant intellectual perspective afforded from Paris. In contrast to Severini, the French sculptor Raymond Duchamp-Villon created his portrait in 1918 of the physician Professor Gosset during a spell in hospital in Cannes after becoming infected with typhoid fever while working as a medical orderly. The Cubo-Futurist abstraction of the posthumously cast portrait evokes, among other visual associations, the gas masks used in the First World War.

A number of German Expressionists pursued their anti-bourgeois and provocative instincts to create pictures of an altogether more unsettling nature of people from the period of the First World War. Walter Gramatté's *Sick Man with Flowers* succeeds in creating the unnerving depiction of a sickly-blue, bony figure (perhaps the debased vision of a dehumanized soldier in a military tunic), who scrutinizes the observer with a penetrating gaze. This look also likely lends expression to the artist's own demoralizing experiences, who as a medical worker had to move back and forth between service on the front line (where he was unable to cope with the strain) and time in Germany (where he was nevertheless declared 'fit for military action').

The Expressionists' self-portraits from the period around 1914 to 1920 in particular provide a radical articulation of the traumas of war and existential angst. A self-portrait within a group portrait, Oskar Kokoschka's *The Emigrants* is the result of a deep crisis experienced of an artist made homeless and forced abroad. Unlike Kokoschka, who had been critically injured fighting on the Eastern Front, Ernst Ludwig Kirchner had no direct experience of the war. While still receiving field artillery training in Halle in 1915, he experienced panic attacks and – addicted to painkillers and alcohol – was eventually discharged. *Self-Portrait as Sick Man* shows the psychologically broken and weakened artist in the Swiss mountain landscape of Davos, a location that would later serve as his magical retreat when he wished to escape the world and convalesce. Wilhelm Lehmbruck remained in Berlin working as a medical orderly and was similarly spared from fighting on the front – and yet his monumental *Fallen Man* (1915–16) bears witness to the shock of war. Lehmbruck intended for *Fallen Man* to serve as a timeless monument to a generation of young soldiers sacrificed in the war effort. At the same time, the figure is the artistic legacy of Lehmbruck himself, who in 1919, suffering from increasingly severe depression, took his own life. It was likely in the wake of his and Richard Dehmel's death that Karl Schmidt-Rottluff in 1920 painted *Conversation on Death*. Produced two years after the war's end, this painting is no longer characterized by the glaring accusation of death or pathos-filled gestures, but is instead a melancholy engagement with the ubiquitous presence of death in survivors' conversations. It is astonishing to note just how much potential for renewal there proved to be against the backdrop of the First World War in works of an older generation of German artists. *The Red Christ*, a late work by Lovis Corinth, was created in 1922 when the artist was 64 years of age. While in 1914 he still belonged to the patriotic supporters of the First World War, this crucified figure represents the shift in mood towards scepticism and pessimism, given visual form through the iconography of the Christian Passion. Corinth does not portray his red Christ as a divine figure of redemption, but rather as a tortured and mutilated human being. Through the dramatic intensity and directness of the impasto and sprayed paint, the painter (born 1858) once again soared to an unprecedented height of late Expressionist pathos.

Oliver Kase

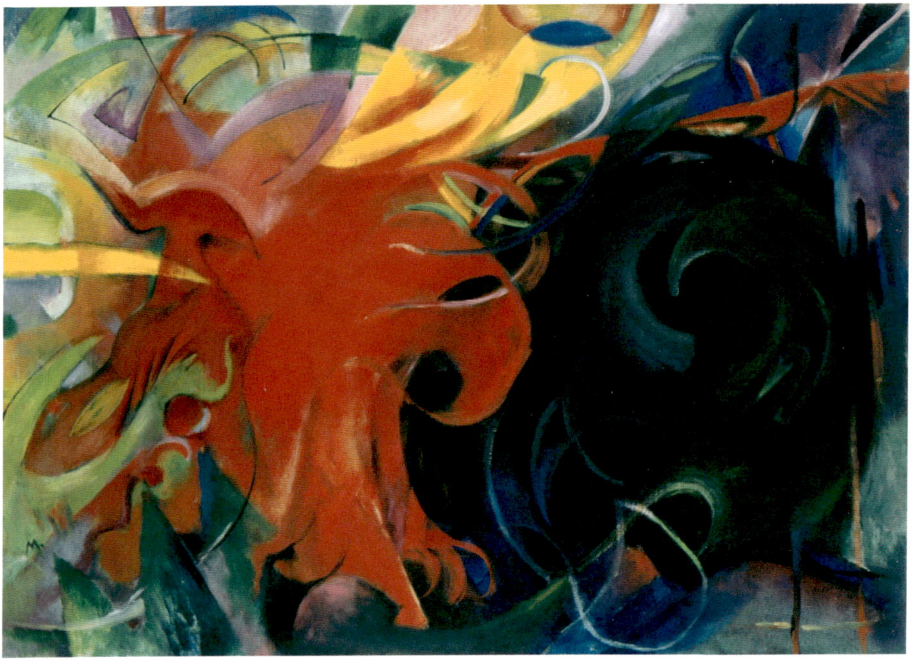

Franz Marc | Kämpfende Formen (Fighting Forms) | 1914
Oil on canvas, 91 × 131.5 cm, inv. no. 10972
Acquired 1949

In Franz Marc's work, the route to abstraction reached its apogee in *Fighting Forms* (1914). This work and other pictures from that year – *Cheerful Forms*, *Playing Forms*, and *Broken Forms* – constitute a group of abstract experiments. The painting has attracted numerous interpretations that revolve around the supposition that it represents a premonition of the world war. The dynamic energy of the red and blue-black forms is captivating: the red form darts out, expanding towards the viewer and the picture's edges; the black forms a spiral that recedes into the depths. OK

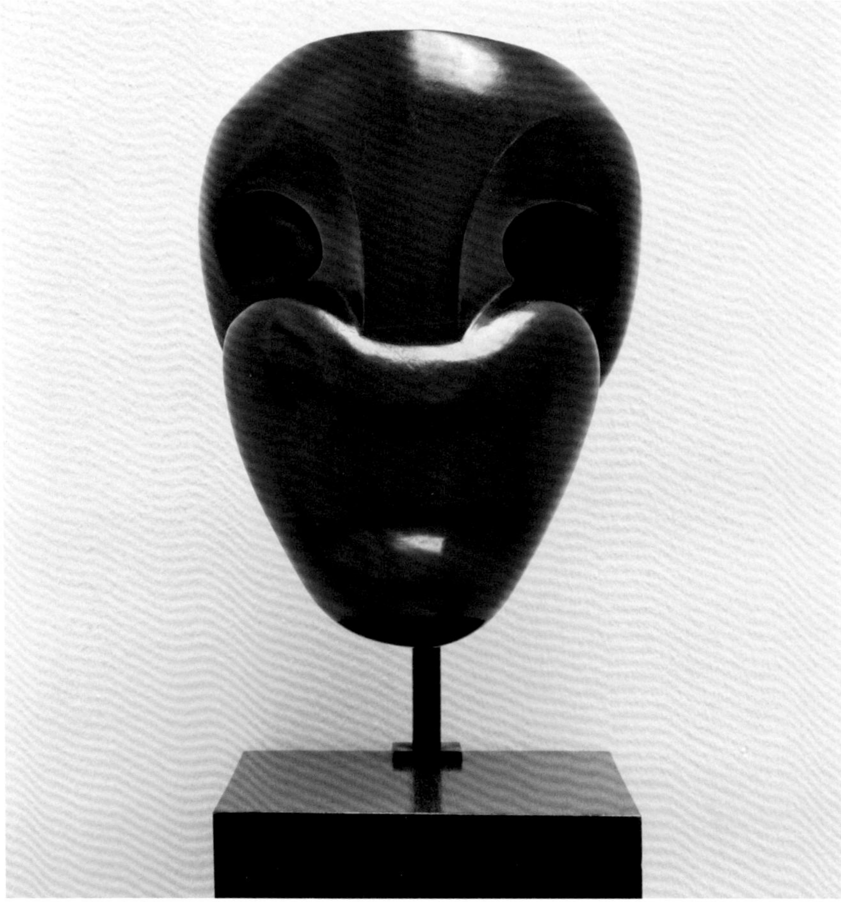

Raymond Duchamp-Villon | Portrait du Professeur Gosset (Portrait of Professor Gosset) | 1917–18 (posthumous cast)
Bronze, height 30.5 cm, inv. no. B 402
Acquired 1963

Duchamp-Villon experienced the First World War as a medical orderly. At the front, he was only able to pursue his artistic work on paper and in plaster. In 1916 he became infected with typhoid fever and died two years later. In a series of studies made shortly before his death, he created a model of the *Portrait du Professeur Gosset*, which was posthumously enlarged and cast in bronze. The radical reduction of the subject's facial features opens up a second level of associations, equally suggestive of an interest in African masks, an impression of a skull, or the sort of mask Gosset would have worn to protect himself against the poison gas used in the war. NE

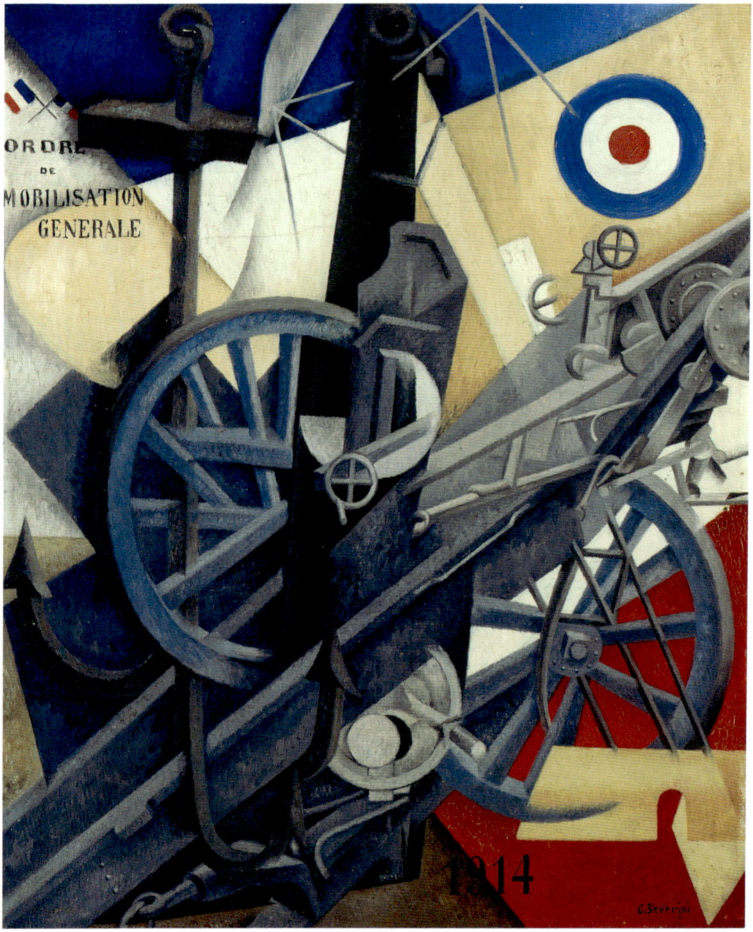

Gino Severini | Synthèse plastique de l'idée: Guerre
(Sculptural Synthesis of the Idea of War) | 1915
Oil on canvas, 60 × 50 cm, inv. no. 15036
Acquired 1987

The Italian Futurist Gino Severini wanted his painting to form a 'sculptural synthesis of the idea of war'. Using Cubist stylistic devises, he composed and created a collage depicting a factory smokestack and the three branches of the military: the navy (anchor), artillery (howitzer), and air force (airplane wing) and thus an aesthetic symbol of the new war machine. Severini selected the French Tricolore for the background, complemented by the year '1914' and the order for general mobilization. With hindsight, the Futurist celebration of progress takes on the aspect of a totem of mass killing in the mechanized war. OK

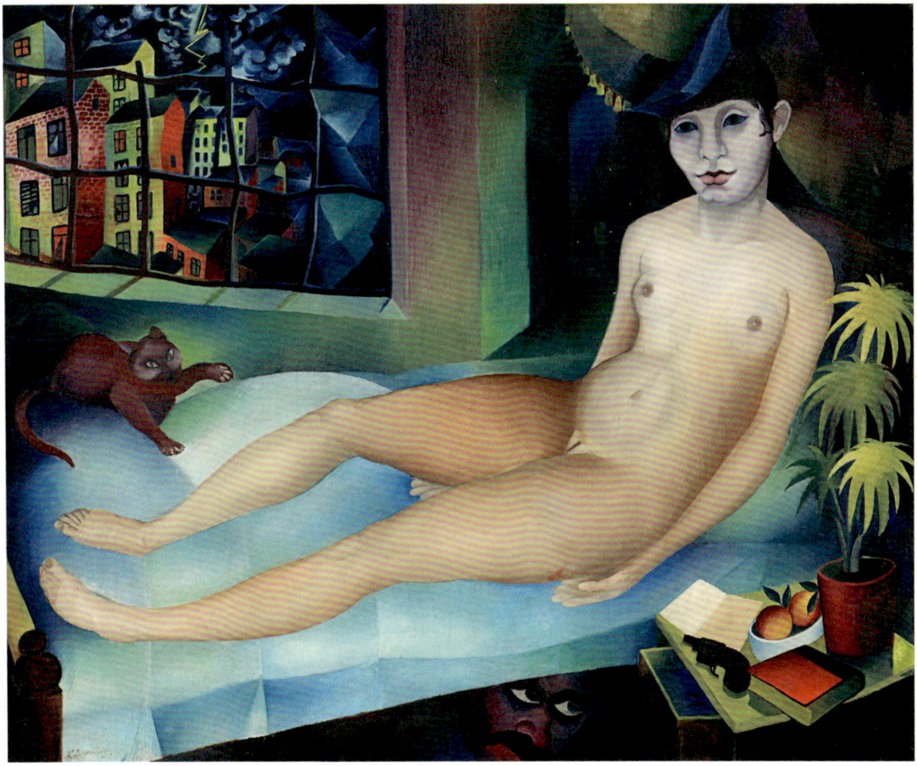

Heinrich Maria Davringhausen | **Der Lustmörder** (The Ripper) | 1917
Oil on canvas, 119.5 × 148.5 cm, inv. no. 14292
Acquired 1972

Boasting seismographically acute sensitivity to the social crises gripping the German Empire, the Berlin artist Davringhausen painted potentially scandalous subjects in toxic, morbid palettes, while at the same time singalling the onset of the *Neue Sachlichkeit* (New Objectivity). *The Ripper* is the earliest representation from the field of sexual violence that was an equal source of fascination for both the sensationalist press and artists. While the city in the background is struck by nocturnal flashes of lightning and the murderer lies in wait under the bed, the viewer is perturbed by the uncanny sight of a nude child-like Venus, simultaneously seductress and victim. OK

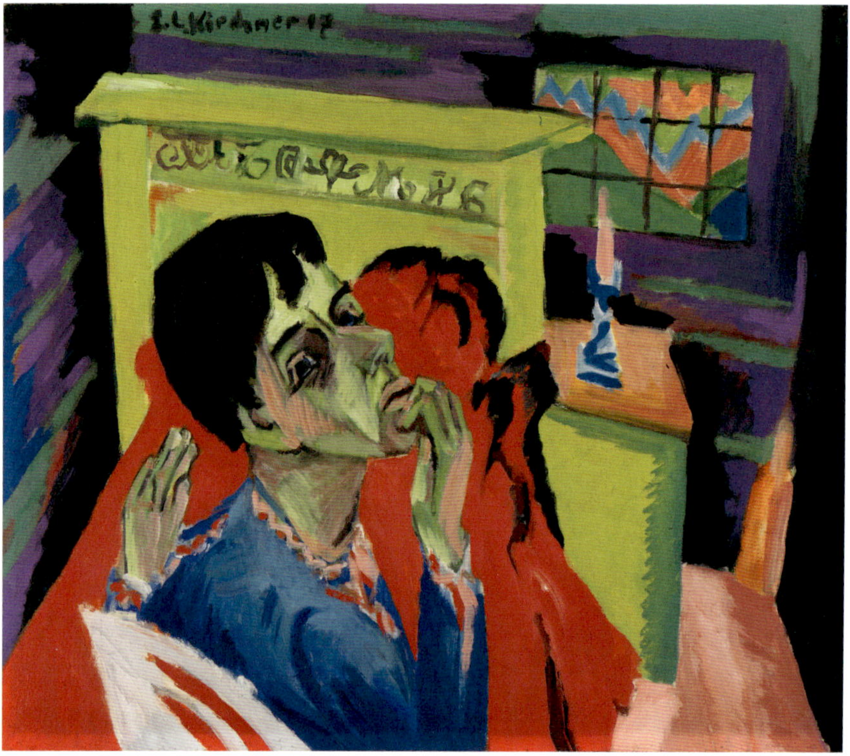

Ernst Ludwig Kirchner | **Selbstbildnis als Kranker** (Self-Portrait as Sick Man) | 1918/30
Oil on canvas, mounted on plywood, 59 × 69.3 cm, inv. no. 15580
Acquired 2002 with support of Kulturstiftung der Länder, Ernst von Siemens Art Fund, Bayerische Landesstiftung, and Federal Government Commissioner for Culture and Media

Kirchner's self-portrait is characterized by Expressionist *Angst*, trauma from the world war, and an approach that merges self-mythologizing and autobiography. The artist created the portrait in 1918 at his home in Davos, depicting himself with a horrified expression, his hand held anxiously to his mouth. After a mental breakdown in 1915, several spells in sanatoriums, and becoming addicted to morphine and the barbiturate Veronal, he battled with symptoms of paralysis and cognitive disorders. He first regained his health in Davos in 1917. In 1930, Kirchner reworked the picture and backdated it to 1917 so that it could be stylized as having emerged at a moment of crisis and transformation. OK

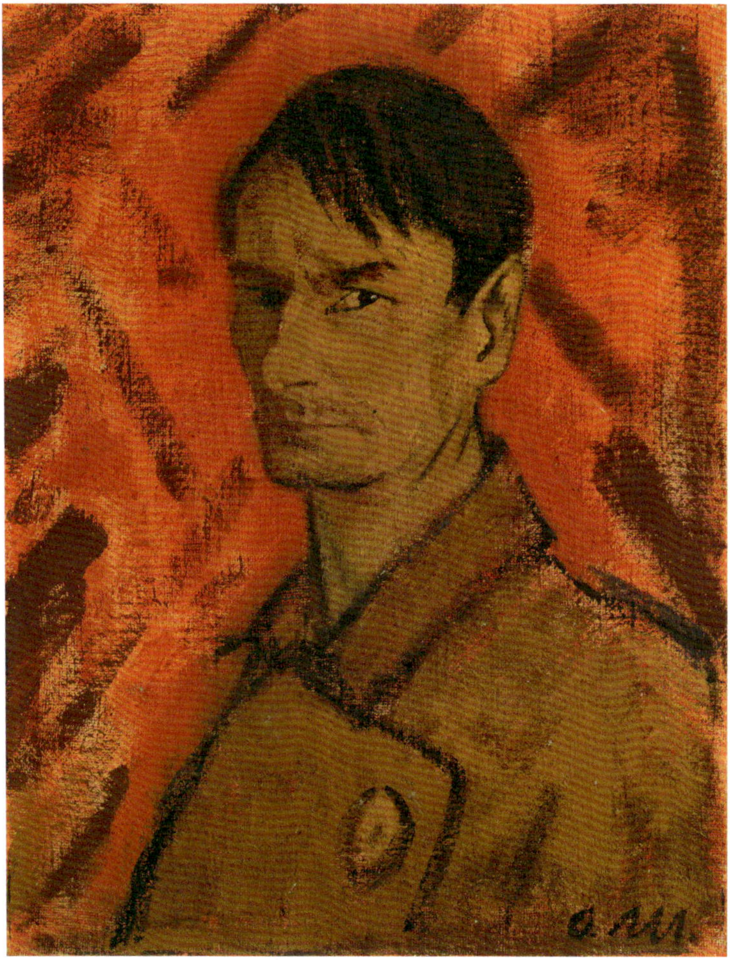

Otto Mueller | Selbstbildnis (Self-Portrait) | 1919
Oil and tempera on canvas, 71 × 54.7 cm, inv. no. 11242
Acquired 1951

Otto Mueller, who first joined the Expressionists of *Brücke* in 1910, served in the First World War as an infantry soldier. In 1917 he contracted a potentially fatal case of pneumonia, and after the war was appointed professor at the Breslau Kunstakadamie in 1919. Mueller sets his self-portrait against a red backdrop with broad dark stripes, which lend the head a diabolical character and intensify his penetrating, aggressive gaze. The sinister expression bespeaks apocalyptic experiences of war, while creating a stark contrast to the image of Mueller as a lyrical, introverted individual. OK

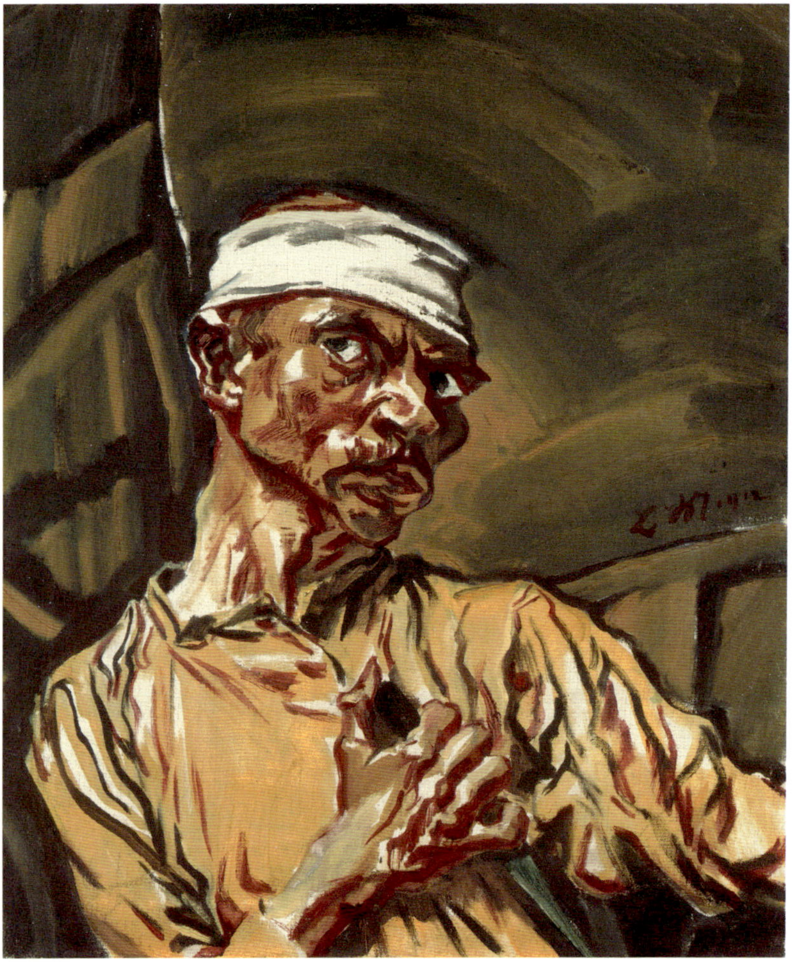

Ludwig Meidner | **Der Selbstmörder** (The Suicide) | 1912
Oil on canvas, 69.7 × 59.5 cm, inv. no. 15255
Acquired 1991

Practically no other 20th century artist achieved a more penetrating self-portrait than the one created by the Berlin poet and painter Ludwig Meidner. From 1912, his style became radicalized by the influence of Futurism and Cubism. Meidner became an 'ecstatic' artist, who intensified Expressionist self-reflection to the point of self-harm. He depicts himself as a man about to commit suicide in the cold light of the night-time city. The brush turns into the knife with which the artist repeatedly hacks at himself, while the dramatic style that characterizes the painting technique echoes the angular aesthetic of woodcuts. OK

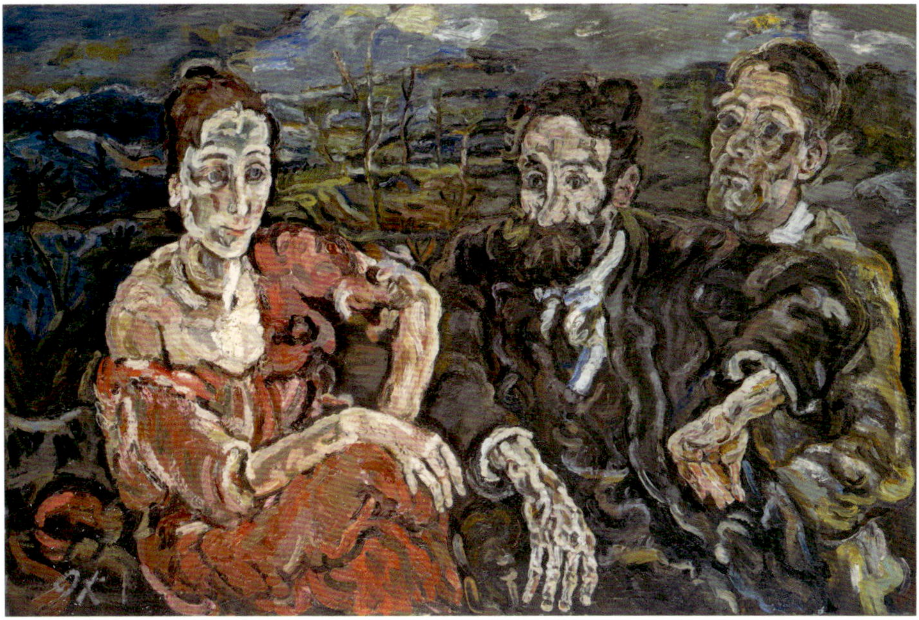

Oskar Kokoschka | Die Auswanderer (The Emigrants) | 1916–17
Oil on canvas, 94 × 145 cm, inv. no. 13465
Donation of Sofie and Emanuel Fohn, 1964

The painting is a masterpiece created during the artist's creatively productive period in Dresden. Having been wounded in the war and following his separation from Alma Mahler, Kokoschka took refuge in Dresden in 1916, where he found a new circle of friends. Both a group portrait and 'friendship picture', *The Emigrants* shows Kokoschka with the actress Käthe Richter and the poet Fritz Neuberger in a bare landscape. It symbolizes a disillusioned and homeless generation of artists, whose desolation Kokoschka successfully lends congenial expression through the use of impasto and restless brushstrokes. OK

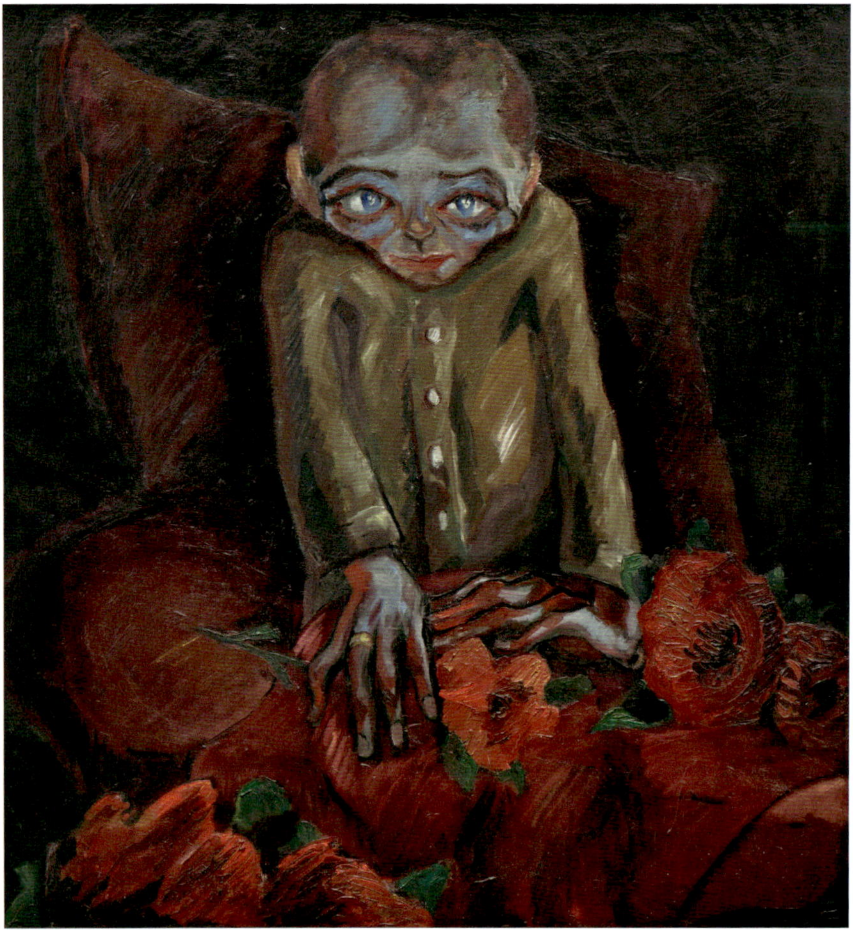

Walter Gramatté | Der Kranke mit den Blumen (Sick Man with Flowers) | 1918
Oil on canvas, 80.5 × 78 cm, inv. no. 15494
Acquired 1998

Walter Gramatté began his artistic training in 1915, one year after being called up to serve on the Western Front aged just 17 years of age. His experiences in Belgium proved formative in his painting, which soon turned its focus to human subjects. The *Sick Man with Flowers*, created in the last months of the war, shows an emaciated soldier who in contrast to the blood-red bed linen appears to have been sapped of the very last remnants of his energies. Under his hand lies the poppy, which in Belgium had attained symbolic status – for its role as an anaesthetic for the injured, and in remembrance of the fallen on whose graves the flower still grows. NE

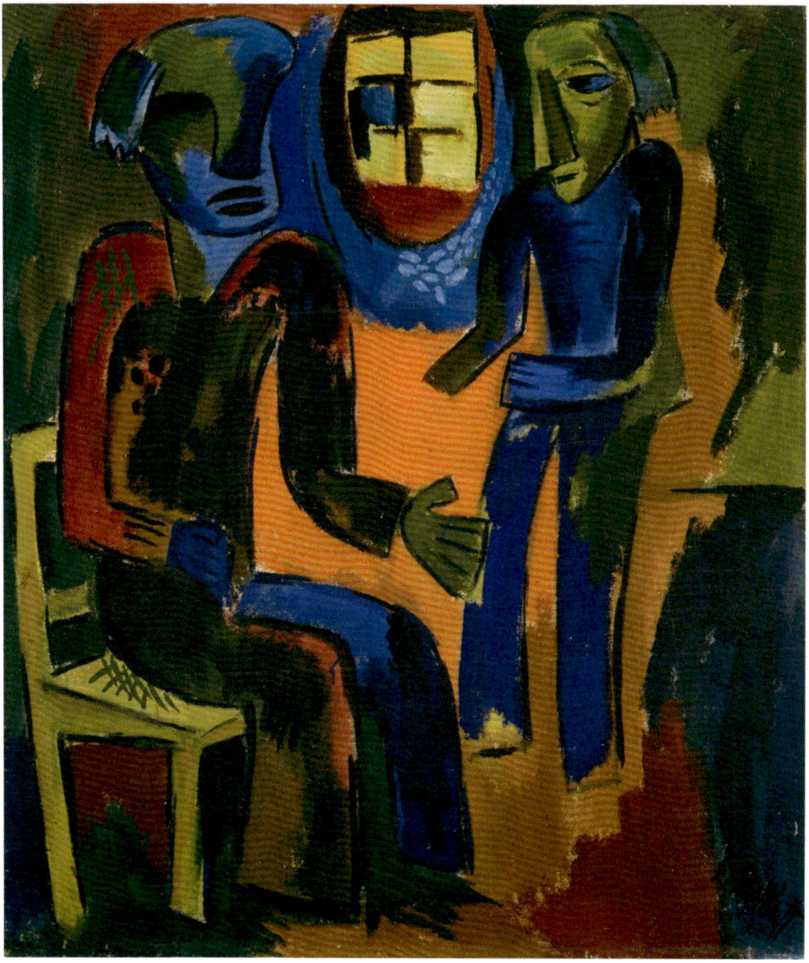

Karl Schmidt-Rottluff | Gespräch vom Tod (Conversation on Death) | 1920
Oil on canvas, 102 × 87 cm, inv. no. 14522
Bequest of Martha and Markus Kruss, 1977

Schmidt-Rottluff created a small group of interior paintings in which conversations are taking place. Among them, *Conversation on Death* stands out for its existential gravity, which arose in connection to the poet Richard Dehmel's death in 1920. A chair and window are the only real objects in the interior, which with the red-brown painted surfaces and the window open up to create 'space for reflection'. The monumental oval, or eye, of the window – signifying death and transcendence – seems to exert a magnetic force that draws the figures' heads towards it. The subjects' grief makes them appear mutilated, blind, and paralysed. OK

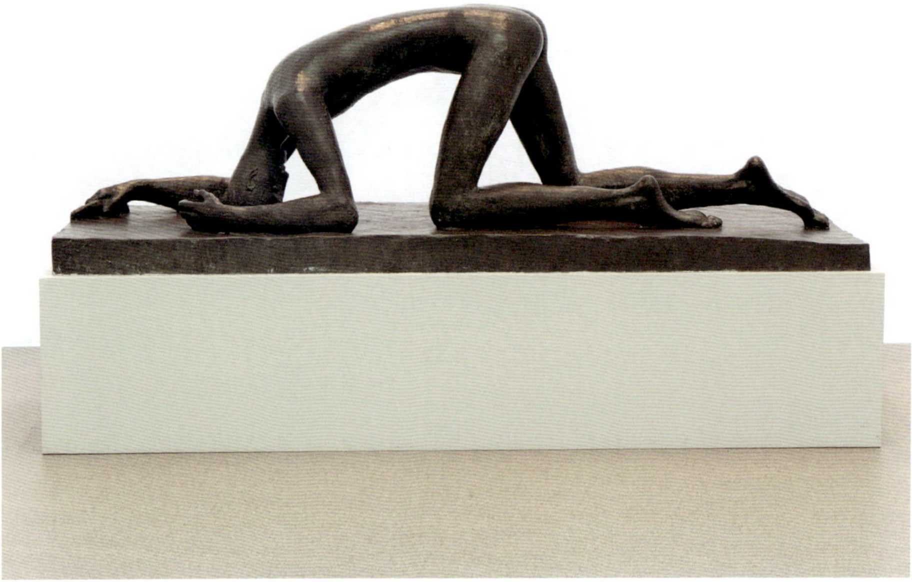

Wilhelm Lehmbruck | Der Gestürzte (The Fallen Man) | 1915–16 (posthumous cast)
Bronze, 65 × 236 × 66.5 cm, inv. no. B 397
Acquired 1963

The Fallen Man is a monument to the youth of Europe who died in the First World War. Only identifiable as a soldier by the stub of a sword, Lehmbruck's larger than life-size sculpture of a naked young man emerges as an anti-war memorial requiring no compositional props or inscription: it is solely the composition of the figure that creates the pathos of grief. The over-long limbs create a bridge that alternate evocatively between the hollows and the body, giving visual expression to the final burst of life and the figure's imminent collapse into death. Working as a medical orderly, Lehmbruck had experienced the consequences of war for himself, and subsequently took his own life in 1919. OK

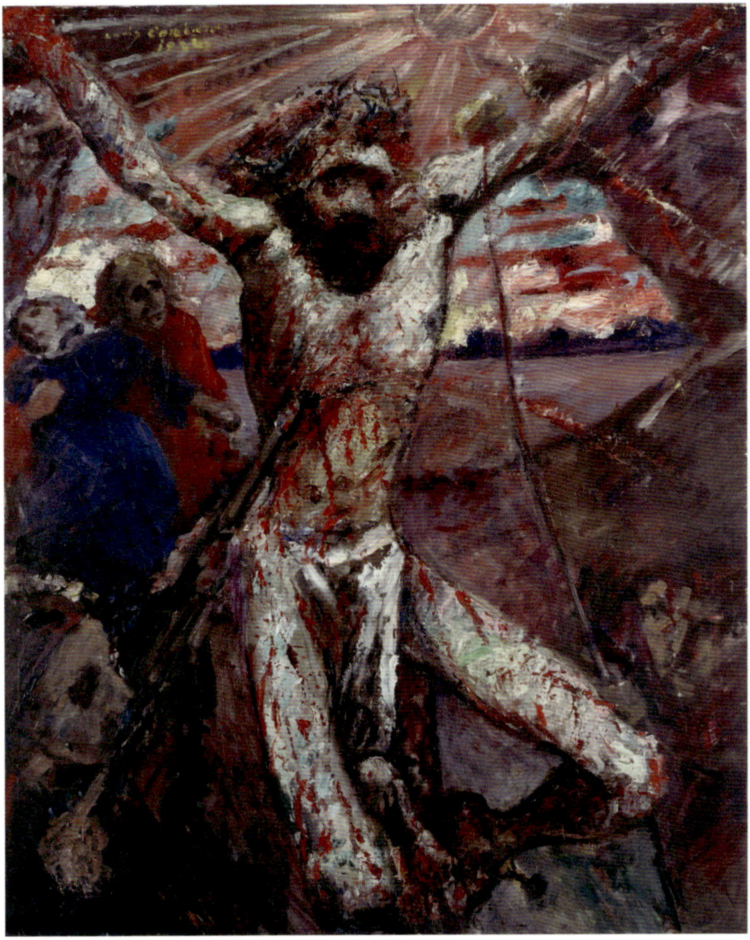

Lovis Corinth | Der rote Christus (The Red Christ) | 1922
Oil on wood, 130.2 × 107.4 cm, inv. no. 12383
Acquired 1956

The Red Christ was created three years before Lovis Corinth's death. Shaken by the effects of the First World War, the artist felt the situation to be empty of meaning and lacking any sign of hope. This bleak work of late Expressionism reflects this pessimism. With intense drama, the work depicts Christ on the cross with blood streaming over his body. The figure shown is a long way from the Christ to whom the faithful look up as their redeemer. The body instead takes on the appearance of a human sacrifice; the artist appears to mete even more violence on the body as he cuts through the figure's limbs with the compositional diagonals that streak across the painting. FS

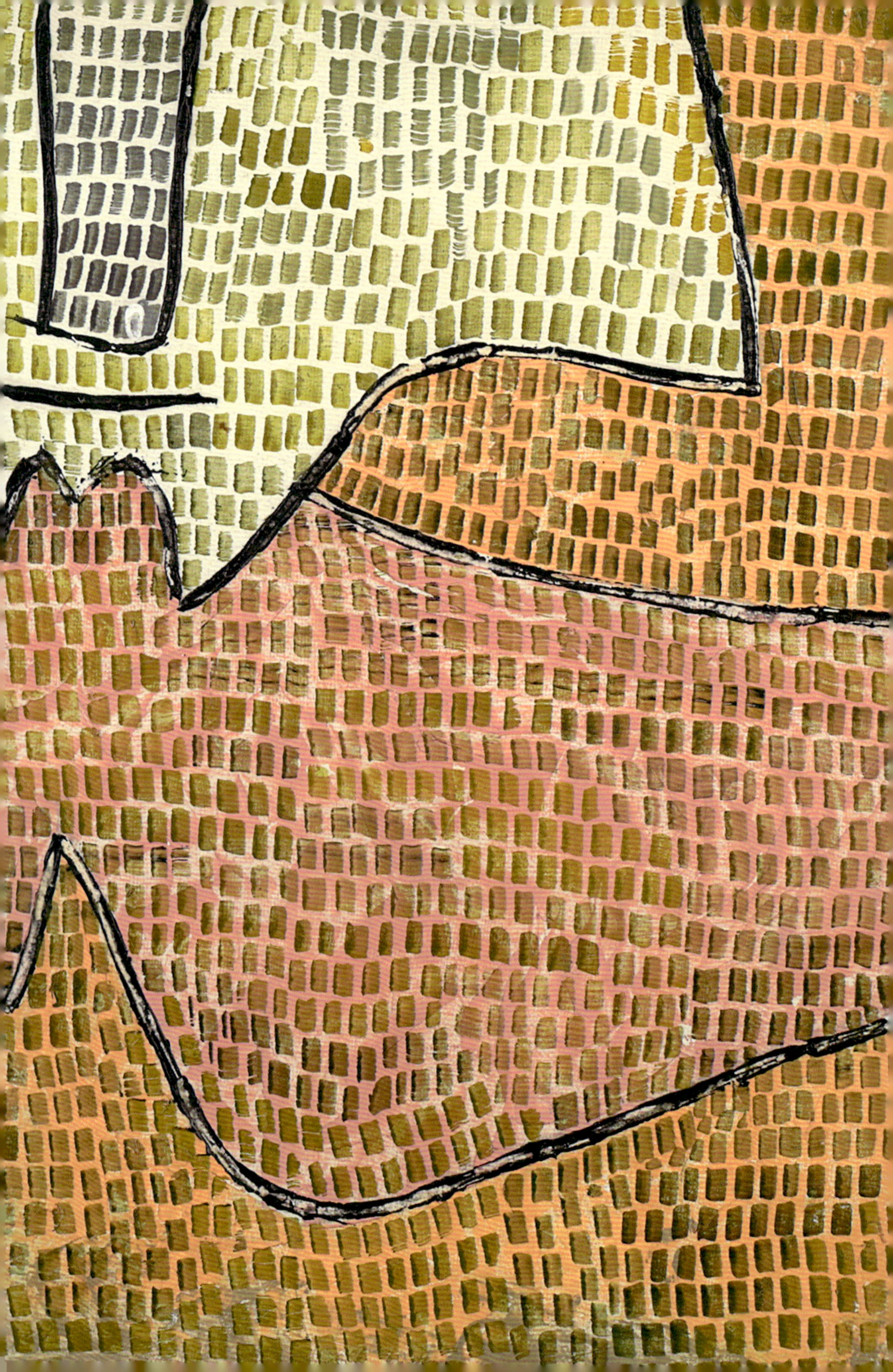

ABSTRACTION AND CONSTRUCTION
THE BAUHAUS AND ITS CIRCLE

Many myths surround the Bauhaus, and its story can be told from many perspectives. It was in Weimar, Dessau, and Berlin – the successive sites of the Bauhaus school – more than anywhere else in Germany that the foundations of functionalist architecture were laid. Some painters, especially those close to *Der Blaue Reiter* in Munich, had already taken important steps towards abandoning figurative art before the First World War. It was at the Bauhaus, however, that fundamental theoretical and practical questions about abstract art (which was to shape the whole of the 20th century) were first addressed systematically. Moreover, despite a certain exclusivity, a profound social consciousness underlay many of the Bauhaus's core ideas. It taught and demonstrated the importance of combining artistry with sound craftsmanship – in other words, uniting the formal and the functional in art, architecture, and design. But, more than this, it aspired to create architecture for ordinary people and recognised the right of everyone to enjoy aesthetically pleasing surroundings. The Bauhaus's model of communal creativity played a central role in the pursuit of its ideas. As a college of design, it strove for close collaboration between teaching and practice, echoing the tradition of the mediaeval stonemasons' guilds. It was no accident that Lyonel Feininger's woodcut *Cathedral* was chosen for the cover of the Bauhaus's first published programme and manifesto in 1919. Backward-looking and socially utopian though this may seem at first glance, it was nevertheless the Bauhaus's lasting achievement to give enormous impetus to the debate about how modernism was to be achieved.

Because of the liberalism of the Bauhaus's teaching and practice, its artists were the target of regular attacks from conservative forces, a continuation of the animosity towards modernism which had already been evident before the First World War. It was not surprising, therefore, that after its foundation in Weimar in 1919, the Bauhaus was forced to move to Dessau in 1925. In 1932, following further attacks, it moved again, to Berlin, where, just a year later, all that was left of the legendary institution was finally dissolved. The biography of László Moholy-Nagy is a reflection of these events. He began work as a teacher in Weimar in 1923 and continued to work in Dessau until 1928. Later he emigrated to the USA, where he helped to win international recognition for the new ideas from Germany by founding the *New Bauhaus* in Chicago. In 1921 he had joined Raoul Hausmann, Hans Arp, and other artists to issue a challenge in the journal *De Stijl*: 'To the artists of the world! We love art's power of bold invention and renewal.' In his manipulation of light and movement, Moholy-Nagy was to become a forerunner of Kinetic Art.

The repeated expulsions of the Bauhaus show how fundamentally reactionary the Weimar Republic was, but its artists nevertheless resisted its narrow outlook and stifling of free expression. They were, after all, long accustomed to anti-modernist attacks. Wassily Kandinsky, who worked for a while at the Bauhaus, had been the victim of one such assault as early as 1913. A critic of his Hamburg exhibition that year derided his work as 'scrawled colours and incoherent lines', 'a frenzy of forms and colours', and evidence of 'mental deficiency', and went on to declare that 'we can now dispose, quickly and quietly, of this Russian Kandinsky'. The hostility which accompanied this widespread chauvinistic incomprehension continued to dog modernism, until it finally culminated in the anti-modernist stance associated with such names as Adolf Ziegler, Hitler's purger of 'degenerate art' (p. 153). In a letter to Will Grohmann, Kandinsky nevertheless expressed his confidence, 'that people will one day see what lies behind my painting [...] and won't be satisfied with simply noticing that I use triangles or circles. I know that the future belongs to abstract art'. He was to be proved right, particularly by the artistic movements which came to the fore during and after the Second World War in the United States and France.

Although one or two artists, such as Fritz Winter, survived in internal exile, the history of the Bauhaus also includes the continuing development of its ideas abroad. Paul Klee initially left the Bauhaus for a teaching post in Düsseldorf, before finally abandoning Germany for exile in Switzerland. Like Kandinsky, he strove to give abstraction in art a spiritual dimension. His stance was a reaction both against Impressionism, with its focus on the outer world and surface appearance, and the exaggerated emotionalism of Expressionism. In the manuscript for his Jena lecture of 1924, *Über die moderne Kunst*, he writes: 'Our beating heart drives us downwards, deep down to the primordial source. What emerges from this activity, whatever it is called – dream, idea, fantasy – must be taken absolutely seriously when it employs the appropriate pictorial means perfectly in form.' For him this was not about the free or deliberate association which interested the Surrealists, or the Dadaists' provocative combinations of objects and imagery, but about fundamental questions to do with creativity itself.

Another artist who provided a link between the Bauhaus and post-war modernism, and between Germany and the outside world, was Lyonel Feininger. Like Klee, he had started out with a style of caricatural figuration. The serious side to his art, however, can be seen in crystalline and translucent images of churches and cathedrals, like his depiction of the market church in Halle. Community architecture had been a central concern of the Bauhaus right from the start. Feiniger – the father of the photographer Lux Feininger – painted this church from a photograph: no contradiction existed between modern technology and historical form and purpose. In 1948, long after his exile, the painter declared: 'Many people write to tell me that I am not forgotten in Germany. Of all the aspects about my so-called "fame" that is the one thing that makes me happy.' There could scarcely be a clearer example of how the best German artistic traditions were destroyed by the doctrine of National Socialism.

One of the most outstanding achievements of the Bauhaus was to integrate all the different art forms into one overarching whole. An example is the work of the painter Oskar Schlemmer, who also created murals, sculptures, the *Triadic Ballet*, and the Bauhaus Theatre. His painting *Dancer (The Gesture)* is linked with the latter. Schlemmer wanted, above all, to challenge the opulent naturalistic realism of the Wagnerian stage. In 1922, Schlemmer noted in his journal: 'The more it strives for reality, the more theatre – the world of illusion – is digging a tomb for itself.' Schlemmer illustrates the breadth of the movement for artistic reform in the Weimar Republic, applying rigorous abstraction even to the performing arts.

In 1929 Kandinsky looked back over the struggles and resistance modernism had experienced since long before the Bauhaus was founded and asked with breathless urgency: 'People will soon have been discussing the same theoretical question for 20 years – is it really possible to paint abstractly? how abstractly? how long can it go on? ("he's still painting abstracts!"), in which countries should it be allowed? Will it be the death of real painting – of art itself?' Almost a hundred years later we know how vital this movement was and, despite all the opposition it faced and the exile of so many artists, what an influence it had on the development of modern art.

Bernhard Maaz

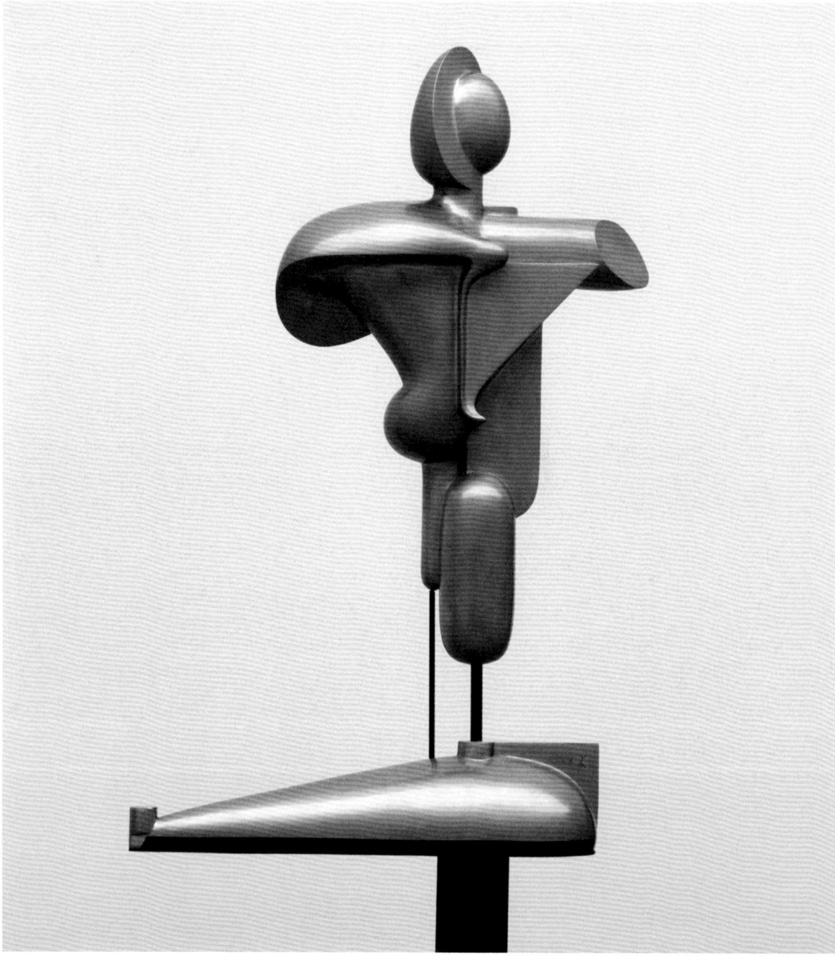

Oskar Schlemmer | Abstrakte Figur (Abstract Figure) | 1921/23 (cast 1961)
Bronze, nickel-plated, 104.5 × 70 × 19 cm, inv. no. B 382
Acquired 1961

Oskar Schlemmer first joined the Weimar Bauhaus in 1921 and in 1922 he became, amongst other things, head of the workshop for wood and stone sculpture. It was in the following year that he completed the original plaster of the *Abstract Figure*. Not cast in bronze until after his death, the model may originally have been intended for a sculpture in stone. The figure, reduced to its basic geometry, expresses Schlemmer's desire to find a purified, contemporary human image, achieving universality by transcending every trace of naturalism and individuality. The impression of floating underlines the idealised nature of the figure. BSO

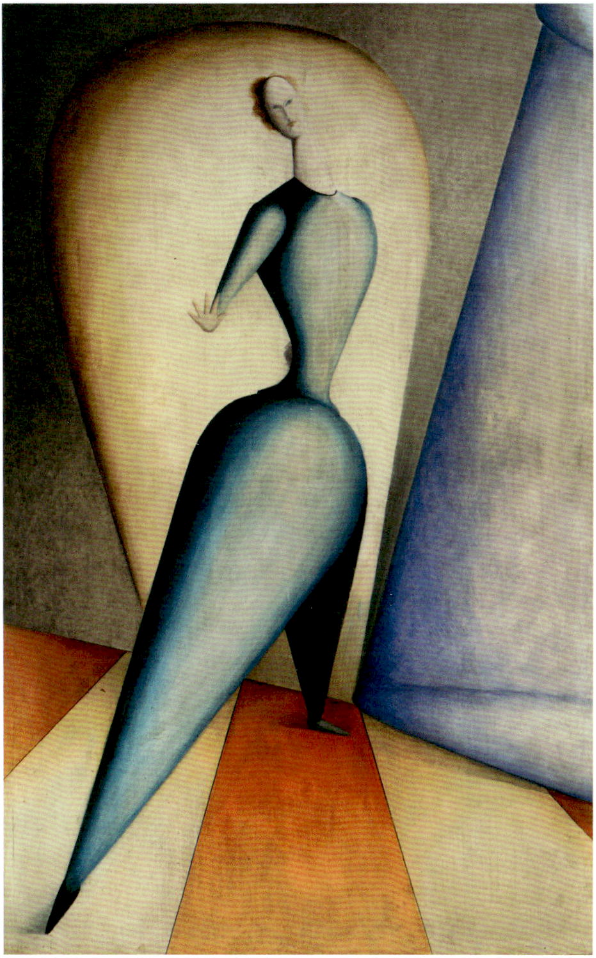

Oskar Schlemmer | **Tänzerin** (Die Geste) (Dancer – The Gesture) | 1922–23
Oil and tempera on canvas, 200 × 130 cm, inv. no. 13421
Acquired 1964

Throughout his life, Schlemmer was fascinated by the human figure in space. The dancer in the picture steps forward towards the viewer, while at the same time raising a warning hand. She seems to exude powers which completely contradict Max Weber's notion of the 'disenchantment of the world'. This corresponded to Schlemmer's experience, both as the creator of the *Triadic Ballet* and as a painter. In the script for a lecture in 1933, he wrote: 'The human figure, released from the crowd and placed in the special world of the stage (or the picture), seems to gather about it a nimbus of magic and become a being bewitched by space'. BSO

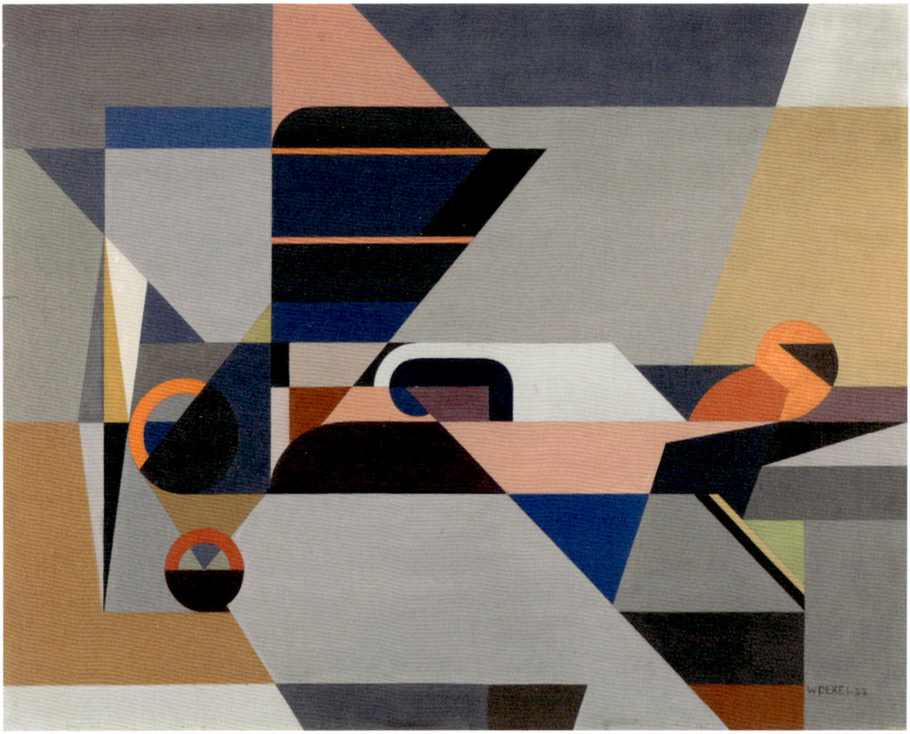

Walter Dexel | **Das Flugzeug** (The Aeroplane) | 1922
Oil on canvas, 66.3 × 85.3 cm, inv. no. 13418
Acquired 1964

Born in Munich, Walter Dexel was among the most important proponents of Constructivism during the 1920s, a decade which he spent mostly in Jena. *The Aeroplane* is an example of figurative Constructivism. The picture may have an identifiable subject, but its faithful representation is subjugated to the striving for a harmonious arrangement of geometric areas of colour. For Dexel, an important source of inspiration in his artistic career was his friendship with Theo van Doesburg, a member of the De Stijl movement who greatly influenced the development of the Bauhaus in neighbouring Weimar from 1921 onwards.
BSO

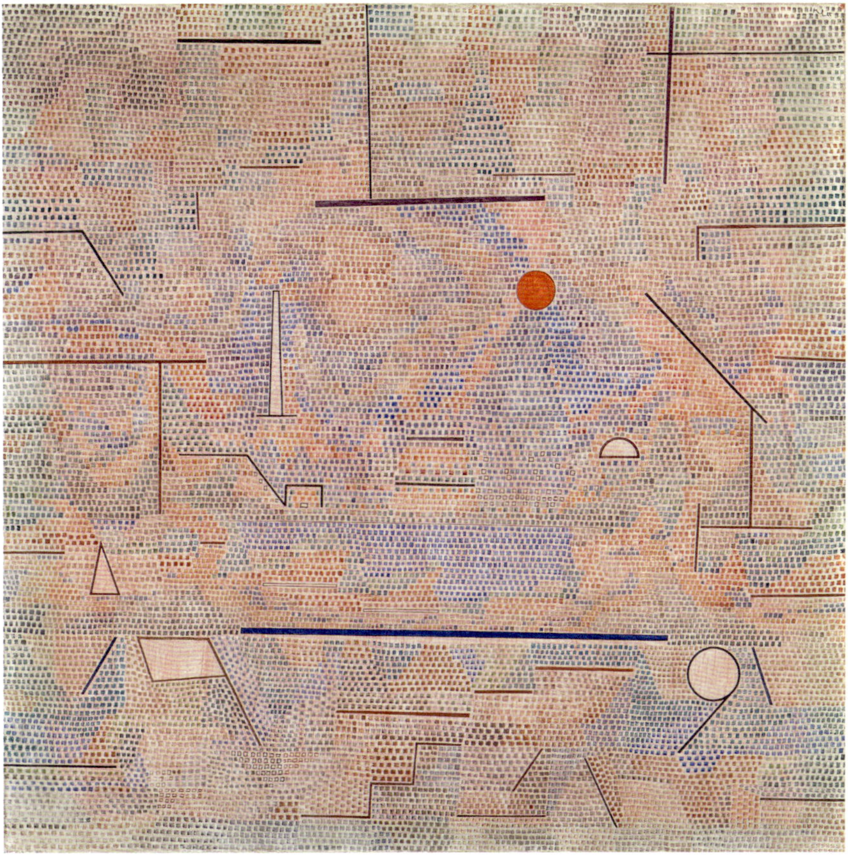

Paul Klee | **Das Licht und Etliche** (The Light and So Much Else) | 1931
Watercolour, pen and ink, and pencil on varnish ground on canvas,
95 × 97.5 cm, inv. no. 14070
Acquired 1968 with support of PIN. Freunde der Pinakothek der Moderne

It was in 1931, after taking up his professorship at the Düsseldorf Kunstakademie, that Klee evolved his 'divisionist' pictures, characterised by the magical brilliance of their colouration. *The Light and So Much Else* is one of the masterpieces from this period that is largest in scale and almost completely abstract. Using a detailed mosaic of coloured squares against a light ground, Klee creates an unreal space of shimmering light and colour. Lines and bars create surface rhythm; the red circle and architectural elements such as the obelisk evoke associations with Klee's travels in the south. OK

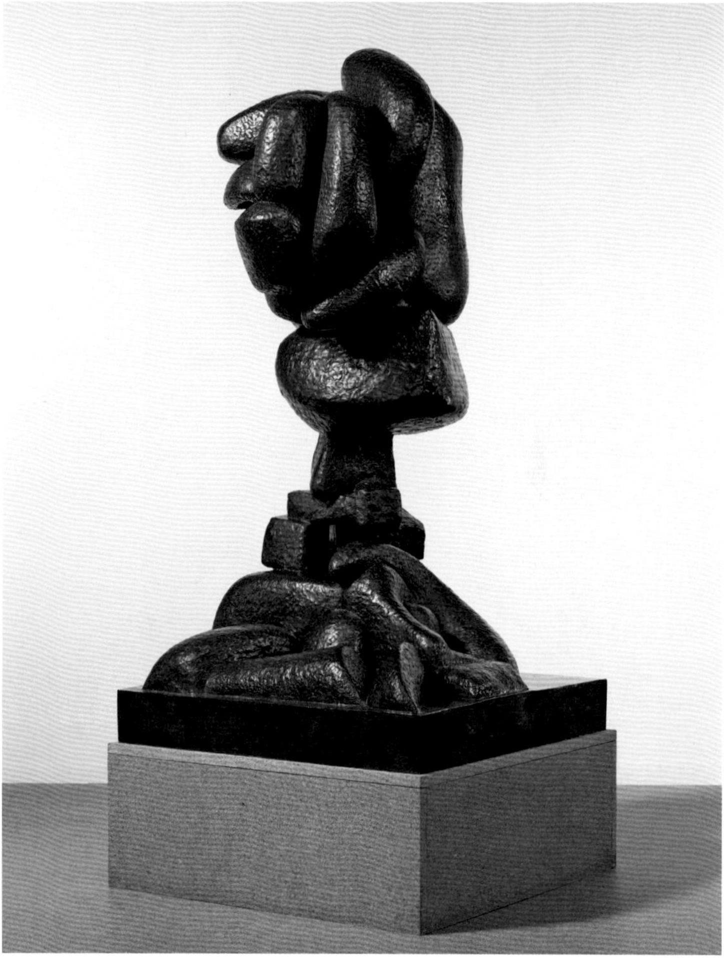

Otto Freundlich | Ascension | 1929 (cast 1979)
Bronze, 200 × 104 × 104 cm, inv. no. B 791
Donation of Theo Wormland Foundation, 1983

Otto Freundlich's works and writings were inspired by his belief in a new social order, where individualism would be renounced in favour of communality. Freundlich, later ostracised and murdered by the National Socialists, was the creator of *Ascension*, the first monumental abstract sculpture of the 20th century. Resting on square stone blocks, and rising from a root-like base, the powerfully convoluted, abstract form seems to defy gravity. With its sophisticated interplay of light and shade, *Ascension* is also a symbol of Freundlich's social utopia.
FS

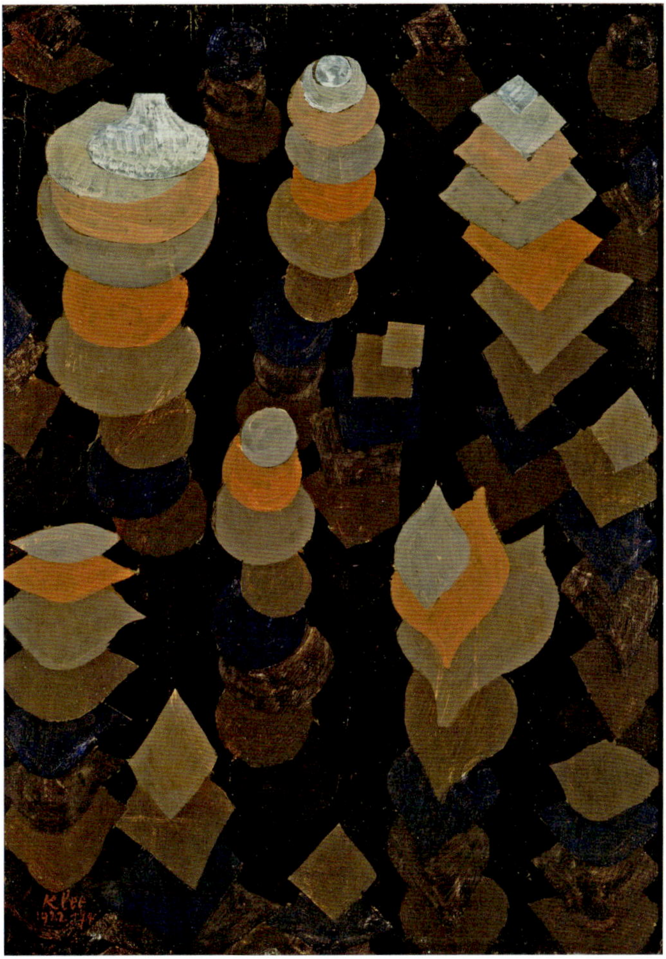

Paul Klee | Wachstum der Nachtpflanzen (Growth of the Night Plants) | 1922
Oil on card, 47.3 × 34 cm, inv. no. 15250
Acquired 1991

This work affords an insight into Paul Klee's Bauhaus lecture series entitled *Ways of Studying Nature*. It illustrates his claim that 'Art does not reproduce the visible; it makes visible.' Here, 'making visible' turns out to be an enigmatic procedure. A succession of geometric shapes – circles, ellipses, rectangles, and trapeziums – rise in close succession out the dark background to form towers. The gradations of colour follow a fixed tonal scheme, moving from dark to light. They are based on the theories Klee taught about colour relations and the universal processes which he believed underlay all types of growth. BSO

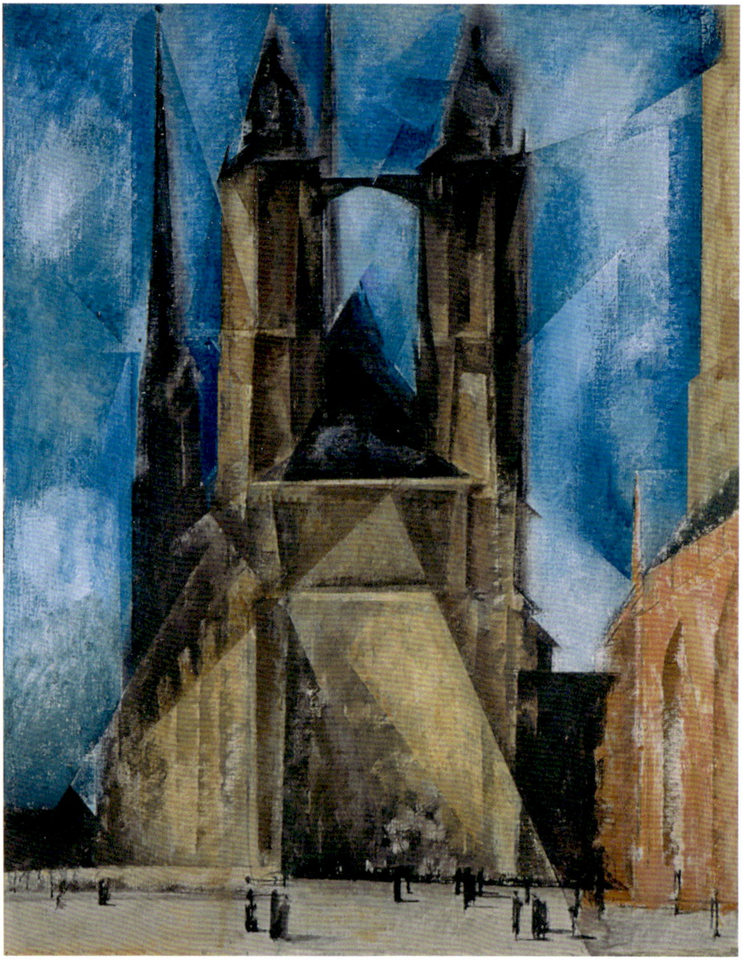

Lyonel Feininger | Marktkirche in Halle (Market Church in Halle) | 1930
Oil on canvas, 102 × 80.4 cm, inv. no. 12013
Acquired 1954

While he was living in Halle (Saale) for a brief period between 1929 and 1931, Lyonel Feininger made images of the town's buildings. One of his favourite motifs was the Marienkirche on the market square. In the Munich painting, the building is illuminated by rays of reflected light. Against the blue prism of the sky they give it the appearance of a dark crystal in which materiality and spirituality are united. The composition echoes visions of cathedrals by German Romantic painters. In 1919, Feiniger had already set himself in this tradition, when he created his woodcut of a cathedral for the cover of the Bauhaus manifesto. BSO

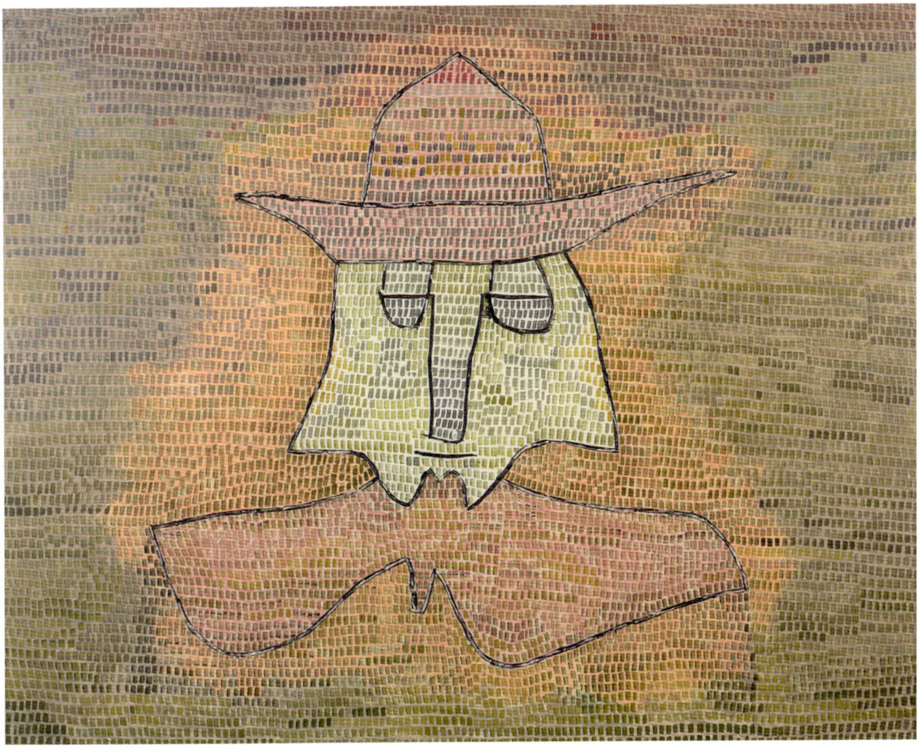

Paul Klee | Pastor Kohl | 1932
Oil on nettle cloth, mounted on plywood, 50 × 65 cm, inv. no. 16428
Acquired 2015 in joint acquisition with Ernst von Siemens Art Foundation, with support of PIN. Freunde der Pinakothek der Moderne and Kulturstiftung der Länder. Purchased directly from the descendants of Paul and Lily Klee

In Klee's work, religious motifs are often given an ironic twist. This is the case here, in a caricature-like portrait of a fictitious pastor, created shortly after Klee finished his spell of teaching at the Bauhaus and moved to the Düsseldorf art school. It is one of his pointillist works, where the colours are applied to give the effect of mosaic. On a trip to Ravenna in 1928, Klee had been fascinated by Byzantine mosaics, including representations of Christ and St. Apollinaris as shepherds (Italian: *pastore*), which may be echoed in *Pastor Kohl*.
BSO

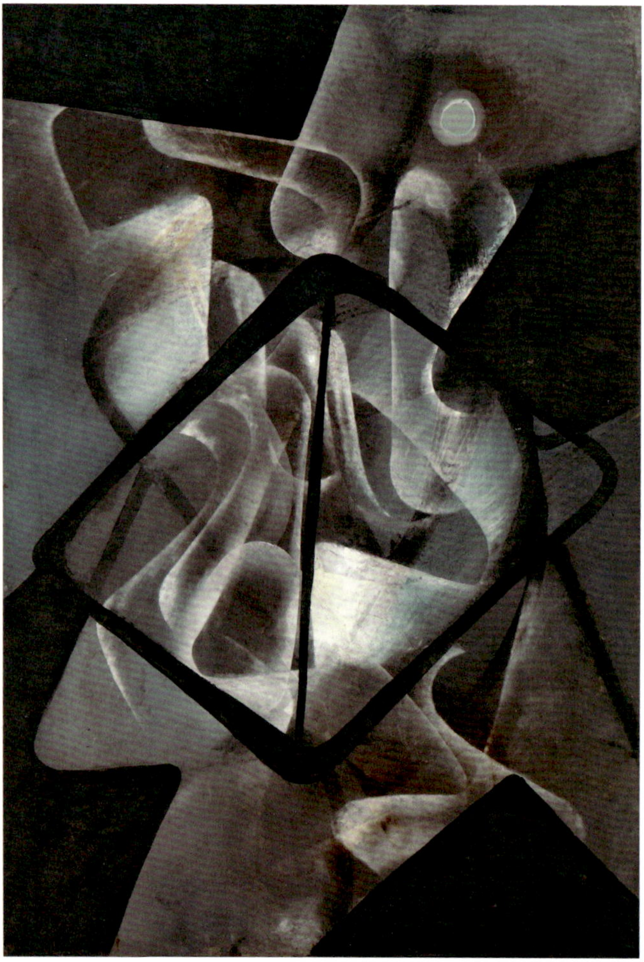

Fritz Winter | K 35 | 1934
Tempera on paper, mounted on canvas, 110 × 75 cm, inv. no. 12984
Acquired 1959

Fritz Winter studied at the Bauhaus in Dessau from 1928 to 1930. Throughout his artistic career, which continued into the 1970s, he returned again and again to his quest for a vital synthesis between the artistic and scientific worldviews. The *Light Pictures* which he created between 1934 and 1936 suggest a response to the immateriality of photography; these abstract works, with their transparent handling of paint, seem make visible the forces of nature – either by microscopic enlargement of minute structures or by gazing into cosmic distances with telescopic vision. BSO

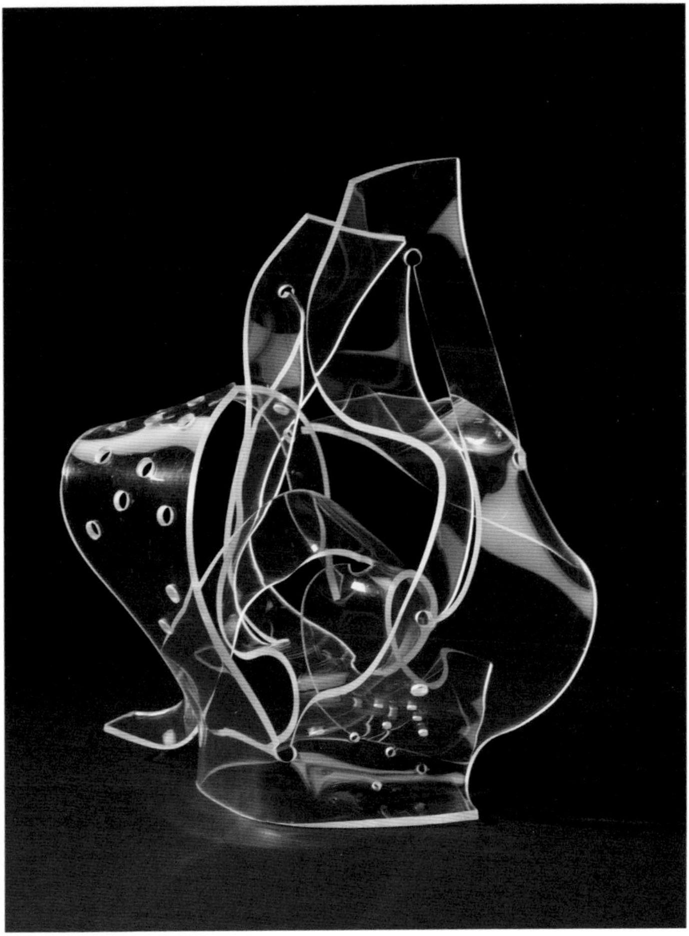

László Moholy-Nagy | Double Loop | 1946
Transparent, thermally formed plastic, max. 45.5 × 34.5 × 38 cm, inv. no. B 357
Acquired 1959

As early as the 1920s, while he was teaching the compulsory introductory course at the Bauhaus in Dessau, László Moholy-Nagy was experimenting with modern synthetic materials such as acrylic glass. He prized this easily moulded material because its transparency allowed him to use light as a means of representing space and movement. *Double Loop* was made in the year of the artist's death. Because of his Hungarian-Jewish birth, Moholy-Nagy left Germany when Hitler came to power, emigrating first to Holland, then to London, and finally to Chicago, where he founded the *New Bauhaus* in 1937. Although it closed after only a year, he later went on to found the *School of Design*. BSO

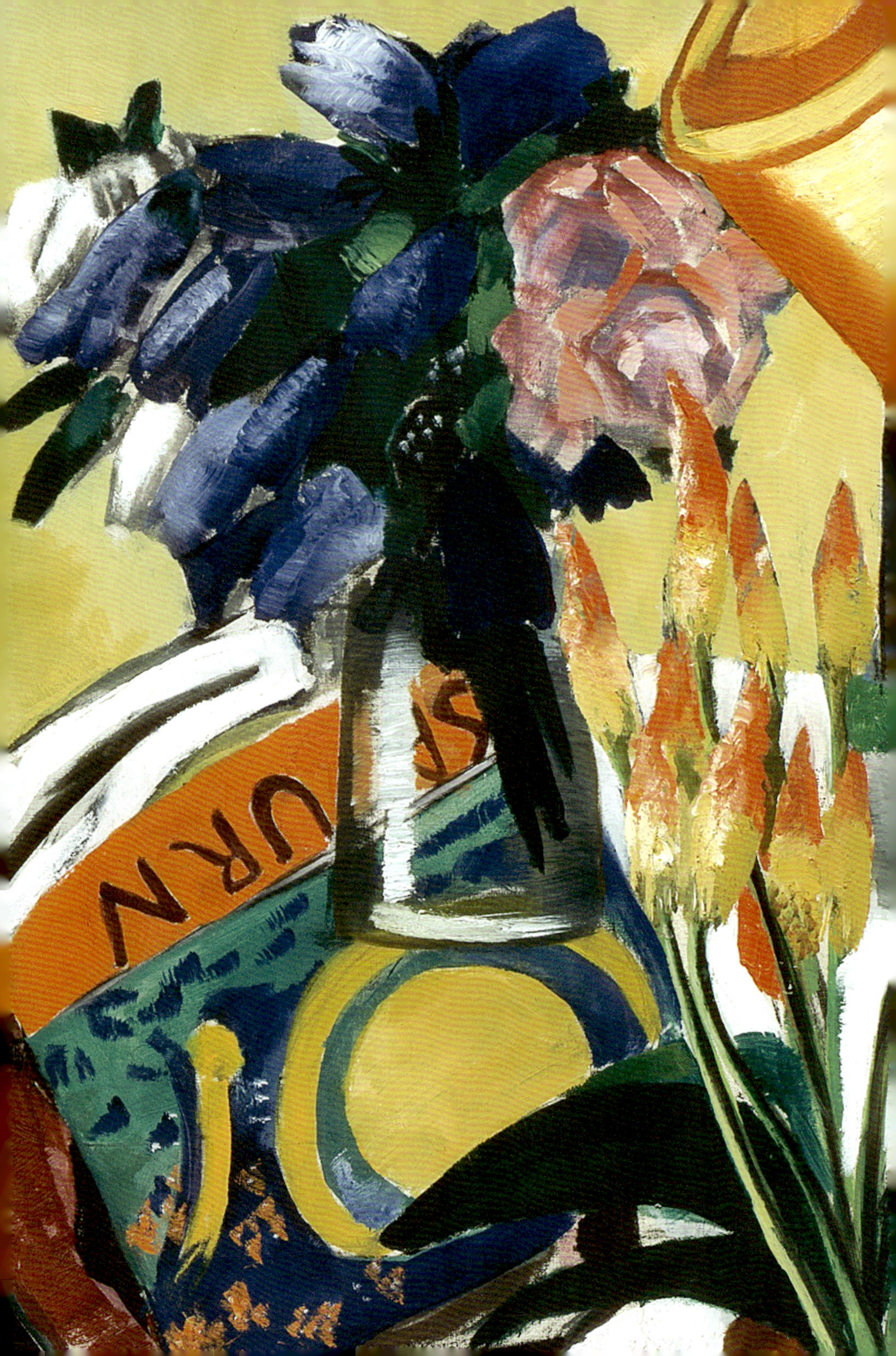

THE GOLDEN TWENTIES?
NEUE SACHLICHKEIT AND NEOCLASSICISM

Were the 1920s really 'golden', as the traditional view would have us believe? What does a 'golden' period actually mean, and do they exist? Considered objectively, the term seems appropriate for the years after the First World War, when artists such as Max Beckmann, Wilhelm Lehmbruck, and Otto Dix returned with their experiences of the conflict and set about developing new areas of activity, and widening existential horizons. This period saw unrelenting ideological conflict in the young Weimar Republic and, as Harry Graf Kessler recounts in his memoirs, numerous political murders. The German people were beginning to see the first signs of something resembling prosperity again, although it was not attainable for everyone. Social inequality surpassed anything people had experienced before the First World War, contemporaries were shaken by the financial crisis and hyperinflation, while movements bent on putsch and political agitation destabilized ideological beliefs. Even before the Weimar Republic had had a chance to establish its democratic foundations, there gathered brutal and energetic opposition forces. These precipitated a reaction that foreshadowed National Socialism and put great pressure on the young republic. Nevertheless, it seemed as though Europe were united and had learned from its experience of the war.

Before the First World War, a new image of man had been formulated by Impressionism and Pointillism, Fauvism and Expressionism, Cubism and Futurism. After the war, artists who had survived (unlike, for example, August Macke and Franz Marc) were frequently confronted by individual catastrophes, social and personal traumas – or at the very least, a worldview that had been shaken to the core. Holders of traditional posts at academies and university were in some institutions replaced by artists who heralded a new kind of innovative freedom in art. The system of academic sinecures from Wilhelmine Germany collapsed. This lent new relevance to public institutions such as the Bauhaus in Weimar. For the Bauhaus celebrated precisely this spirit of artistic experimentation and intellectual anarchy in its efforts to conquer new terrain for the arts and crafts – in design, architecture, and decoration. Inevitably, this branch of modernism soon encountered radical opponents both in the art business and wider society. Long before the Nazis launched attacks on so-called 'degenerate' art, conservatives staged campaigns first in Weimar, then in Dessau, repeatedly forcing the Bauhaus to move home, until in 1933 it finally became (briefly) active in Berlin.

Alongside the great masters of the Bauhaus – Feininger, Kandinsky, Klee, Schlemmer, et al. – Max Beckmann numbers among the most influential artistic figures in 1920s Germany. Our museum collection boasts exceptional examples of Beckmann's work that bear the hallmark of his unmistakable artistic rigour. His expressive, richly symbolic, and cryptic visual world – that nonetheless never strayed far from fundamental human questions – is a unique presence in a period in which the form-destroying painting of late Expressionism predominated alongside the *Neue Sachlichkeit* or 'New Objectivity'. The first generation of Expressionists had since become figures of the establishment or, like Ernst Ludwig Kirchner, emigrated; the second generation of painters, such as Conrad Felixmüller and Carl Lohse, still today remain less appreciated than their predecessors. Some of the artists from *Der Blaue Reiter* had been killed in the First World War, as was the case for Franz Marc and August Macke, while others – such as Wassily Kandinsky – were working at the Bauhaus. In Paris during this period, artists like Salvador Dalí, Juan Gris, and Pablo Picasso were actively shaping the French-dominated face of international modern art.

The *Neue Sachlichkeit* heralded a shift towards a focus on the external world, or the world of 'things', which gave rise to works of traditional painting genres, such as landscape, still life, and portrait. The director of the Mannheim Museum, Gustav Hartlaub, coined the term *Neue Sachlichkeit* for the 1925 exhibition that displayed the latest generation of paintings. Artists such as Schrimpf and Kanoldt explored subjects borrowed from German Romanticism and the Biedermeier period; others continued down the path first explored by the likes of Giorgio de Chirico and Carlo Carrà and transposed the style of the *Pittura metafisica* to Germany. They depicted local landscapes in an objective and/or alienating manner, capturing still lifes (often featuring tropical plants) with a cool and even estranged eye. At times, they would stylize human figures with a sense of doll-like, inanimate coolness – as though memories of the conflict, the global economic crisis, and reparations payments were such a burden that it was not permitted in the post-war period to acknowledge emotions, but only a person's social class and appearance. Such is the mood that pervades Otto Dix's portrait of Hugo Erfurth. With *Woman in Black Coat*, George Grosz created a picture suffused with objective coolness and sceptical distance, while (somewhat disconcertingly) exalting the traditional roles played by simple, though independent, women. How a studiously observant American woman from the period perceived her German counterparts is revealed in a letter from Berlin written in 1922 by Berenice Abbott: 'Everything here is different. Generally speaking, the women look "provincial" – at first glance – sometimes you really have to hold back from laughing. They want for chic-ness, but they're more independent and "modern" than French women.' As is evident in Beckmann's *Dance in Baden-Baden*, there did exist a cryptic, moribund, and soulless sense of chic, but it had retreated to fashionable locations and kept to itself. In addition to Beckmann, the most radically analytical artworks of this period were by George Grosz and Otto Dix, who created group and solo portraits that were part-sceptical, part-social critique, while Helmut Kolle painted scenes suffused with melancholy. The latter artist also embodied the shift to Neoclassicism initiated in the 1920s by Picasso and De Chirico, which laid the groundwork for re-establishing an ideal of beauty – or of the world – based on classical precepts, but which had been torn asunder during the war. The way Nazi art doctrine drew upon this aesthetic idea is explored elsewhere in this book (pp. 147–161).

Observed from afar, the Golden Twenties were anything but ideal. As Kessler detailed in his diaries, the decade was characterized and sometimes even scarred by struggles between rival political camps. These laid siege to an inexperienced democracy named after the city in which it had been established: the Weimar Republic. However, the humanity and humanism of Weimar Classicism could only be laboriously translated into political life, and ultimately (as demonstrated in 1933) without lasting effect in Germany. Traditional media, particularly newspapers, were challenged by newcomers such as the radio; cars, radios, and airplanes became features of everyday life. In short, the 1920s were only ever 'golden' for the wealthy.

Bernhard Maaz

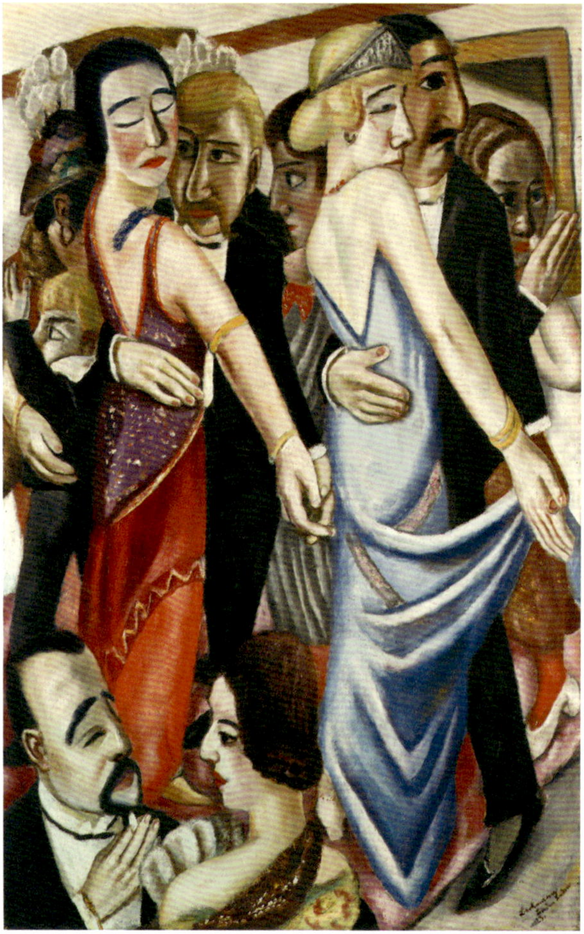

Max Beckmann | Tanz in Baden-Baden (Dance in Baden-Baden) | 1923
Oil on canvas, 108 × 66 cm, inv. no. 14367
Günther Franke Endowment, 1974

Max Beckmann had already begun his artistic development prior to 1914, creating compositions that were melancholy, clayey, and replete with figures. He subsequently returned home marked by bleak wartime experiences. After making prints during the war years, he developed a new creative prowess that culminated in paintings such as *Dance in Baden-Baden*. The picture, shown at the 1925 *Neue Sachlichkeit* exhibition in Mannheim, reflects German society and its questionable attempts at regaining its sense of pleasure in life. The elegant evening gowns cannot conceal a pervading sense of reserve, greed, and coldness.

BM

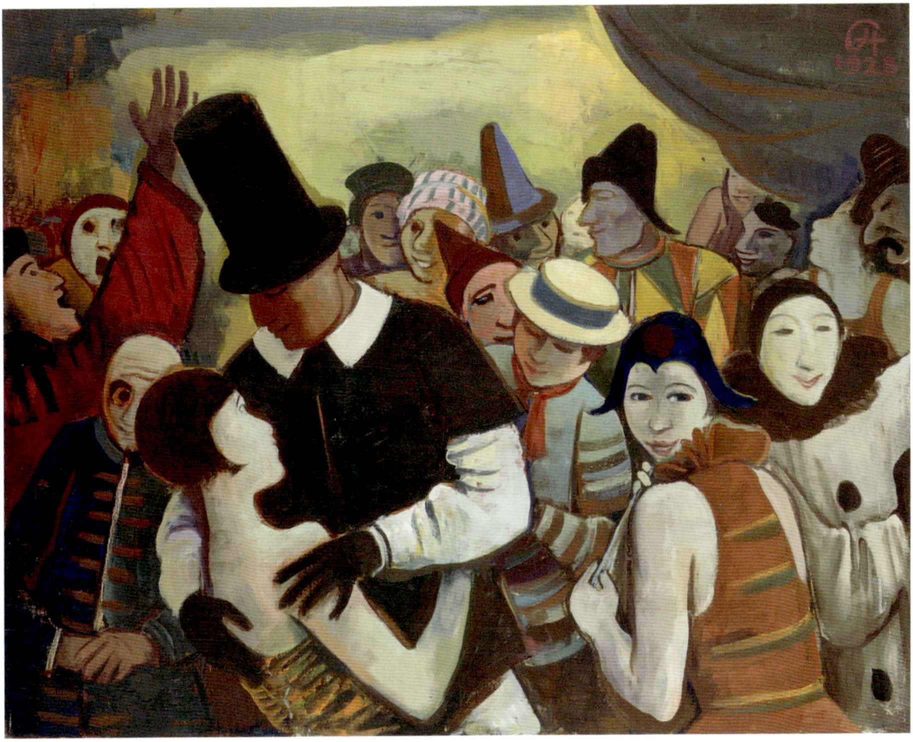

Karl Hofer | **Großer Karneval** (Big Carnival) | 1928
Oil on canvas, 102.5 × 130.5 cm, inv. no. 13461
Donation of Sofie and Emanuel Fohn, 1964

As early as the turn of the 20th century, James Ensor was motivated by the desire to hold up a mirror to society with his depictions of masks. In his painting *Big Carnival* from 1928, Karl Hofer also reflects a downright bizarre interplay of closeness and withdrawal amidst a great jumble of humanity. Harlequin, sailor, courtesan, and magician whiz past one another, seeking somewhere to stop, some locked briefly in a dance, some gesticulating into the void. This motley crew – including, for example, the incongruous couple of a man in a top hat and a young girl – collectively create a vision of the grotesque and unstable. BM

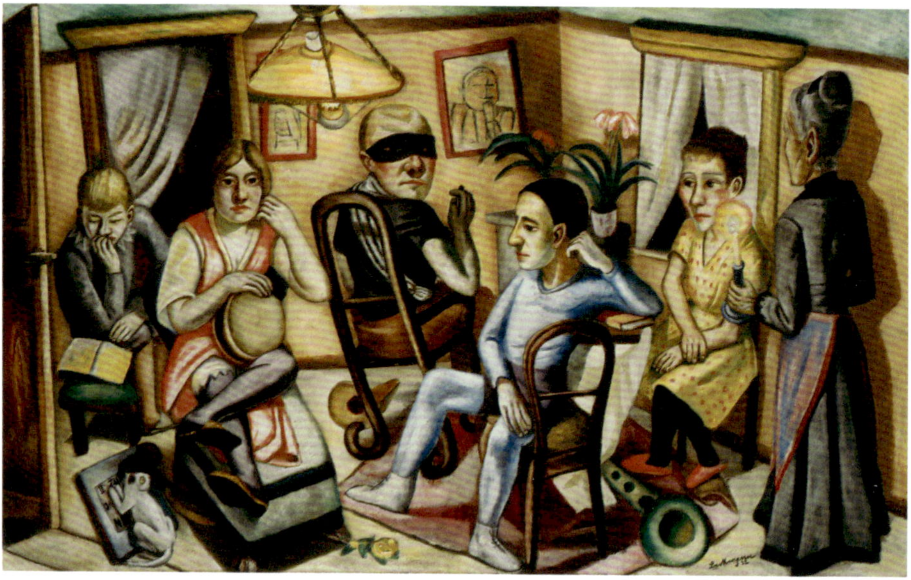

Max Beckmann | Vor dem Maskenball (Before the Masked Ball) | 1922
Oil on canvas, 80.4 × 130.5 cm, inv. no. 13402
Acquired 1963

One might imagine that spirits would be high before a masked ball, with guests looking forward to an evening free of boundaries, reserve, and social convention. Not so in this work by Beckmann. Half a dozen people have gathered in an insipidly lit room, though without quite being able (or wanting) to strike any sort of rapport with one another. On the left, the adolescent son is reading, the slightly goggle-eyed figure next to him is the painter's first wife, and Beckmann himself is portrayed wearing an eye mask, his back turned in a peculiar pose. A couple of friends and the artist's mother-in-law are next in sequence; each and every person is portrayed in joyless isolation.
BM

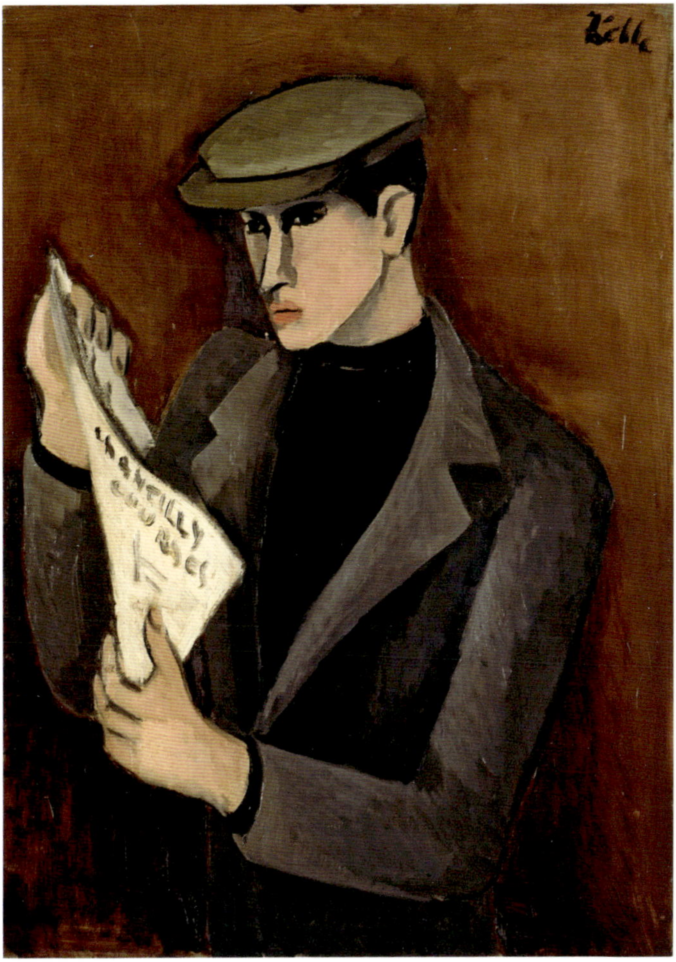

Helmut Kolle | Der Zeitungsleser (The Newspaper Reader) | c. 1928/30
Oil on canvas, 100 × 73 cm, inv. no. L 2369
Private loan, accessioned 1998

A resident of Paris from 1924, Helmut Kolle painted in a late-Expressionist and monumentalizing style. Using an earthy palette, he created numerous pictures of lugubrious, heavy-hearted young men, which give expression to his own sense of bewilderment and rootlessness. Introversion and isolation characterize his figures, and the depiction of a man reading a newspaper here becomes emblematic of attempts to regain a sense of temporality. At the time, the newspaper was still the preeminent medium and dominant shaper of public opinion; soon after saw the unstoppable rise of the radio. BM

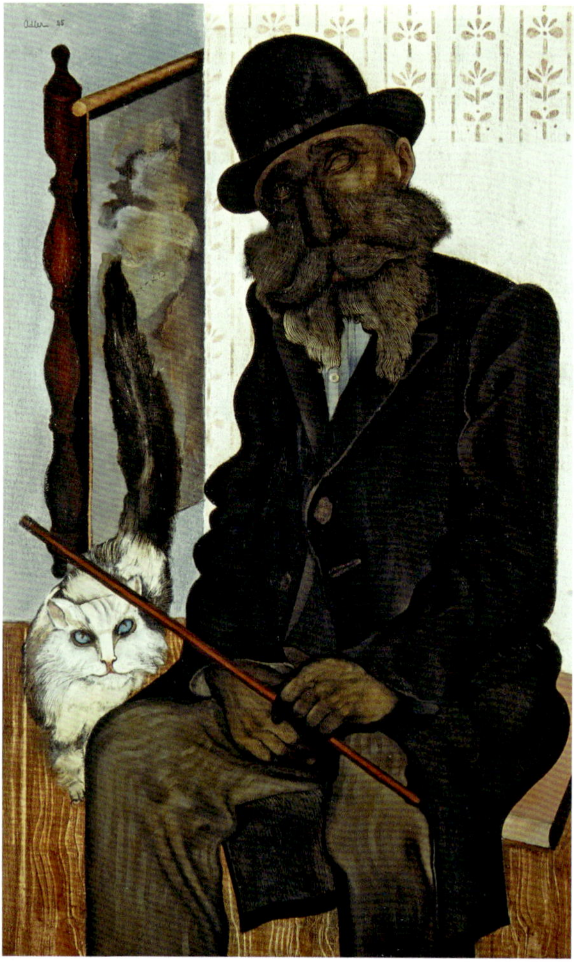

Jankel Adler | Herr Cléron, der Katzenzüchter (Mr. Cléron, the Cat Breeder) | 1925
Oil on canvas, 110.2 × 70.3 cm, inv. no. 13453
Donation of Sofie and Emanuel Fohn, 1964

A blue-eyed white cat fixes its gaze on the cat breeder, who is seated on a bench in an unspecified interior space in front of patterned wallpaper, sunk in thought. The man has lost his sight, as is evident from his unseeing eyes and the way he tilts his head to pay attention. Cat breeding is depicted here as a form of retreat from society and limitation to contact with animals. Jankel Adler's Eastern European Jewish origins are poetically reflected in the style of the subject's beard and clothing. BM

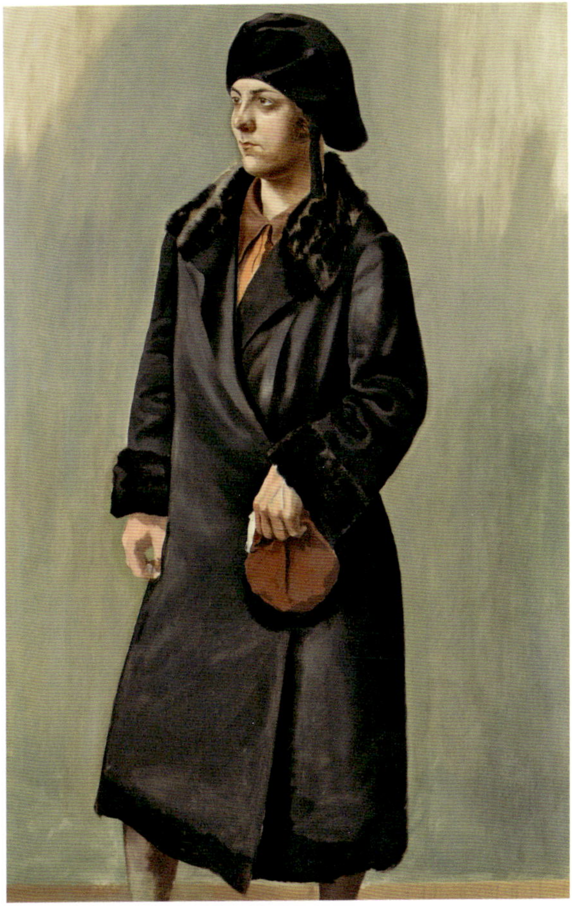

George Grosz | **Frau im schwarzen Mantel** (Woman in Black Coat) | 1927
Oil on canvas, 128.5 × 83.2 cm, inv. no. 15753
Acquired 2008 with support of Kulturstiftung der Länder,
Dr. Winterstein, and Theo Wormland Foundation

Having gained fame for radical works with socially critical and analytical subjects, in the 1920s George Grosz went on to paint a number of portraits that testify to an eye for precision almost equal to that of the Old Masters. These works depicted notable contemporaries such as the poet Max Herrmann-Neisse and the boxer Max Schmeling. Created at around the same period, this picture of a darkly garbed woman with resolute poise and a provocative expression shows an (as yet) unidentified – though evidently independent – woman from the 1920s. The subject seems not to have been able to decide on whether to defensively withdraw or be the first to accost with a pert suggestion. BM

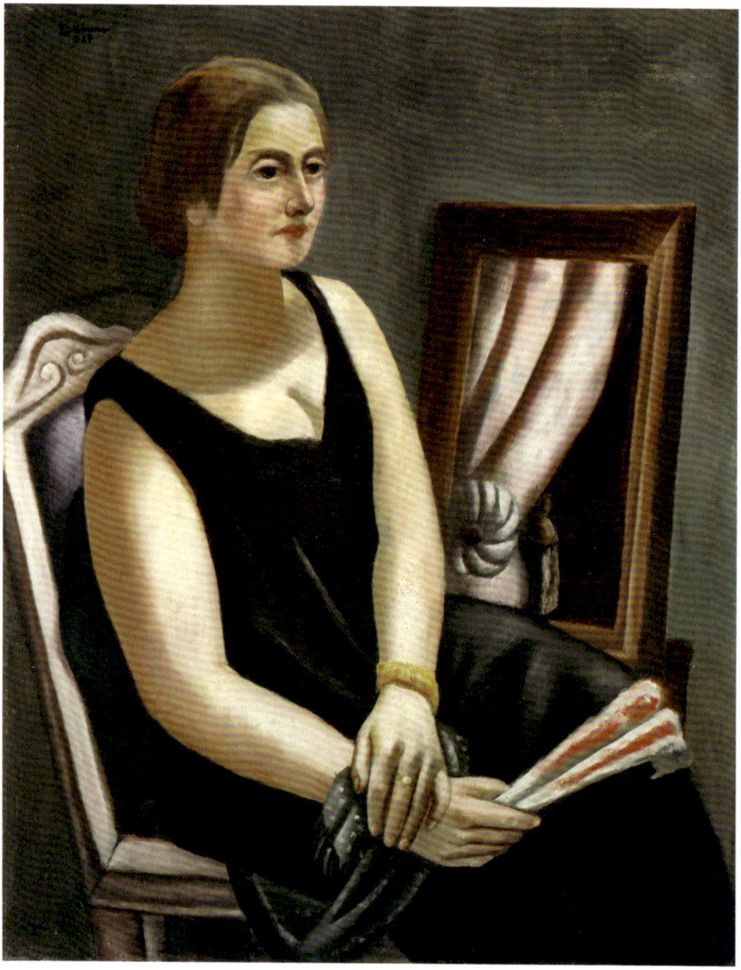

Max Beckmann | Bildnis Minna Beckmann-Tube (Portrait of Minna Beckmann-Tube) | 1924
Oil on canvas, 92.8 × 73 cm, inv. no. 14368
Günther Franke Endowment, 1974

Beckmann met his first wife, Minna, at the Weimar School of Art. The couple became increasingly estranged after the end of the First World War, leading to their divorce in 1925. The previous year, the artist met his future partner Mathilde, known as Quappi, whom he married in 1925. A woman in her early 40s, Minna sits with a vacant expression next to a mirror, which does not capture her mature beauty, but rather the banal reflection of a curtain – which looks as though it is about to fall. The curtain does however serve as a reference to the subject's stage career, having worked since 1918 as a successful singer in Graz. BM

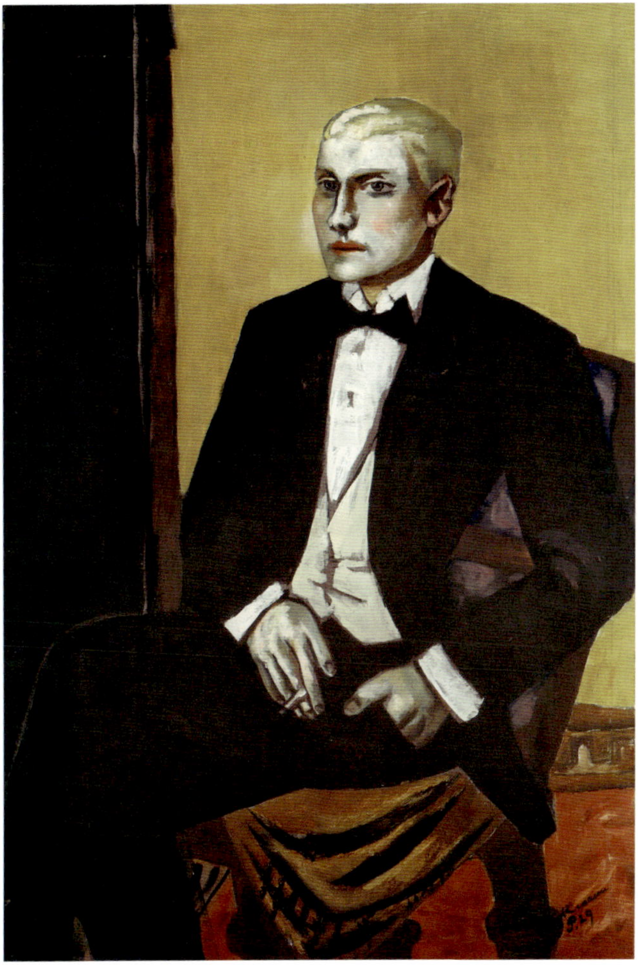

Max Beckmann | Bildnis eines Argentiniers (Portrait of an Argentinian) | 1929
Oil on canvas, 125.5 × 83.5 cm, inv. no. 14375
Günther Franke Endowment, 1974

Beckmann and his wife Quappi spent the turn of the year 1928–29 at the Grand Hotel in St. Moritz. There, so Quappi, 'a young Argentinian' who seemed 'quiet, introverted, and enigmatic' caught the painter's attention. Beckmann embarked on the portrait after his return to Frankfurt. Working from memory, he captured the stranger's inscrutable melancholy and casual elegance and invested his model with classical grandeur and dramatic presence through his use of a pared-down palette of contrasting blacks and whites and his old-masterish composition. OK

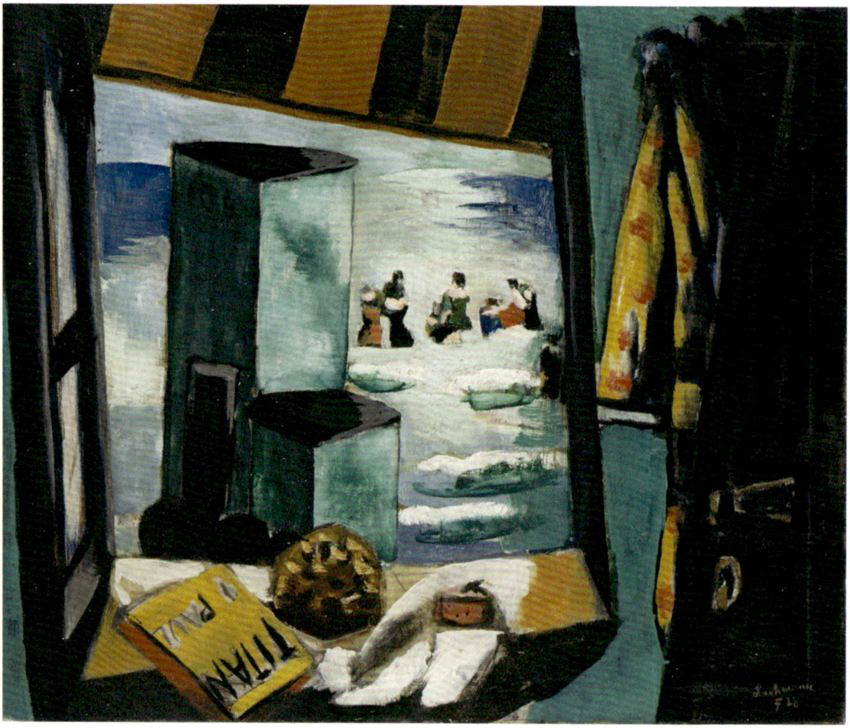

Max Beckmann | Badekabine (grün) (Bathing Hut, green) | 1928
Oil on canvas, 70.6 × 85.7 cm, inv. no. 9651
Donation of Curt Valentin, Buchholz Gallery, New York, 1949

After spending a holiday at the bathing resort of Scheveningen in the summer of 1928, Beckmann created this ingenious composition, showing a window with a view of a mobile beach hut and people frolicking in the waves. Contrasting with the wide expanse of sea is the contained space of the interior, where Beckmann has inscribed a personal note: on the window ledge lies the coming-of-age novel *Titan* by Jean Paul, which the painter greatly admired. In 1930 the painting was the first work by Beckmann to be acquired for the Staatsgalerie; in 1937 it was confiscated by the Nazis as 'degenerate' art. Karl Buchholz sold it in 1941 to Curt Valentin in New York, who gifted the painting back to Munich in 1949 OK

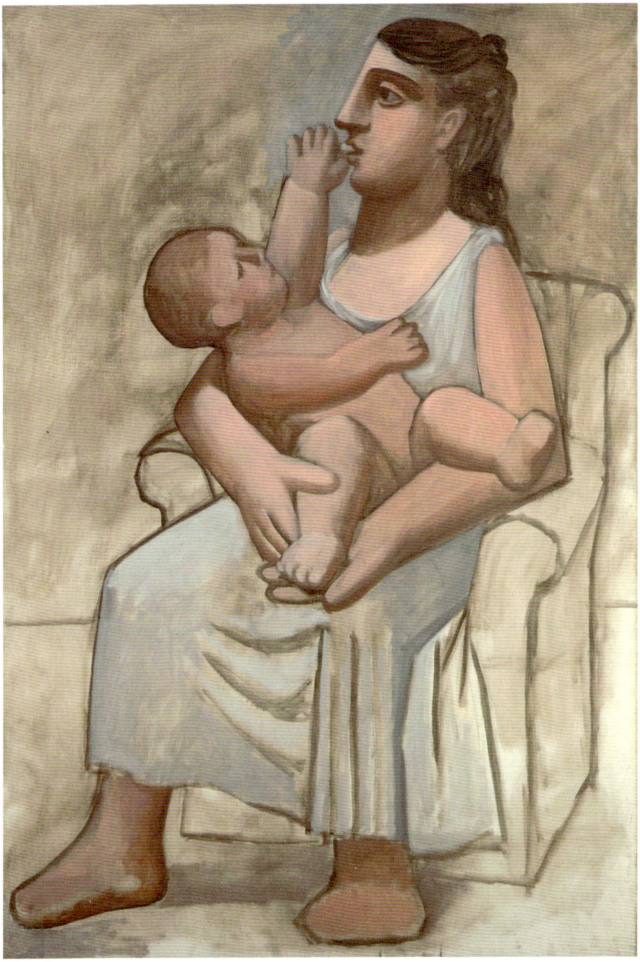

Pablo Picasso | Maternité | 1921
Oil on canvas, 154 × 104 cm, inv. no. 14635
Acquired 1980

Having left behind his Blue, Pink, and Cubist periods, at 45 years of age Picasso painted this classically inspired, serene picture known by the title *Mother with Child*, or *Maternity*. The traditional Renaissance depictions of the Madonna, which bear witness to the interaction between the lively infant and his caring mother, evidently served as the historical inspiration for this subject. However, the painting's sculptural monumentality and the modelling effect of a monochrome palette also allude to the *Pittura metafisica* of the 1920s – specifically to the work of Giorgio de Chirico. BM

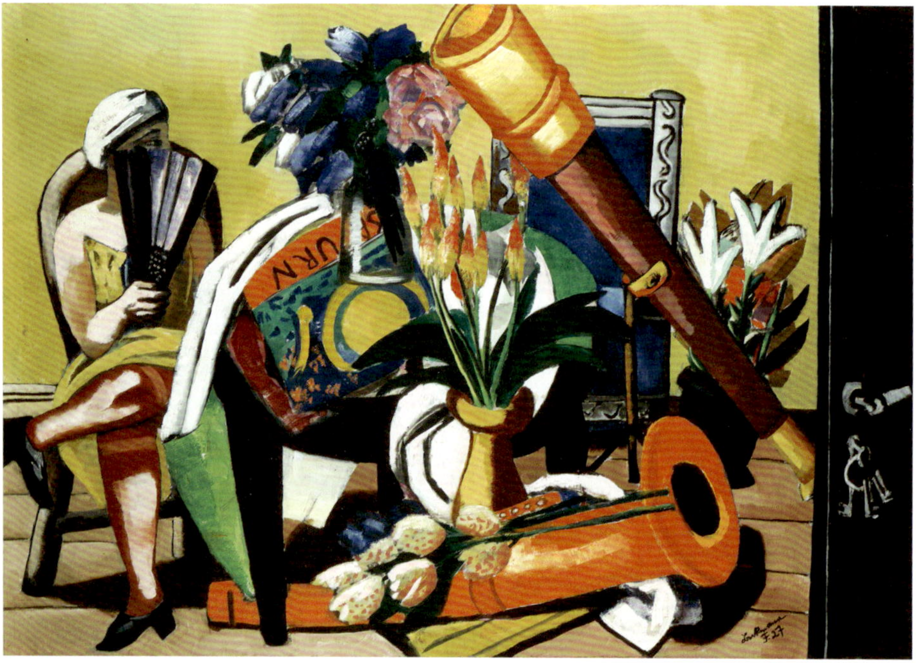

Max Beckmann | Großes Stillleben mit Fernrohr (Large Still Life with Telescope) | 1927
Oil on canvas, 140.7 × 200 cm, inv. no. 13454
Donation of Sofie and Emanuel Fohn, 1964

Max Beckmann was a subtle thinker who was never content just to paint an easily comprehensible subject. 'My motivation has been to re-open the debate on representationalism in a new form of art,' wrote Beckmann in a letter to Wilhelm Hausenstein in 1926, and hence at a time when faithful depiction had become the norm both for the *Neue Sachlichkeit* and Bauhaus. The flowers and props seen in this interior still life, which include an allusion to Saturn and by extension to melancholy, alternate between gloom and *joie de vivre*. The painter is absent; the paraphernalia (objects that have been either found or left abandoned) strike an enigmatic note.
BM

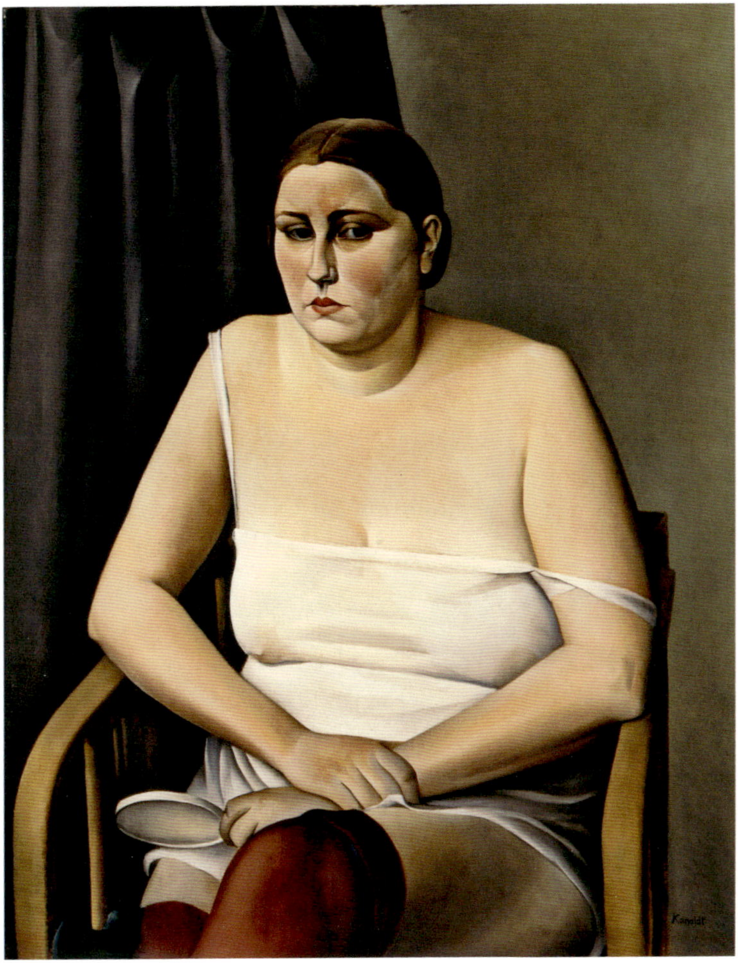

Alexander Kanoldt | Halbakt II (Half Nude II) | 1926
Oil on canvas, 90.5 × 71 cm, inv. no. 14157
Acquired 1971

Alexander Kanoldt's full-figured half-nude has the aloof scepticism of the jaded courtesans portrayed by George Grosz and Otto Dix, the ponderousness of a prostitute selling her body, and the facial expression of an emotionally numbed worker: this is not how happiness looks. The hand mirror calls to mind the age-old visual trope of Venus, goddess of love. Yet everything appears full of disappointment and far removed from any hope of life or love. Kanoldt, an extremely gifted painter of still lifes, here translates the human figure into an idiom of unmoving, soulless objects. BM

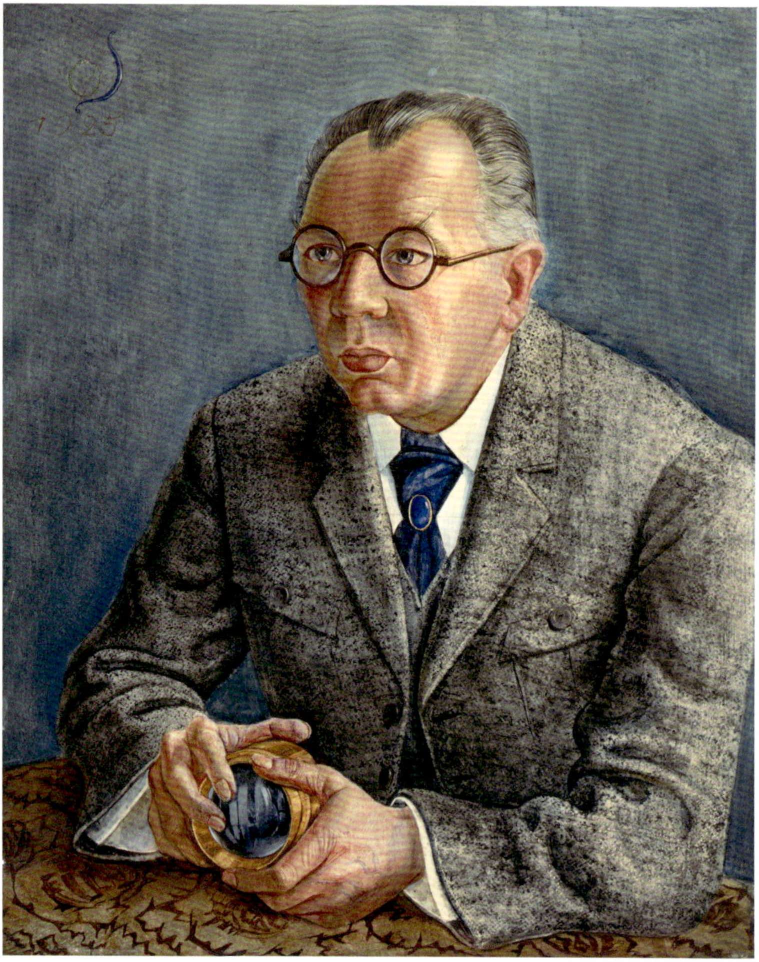

Otto Dix | Bildnis des Photographen Hugo Erfurth (Portrait of the Photographer Hugo Erfurth) | 1925
Tempura on plywood, 75.1 × 60.6 cm, inv. no. 13459
Donation of Sofie and Emanuel Fohn, 1964

In 1918, Otto Dix returned from the war a psychologically broken man, only gradually able to return to the art world. During the mid-1920s he lived in Berlin, where he created a number of portraits. These included a portrait of the photographer Hugo Erfurth, a friend of the artist. The work was acquired by the Dresdener Museumssammlung, only to be confiscated as 'degenerate' in 1937. It came to Munich as part of the Sofie and Emanuel Fohn Collection in 1964.
BM

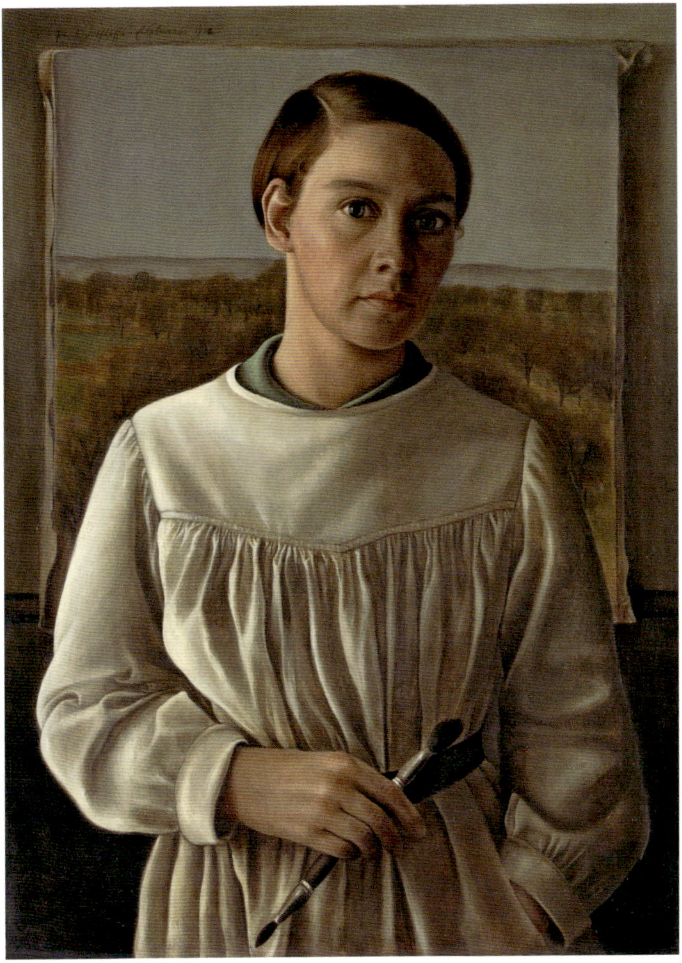

Fridel Dethleffs-Edelmann | Selbstbildnis (Self-Portrait) | 1932
Oil on canvas, 74 × 55 cm, inv. no. 10019
Acquired 1935

Many women artists and female poets famously made a significant impact on 20th century cultural life. Nevertheless, there remain many names yet to be discovered. When Fridel Dethleffs-Edelmann depicted herself in this work, which brings together artistic production and serious self-interrogation to create a simultaneously objective and sensitive self-portrait, the artist was a little over 30 years old. In the old traditional manner, she portrays herself in front of a landscape – though not at a window, but in front of a painting that she has evidently painted herself. Thus the picture functions as a twofold self-portrait. BM

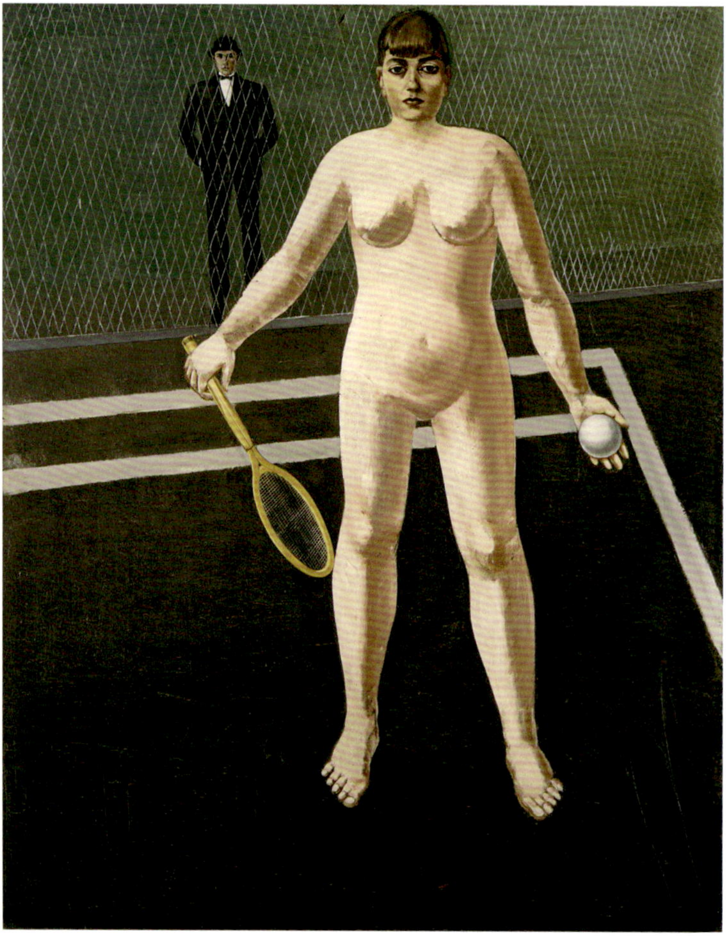

Anton Räderscheidt | Tennisspielerin (The Tennis Player) | 1926
Oil on canvas, 100.5 × 80.3 cm, inv. no. 14311
Acquired 1973

This picture of a tennis player, frozen in motion as she serves the ball, is lent a disconcerting quality by the provocative approach it adopts both to bodily conventions and traditional femininity. The clothed man stands like a warden at the edge of the court with his arms folded behind his back, like a figurine in the work of Oskar Schlemmer. Sporting a fringed haircut, the buxom woman fills the space of the court and the picture. The female body on show becomes the subject of an extraordinarily cold and mercilessly isolating depiction. There is no sign of the 'Golden Twenties', or at least no indication that the individual is liberated from the constraints of convention.
BM

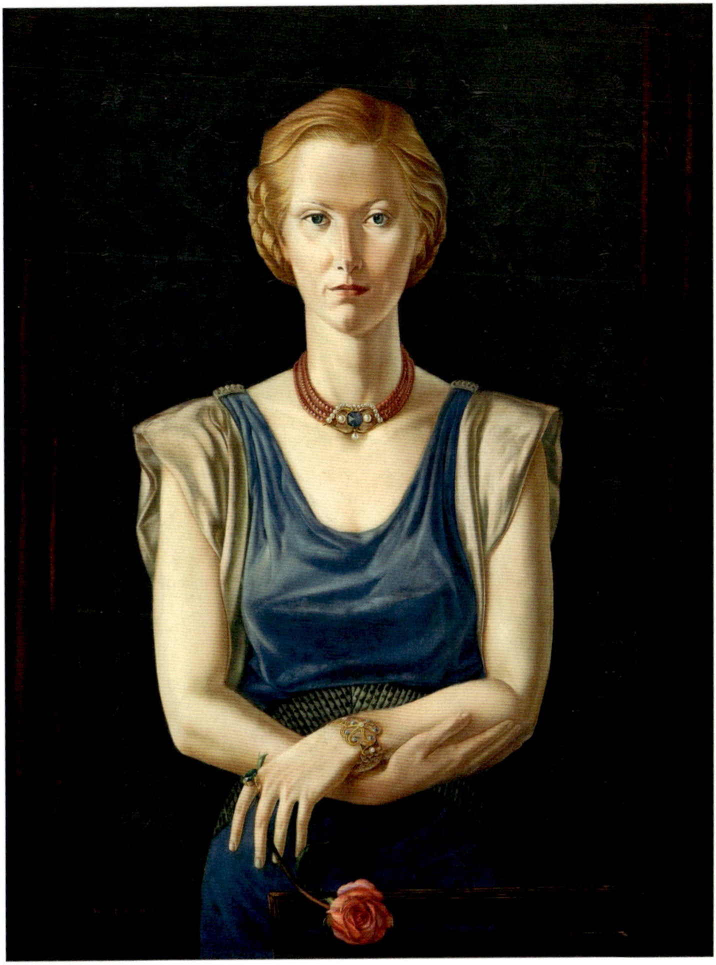

Wilhelm Lachnit | Mädchen mit Schmuck (Girl with Jewellery) | 1936
Oil on wood, 92 × 74 cm, inv. no. L 2563
Private loan, accessioned 2016

The coral jewellery and rose evoke culture and nature; they call to mind the water and land that serve as their respective habitats. Wilhelm Lachnit painted this work for a competition held by the German Society of Goldsmithery in Bremen, which invited entrants to create portraits of women wearing jewellery. His inclusion of traditional attributes, which could well derive from knowledge of Early German painting, and his debt to (for example) the frontal portrait art of Barthel Beham, with which he would have been familiar from the Dresdener Galerie, can be assumed with some certainty. BM

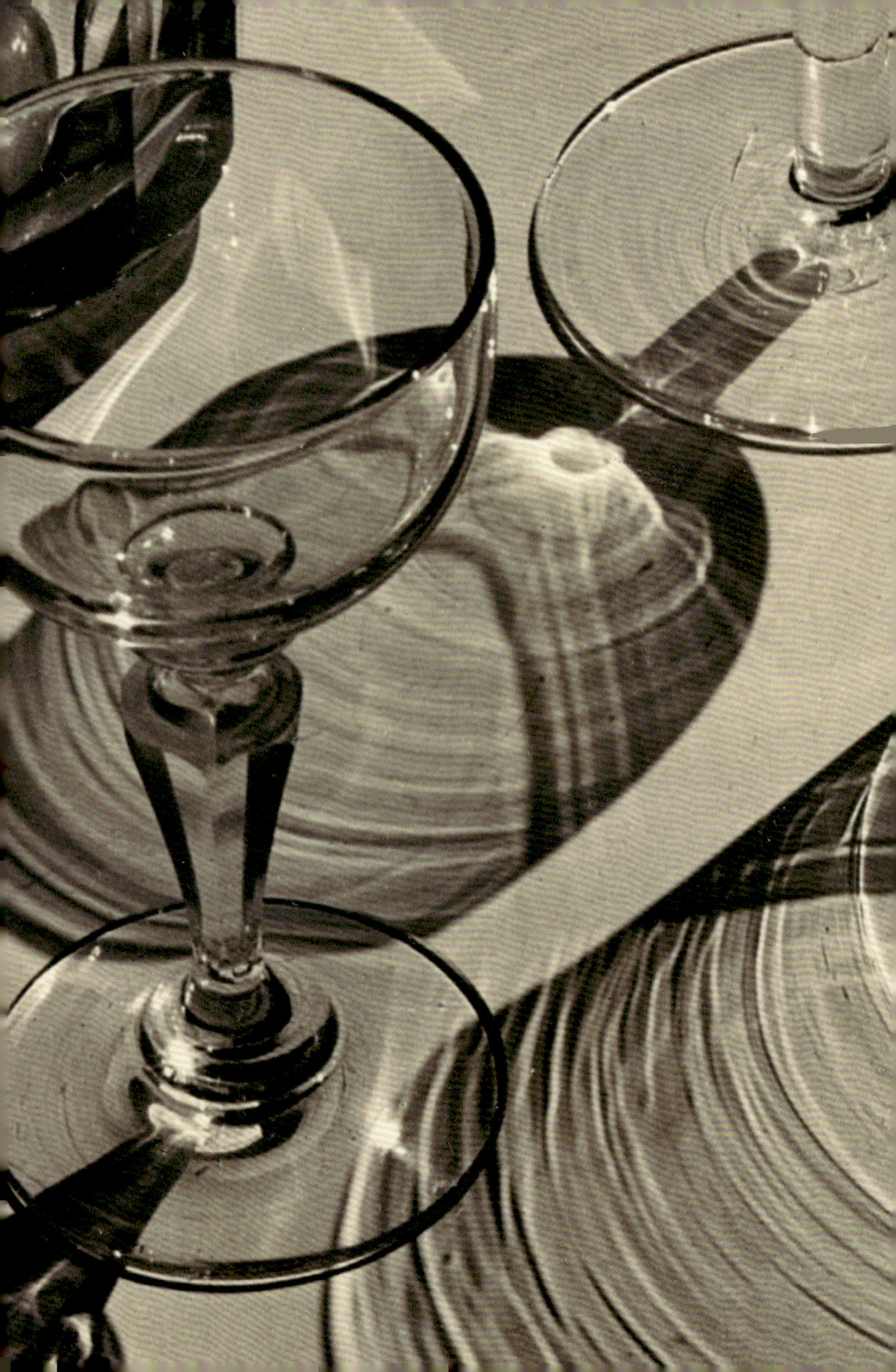

NEUES SEHEN
PHOTOGRAPHY IN THE 1920S AND 1930S

The first public exhibition of Karl Blossfeldt's plant photography, in the Galerie Neumann-Nierendorf in Berlin in 1926, heralded the arrival of a new wave of photography, which had been evolving in Germany since the mid-1920s. Although Blossfeldt's photographs of natural forms were intended only as the basis for drawings and models, the images almost perfectly fulfilled important stylistic criteria. He dispensed with Pictorialist effects – large-scale retouching and fine printing techniques – which had been in widespread use in the early 1920s, meant to give a painterly appearance to artistic photography. Blossfeldt reduced his subject matter to its elementary forms, presenting the material in a neutral, objective style, in the name of comparative visual analysis. For photography's *Neues Sehen* (New Vision), the key criteria were a use of the camera specifically befitting the medium of photography – not some other medium – precision and objectivity in the images, and an overall approach which aimed at a new vision of reality, a new way of seeing what was there. Blossfeldt's stylistic tendencies led him to be regarded as a forerunner and ancestor of the movement. The publication of his photographs under the title *Urformen der Kunst* (1928, published the following year in English as *Art Forms in Nature*) laid the stylistic groundwork for *Neues Sehen*, alongside books like László Moholy-Nagy's programmatic *Painting, Photography, Film* (1925), Albert Renger-Patzsch's *The World is Beautiful* (1928) and August Sander's *Face of Our Time* (1929).

The new photography of the 1920s encompasses a wide spectrum of greatly differing aesthetic approaches. But what they all had in common was an insistence on using genuinely photographic means of expression. A new formal vocabulary emerged, which found particular popularity in portrait photography, images of everyday manufactured products, and real urban life, as well as in landscape and nature photography. The new style emphasized formal structures and the materiality of the subject, and made use of dynamic perspectives from below or above, fragmentation, extreme close-ups, and montage techniques. *Neues Sehen* and *Neue Sachlichkeit* were generally seen as the two most important movements within German photography. The two styles were often respectively seen as epitomized by their most important exponents: for *Neues Sehen*, the Bauhaus master László Moholy-Nagy, an autodidact working in a variety of media, and for *Neue Sachlichkeit*, the Essen-based professional photographer Albert Renger-Patzsch. In 'Aims', a programmatic text published in 1927, Renger-Patzsch pleaded that objects should be represented 'in a mode of appearance optimal to their structure, taking into account the photographic means used to emphasize this intention'. By contrast, Moholy-Nagy propounded a view of photography as a 'technical medium, which uses light and the camera-machine as a basis for an expansion of the field of perception'. The Hungarian artist understood photography as the action of shaping light. He promoted the expansion of photographic vocabulary through experimental procedures, and saw the medium of film as the logical evolution and ultimate perfection of photography. For his part, Renger-Patzsch emphasized that photography's decisive quality was its realism, and felt a duty to faithful representation.

Photographers renewing the language of the medium consciously and radically broke with current photographic conventions by embracing visual characteristics such as sharp focus, objectivity, detail, and precision, which had previously been deemed unartistic. Most of these 'iconoclasts' – many of whom were women, including Aenne Biermann, Florence Henri, and Germaine Krull – did not come from the dominant milieu of trained studio and professional photographers. In fact, they were mostly self-taught, having come to photography from backgrounds in other creative and artistic fields, like the Bauhaus or the artists' group *Cercle et carré*. Around this time, traditions in the history of photography were being newly defined – the 1920s saw the rediscovery of daguerrotypes and calotypes, with photography's earliest years now reinterpreted as its first golden age. There was praise and acclaim for photographers, like Blossfeldt and Eugène Atget, whose work had been marked by a detached, descriptive intent. Scientific and anonymous photography also came to the attention of artists, as long as these new kinds of images were characterized by a modern aesthetic, in the manner of *Neues Sehen*.

Works from this euphoric and increasingly popular movement were collected in the exhibition *Film und Foto* (FiFo) in 1929. Originally organized as part of the Deutscher Werkbund design show in Stuttgart, in the following years the exhibition went on tour, visiting Berlin, Zürich, Vienna, Japan, and other locations. Today, *Film und Foto* is still regarded as the most important exhibition in photography and film in the early decades of the 20th century. The ambitious goal of the exhibition – organized by the Russian Constructivist El Lissitzky and the American photographer Edward Steichen among others – was to present, in as continuous a way as possible, all historical figures who had embraced the camera as a contemporary creative medium. Encompassing around 1200 works by European, American, and Russian artists, the FiFo exhibition successfully presented a knowledgeable, international survey of the innovation in photography and film. In Germany, the event marked the zenith of modern photography, and was vividly documented in the bibliophile volume *fotoauge* ('photo eye') edited by Franz Roh and Jan Tschichold, which contained a selection of works from FiFo. In subsequent years, the stylistic innovations of *Neues Sehen* were appropriated by advertising and magazine photography, a rapidly-expanding sector, as well as by National Socialist propaganda. But many of the style's actual innovators were persecuted after 1933, often forced into exile, where many were unable to continue their professional and artistic careers.

Inka Graeve Ingelmann and Simone Förster

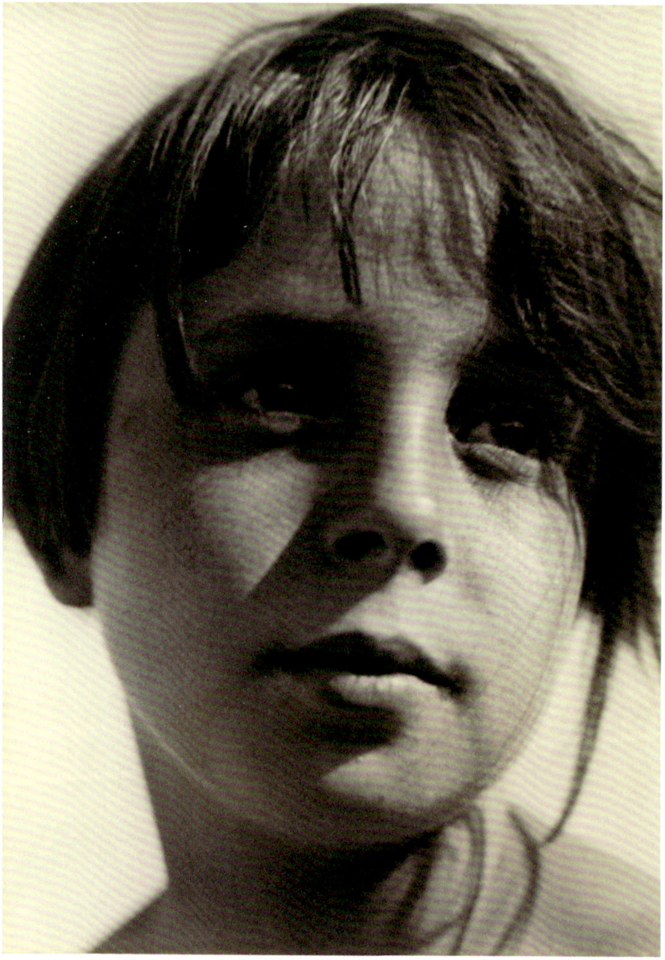

Aenne Biermann | View | c. 1930
Gelatin silver print, 58 × 42 cm, inv. no. AJW 429
Ann and Jürgen Wilde Foundation, accessioned 2010

The declared aim of photographer Aenne Biermann was to achieve a 'greater intimacy with things'. Using tight cropping, unconventional perspectives, and high-contrast lighting, she captured the detail and characteristic features of her subjects. Biermann used her lens to reveal the surprising, delightful charm of everyday phenomena. The candid childish gaze of Biermann's daughter Helga is thus more than simply the subject of this photographic 'View' – it is at the heart of the photographer's approach to her work. AV

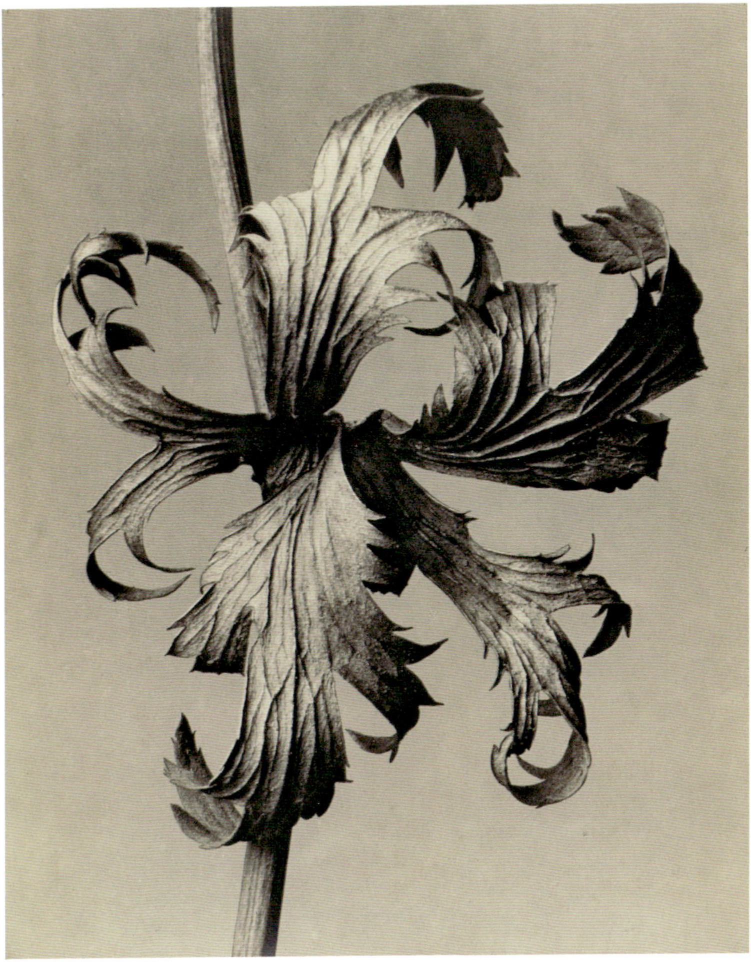

Karl Blossfeldt | Trollius europaeus (Common Globeflower) | 1915/25
Gelatin silver print, 29.7 × 23.8 cm, inv. no. 16099
Acquired 2010

The globeflower's stem-leaves dry out easily: here, they have already begun to contract. In close-up, the plant's entire form, including the leaf veins, seem to protrude forward sculpturally. Cropping and lighting give the plant the look of a delicate bronze sculpture. Blossfeldt found the 'basic forms of art' within nature, and he reflected this in the title of his groundbreaking photo book, *Art Forms in Nature*. His radically-reduced visual idiom – a style developed from the immanent qualities of the medium – made him the doyen of the New Photography.
IGI

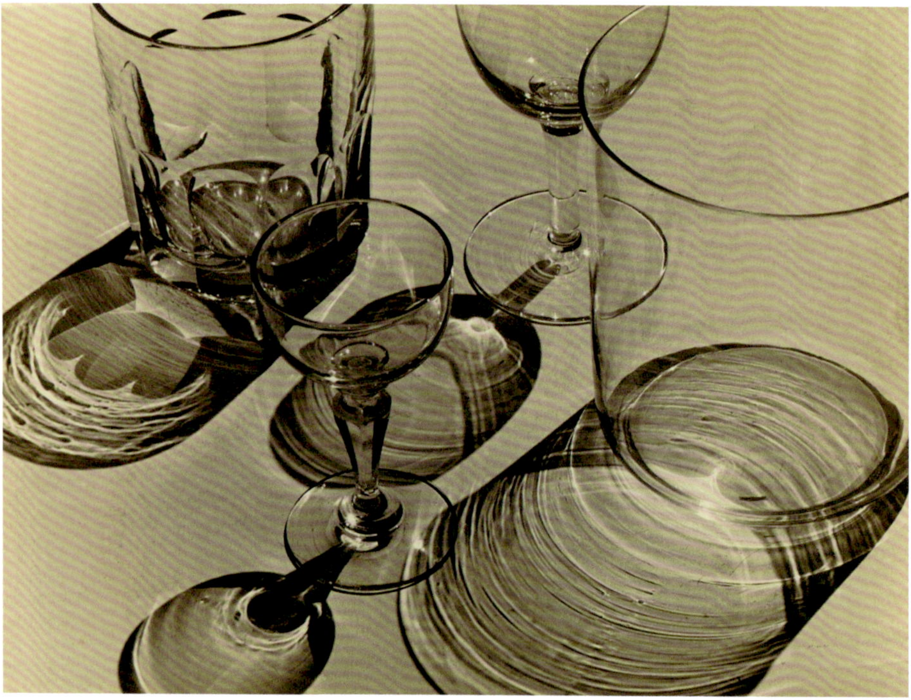

Albert Renger-Patzsch | Glass | 1926–27
Ggelatin silver print, 16.8 × 22.7 cm, inv. no. AJW 887
Ann and Jürgen Wilde Foundation, accessioned 2011

Alongside Karl Blossfeldt and August Sander, Albert Renger-Patzsch was among the most important representatives of *Neue Sachlichkeit* photography in Germany in the 1920s and 1930s. The guiding principle of his work was not the development of a personal style, but rather an objective photographic reproduction of the 'essence of things'. Renger-Patzsch's clear, objective representations of industrial objects, architecture, and everyday items that he made on commission from industry and business had a profound influence on the aesthetics of modern photography.
SF

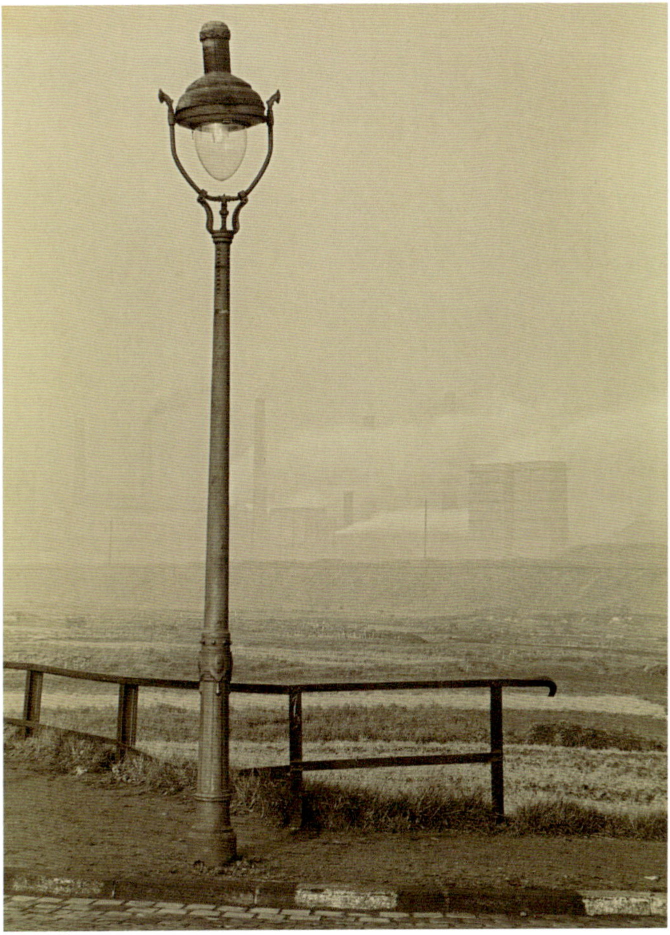

Albert Renger-Patzsch | Industrial Landscape at Oberhausen | 1931
Gelatin silver print, 37.6 × 27.4 cm, inv. no. AJW 106
Ann and Jürgen Wilde Foundation, accessioned 2010

Between 1927 and 1935, Albert Renger-Patzsch took photographs of the industrial Ruhr region, capturing images of landscapes on the edge of cities, slagheaps, inner courtyards, suburban houses, and industrial and mining facilities. The series was the only major non-commissioned work that Renger-Patzsch ever carried out. With their reticent emotionality and compositional clarity, these images make an important contribution to the representation of modern industry and landscapes. Today, the Ruhr photographs can also be read as a visual commentary on contemporary discussions of urbanism, landscape conservation, and post-industrial landscapes. SF

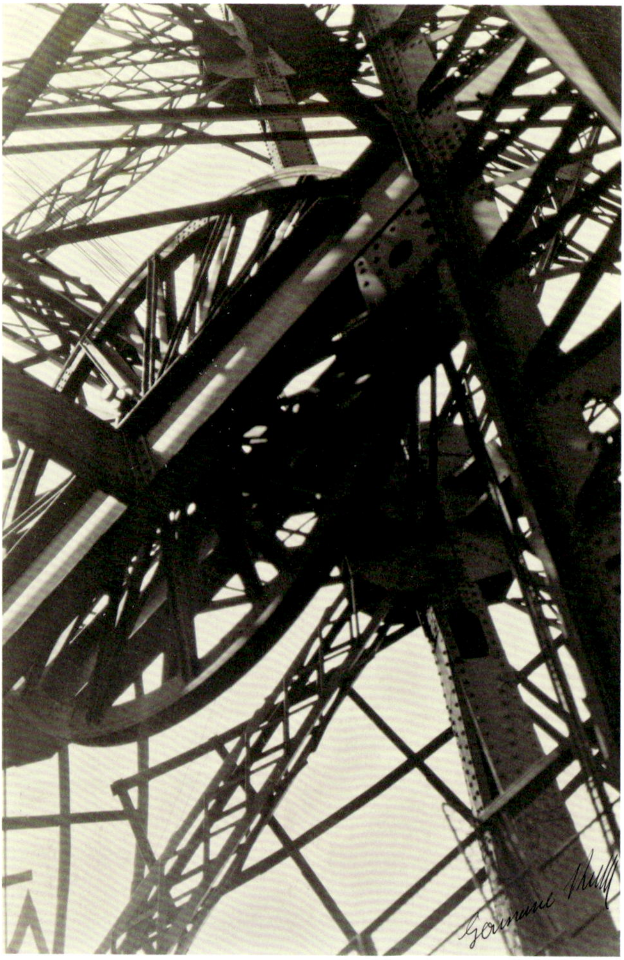

Germaine Krull | Tour Eiffel (Eiffel Tower) | 1927
Gelatin silver print, 36.1 × 24.2 cm, inv. no. AJW 564
Ann and Jürgen Wilde Foundation, accessioned 2010

Germaine Krull first trained in photography in Munich. Later, after sojourns in Moscow, Berlin, and Amsterdam, she moved to Paris, where she worked as a photojournalist and became a successful advertising and portrait photographer. Her significance as an avant-garde artist is partly due to her portfolio *Métal* (1928), in which she took cranes, bridges, machines, and the Eiffel Tower as her subject matter. Through unusual camera angles and cropped details, Krull stylized the gigantic iron constructions, presenting them as dynamic monuments to modern life.
SF

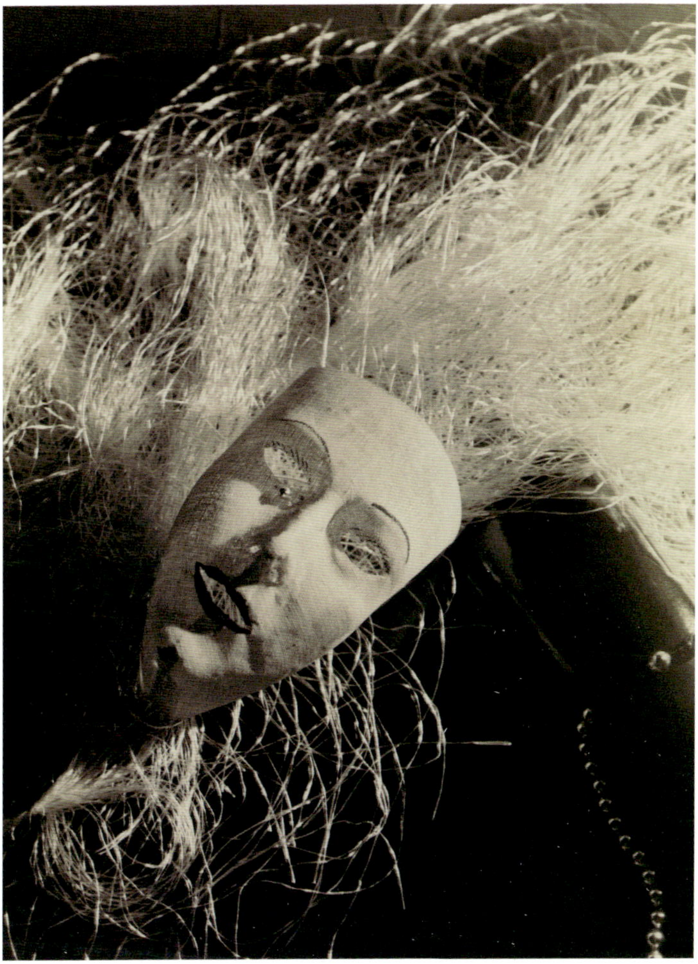

Werner Rohde | Carnival | 1928
Gelatin silver print, 22.6 × 16.9 cm, inv. no. AJW 601
Ann and Jürgen Wilde Foundation, accessioned 2010

By his own account, Rohde, who came from a family of church painters, saw photography as a chance to develop freely as an artist. Rohde first worked as a fashion photographer, but his work became increasingly free in form, playing with theatrical masquerades and staged identities. Elaborately costumed figures and still lifes make his photographs look like citations from films of the 1920s and 1930s. In 1929, *Carnival* was included in the travelling exhibition *Film und Foto*, alongside six other photographs by Rohde. SF

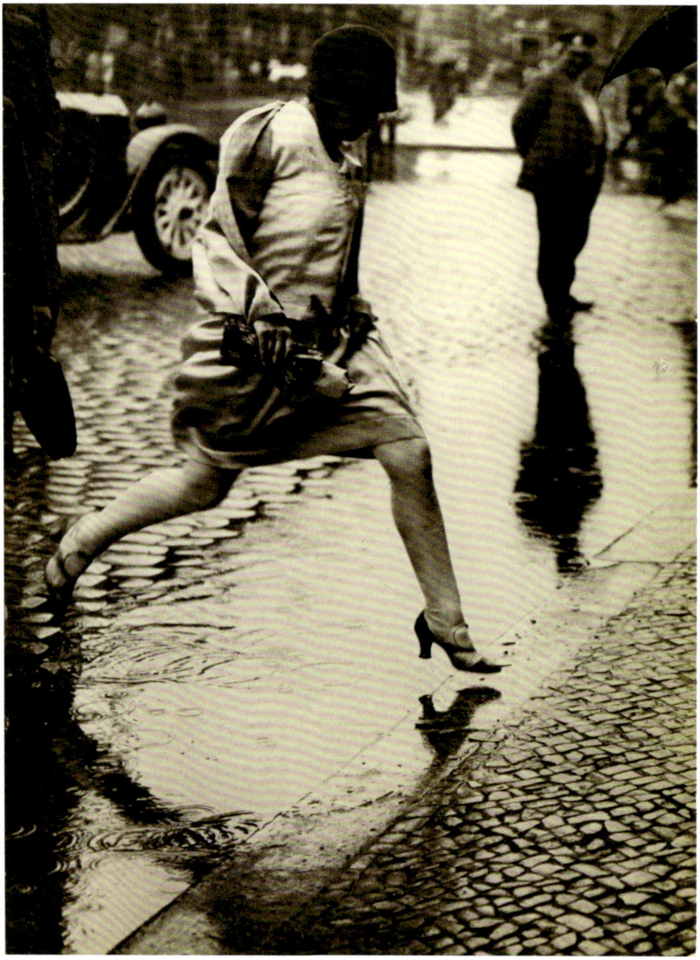

Friedrich Seidenstücker | Untitled (Puddle Jumper) | c. 1925
Gelatin silver print, 16.5 × 12.2 cm, inv. no. AJW 217
Ann and Jürgen Wilde Foundation, accessioned 2010

Friedrich Seidenstücker was among the most important chroniclers of Berlin's everyday life during the Weimar Republic. His photographs narrate inconspicuous events and incidents, telling of easy Sunday pleasures and exhausting working lives, children's games on the street and crowds in railway stations or at the zoo. Seidenstücker casts an ironic and sometimes humorous eye on people and life in the metropolis. However, in the background and at the margins of his photographs, the social reality of the 1920s and 1930s can clearly be seen.
SF

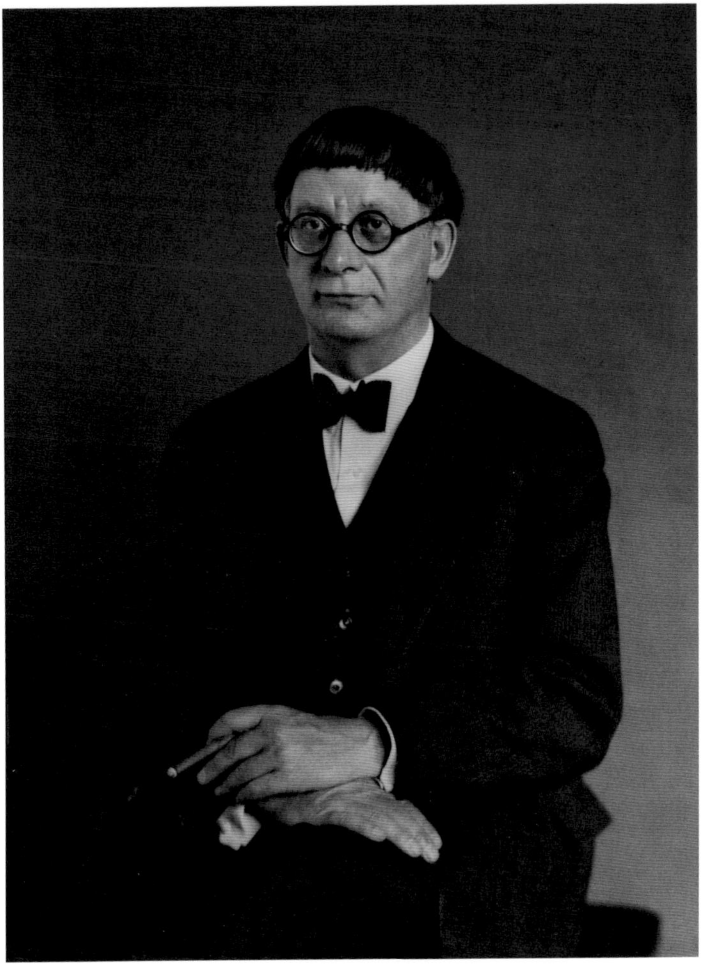

August Sander | The Architect (Hans Poelzig) | 1928
Gelatin silver print, 40 × 29.8 cm, inv. no. 16349
Donation of Lothar Schirmer, 2014

In his epochal work *People of the Twentieth Century*, August Sander devoted an entire chapter to architects as a human type. Here, Sander depicts Hans Poelzig in seated posture, as he did with most of the architects he portrayed. Poelzig was the co-founder of the *Neue Sachlichkeit* school of architecture: his three-piece suit, bowtie, and the cigar loosely held in the left hand point to his status within the prosperous bourgeoisie, but his unusual haircut and striking spectacles emphasize his artistic, avant-garde attitude. IGI

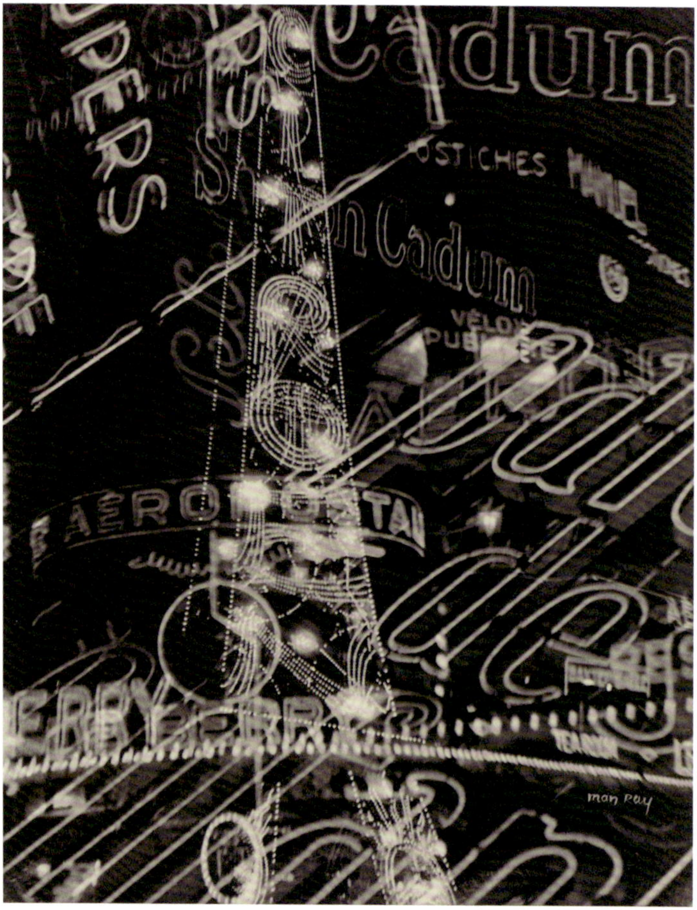

Man Ray | La Ville (The City) | 1931, from the portfolio *Électricité: Dix rayogrammes de Man Ray et un texte de Pierre Bost, Compagnie générale d'électricité,* Paris 1931
Photogravure, 26 × 20.5 cm, inv. no. AJW 661 3/10
Ann and Jürgen Wilde Foundation, accessioned 2010

Man Ray had a radical influence on modern art, as a photographer, a painter, a filmmaker, and a maker of assemblages. In his photographic work, he experimented with cameraless photography, multiple exposures, montage, and manipulation. The elegant portfolio *Électricité* was originally a commission for the Paris electricity provider, intended to advertise electricity. In ten photogravures made from what were called rayographs, Man Ray makes light, vibration, energy, and tension visible – electricity here appears as a metaphor for modern life.
SF

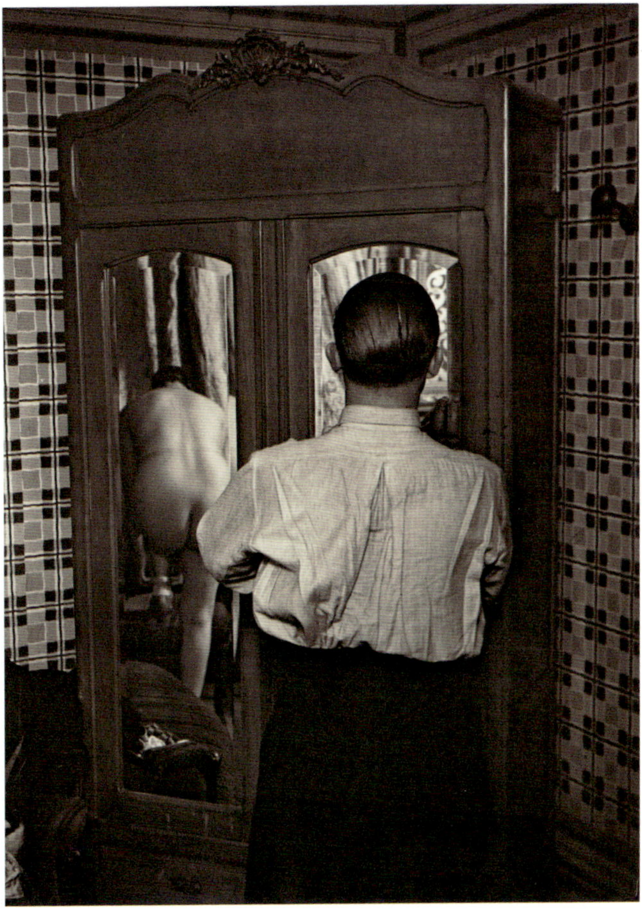

Brassaï (Gyula Halàsz) | **L'armoire à glace: Dans un hôtel de passe, rue Quicampoix**
(Mirror Cabinet: In a Hotel-Brothel, Rue Quicampoix) | 1938–39
Gelatin silver print (later print), 38.9 × 28.5 cm, inv. no. 15683
Donation of the art business, 2006

The photographer Brassaï wandered the streets of Paris by night, driven by fascination for the 'world at the margins of our own'. This pushed him out into the streets and commercial establishments, and away from the splendid avenues and art monuments. Using photo-plates, Brassaï captured impressions otherwise only seen by criminals, pimps, prostitutes, and their clients. Deep shadows, faces concealed in darkness, glances obscured or exchanged in reflective surfaces: these are all characteristic of his photographs. Even today, Brassaï's pictures have considerable influence on our image of seedy Parisian milieus of the 1930s.
AV

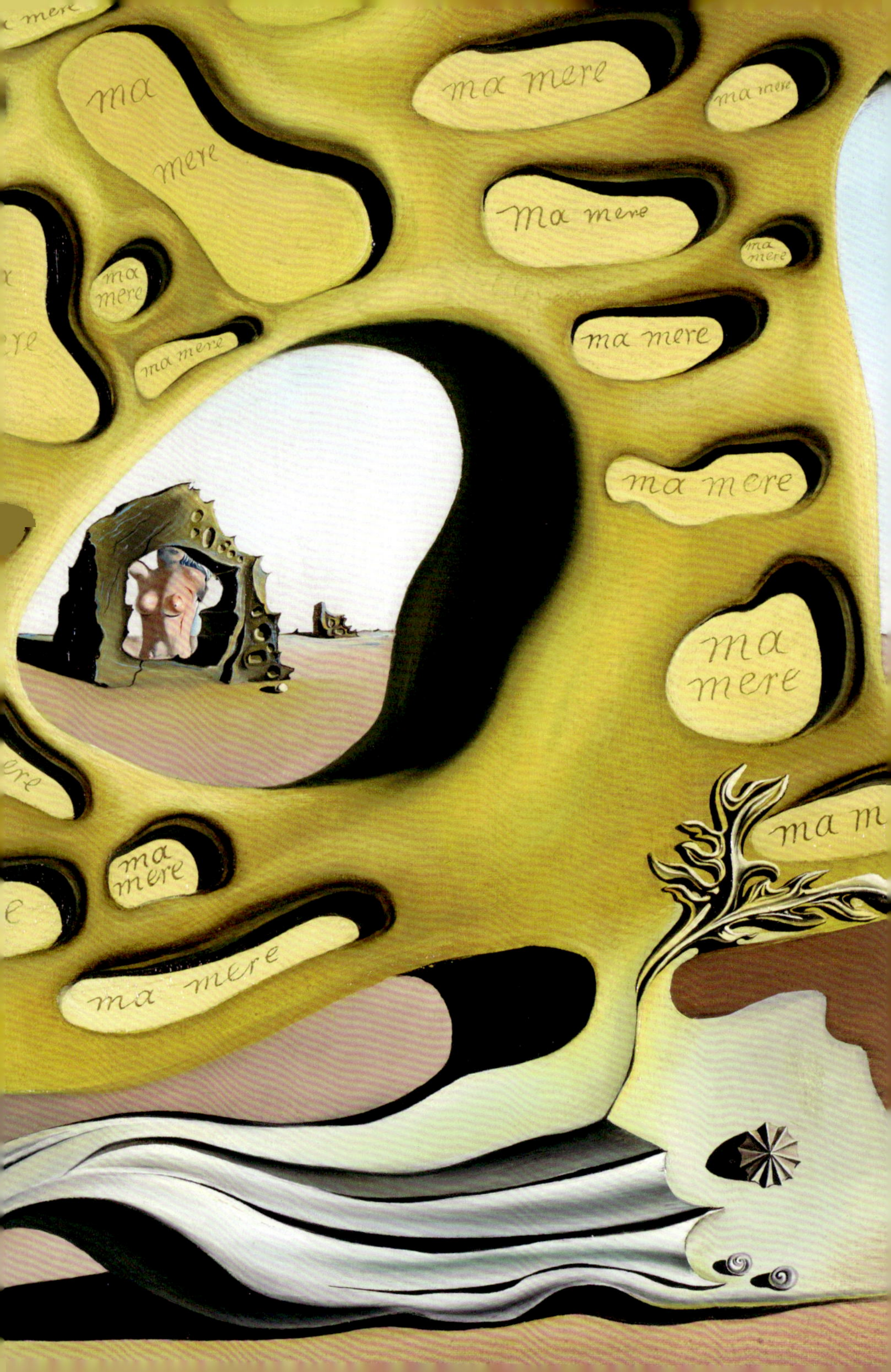
ma mere
ma mere
ma mere
ma mere
ma mere
ma mere
ma mere
ma mere
ma mere
ma mere
ma mere
ma mere

VISIONS
SURREALISM AND MAGIC REALISM

The 1920s saw the emergence of Surrealism, Magic Realism and *Neue Sachlichkeit*, all of which were conceptually and visually opposed to the abstract art which preceded them. These trends were strong in France, Belgium, and Germany, but also had an important predecessor in pre-war Italy, where *Pittura metafisica* had sprung up in the 1910s. *Self-Portrait* by Giorgio de Chirico – *Pittura metafisica*'s most prominent representative – reveals a number of key aspects of both content and form: first, an interest in metaphysics, in other words, in what lies behind the visible world, and second, an affinity with precisely-executed figuration. This showed a debt to both Renaissance and Neoclassical art, and stood in sharp contrast to Italian Futurism, which had emerged just a few years before *Pittura metafisica*.

Emerging in France and Belgium in the 1920s, Surrealism was a programmatic movement of artists and writers, loosely grouped around the writer André Breton. Magic Realism, on the other hand, was a concept introduced by art criticism, which took on a number of meanings over time and was applied to a variety of artworks. The term Magic Realism was first proposed by Franz Roh in 1925, used to refer to a kind of post-Expressionist art characterized by sober, figurative representations. In this context, 'magic' should not be understood as an opposed term to 'mystical'. The 'realism' in 'Magic Realism' addressed the 'magic of being': in other words, it emphasized the existence of the world of things. Thanks to a Gustav Hartlaub exhibition in Mannheim in 1925, the term *Neue Sachlichkeit* became established as a general term for post-Expressionist art, used in parallel with 'Magic Realism'. Essentially, *Neue Sachlichkeit* thus applied to two distinct styles: first, the veristic, bitingly social-critical work of the likes of George Grosz and Otto Dix, and second, the idealistic, rather uncritical work of artists like Georg Schrimpf and Alexander Kanoldt. From around 1926, this latter style was increasingly named Magic Realism, not least because of the palpable thematic influence of *Pittura metafisica*, including its strange, cool, and unreal moods. Although nowadays the term Magic Realism is often used without a specific temporal or geographic referent, in the 1930s and especially in the 1950s, the term was applied to interwar German painting which had a clear relation to French and Belgian Surrealism, and to *Pittura metafisica*. In a 1957 article, Franz Roh distinguished between Surrealism's concrete 'phantasmagoria', in which 'strange objects and constellations are invented', and the way Magic Realism 'only seeks to subject our continuously existing environment to a hidden shaping'. By making this distinction, Roh sought to distinguish between impossible scenarios and ones which were improbable, but nonetheless possible. However, it is often impossible to draw such a neat line between the two, either in terms of individual works or of entire oeuvres. Thus Richard Oelze's *The Brother-in-Law (Couple with Dog)* contains some elements of Magic Realism along with some drawn from Surrealism. All his life, the painter Edgar Ende rejected classification in one or the other genre, describing his works simply as 'Visionary Art'. But his painting *The Woman on the Tortoise*, for example, unquestionably reveals the influence of Surrealism.

The Surrealist movement included the painters René Magritte, Salvador Dalí, Joan Miró, André Masson, Hans Bellmer, and Paul Delvaux. Other members included Max Ernst and Hans Arp, both of whom had previously been involved with Dadaism. In the wake of the traumatic experience of the First World War, these artists regarded bourgeois ideas and categories as morally dubious; a belief in reason and order had dwindled away. However, Surrealism was based on a programme with strong theoretical and thematic inclinations: in this respect, it was unlike Dadaism, which was far more marked by anarchist spontaneity, although it, too, sought to mock and subvert a bourgeois sense of order.

In the *First Surrealist Manifesto*, written in 1924, Breton wrote: 'I am defining it once and for all: SURREALISM, *n.* Psychic automatism in its pure state, by which one proposes to express – verbally, by means of the written word, or in any other manner – the actual functioning of thought. Dictated by the thought, in the absence of any control exercised by reason, exempt from any aesthetic or moral concern. [...] Surrealism is based on the belief in the superior reality of certain forms of previously neglected associations, in the omnipotence of dream, in the disinterested play of thought. It tends to ruin once and for all all other psychic mechanisms and to substitute itself for them in solving all the principal problems of life.' Breton's manifesto formulates basic aesthetic goals and intellectual ideas, but gives no indication of how they are to be implemented in artistic terms. In their actual works, the Surrealists used a wide variety of abstract and figurative forms to express their preoccupation with dreams, the unconscious, automatism, and chance.

Examining the paintings gathered here at the Pinakothek der Moderne, the range of Surrealist art becomes clear. Dalí and Magritte tended to a veristic, Old-Master style, excluding any form of chance: instead, they carefully applied one brushstroke after another, achieving an extreme degree of precision. While Dalí's *The Enigma of My Desire or 'My Mother, My Mother, My Mother'* confronts the painter's anxieties, longings, and fantasies, Magritte's work was often driven by semiotic and philosophical reflections. In a painting like *The Key to Dreams*, Magritte addresses the arbitrariness of signs, a theme connecting his work with the writings of Swiss linguist Ferdinand de Saussure, who described the relation of signifier and signified as an arbitrary result of human conventions.

By contrast, other Surrealists – like Joan Miró in his abstract *Composition* – were committed to using chance within their work. Max Ernst employed a wide variety of automatic and semi-automatic procedures: in frottage, the structure of objects was transferred to paper by rubbing their surfaces with a soft pencil, while grattage involved scraping away several layers of paint from a canvas, thus allowing the object of the painting to emerge. Above all in forest paintings like *Totem and Taboo*, Ernst used the technique of decalcomania, by which a thin piece of freshly painted glass was pressed onto a canvas, then pulled away, leaving behind a random pattern. However, while this was a form of automatism, the artist's actions always remained subordinate to an exact conception of the picture, with surfaces and other elements arranged with considerable deliberation. Ernst consistently combined semi-automatic procedures with processes of revision: this allowed him to concretize what had emerged, completing the composition.

From the mid-1930s, political reality caught up with the Surrealists' immersion in dreams, longing, the unconscious, and the irrational. Reality intervened in both life and art: under National Socialism, avant-garde artists were ostracized and even murdered, forced to emigrate or to go into 'internal exile'. For all their surreal qualities, paintings like Magritte's *The Third Dimension* or Ernst's *The Angel of Hearth and Home* are reflections on contemporary events, specifically on Nazism's threat to both art and society.

Franziska Stöhr

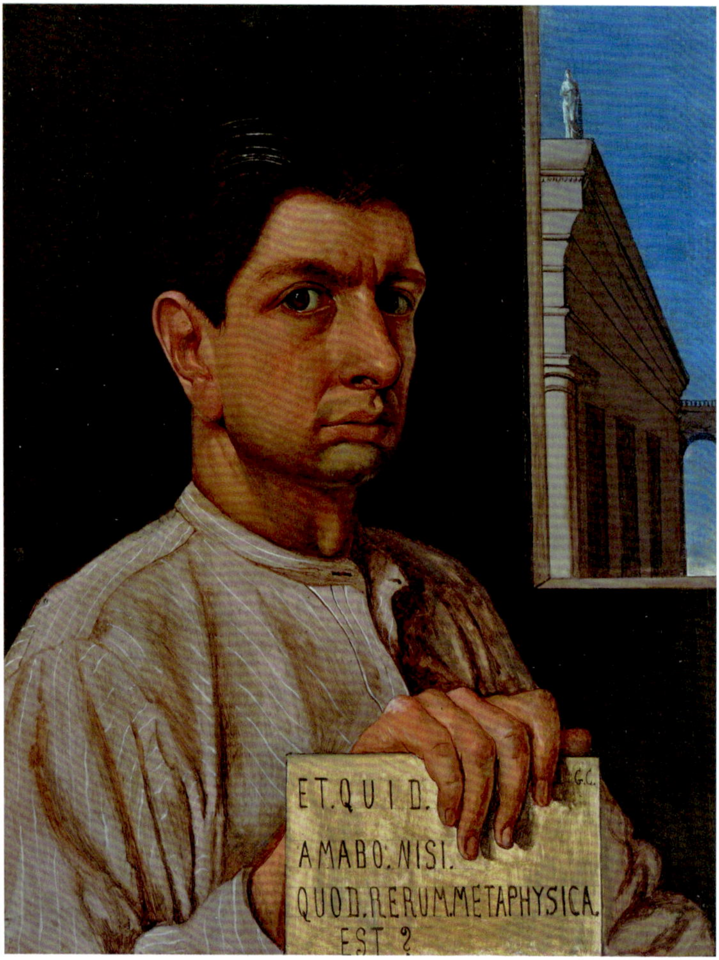

Giorgio de Chirico | **Autoritratto** (Self-Portrait) | 1920
Oil on wood, 50.2 × 39.5 cm, inv. no. 14682
Acquired 1981

In his 1919 essay 'The Return to Craft', Giorgio de Chirico wrote 'I am a classical painter'. However, his *Self-Portrait* does not show him with a brush and palette, but rather with a tablet whose Latin inscription reads: 'And what will I love, if not that which is the metaphysics of things?' In this way, De Chirico, the co-founder of *Pittura metafisica*, announces a programmatic aesthetic interest in the enigma hidden behind visible things. In the image, he formally places himself in the tradition of Italian Renaissance painting, by virtue of the architecture in the background, and the visible section of the window. FS

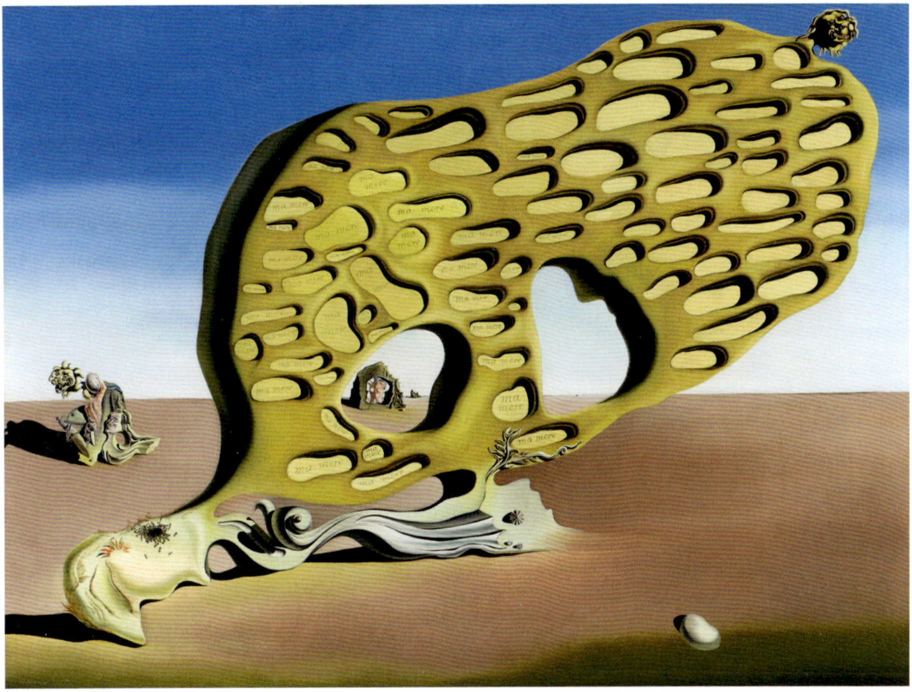

Salvador Dalí | L'Ènigme du desir – ma mère, ma mère, ma mère
(The Enigma of My Desire or 'My Mother, My Mother, My Mother') | 1929
Oil on canvas, 110.5 × 150.5 cm, inv. no. 14734
Acquired 1982 with support of Theo Wormland Foundation

Salvador Dalí's key veristic work reveals the effort he put into visualizing his dreams, fears, and desires. The central figure thematizes the painter's longing for his mother, who died young, while his ambivalent relation to his father is addressed in the group of figures in the left of the picture. Here a young man embraces an older man, while a hand with a knife, a murder weapon, appears behind both of their backs. In the background, our gaze is directed towards another female body, possibly alluding to Dalí's wife Gala, whom he met in 1929. FS

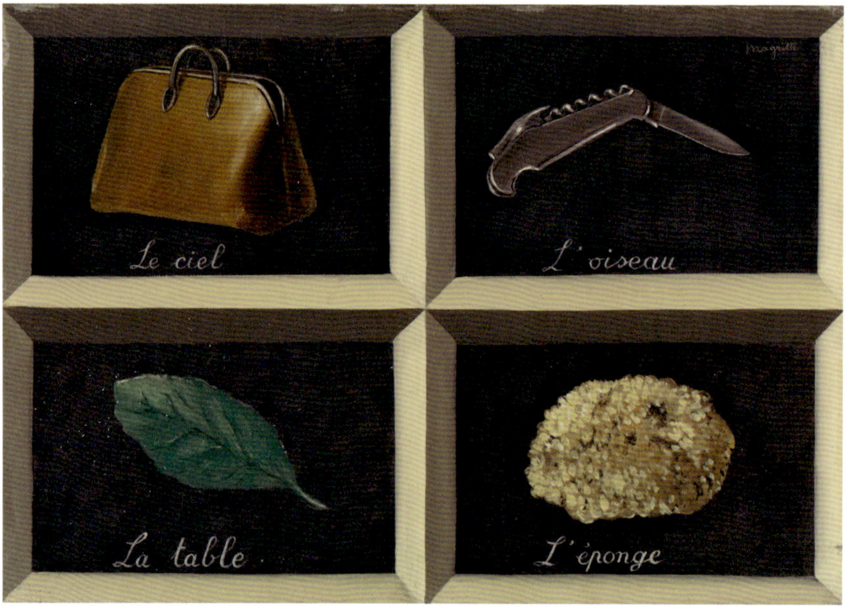

René Magritte | La Clef des songes (The Key to Dreams) | 1927
Oil on canvas, 38 × 53 cm, inv. no. 16260
Donation of Theo Wormland Foundation, 2013

Four everyday items in four separate fields, combined with four nouns. Image and concept do not match up here: only the image of a sponge has the correct French word for 'sponge' underneath. This was the first of René Magritte's many word-pictures, which were prompted by the following thought: 'An object is not so attached to its name that we cannot find another one that would suit it better.' Magritte creates a game between word and picture: here, conventional associations are dissolved, and painting reveals poetic potential between word and image.
FS

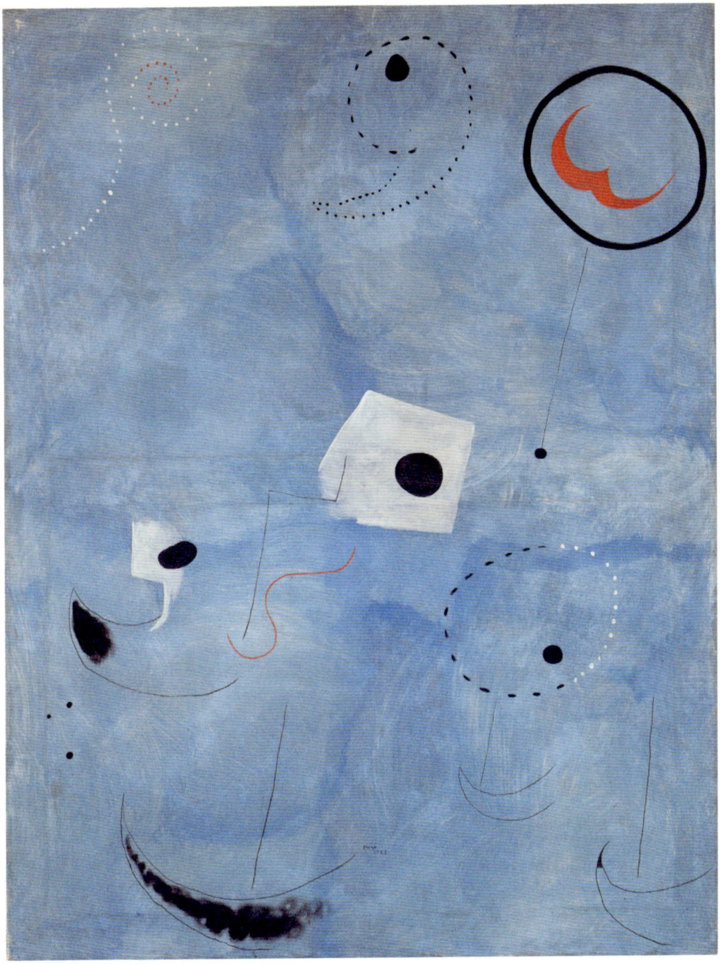

Joan Miró | Composition | 1925
Oil and tempera on canvas, 116 × 89 cm, inv. no. 14250
Acquired 1971

In *Composition*, an early work by Joan Miró, apparently weightless forms are placed playfully on a blue background. The forms are far removed from figurative narration, but nonetheless appear marked by a certain cheerfulness. Chance as a source of inspiration was central to Miró's spontaneously created work, which thus links up with André Breton's theory of automatism. Miró's work contrasted sharply with the veristic work of a painter like Salvador Dalí and his paintings would later become an important model for the American avant-garde.
FS

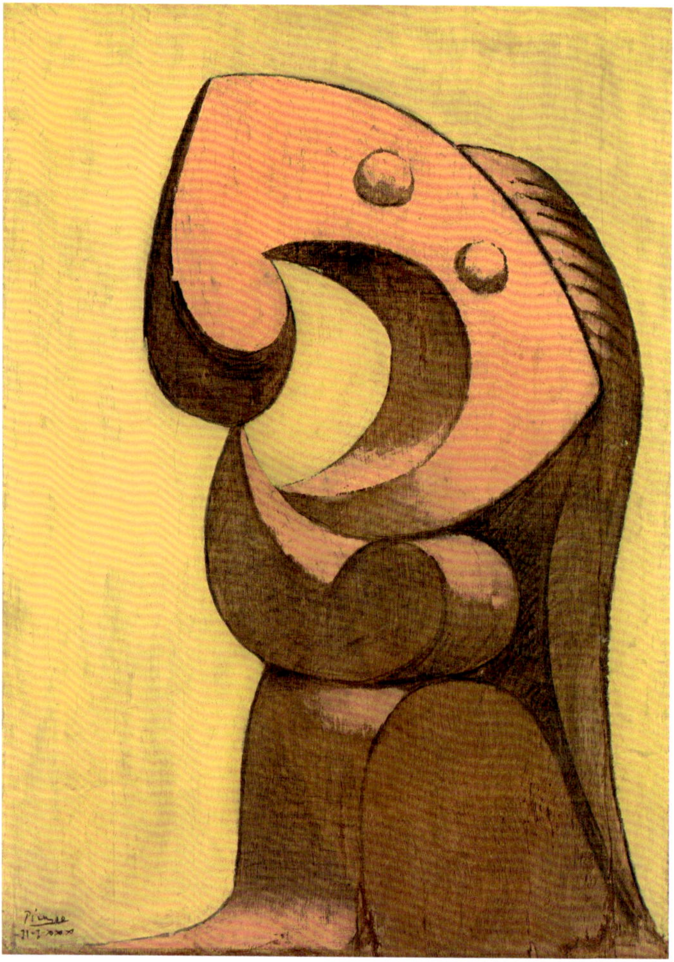

Pablo Picasso | **Femme** (Woman) | 1930
Oil on wood, 68 × 49 cm, inv. no. 14834
Donation of Theo Wormland Foundation, 1983

Against a luminous yellow background but with the underlying wood left partly visible, Picasso employs distinctive forms which come together to form a partly flesh-coloured figure. *Femme* was created during Picasso's short Surrealist phase (between around 1927 and 1933). During this period, he made numerous works which represented fragmented female figures and fragmented limbs. They seem to be an expression of pain, while at the same time radiating aggression. Thus the arch-shaped opening within the woman in the painting can also be viewed as a scream from an open mouth. FS

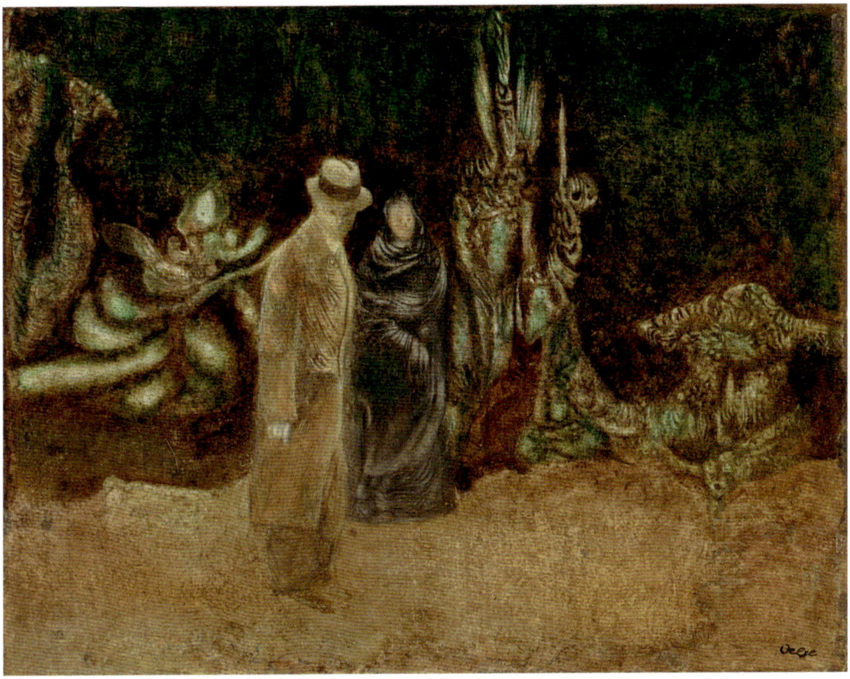

Richard Oelze | Der Schwager (Paar mit Hund)
(The Brother-in-Law – Couple with Dog) | 1935
Oil on cardboard on wood, 23 × 30 cm, inv. no. 15640
Donation of Theo Wormland Foundation, 2004

This painting, with its dark and mystic setting, went by the name *Couple with Dog* until the 1950s; at that point, Oelze put it into a smaller format, renaming it *The Brother-in-Law*. Oelze, once a student of Johannes Itten at the Bauhaus, created the painting during his time in Paris, where he had close relations with Surrealists like André Breton and Max Ernst. Although the woman and the dog almost blend into their surroundings, the man, in urban clothing, seems an alien presence here. Is he looking at the spectator? The lack of unambiguous points of reference means that interpretation of the painting is left up to the spectator. FS

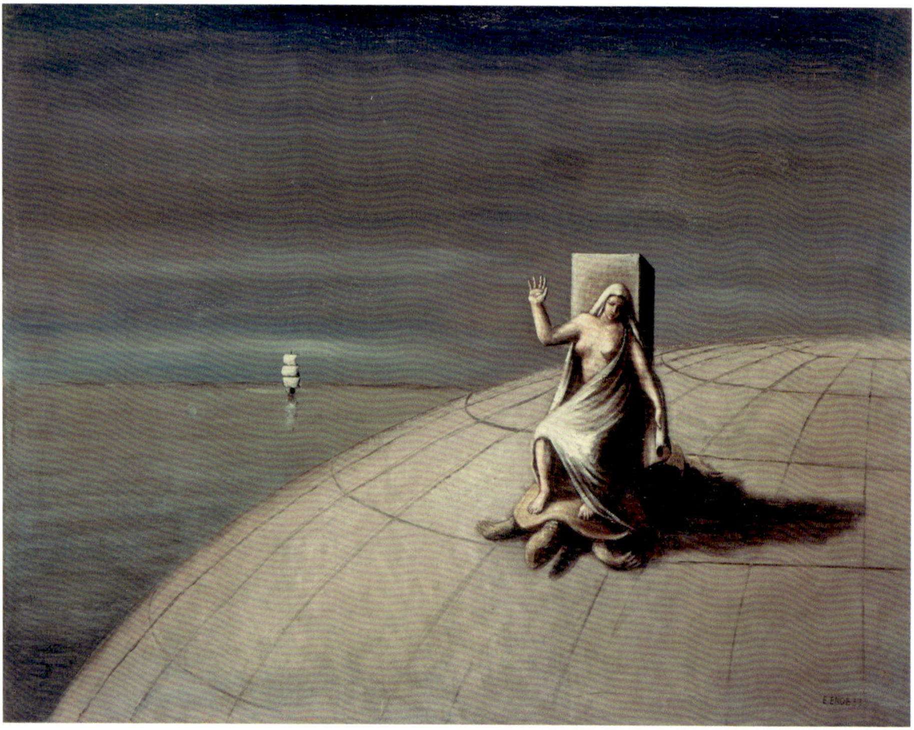

Edgar Ende | Die Frau auf der Schildkröte (The Woman on the Tortoise) | 1933
Oil on canvas, 60 × 80 cm, inv. no. 15572
Donation of Mariko Sato-Ende Foundation, 2002

Typically for his work, Edgar Ende's painting opens onto a fantastical and apparently surreal setting: a female figure is seated on a stone throne, carried across the globe by a tortoise. It remains unclear if she is holding up her hand as a warning to the ship, or as a greeting. Ende created this bleak cosmos in a very productive period, but a time when he also came under threat from the increasingly powerful National Socialists. More than as a specific position on political events, it should be understood as an engagement with fundamental human themes like loss and mourning. FS

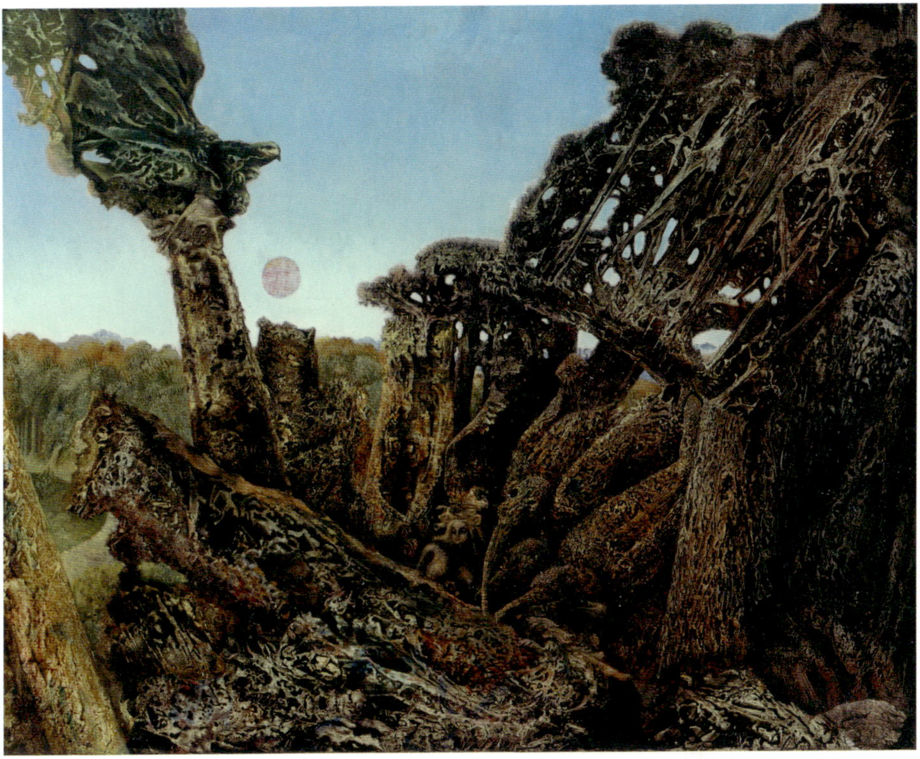

Max Ernst | Totem und Tabu (Totem and Taboo) | 1941–42
Oil on canvas, 72 × 92 cm, inv. no. 16254
Donation of Theo Wormland Foundation, 2013

Totem and Taboo refers to Sigmund Freud's book of that name, in which the psychoanalyst discusses the primal horde's murder of an over-powerful father figure, which is followed by remorse and the establishment of totems and taboos. The painting, made during Ernst's exile in the United States, represents a morbid forest landscape. In the centre, a bare-breasted woman is placed next to three birds feasting on a meal – a cannibalistic act? Above and to the left, a bird which could be read as a possible representation of the artist as his alter ego Loplop looks down onto the scene where the forest, once a promise of freedom, has ossified into a bleak world. FS

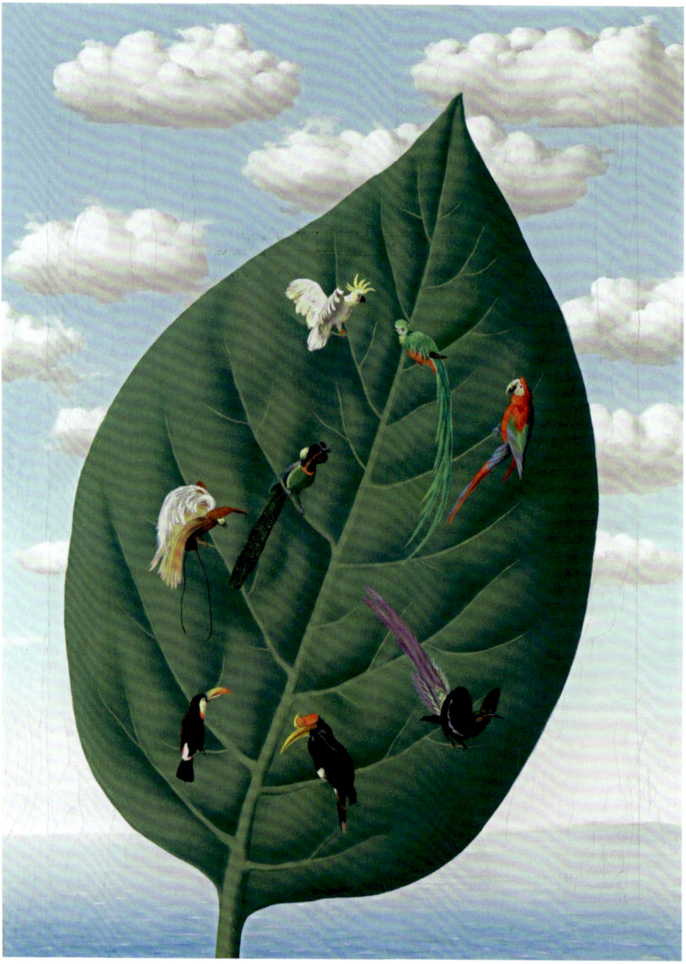

René Magritte | La Troisième Dimension (The Third Dimension) | 1942
Oil on canvas, 74 × 55 cm, inv. no. 16259
Donation of Theo Wormland Foundation, 2013

Birds have come to rest on an isolated leaf; in the background, only the open sea and a sky with clouds are visible. Yet the composition poses questions: can we correlate the relative size of birds and leaf? How can the birds hold on to the leaf's veins? Magritte made the painting during the German occupation of Belgium. In a composition alluding to Dutch Baroque images of paradise, he assembled identifiable birds of paradise, thus formulating his resistance to political reality.
FS

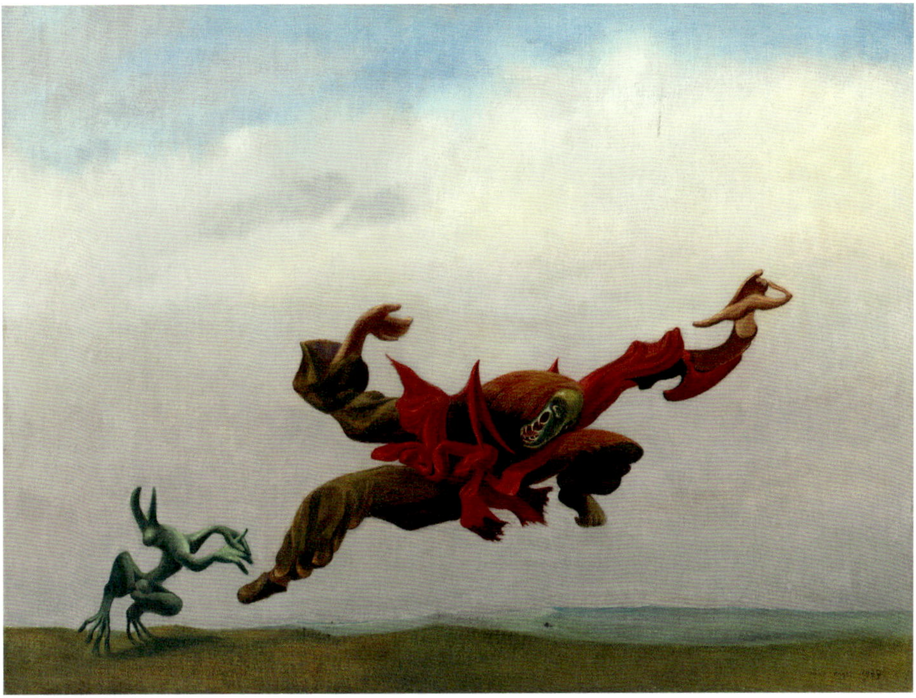

Max Ernst | L'ange du foyer (The Angel of Hearth and Home) | 1937
Oil on canvas, 54 × 74 cm, inv. no. 16253
Donation of Theo Wormland Foundation, 2013

A grotesque figure – half-human, half-monster – rages through a barren landscape. *The Angel of Hearth and Home*, described by Ernst as a 'clumsy oaf', was a reaction to the Spanish Republicans' fatal defeat at the hands of Franco. The artist saw the angel as a symbolic representation of a rampant fascism. The green creature, making obscene gestures at its feet, can be read as representing Surrealism, mocking while also lamenting. However, *The Triumph of Surrealism*, the temporary title given to the picture in 1938, makes clear the irony of the Surrealists' mockery and futile protests. FS

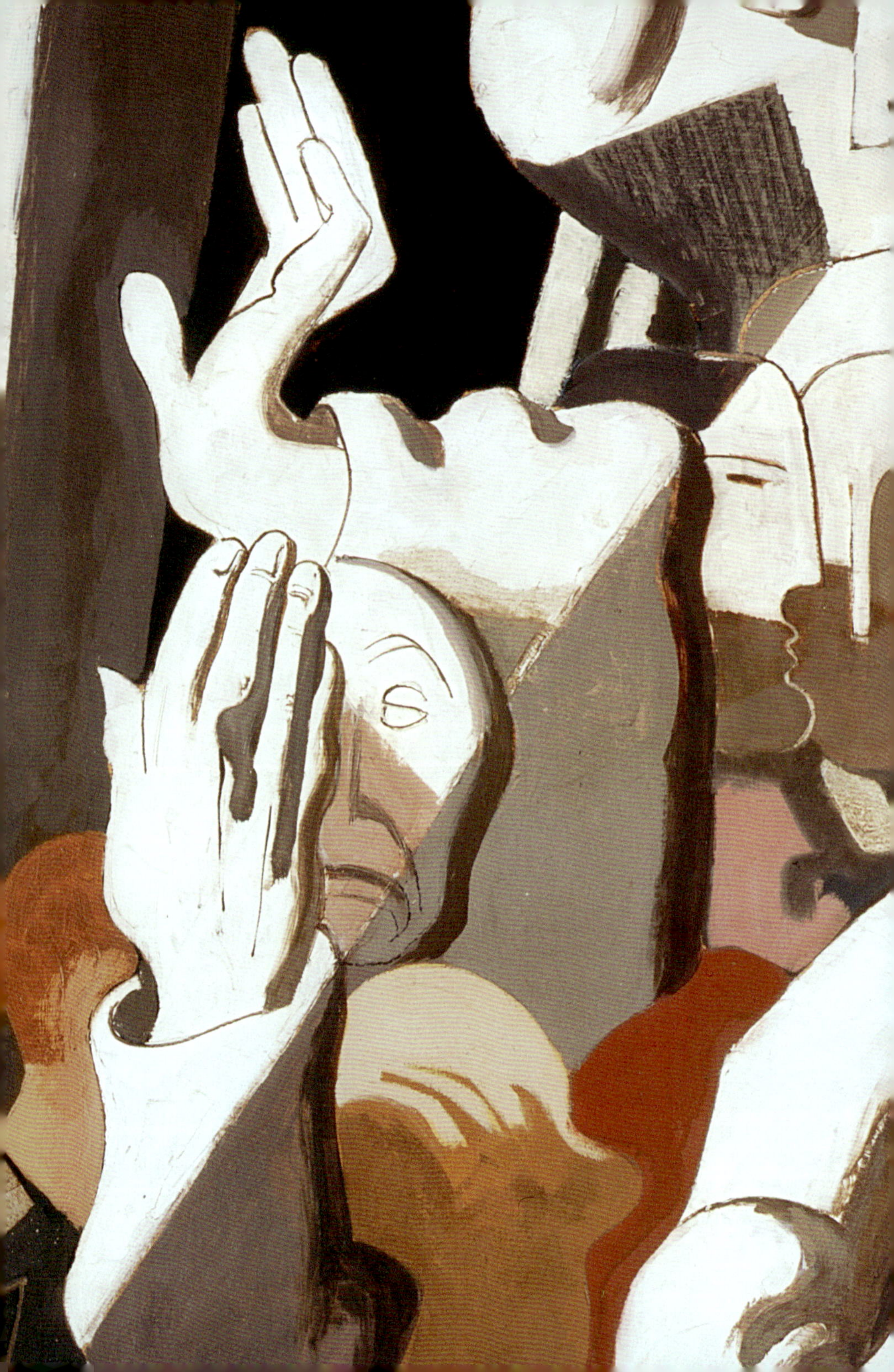

PROPAGANDA, CONFORMISM, WITHDRAWAL, CRITICISM, EXCLUSION, AND EXILE
THE NAZI PERIOD

Even the painted icons of strict, ruthless power can sometimes also be of art-historical importance. We know this from Bernhard Strigel's portraits of Emperor Maximilian I or – a more ambiguous, literally dictatorial figure – Jacques-Louis David's images of Napoleon crossing the Alps in triumph. The icons of National Socialism, a regime of a brutality far exceeding Napoleon and the Holy Roman Empire, included portraits of Hitler and the regime's senior functionaries, but also a work like Adolf Ziegler's triptych *The Four Elements*. This image makes use of national(ist) doctrine, transposing the sacred traditions of the altarpiece to the utterly profane. For many years, Ziegler's painting has been used in publications and exhibitions to illustrate the aesthetic norms and visual language of that dark historical period, mostly recently in Neil McGregor's 2014 book, *Germany: Memories of a Nation*. The apparent harmlessness of the image cannot disguise its problematic transmission of a blonde, 'Germanic' racialized image. It is time to stop using Ziegler's picture merely as a comparative illustration in history books. All this does is lend the painting auratic power, however negatively connoted, while actually distracting us from seeing it clearly. Instead, Ziegler's picture should be discussed within the broader art-historical survey of a period or century, such that a museum offers. Just as affirmative art from earlier centuries is now part of the discourse, we can trace the stylistic evolution of this picture by seeing it juxtaposed with other Neoclassical works, and with images from the interwar *Neue Sachlichkeit* movement. Then there is the important question of artistic quality: there is little enough of that in Ziegler's picture, something made clearer by the original than the standard reproductions.

Despite his early Expressionist connections, Ziegler is representative of art and artists hostile to modernism, both before and after the First World War. Before 1914, German 'salon painters' like Carl Vinnen were opposed to the acquisition of French art, for example by the Impressionists or Vincent van Gogh. In the 1920s, this struggle against modernism continued unabated, albeit at first with less success. In 1909, Hugo von Tschudi arrived from Berlin to take up the position of director-general of Munich's Pinakotheken, ushering in a new era for the acquisition of international modern art. Between the wars, tolerance seemed to reign at first: one only has to think of the collection assembled at the Nationalgalerie in Berlin by Ludwig Justi (although it should be noted that Munich, by comparison, long remained highly conservative). However, the conflict over modernism soon intensified again, and when the Nazis took power, Justi was swiftly dismissed, along with many other progressive-minded directors. The same happened in universities and academies: progressive artists were among the first victims of the new National Socialist regime.

This change had radical consequences, since if artists cannot exhibit and are banned from teaching, they are also limited in their capacity to sell their work. This chapter outlines the varied destinies of artists' lives and careers in that era. Some painters set about creating state propaganda, making allegories like Ziegler's bored, standardized women: these were meant to symbolize opposed elements like fire and water, but actually exhibit nothing but a lifeless female ideal – 'pose and indoctrination', as Max Imdahl put it. Landscape painting could also be conformist, helping to support the state, for example through commissions to depict the building of the *Autobahn* network. At the end of the war, any surviving paintings with a directly military subject were seized by the Allies. These were initially transported to the United States, as the 'German War Art Collection'; later, part of the collection was returned to Germany, and can be seen in the Deutsches Historisches Museum in Berlin. The surviving works were regarded as tolerable. This is another aspect of the reception history of conformist art from the Nazi period: the Americans did not want to destroy it, instead, they hoped it would give future generations 'a full and just estimate of the Nazi character, spirit, and times', as Herbert S. Leonard emphasized in September 1947. At the time, Leonard was director of the Munich Central Collecting Point, in a building now occupied by the Zentralinstitut für Kunstgeschichte (Central Institute for Art History) at Königsplatz.

Of course, many German artists took the path of conformity to a greater or lesser degree, often expressing this in landscape painting of exceptional triviality. Others chose withdrawal and precaution, giving up artistic work so as not to be declared 'degenerate', forbidden to exhibit, or even entirely banned from artistic work. The public critique of modernism under Nazism has been well researched for decades, much more so than themes like the looting of art. Scholarly work has been carried out on the exclusion of artists, on 'ostracized art' (for example, Werner Haftmann, 1986), on the 'art of the disappeared generation' (for example Rainer Zimmermann, 1986), as well as on the Munich *Degenerate Art* exhibition (for example Peter-Klaus Schuster, 1987), and other themes, including exile. The opponents of modernism succeeded in driving many significant artists into exile, including Max Beckmann and the members of the Bauhaus. But these opponents must be taken into account in any close look at modernism's ambivalent paths: only in this way can we obtain a coherent image of German art and German history. The resulting image is sometimes of necessity an unpleasant one, but this is what we must confront.

After the Second World War, the Bayerische Staatsgemäldesammlungen was able to build up a modern art collection without parallel in Germany, thanks to the efforts of many highly active collectors and patrons. For the generation that came after the Nazis, it seemed the right thing to atone for the ideologically-inspired iniquities done to art and to repair what could possibly be repaired. This reparation took place in the Haus der Kunst, originally called the 'House of German Art' and created as the venue for the Nazis' 'Great German Art Exhibition', close to the venue of the *Degenerate Art* exhibition, in the nearby Hofgartenarkaden. The Pinakothek der Moderne owes its fascinating collection to this very human attitude of atonement. It is thus all the more important to pay particular attention to the phenomena discussed here, and their causes. This should be understood as the precise opposite to any kind of sign of reverence.

The sensitive way artists reflected this dramatic epoch, in Germany and in exile, is clear in Max Beckmann's work from the early period of National Socialism and Karl Hofer's art produced at the very end of the war. Their works achieve the highest intensity of expression, creating space for danger and hardship: these deeply human pictures contrast with the superficiality of a work by Adolf Ziegler. Learning to recognize the difference will always be a challenge, but a discriminating eye allows the spectator, above all, to unmask art that is saturated in ideology.

Bernhard Maaz

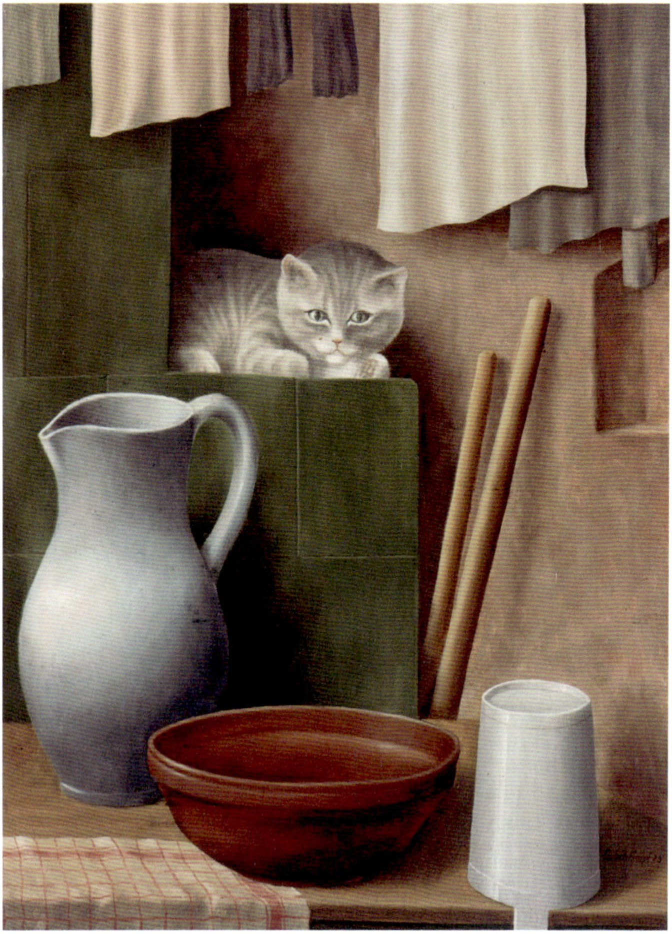

Georg Schrimpf | Stillleben mit Katze (Ofenecke) (Still Life with Cat – Oven Corner) | 1923
Oil on canvas, 60.7 × 45.4 cm, inv. no. 14099
Bequest of Babette Susanna Heller, 1969

Beginning in the 1920s, Schrimpf earned a good reputation and was generally regarded as a (neo-)Romantic. Among the most significant painters of the *Neue Sachlichkeit*, he was awarded a professorship in Berlin as early as 1934. The rigor of this noiseless, timeless still life, featuring tableware, drying washing, and a cat, prompts the question of why this idyllic painter ultimately had dozens of his works declared 'degenerate' and confiscated. The explanation lies in the details of his biography: since 1912, Schrimpf had been a close associate of the anarchist Erich Mühsam, and was later a member of the Communist party. The judgement was not about his art, but about him. BM

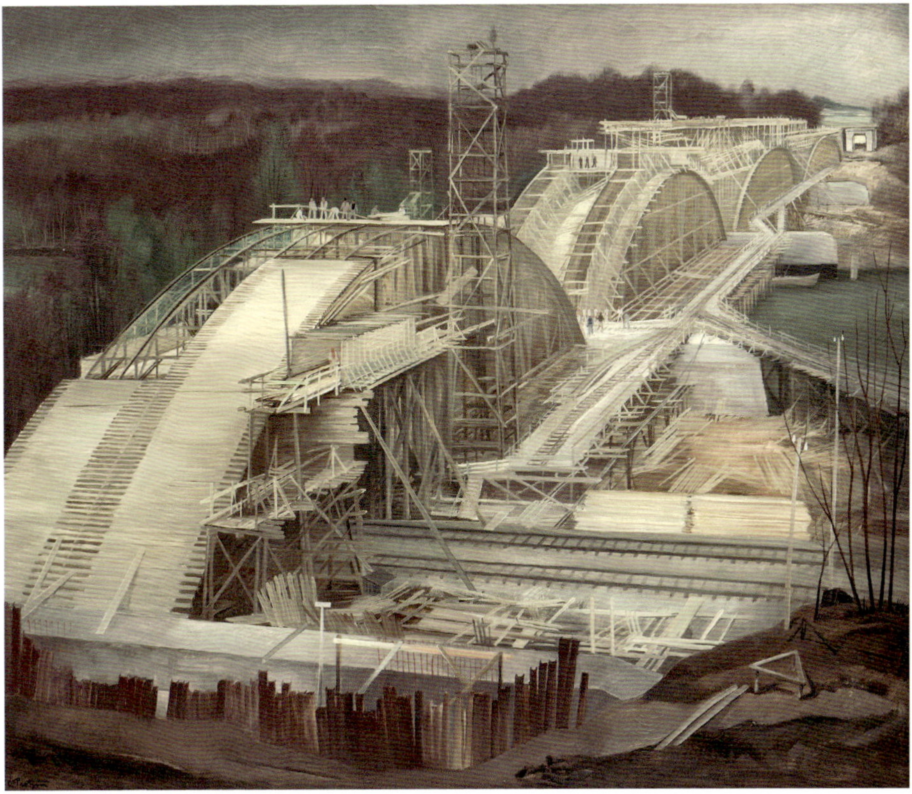

Carl Protzen | Donaubrücke bei Leipheim (Danube Bridge at Leipheim) | 1935–36
Oil on canvas, 111 × 130.5 cm, inv. no. 11926
Relocation of state property in 1953 (former property of the Nazi Party)

While the Futurists' pictures expressed their intoxication with speed, the painters of the *Neue Sachlichkeit* were captivated by enormous, unmoving industrial buildings and traffic infrastructure, as in the work of Georg Schrimpf, who painted *Level Crossing* and *Radio Station* in 1932–33. Carl Protzen and others followed his example: in 1935–36, they went on to create dramatic images of the biggest-ever German traffic project, the building of the *Autobahn* system. Their pictures documented the work, while also rendering it heroic. Later, the dubious place of these roads in the National-Socialist infrastructure programme became clear. BM

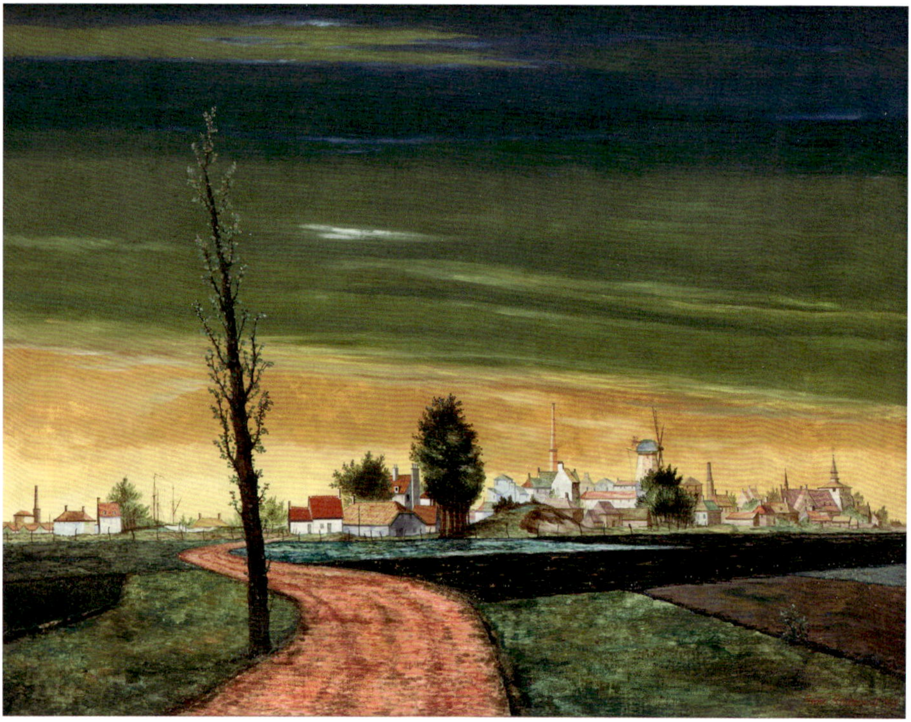

Franz Radziwill | Grodenstraße nach Varelerhafen (Grodenstrasse to Varel Harbour) | 1938
Oil on canvas on wood, 72 × 97 cm, inv. no. L 2490
Loan from a private collection, accessioned 2005

As a painter, Franz Radziwill began as devotee of *Neue Sachlichkeit*, but soon emerged as a highly inventive visionary. His pictures anticipated the coming global conflagration, expressing the turmoil of life on earth in what are, at times, deeply disturbing compositions. The gleaming light here is suggestive of something more than just the light of sunrise or sunset, seeming closer to the glow of a burning city on the horizon. This contrasts with the lonely, gently blossoming tree, a form taken from German Romanticism, here a weak sign of hope.
BM

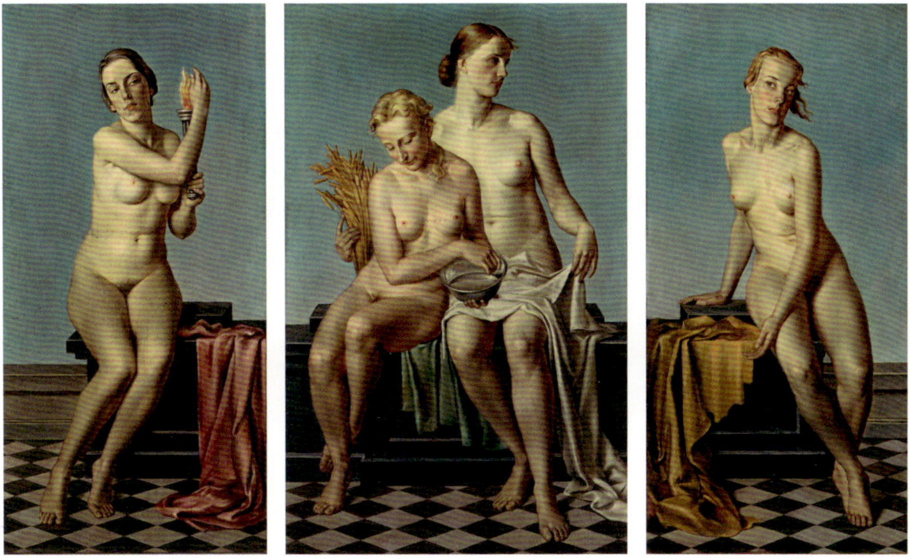

Adolf Ziegler | Die Vier Elemente (Feuer, Wasser und Erde, Luft)
(The Four Elements – Fire, Water and Earth, Air) | before 1937
Oil on canvas, tripartite, 171.5 × 86 cm, 171.3 × 110.5 cm, 171.2 × 86 cm, inv. no. 11931, 11925, 15348
Relocation of state property in 1953 (former property of the Nazi Party, 11931, 11925),
acquired 1993 (15348)

Ziegler's painting of the four elements is not worth exhibiting on artistic grounds, but rather because it was once hailed as the epitome of National Socialist visual propaganda. In addition, the picture has been widely exhibited in recent years as an illustration of the Nazis' doctrine on art. Disturbingly, the Nazis were seen as appreciating an innocuous kind of art. If we want to understand the attacks of the *Degenerate Art* action, mostly directed against the Expressionists, we must carefully observe the stilted, artificial triviality of works like this. BM

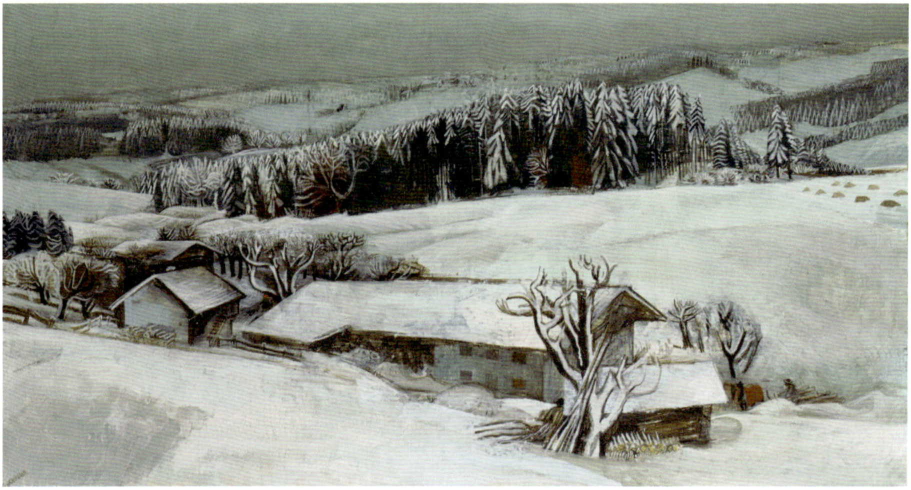

Günther Graßmann | Bauernhöfe im Chiemgau (Farms in the Chiemgau) | 1933
Oil and tempera on canvas, 64.5 × 122 cm, inv. no. 9978
Acquired 1934

In 1934, what is now the Bayerische Staatsgemäldesammlungen acquired this painting of farms in Bavaria's Chiemgau region. Three years later this somewhat melancholy landscape painting, with its neutral subject matter, was seized as 'degenerate art' but then returned to the museum: a good illustration of the contradictory and arbitrary nature of decisions of this kind. In the 1920s, Günther Graßmann painted late Expressionist works; beginning in 1941, he taught at the Städel School in Frankfurt, while from 1968 on he lived at the Starnberger See. In 1983, he was given a solo exhibition at Munich's Stadtmuseum. BM

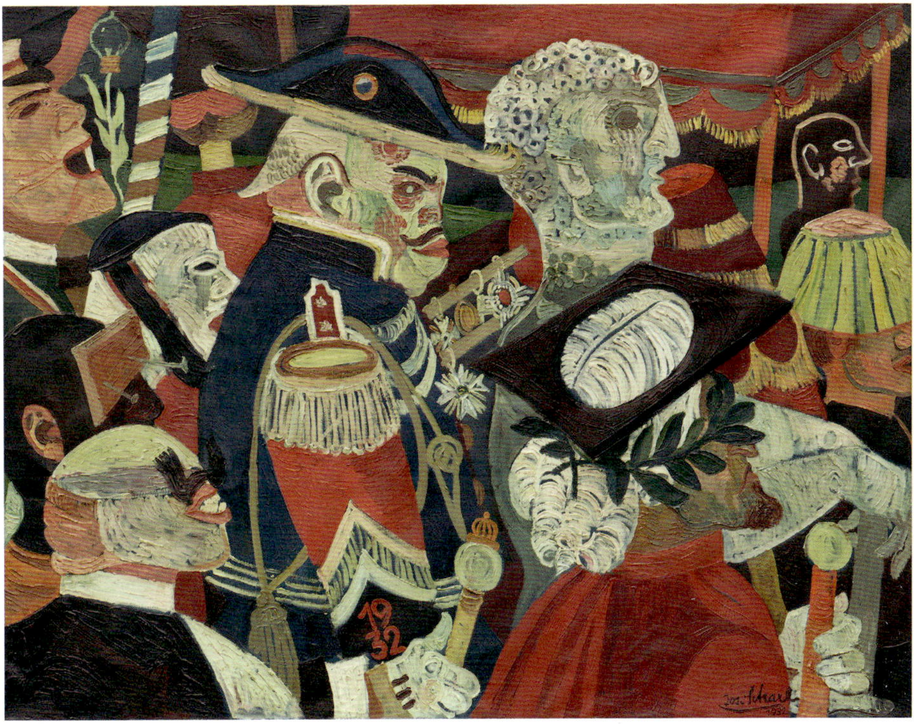

Josef Scharl | Triumphzug (Victory Parade) | 1932
Oil on canvas, 76 × 99.2 cm, inv. no. 14950
Donation of Professor Dr. Dr. Aloys Greither, 1985

Like Graßmann, Josef Scharl began as a late Expressionist. Even in the late 1920s, his pictures attracted savage criticism and even attempts at their destruction. This was a result of Scharl's corrosive, biting, and nihilist view of society's elites, and his depictions of what Dostoyevsky called the 'insulted and humiliated', in representations which were simultaneously critical, compassionate, and sceptical. Scharl shows both extremes of society, but not the centre. Opponents attacked his aggressive dissection of the depravity of the 'pillars of society' (George Grosz). He went into exile in 1938. BM

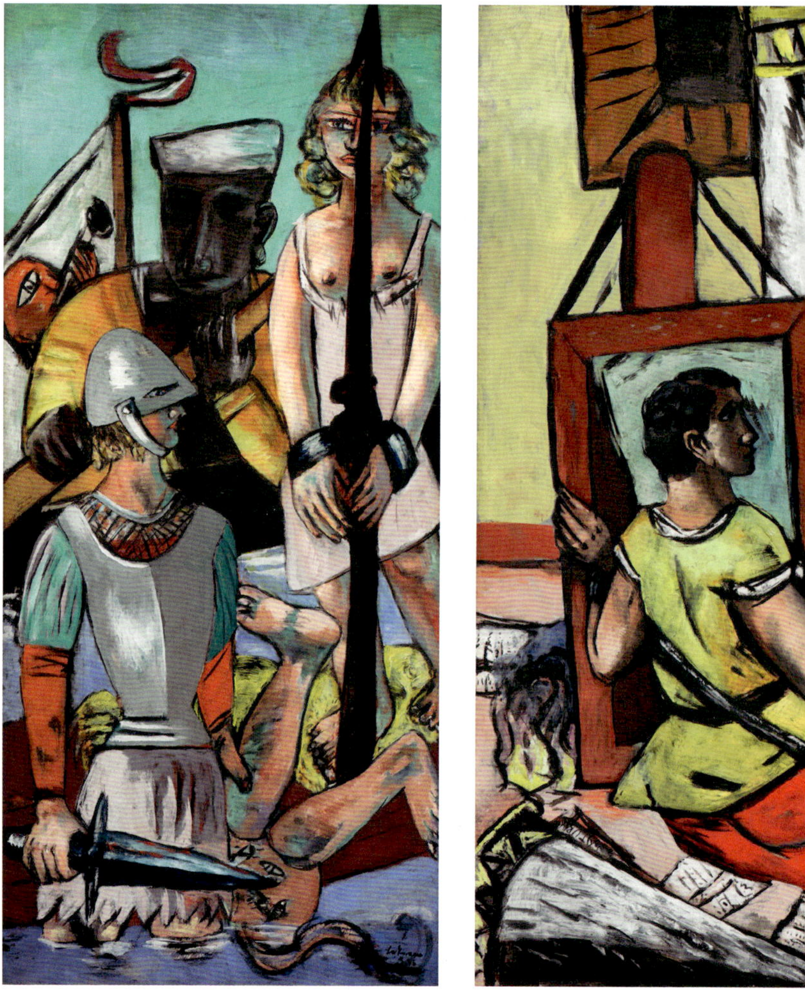

Max Beckmann | Versuchung (Versuchung des heiligen Antonius)
(Temptation – Temptation of St. Anthony) | 1936–37
Oil on canvas, tripartite, 215.5 × 100 cm, 200.5 × 1705 cm, 215.5 × 100 cm,
Inv. no. 14487, 14486, 14488
Acquired 1977

Beckmann had been familiar with the work of the French writer Gustave Flaubert since 1923, and had been given his novel *The Temptation of St. Anthony* in 1935. He intermittently toyed with the idea of illustrating the text, which was itself indebted to David Teniers's 17th century paintings on the same subject. The theme here was always virtuous and cou-

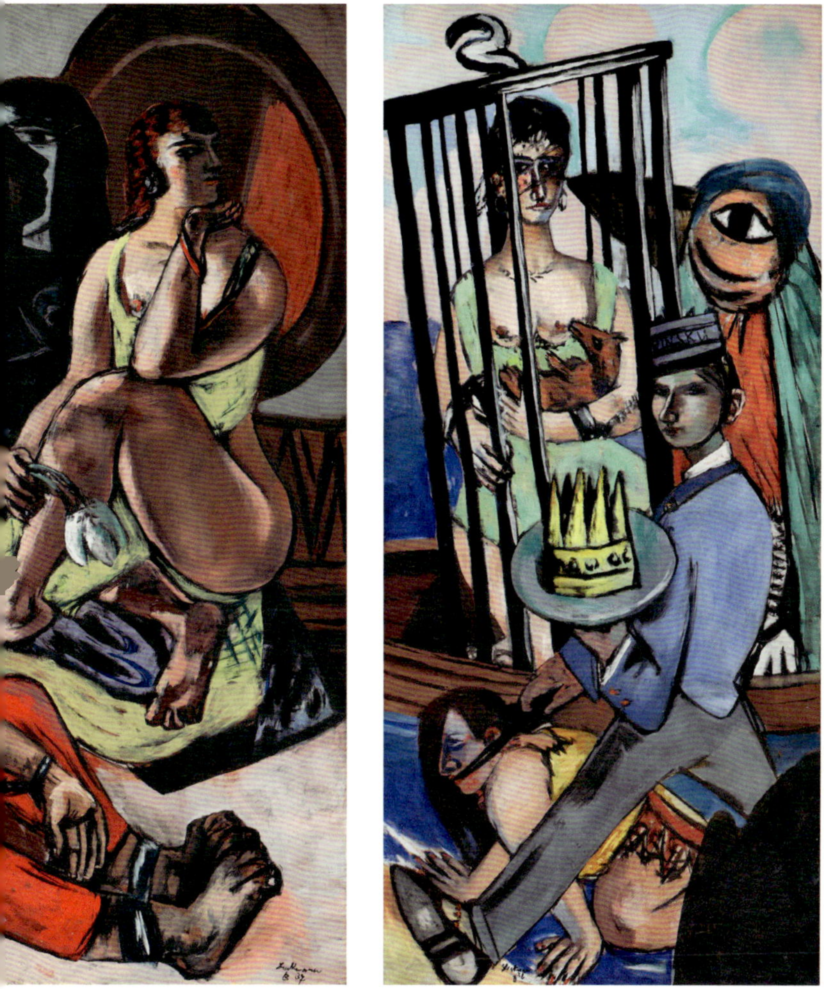

rageous resistance to temptation: this included temptation's erotic and sensual aspects, but also a broader sense of human beings' general susceptibility. Of course, this touches on questions of attitude, at a time when an artist like Beckmann, who sought international success and recognition and knew how to enjoy his life (including in an erotic sense), was under constant political pressure. The three scenes cover a range of temptations, from humiliation to beauty. The man in the central panel is thus captivated before (or by) beauty: in front of him sits the goddess of temptation. On the left, the seductive Helen is bound to a lance, while on the right, the Queen of Sheba is a seductress in a cage, in front of whom a page is humiliating a female slave. The theme is bondage, in both an erotic and a social sense. BM

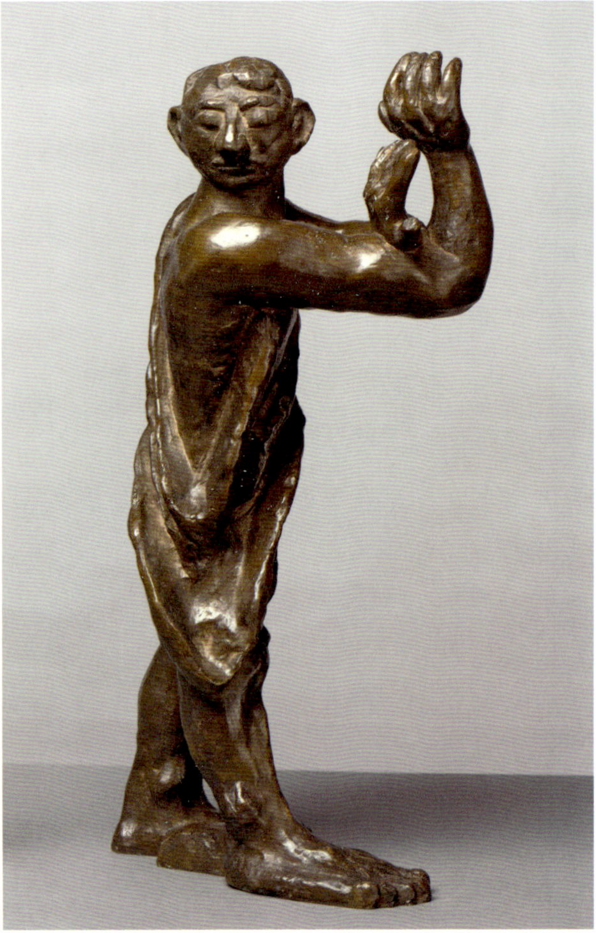

Max Beckmann | Mann im Dunkeln (Man in the Dark) | 1934
Bronze, height 57.3 cm, inv. no. B 350
Acquired 1958

As early as 1934, Beckmann created this highly expressive metaphor for uncertainty and incalculability: the large listening ears cannot hide the unseeing eyes, and arms raised in protection. Defence and uncertainty leave the man, dressed in timeless clothes, caught in a position of thoughtful stasis. By 1933, Beckmann had seen the room containing his works in Berlin's Kronprinzenpalais, part of the Nationalgalerie, closed on the orders of the National Socialist regime. The display featured many of his best works to date and, from a critical standpoint, was the best showing of his art up to that point in time. BM

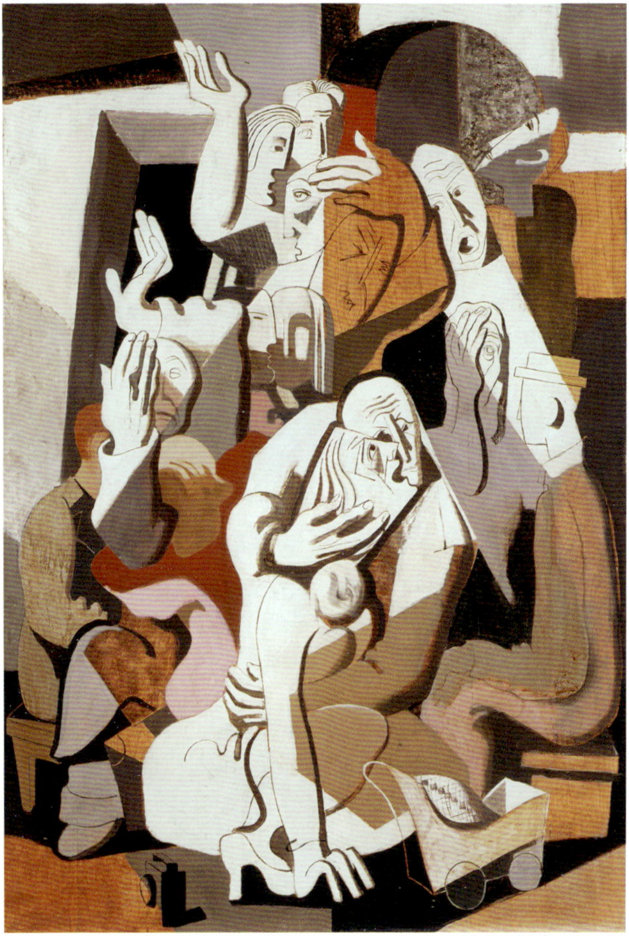

Karl Kunz | Augsburger Bombennacht (Im Keller)
(Augsburg Bombing by Night – In the Cellar) | 1945
Oil on plywood, 122.5 × 85 cm, inv. no. 11244
Acquired 1951

It would be good to know whether Karl Kunz, who survived National Socialism through inner exile, made this picture before or after the end of the war, particularly since reports suggest that in 1944, a year before the picture was made, his studio was burned down. Kunz had been defamed as a 'degenerate artist' and fired from his teaching position, thereafter only painting in secret. This painting, which shows the influence of Picasso's *Guernica*, is filled with gestures of guarding and protection, and expressions of sighing and screaming: a painted inferno, emaciated human figures between swaying walls in the cold light. BM

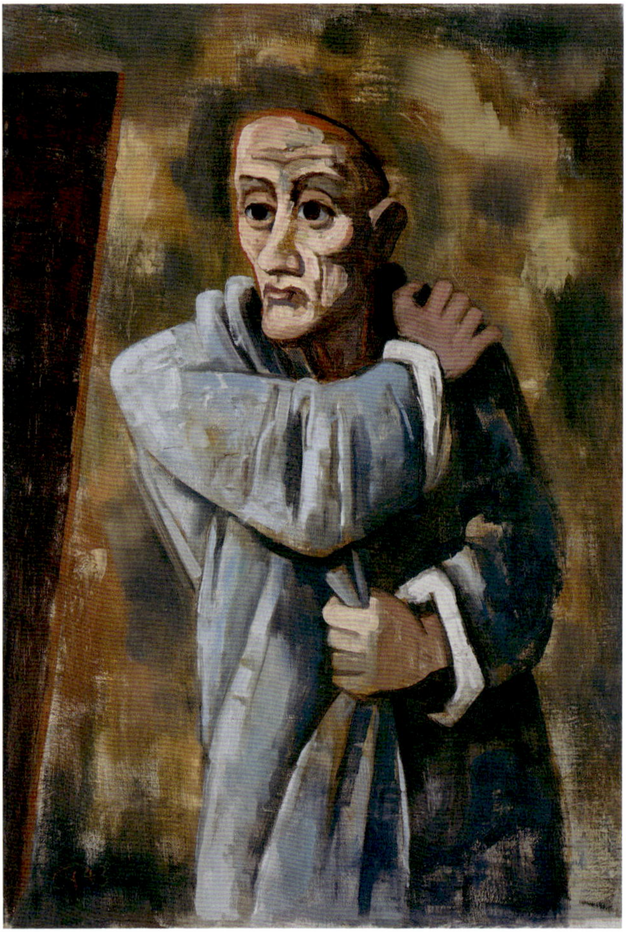

Karl Hofer | **Mann vor dem Spiegel** (Man in Front of the Mirror) | 1943
Oil on canvas, 100.5 × 69.6 cm, inv. no. 12801
Acquired 1958

Like Beckmann's *Man in the Dark*, Hofer's *Man in Front of the Mirror* can be read as a coded image of its time, except that by the time this image was made, uncertainty had crystallized into the unsparing clarity of failure. Alert contemporaries could not regard the end of the war, so long hoped for, in terms of the 'final victory' of Nazi propaganda. Instead, the end came as a final collapse. For many, life had already shrunk to the barest hopes for survival. Stepping over to look in the mirror held the risk of sudden insight and bitter realization. The blue apron is roughly gathered up, the hand has ghostly spasms. BM

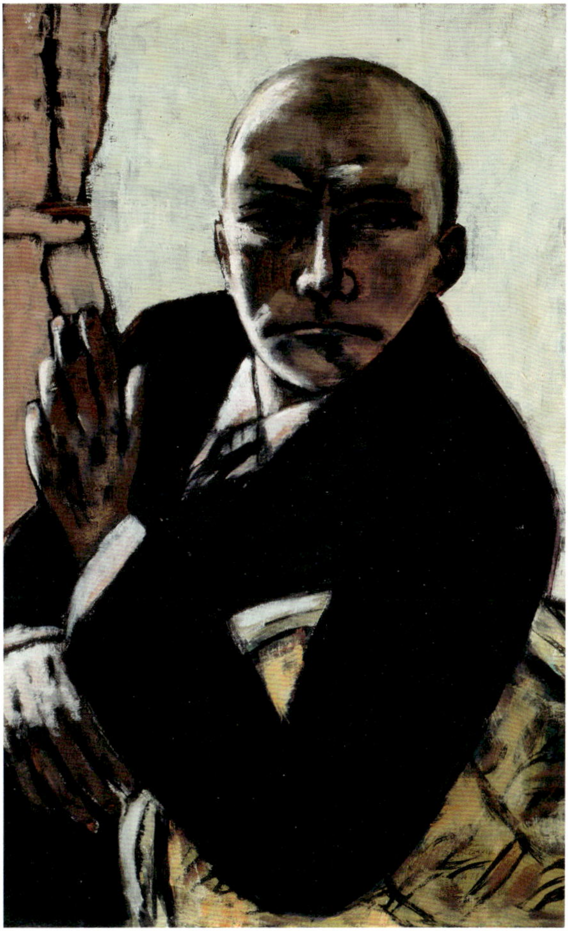

Max Beckmann | Selbstbildnis in Schwarz (Self-Portrait in Black) | 1944
Oil on canvas, 95 × 60 cm, inv. no. 10974
Acquired 1949

Beckmann lived in exile for many years, and this self-portrait was created during those years. He chose Amsterdam, although it was occupied by the Germans: in the Netherlands, Beckmann could observe his homeland as if looking back over his shoulder, while also passing on works to collector friends. At the end of the war, he set out from here for the United States to gain the acceptance he had once wanted in Paris as a rival of Picasso. On the other side of the Atlantic, Beckmann was honoured as a subtle colourist, as a great painter of enigmatic compositions, and as a fascinating printmaker, able to give timeless expression to the obsessions of his time. BM

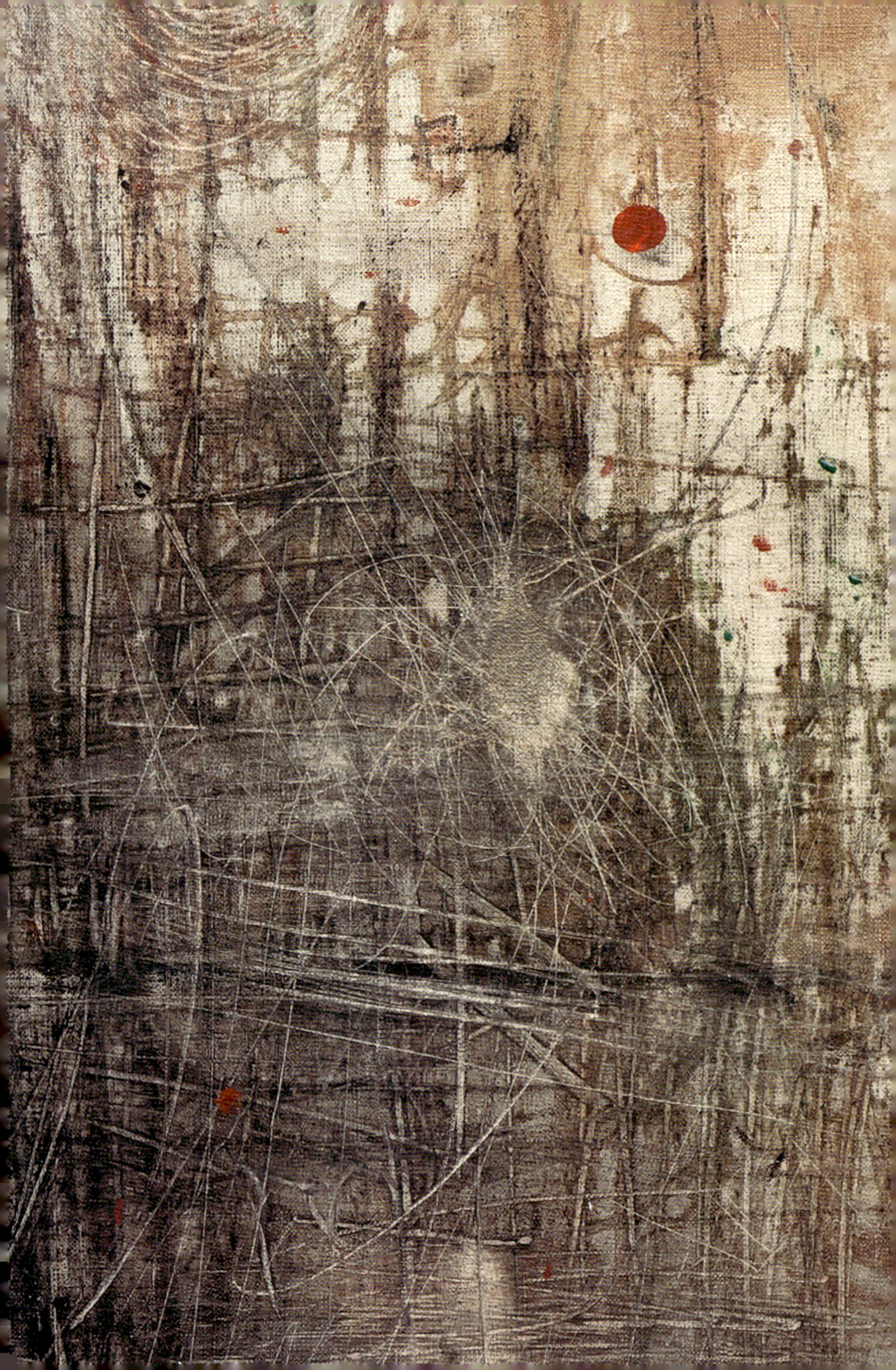

PAIN AND HOPE
AFTER THE SECOND WORLD WAR

In the wake of the Second World War, Europe – and other continents as well – appeared brutally covered in ruins and battlefields. People's understanding of the world was shaped by an awareness of omnipresent failure, the relativity of worldly glory, the fragility of human life, a generation's guilt, and the fallibility of the European Enlightenment. With the onset of the Cold War within just a few years, peace fixed its icy, menacing stare on the continent. The awareness of atomic powers co-existing in a state of hostile rivalry lurked in people's minds as they went about their day-to-day business. A significant number of people felt that the Third (and, so they thought, final) World War was imminent. Confronting one another were two opposing sides: a deeply insecure existentialism, versus a corrupted form of communism that had initially harboured socially progressive intentions. Only the idea (again under threat today) of a united Europe brought hope, soon bolstered by the clearance of rubble and the upturn in economic growth.

One artist who gave expression to this post-war sentiment was Wolfgang Schulze (known as Wols). A sensitive and creative artist, Wols suffered enormously throughout his life from an urge to flee his surroundings and was plagued by periods of homelessness. His 1946 painting *Composition* echoes some of his earlier photography and its interest in textural qualities and surface, but refrains from any form of narrative element – as though there were nothing more to report after the horror of war and internment. When witnesses fall silent, it is the expression of terror that prevails. In Wols' work, picture surfaces seem furious and jittery, clawed and furrowed. This seemingly destructive painting process flows into the completed work, forming expressive gestures that reflect a sensitive, introverted vulnerability. This painter, graphic artist, and photographer had long since left behind his artistic roots in Surrealism; for him, experiencing the world through the prism of the sur-real (in the sense of preternatural, incredible) hindered the creation of harmonious narratives in constellations of figures. The sceptical and at times nihilistic-seeming worldview articulated by Wols, a German artist estranged from his own country, was taken up by the next generation. Not coincidentally, Joseph Beuys's evocatively titled *Show Your Wound* (Munich, Lenbachhaus) thematizes the modern practice of displaying our wounded condition, but not the origin of the wounds (though he did pursue this theme in spoken statements). Even *The End of the 20th Century* (pp. 254–255), a work that features 'wounded' rocks, resounds with the theme of the burden and pain weighing down upon the era.

Just how unreliable the old world orders had become is exemplified by the hugely successful Italian sculptor Marino Marini. Although *Rider* signals Marini's indebtedness to an age-old compositional form, passed down in innumerable variations from antiquity onwards – specifically, the connection between horse and rider – he nevertheless endows the subject with an innovative form. As the most prominent class of artworks to juxtapose man with animal, the equestrian statue has always served to proclaim the glory and splendour of rulers, while underscoring their claim to hegemony. Depicting their subjects in regal poses, the statues give expression to imperial conceptions of power. However, by depicting the horse's downward gaze towards the ground, Marini instead highlights elementary animal existence and the primal hunger for sustenance. Furthermore, the horseman's skyward gaze produces what might plausibly be described as a gesture emanating from the hunger of the soul, lending visual form to a search for a higher or even divine presence: a yearning for redemption from earthly existence, a harkening for the infinite and eternal. The animal is not galloping but at rest; the human subject, meanwhile, is a stargazer, perhaps recognizable from the works of such artists as the German sculptor Hermann Blumenthal, who interwove the motif of an indefinite upward gaze with the figure of a young man seated on the ground. In such depictions, the gaze conveys a sense of looking away from terrestrial concerns towards a higher presence – which remains mute, revealing nothing of its existence. Painting had to a large extent committed itself to refraining from mimetic representation, creating work that traced its origins to the abstract painting of Russian artists such as Kazimir Malevich, *Der Blaue Reiter*, and the Bauhaus. Sculpture, by contrast, continued for a long period to remain emphatically faithful to figurative representation, as is evident from the work of artists not featured in this volume – think, for example, of Alberto Giacometti, Germaine Richier, and Louise Bourgeois. Even Joseph Beuys's clamp (ironically entitled *Bed*) remains faithful to representational depiction, albeit via a process of surreal elongation in which a figure appears locked like an object turned on the lathe. Here the clamp and constraining forces serve as ciphers of compression and painful relentlessness representing all forms of human bondage.

Francis Bacon was the most intense, expressive, and passionate creator of painted figures and spaces in the decades following the war. He was able to portray the essence of being oppressed, of being 'thrown' (in the sense defined by Martin Heidegger) as the unmistakable symbol of an age, which he conveyed through unambiguous body language. Bacon's *Crucifixion* refers to the biblical account of Christ's death – the sacrificial, agonizing death suffered in the name of a divine, or perhaps even human, mission. By interweaving symbols such as the swastika, Bacon turns crystal-clear metaphors for violence, interrogation, and crime into images of timeless relevance, symbols of pain, torture, and helplessness. In Bacon's lifetime, these were not merely historical, bygone (and thus concluded) events from the years of Nazism between 1933 and 1945; no, these inhuman tortures were as much a feature of Stalinist Soviet Union as post-war Korea, China, or Algeria.

Bacon was of course not the only artist dealing with encrypted symbols of violence. Like him, Antonio Saura evoked traditional biblical themes such as Christ's Passion, using a work entitled *Crucifixion* to explore the dismemberment of the human body (a theme similarly inherent in the merciless violence to which Bacon gives visual expression). In the process, Saura cites the formal language of Pablo Picasso, specifically that articulated in his iconic work *Guernica*, which in 1937 took initial stock of violence in the twentieth century through the depiction of an atrocity that would subsequently pale by comparison to even worse horrors. This recourse to the Bible was another typical feature of art from the early post-war period, serving as a repertory of figural arrangements, gestures, and forms that would have resonated with all educated people. Writing in around 1960, one of the most important authors of the period, Albert Camus, stated in *The First Man* that Christ had never travelled as far as Algeria – a country where, as is widely known, the collapse of colonialism created fissures that remain to this day unhealed. Such a statement is indicative of how people's view of the world in this period remained compatible with biblical myths, since both art and politics still existed in a context permeated by Christianity.

Everything seemed unstable, despite people's prosperity; everything evoked doubt, in spite of their convictions. The contemporary world was interwoven with visual traditions in ways as disconcerting as they were creatively productive. Antoni Tàpies' *Ochre-Coloured Oval with Black Incisions* creates the impression of a blocked, walled-off picture space, which the artist imbues with elevated iconographical potency and the promise of transcendence, perhaps reminiscent of Alexei Jawlensky's painted face(s). Does the barbed wire serve as a signifier of division, the wall as a metaphor? The division between Eastern and Western Europe seemed like an inevitable, irrevocable breach within European life and culture. It was only years later and the movement precipitated by the student protests of 1968 that new, liberating questions emerged and came into their own.

Bernhard Maaz

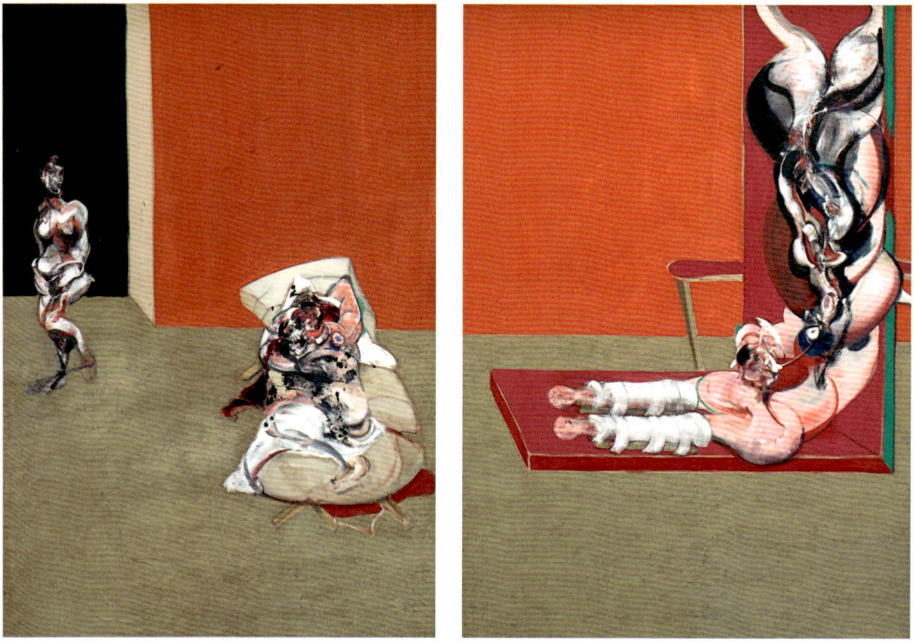

Francis Bacon | Crucifixion | 1965
Oil and acrylic on canvas, 3 parts, 197.5 × 147 cm, 197.3 × 147 cm, 197.3 × 147 cm, inv. no. GST 1-3
Acquired 1967 by PIN. Freunde der Pinakothek der Moderne, endowed in 1999 as initial donation to the Collective Foundation in support of Bavarian Stately Museums

The religious pathos formula betokened by the triptych draws the observer into a horrifying scene composed of lumps of bloody flesh, decay, and disintegration. These form a shocking contrast to the coolly ordered visual stage. On the left-hand table, a naked woman averts her gaze from a physically annihilated figure laid on a camp bed. Only the French cockade remains intact as an identifiable sign. On the central table, the crucified

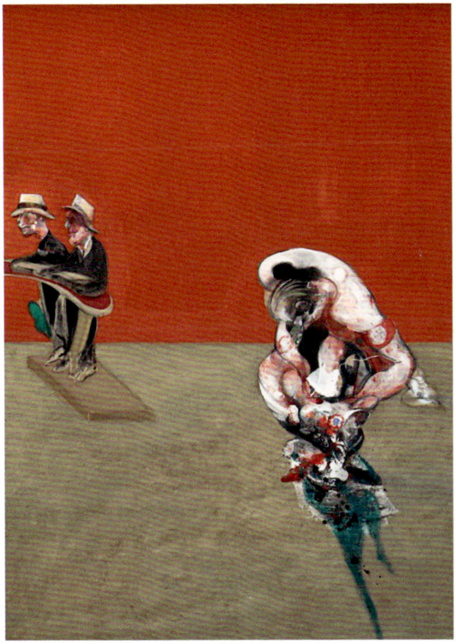

figure is displayed like a slaughtered animal. To the rear right are two bystanders who are neither involved in the events nor paying any attention to the scene on the right. Here, an athletic blond man wearing a swastika armband throttles his victim, of whom only a ghostly smudge remains. There is a thin line between murderer and victim, resistance fighter and sympathiser, historical and contemporary figures – without it being possible to identify the contrasts conclusively. Francis Bacon shows the nightmare of history and draws the present-day observer knowingly into the events. For there is a glass pane attached to the decorative gold frame in which, like it or not, viewers see their own reflection. Unlike in the medieval triptychs that inspired the artist's work, there is no expectation of salvation – instead it creates imagination space beyond the reality of the picture. CT

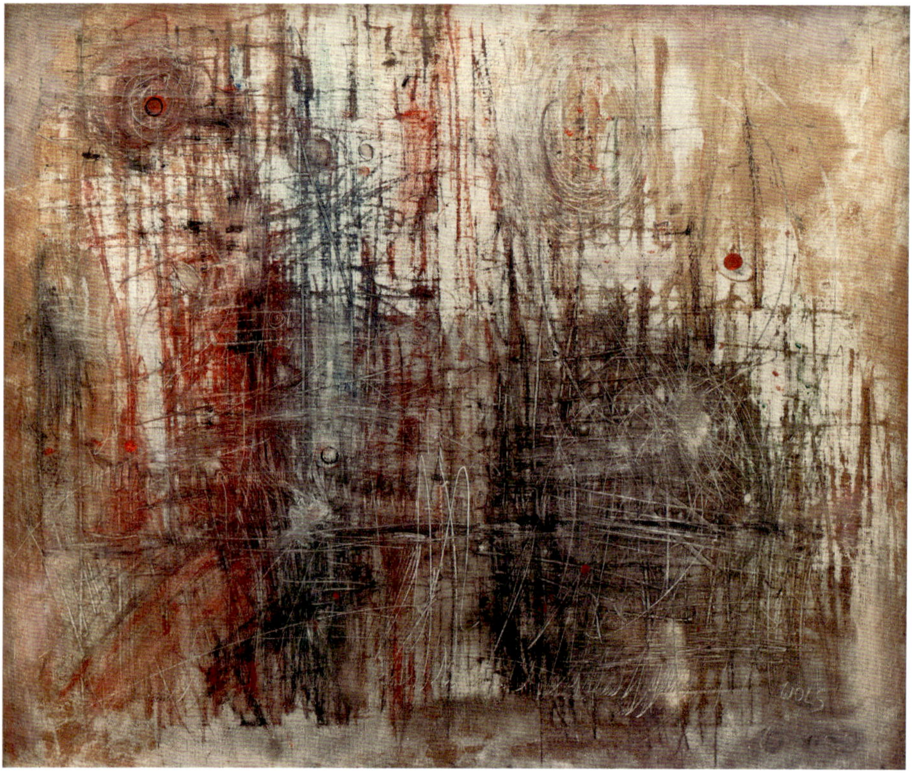

Wols (Alfred Otto Wolfgang Schulze) | **Composition** | 1946
Oil on canvas, 53.8 × 65 cm, inv. no. 13178
Acquired 1962

During a career cut short by his early death, Wols created works that directly articulate the artist's own existentially fraught experience. Stylistically, *Composition* occupies the interface between 'the dissolution and coming together of form' (Rolf Wedewer). Wols ran diluted paint over the canvas, wiping several rivulets to create messy fields of colour reminiscent of congealed blood, and scored wounding marks into those lines and fields. Instead of a deliberate composition, the work bears witness to intuitive actions. These expressive gestures effectively situate Wols as a protagonist of Informal Art and Tachisme. CT

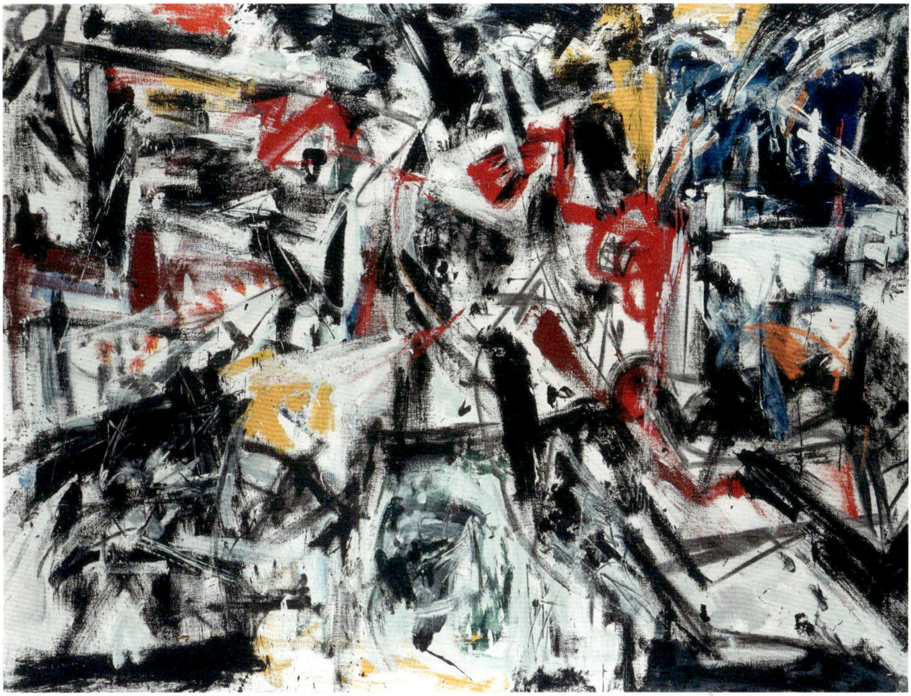

Emilio Vedova | Scontro di situazioni (Collision of Situations) | 1958
Tempera and mixed media on canvas, 145 × 195 cm, inv. no. 14624
Acquired 1979

A looming sense of unrest and war-like forces flow together to form the exaggerated gestural art of the Italian Emilio Vedova, the central figure of the Italian Informal movement. The working title *Collision of Situations* evokes the sort of explosive energy inherent in the post-war period. However it is presented as a potentially destructive force, which is in no way positive or life-giving. The ground, painting process, and paint rage across the surface (in some of the artist's works they also protrude into the room). Facture and fracture come together in painful proximity; painting becomes consternation and aesthetic opposition. BM

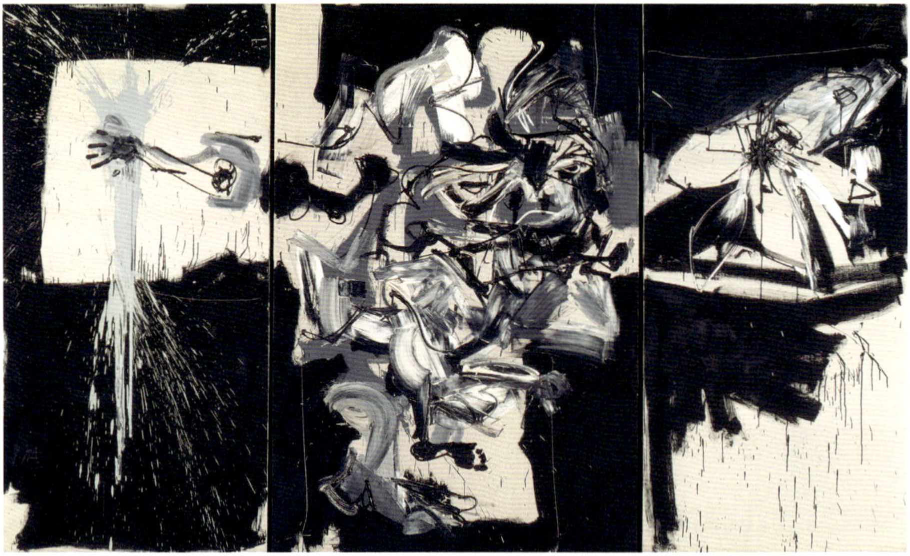

Antonio Saura | Crucifixión (Crucifixion) | 1959
Oil on canvas, three-part, 195.5 × 96.5 cm, 195.5 × 129.5 cm, 195.5 × 96.5 cm,
inv. no. GST 16 1/3 3/3
Donation of Otto van de Loo to the Collective Foundation in support of
Bavarian Stately Museums, 2014

The fact that this bleak picture, entitled *Crucifixion*, breaks down into three parts (and consequently bears the secondary title *Triptych*) is a reflection of two factors. Firstly, it derives from the gesture created by the figure's horizontally outstretched arms. Secondly, since the Middle Ages the triptych has served as an established formula for inspiring observers to pause, take mental stock, and empathize with the crucified Christ (or Christian martyr). The wounding of the body is transformed in Antonio Saura's work into its dismemberment, and thus depicts the highest form of suffering. BM

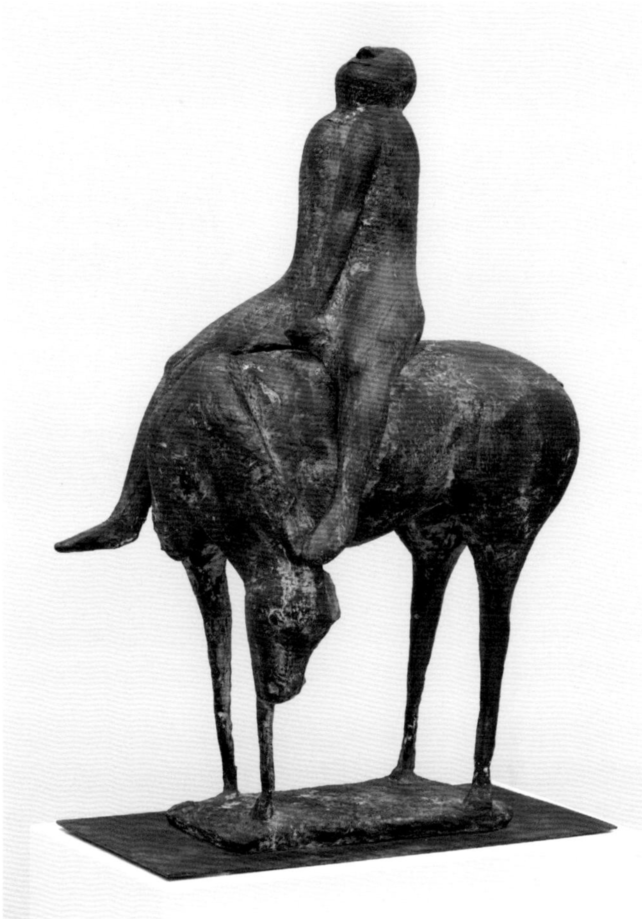

Marino Marini | Cavaliere (Rider) | 1947
Bronze, 100.05 × 67 × 49 cm, inv. no. B 702
Donation of Marino Marini, 1976

What initially resembles a classical or traditional bronze sculpture of a horse and rider is revealed upon closer inspection to be the direct forerunner of a refreshingly free-spirited work by the artist. One year after completing the sculpture displayed here in Munich, Marini created his popular work *Angel in the City*, which similarly depicts a horse and rider. This horseman and his steed have since greeted visitors at the entrance of the Fondazione Guggenheim in Venice. Like its counterpart bronze in Munich, the horseman gazes upwards, and yet his arms are outstretched and his phallus is unmistakably erect. In our sculpture, the heavenly delights experienced by the horseman are on rather less exuberant display. CT

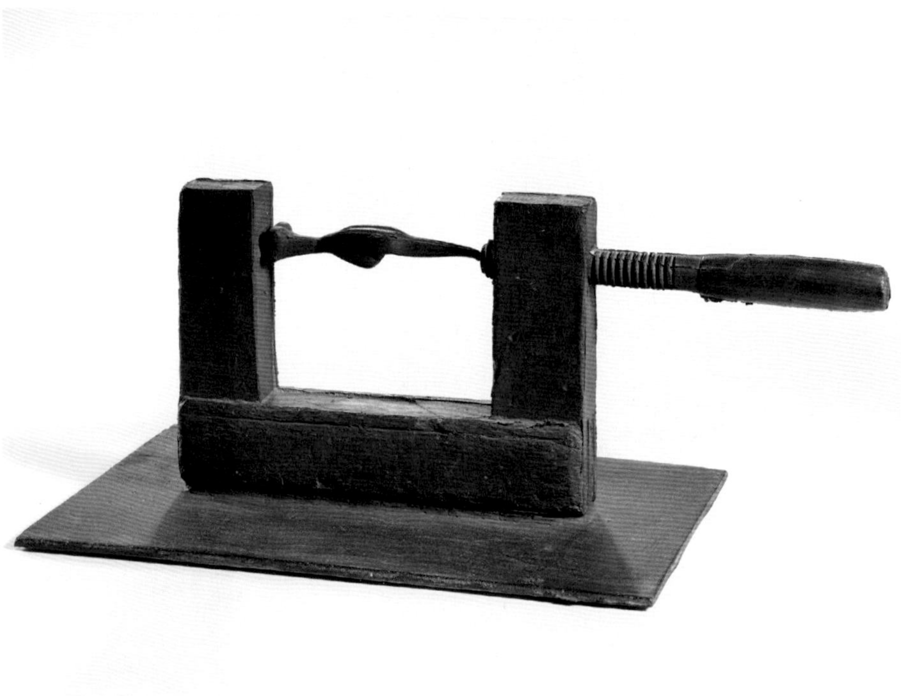

Joseph Beuys | Bett (Bed) | 1950
Bronze, 53 × 25 × 21.5 cm, edition of 6 + a. p., ed. 3/6, inv. no. B 996
Donation of Christof and Ursula Engelhorn, Art Mentor Foundation, Lucerne, 2014

Beuys' *Bed* shows the sculptural representation of a woman's body – without head or feet – in a clamp. At first glance, the work appears to be something like an artefact salvaged from a sculptor's studio that can be separated into two parts. However, closer inspection reveals a rigid and self-contained bronze sculpture. It is a 'thought-image' developed by Beuys to explore the confrontation between man and equipment, organic and geometric form, potential freedom and control. It is through her own growth that the victim will be able to free herself from the corset and develop into an autonomous 'sculptural' form, a creative being.

CT

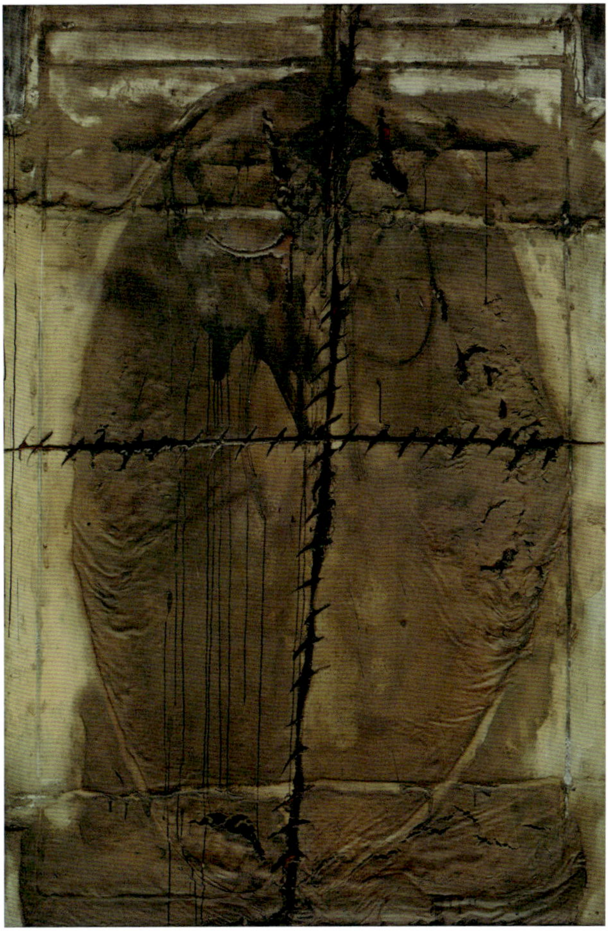

Antoni Tàpies | Ocre oval aux incisions noires
(Ochre-Coloured Oval with Black Incisions) | 1965
Plastic (mass) on wood on canvas, 194.8 × 129.6 cm, inv. no. 13827
Acquired 1967

Scepticism and unrest pervade Antoni Tàpies' pictures. Although painted on a rectangular format, the dynamic oval depicted there – described laconically in the work's title as *Ochre-Coloured Oval with Black Incisions* – functions as an allusion to the shape's role in Spanish painting since the Baroque, not least as a picture form with Catholic and sacred connotations. The oval has enjoyed a deep and solid anchoring in art history. Here it is subversively undermined by the crucifix shape formed by what appears to be barbed wire, becoming interwoven with a sense of impenetrable materiality. BM

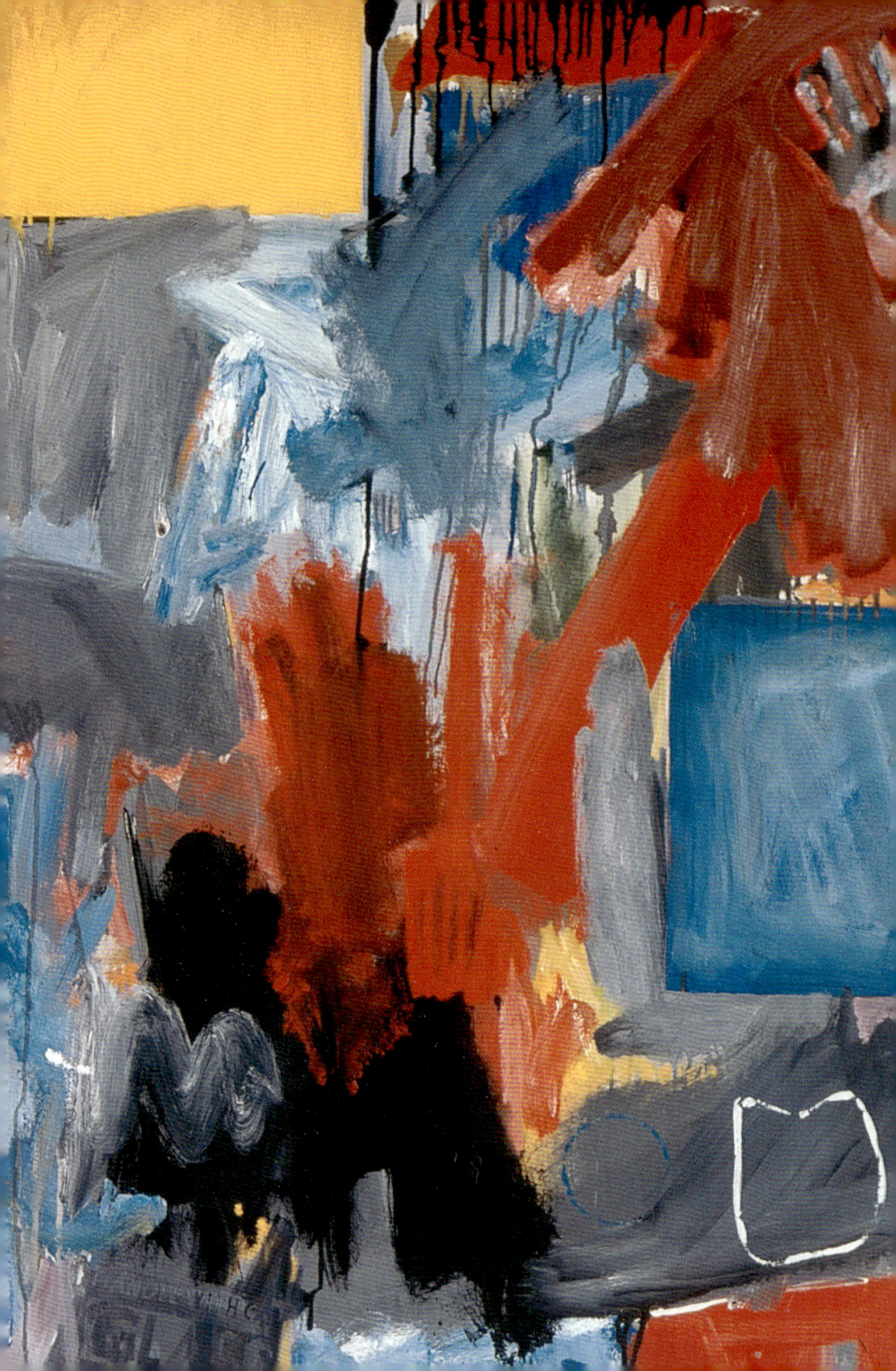

'THE GLOBAL LANGUAGE OF ABSTRACTION'
GESTURES AND CONSTRUCTIONS

Within the spectrum of human expression, spontaneous gestures and planned constructions form poles that are as oppositional as they are elementary. Gestural painting has been around since the birth of visual art. Even in Stone Age caves, handprints and abstract, gestural paintings provide authentic evidence of human existence, and reveal the search for an existential and subjective mode of expression in which the strengths of one's personality are pitted against the unfathomable, spatial, and temporal dimension between 'now' and eternity. It is not really much different when it comes to architectural constructions: had there been a single, first human being, thrust alone into nature and endowed with rationality, then they might have one day started piling stones on top of each another in order to place the size of their own body and the things they could create with their own hands in a spatial relation with the impossibly distant heavens. In doing so, they would have come to recognize the limits of their own creative capabilities, and at the same time, been the fountainhead for a structured civilization. It is conceivable that in order to measure their world, this person might have fixed a string to the ground to create an absolutely straight line which could be distinguished from the pliable, swaying forms of nature. This strictly measured line is an expression of rational thought, and as such, sets itself apart from the natural world's endlessly shifting forms.

Both expressive variants – gestural painting, which captures the physical and psychic energy of the artist on a canvas, and the search for objective and neutral discoveries about matter, dimension, and space – experienced a renaissance in the period following the Second World War. It is as if, in a complex, increasingly global world, after epochs of exhausting countless expressive variations of the brushstroke and the long evolution – stretching back to prehistory – of the history of the figurative representation of the subject, there was a need to once again gain access to the immediate and solid foundations under our feet. If we call to mind the length of time that elapsed between the initial manifestations of this form of expression and its re-emergence in the late 1940s, then it is hardly surprising that in the 20th century people saw in these trends the possibility of unlocking seemingly untapped artistic possibilities, and hoped to harness their (re)discovery for society as a whole. The major milestones in this evolution are formed by artistic movements which art historians in the USA referred to as Abstract Expressionism, in Europe as Art Informel, and, from the 1960s onwards in America, as Minimal Art. The artists belonging to these movements dedicated themselves to the act of spontaneous painting without studious preparatory drawings, exhibiting an interest in the actual process of painting and in the immediate expressive content of form and colour. Artists who worked gesturally observed the trace of a brushstroke across the canvas: at the outset loaded with paint and then gradually depleting. In doing so, their aim was not to manipulate physical and psychological conditions, but rather much the opposite, to investigate these conditions both in the process and in their final form for their own sake, and to strike a harmony with them. Painters such as Willem de Kooning and Franz Kline did not work in a restrained manner, from the wrist, but rather used the entire radius of movement of their arms, (which is evidenced by the size of the central triangular figure in de Kooning's *Detour*) and of their entire bodies, which come to function as individual determinants of scale, significantly influencing the ultimate size of the subject and the canvas.

The Constructivist line investigated the relation between exact dimensions and subjective perception, and observed the shifting effects of colour on a set form through extensive series. The earliest example here is a work by Josef Albers, an influential teacher – originally in Germany and then, from 1933, in America – who analysed how colours seemed to edge forwards out of the visual field of the image towards the viewer, or to repel surrounding colours, despite being applied evenly to a precisely measured, two-dimensional field. Focusing on the analysis of facts, artists such as Carl Andre and Donald Judd subsequently moved towards the creation of precisely planned works in which there was no room for the artist's 'signature', mark-making by hand or individual gesture. In fact, the objects seem entirely anonymous, with their parts being produced by machines. Colour is not applied in the form of paint, but is rather inherent to the working materials such as perspex and metal. In these works, there is no object that is merely painted – and therefore fictional. In order to reduce references to content that was extraneous to the artwork, in their often multi-part works, these artists also eschewed the pathos formulae, identified by Aby Warburg, of older, European art (such as the religiously charged triad of the triptych with its foregrounded central panel), instead seeking out democratic, non-hierarchical arrangements. Andre built his *Steel Row* from ten panels, each measuring one metre by one metre and following a standardized metric. The focus here is on naked facts and their perception, and precisely because of their facticity, the objects are able to become charged with a magical charisma. This was fully intended by the artists, who developed the matter-of-factness of the form of their works in critical dialogue with the confusing referential world of consumer society and media culture – just consider, for example, the substantial gulf which can exist between a commercial product and the advertisements which promote it.

In the years following the Second World War, abstract styles held sway, above all in the USA, but also in Europe. In Europe, the expressivity tended to be introverted, the paintings having smaller formats, while in the USA, many artists – including, for example Franz Kline – turned to large or even monumental formats. Both here and in America however, the artists were equally concerned with the fundamental and universal possibilities of expression. In light of the desired universality of this content, at *documenta II* in 1959, Werner Haftmann came up with the notion of a 'global language of abstraction', which was capable of engaging in a supra-historical exchange, traversing continents and cultures, while at the same time reflecting Western freedoms and independence. The latter reveals how strongly Haftmann's handy conception was beholden to the context of the Cold War, for his remarks must be regarded as a reflexive response to the targeted programme developed by the American government and the CIA. Over the course of the Cold War, these two organizations attempted to promote to European artists and intellectuals the supposedly uniquely American free gesture as proof of the liberal values of the USA, and viewed the large format of these works as an expression of the expansiveness of the unifying central idea underlying the American nation. In doing so, they also hoped to emphasize the successful deployment of these ideas against fascism and barbarism in Europe, and thus also against the artistic doctrines of the Third Reich and Socialist Realism. This 'triumph of American painting' (Irving Sandler) conquered – albeit with the 'peaceful means' (Dwight D. Eisenhower) of cultural understanding – the more restrained expressive tradition of the Nouvelle École de Paris, which included artists such as Jean Dubuffet, Hans Hartung (p. 208) Serge Poliakoff, Wols (p. 168) and the artists of *CoBrA*, such as Karel Appel, Asger Jorn, and later, K. O. Götz. Thus, the hegemonic position which American art reached was not based exclusively on aesthetic criteria, but also on economic, political, and ideological factors. Jackson Pollock summed up the situation well in 1944 when he remarked that 'the idea of an isolated American painting [...] seems absurd to me, just as the idea of [...] a purely American mathematics or physics would seem absurd. [...] the basic problems of contemporary painting are independent of any one country.'

Corinna Thierolf

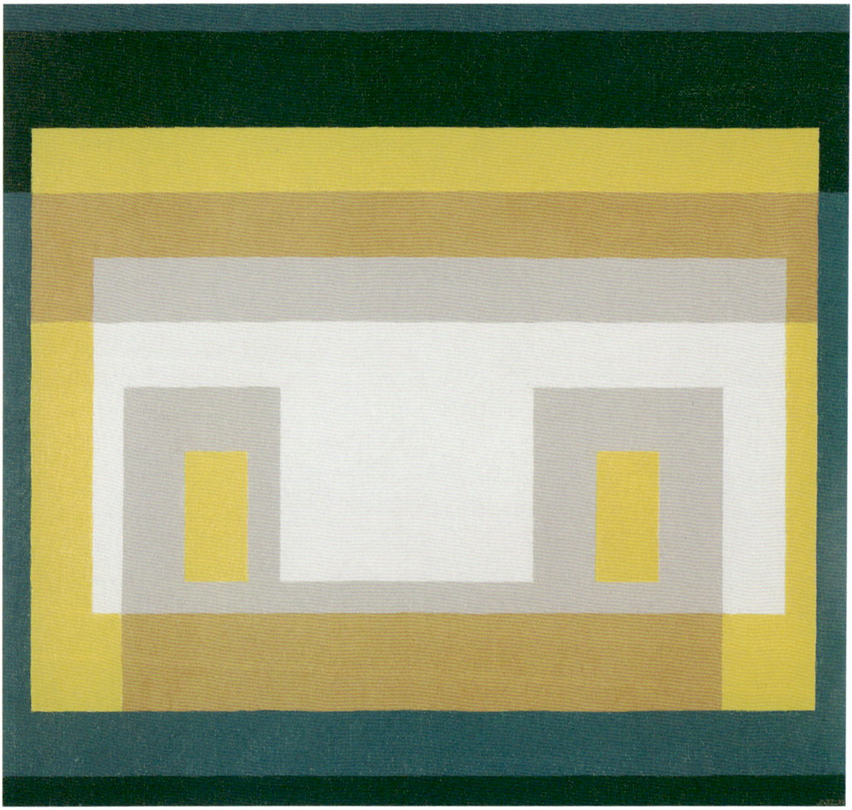

Josef Albers | White and Gray with Two Yellows and Two Greens | 1947/55
Oil on masonite, 63.6 × 68.6 cm, inv. no. 16442
Donation of Christof and Ursula Engelhorn, Art Mentor Foundation, Lucerne, 2016

Josef Albers was deeply preoccupied with the effect of colour in relation to other surrounding colours. In his works he was able to reveal the contradiction between physical and experiential reality. The sequence of colours in these nested squares creates a three-dimensionality: in front of the darker frames of two tones of green, two tones of yellow and white and grey inch towards the viewer. As in his other works that follow a similar compositional plan, Albers provides us here with an example of reduction as a prerequisite for complexity. CT

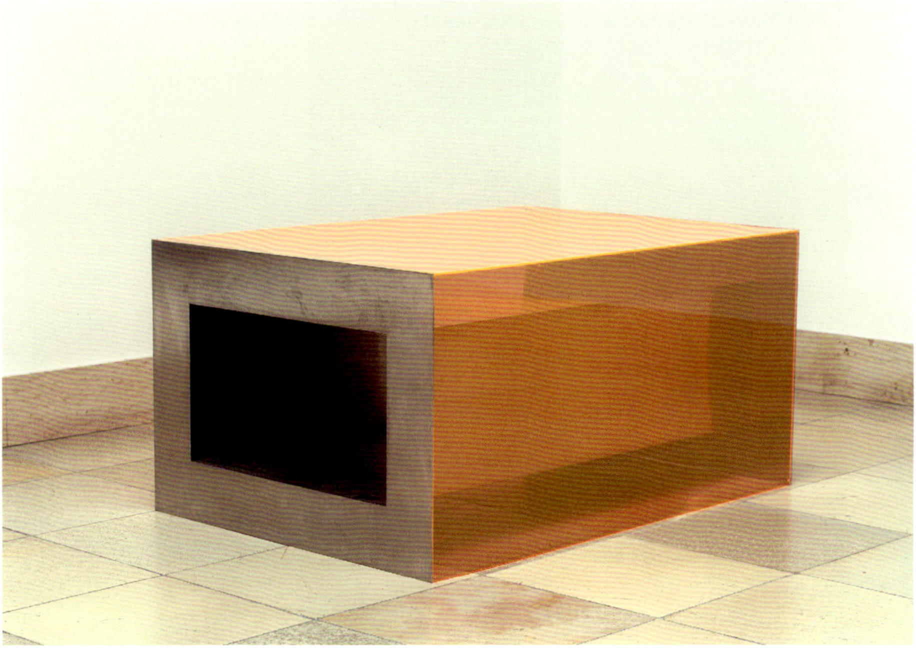

Donald Judd | Untitled (Core Piece) | 1969
Fluorescent yellow Perspex, stainless steel, 84 × 122 × 172.5 cm, inv. no. B 663
Acquired 1973

From 1963 onwards, Donald Judd, one of the main protagonists of Minimal Art, worked with free-standing, three-dimensional objects in order to overcome the illusionism of the image and to lend genuine presence to colour and form. In his floor sculpture *Untitled (Core Piece)*, reflections of the fluorescent Perspex appear on the internal metal structure. The multiplicity of the visual experience, which shifts according to location and lighting, reacts with a formal and material facticity, an uncompromising and exact logic, which can be understood as a basis for beauty. CT

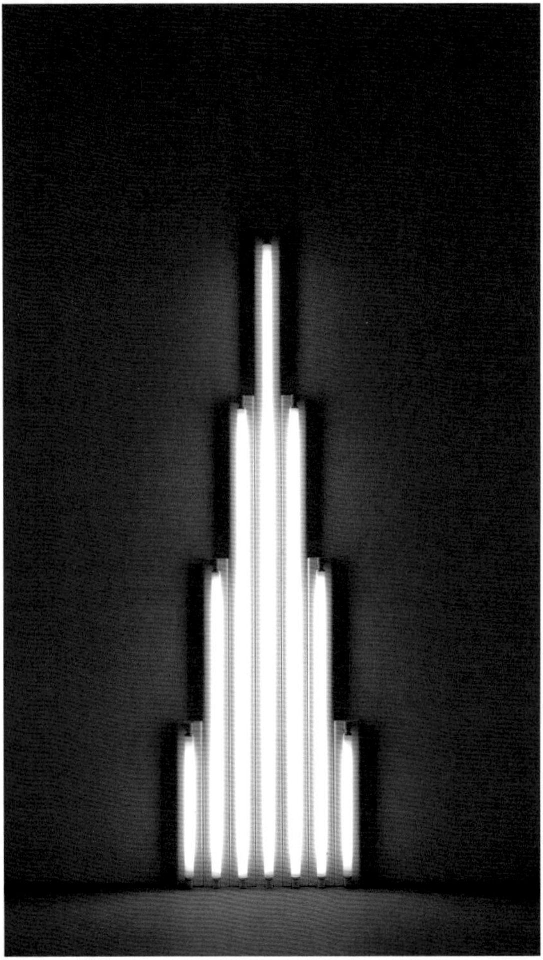

Dan Flavin | monument for V. Tatlin I | 1964
Seven cool-white neon tubes, 244 × 71.5 × 12 cm, inv. no. 15836
Donation of American Patrons of the Pinakothek Trust, 2008

The work of Dan Flavin is represented here with the first of his 39 variations on the theme of the 'monument'. The arrangement of these commercially available neon tubes calls to mind the Empire State Building. The work is dedicated to the Constructivist Vladimir Tatlin, who in 1920, in the early years of the Soviet state, sought to erect a monument to the Russian Revolution. In the era of the Cold War, Flavin paid homage to Tatlin's oeuvre with this work, while at the same time asking the question: what works can an artist create if he is not in the service of politics and ideology. His lower-case title is programmatic. CT

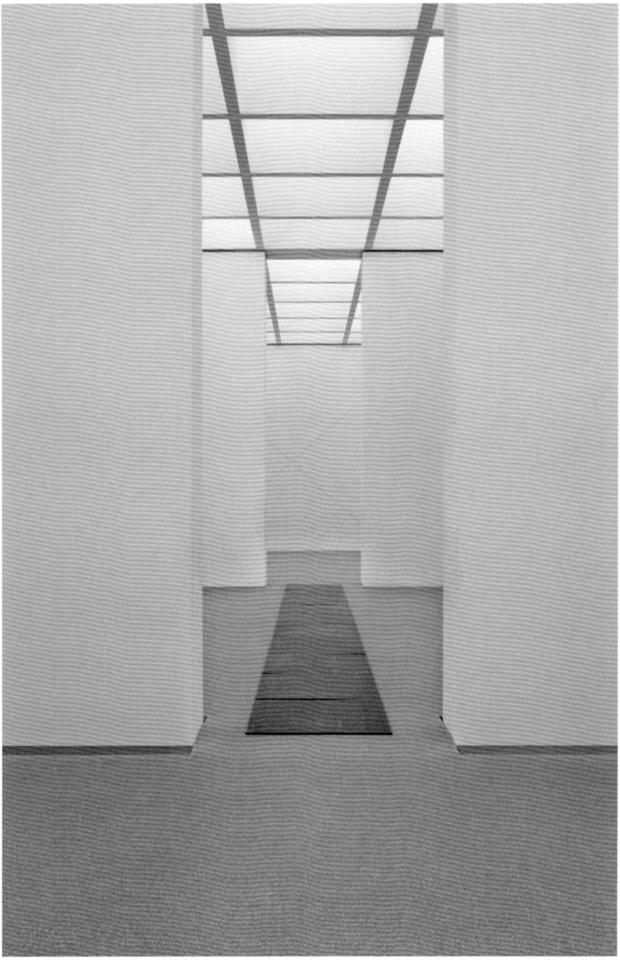

Carl Andre | 10 Steel Row | 1968
Hot-rolled steel panels, 1 × 100 × 100 cm, inv. no. B 711 a-k + GV 21
Acquired 1977 with support of PIN. Freunde der Pinakothek der Moderne

Carl Andre's *Steel Row* is made up of 10 simple, uniform, and quadratic steel panels. The panels in this 'democratized' composition can be exchanged at will, with no single panel being privileged or disadvantaged. The viewer perceives the object as a 'path' and is invited to use it as such, being able to walk around or across the work. It is only through this active participation of the viewer that the meaning of the object is revealed: its precise dimensions enable a spatial understanding of its surroundings, and the specific character of the material of steel, which contrasts with the surface texture of the floor. CT

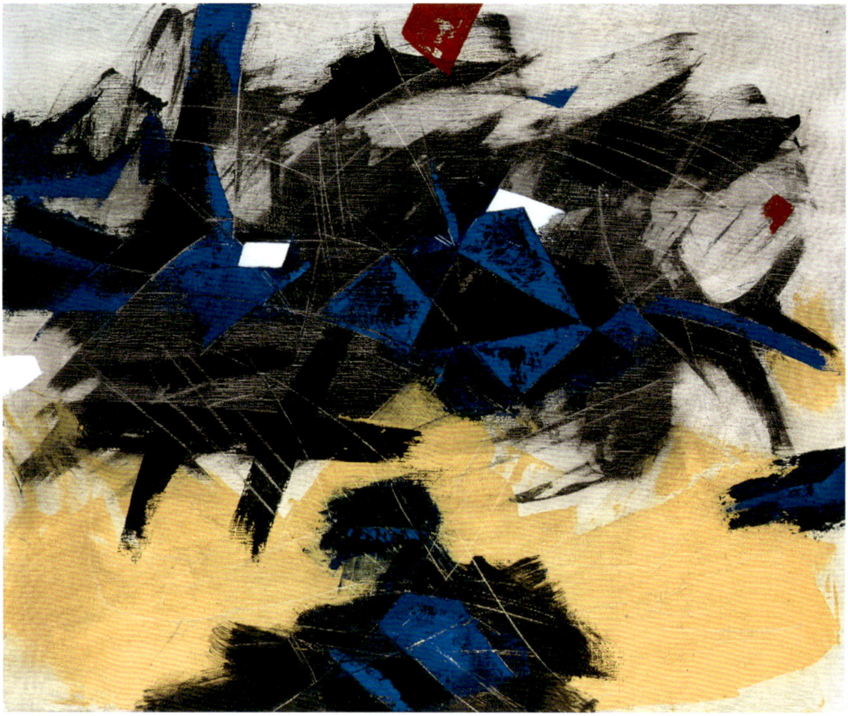

Theodor Werner | **Aufbau** (Composition) | 1951
Oil on canvas, 100.3 × 81.6 cm, inv. no. 11326
Acquired 1951

This work by Theodor Werner is characteristic of the non-objective painting of Art Informel and, in particular, of the artist group *ZEN 49*, of which Werner was a member. The work was exhibited in Munich's Galerie Franke in the year of its creation and subsequently acquired by the Bayerische Staatsgemäldesammlungen. In the catalogue for that show, Werner articulated his artistic credo: 'to the extent that we forego the representation of specific content, associative, metaphorical, or symbolic elements, to the extent that we manage to reach form, this form corresponds to and participates in being, is truth.' BSO

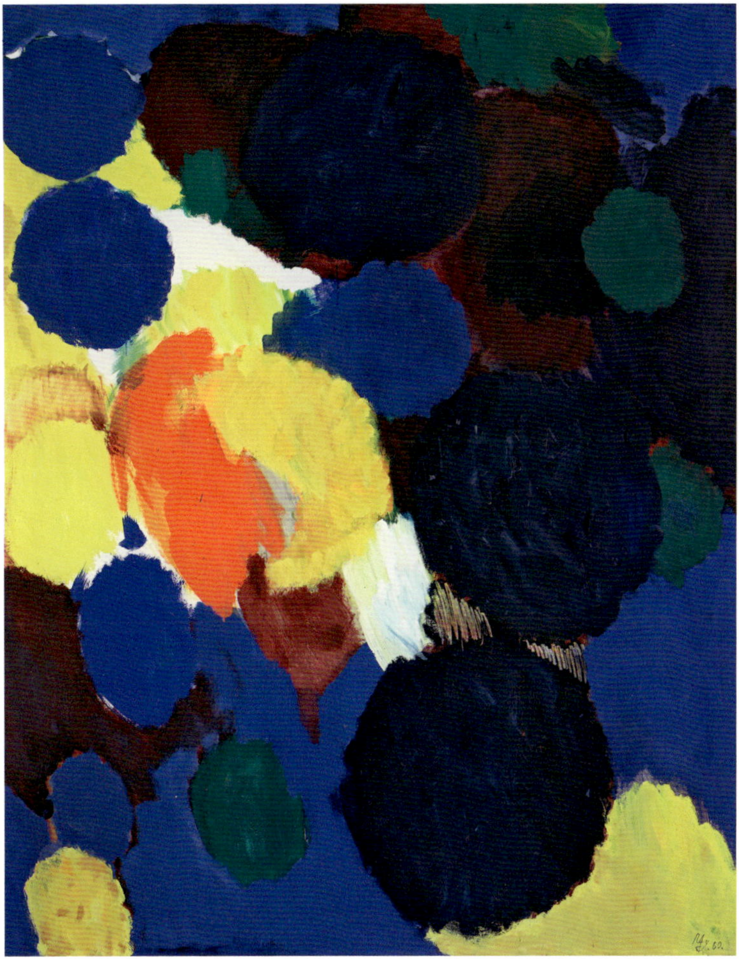

Ernst Wilhelm Nay | Ultramarin und Gelb (Ultramarine and Yellow) | 1960
Oil on canvas, 162 × 130 cm, inv. no. 16276
Donation of Theo Wormland Foundation, 2013

Colour is central to Ernst Wilhelm Nay's oeuvre. In long series of works, he dedicated himself to the confrontation between colours. The *Fugale Bilder* (Fugal Paintings) of the early post-war era were followed in the 1950s by the *Scheibenbilder* (Disc Paintings), in which he grouped together circular and misshapen daubs of colour. The *Fugal Paintings* were usually dominated by a single colour, with Nay experimentally exploring the relation between this colour and others. In this picture, blue sets the tone, confronted by yellow and a patch of red, all over a background of dark and ominous colours. CT

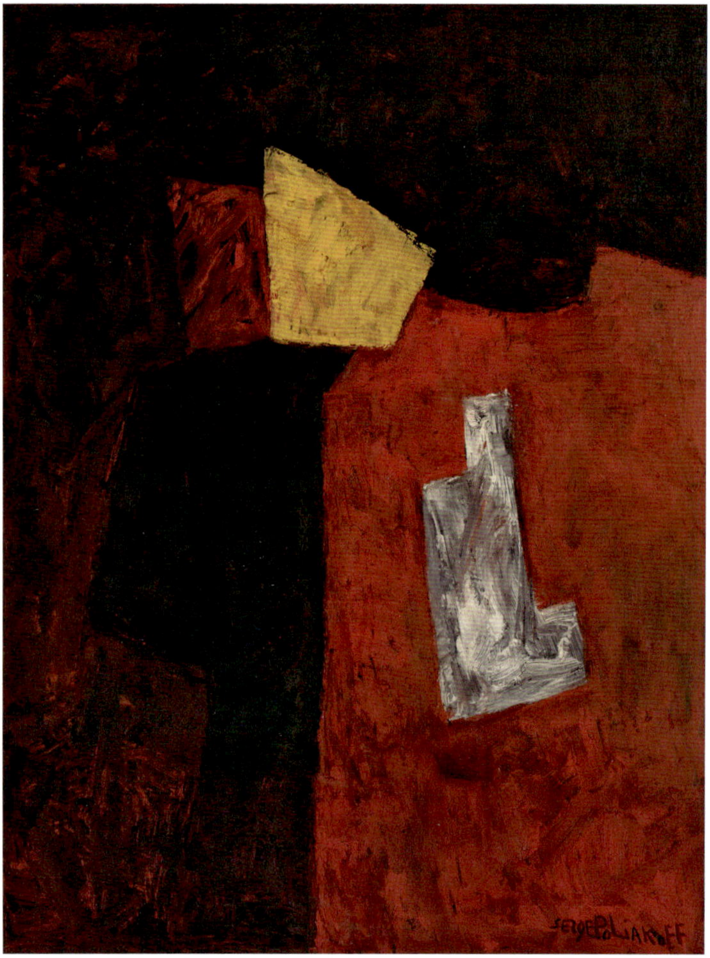

Serge Poliakoff | Composition | 1961
Oil on canvas, 116 × 89 cm, inv. no. MES 201
Permanent loan from the Michael & Eleonore Stoffel Foundation, accessioned 2008

Serge Poliakoff combines large expanses of red and black, delineated by polygonal forms, with a small, irregular field of greyish white and yellow. The painting exudes a solemn silence, which was characteristic for the creative process of the artist. He always produced his works in total calm – in this way, he could be compared to an icon painter. As it happens, aesthetic traditions from his Russian homeland continued to exert an influence on Poliakoff after he settled in Paris in 1923. There, after years of searching, he began his studies in painting, which from the 1940s would lead him towards abstraction. BSO

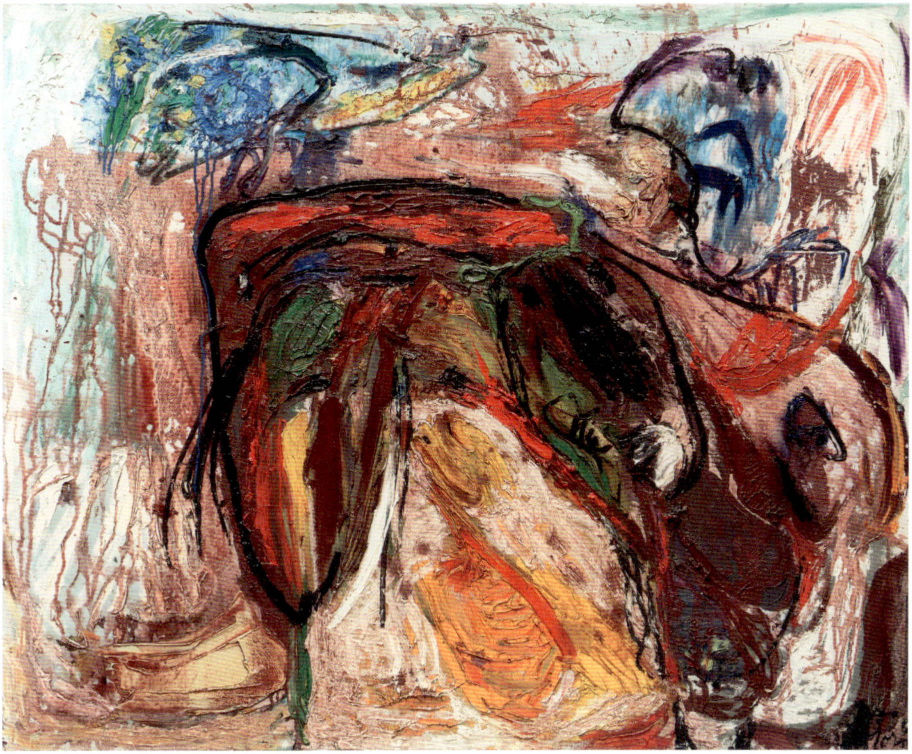

Asger Jorn | **Paradentose des Adlers** (The Eagle's Periodontosis) | 1958
Oil on canvas, 80.5 × 100.2 cm, inv. no. 15208
Acquired 1990

If we do not take the title as a demand to search for the eagle in the picture, the painting reads like a piercing, radiating pain that transcends all identifiable forms. Exploding with a sense of revolt, it seems to be only bearable in ecstasy. Where does this pain originate? Who suffers it? The only certainty seems to be Asger Jorn's complete investment in the production of the picture – as a corporeal, intellectual, and social being. Does painting provoke or soothe him? Is he engaged here in painting, or in iconoclasm? CT

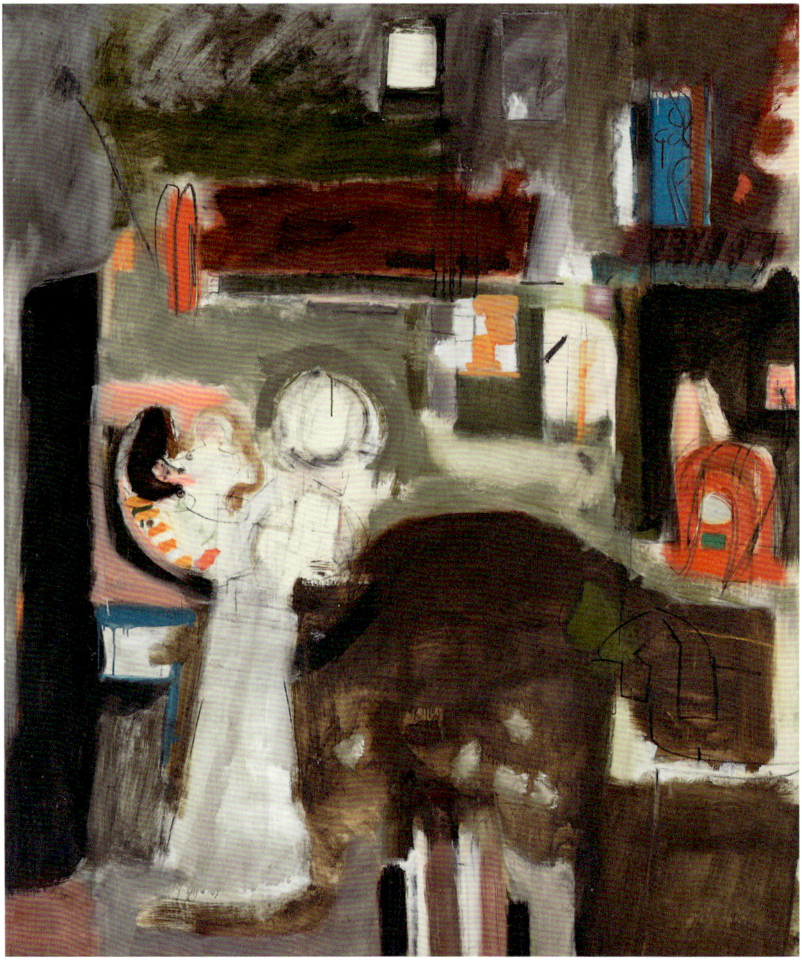

Larry Rivers | **Studio** | 1959–60
Oil and black coloured pencil on canvas, 198 × 173 cm, inv. no. 16279 + GV 57
Donation of Theo Wormland Foundation, 2013

It is only through the title that the rectangular elements in this painting and the organic and amorphous forms become recognizable as components of, and objects in, a studio, or as ideas which preoccupy the painter Larry Rivers in this working environment. The work rejects the illusion, held dear by the chattering classes, of our ability to unpack the content of the image through iconographic deductions and the unmistakable legibility of the objects depicted therein. The composition challenges the viewer to continually and independently reflect upon the possibilities of colour and form on the canvas. CT

Franz Josef Kline | 1960 New Year Wall, Night | 1960
Oil on soft fibreboard, 305 × 488 cm, inv. no. GV 19, 14437 A-D
Acquired for the Modern Art Collection in 1975 by PIN. Freunde der Pinakothek der Moderne

Along with Pollock and de Kooning, Kline is one of the American artists who lost interest in the intricate intellectual painting of Surrealism in the 1940s. In *1960 New Year Wall, Night*, the enormous gestural lines, expanses, and dense blobs of paint in black, white, and grey embody a kind of pure painting. The inspiration for his work came, according to Kline, not from the visible world 'out there', but from 'somewhere else'. Dalí noted an affinity to St. John of the Cross, however Kline had never read the works of this mystic, such as *The Dark Night of the Soul*. CT

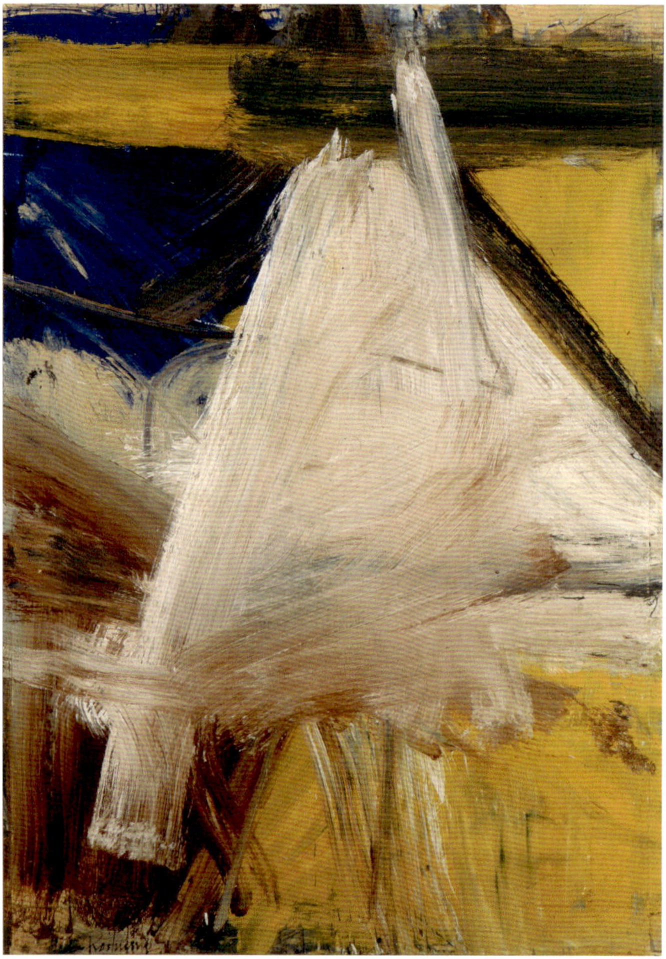

Willem de Kooning | Detour | 1958
Oil on paper on canvas, 150 × 108 cm, inv. no. 14614 + GV 57
Acquired 1979 with support of PIN. Freunde der Pinakothek der Moderne

Detour is a work which is constructed with stark, gestural brushstrokes, and provides a prime example of Abstract Expressionist painting in the USA. And yet, as Willem de Kooning himself recalled, despite all the non-objectivity of the painting, it depicts the experience of a jaunt to the sea in a car. Sun, water, and sand are evoked through the use of colour, the rapid car trip through the dynamic brushstrokes. This unusual 'landscape painting' is not a view of nature, but rather depicts an experience with it. CT

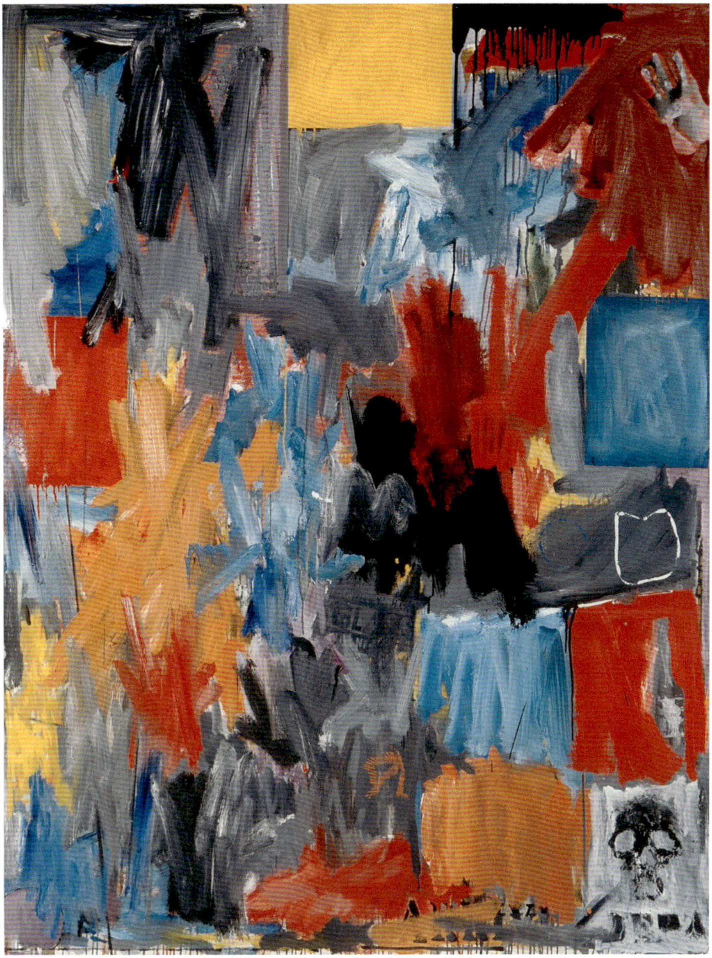

Jasper Johns | Arrive/Depart | 1963–64
Oil on canvas, 173 × 131 cm, inv. no. 14465
Bequest of Klaus Gebhard, 1976

Jasper Johns's painting can be read like an encyclopaedia of different expression: geometric forms alternate with gesturally formed passages, which are either added to the image spontaneously and expressively, or with a measured hand. On top of this, there are impressions (of a hand and a skull, for example), painted forms that are left vague (the red fork), and elements of type that are then partially erased. In Johns's art, content and meaning are as complex as they are uncertain. Might that be the reason why he has included the almost illegible message 'HANDLE WITH CARE/GLASS' in the composition? CT

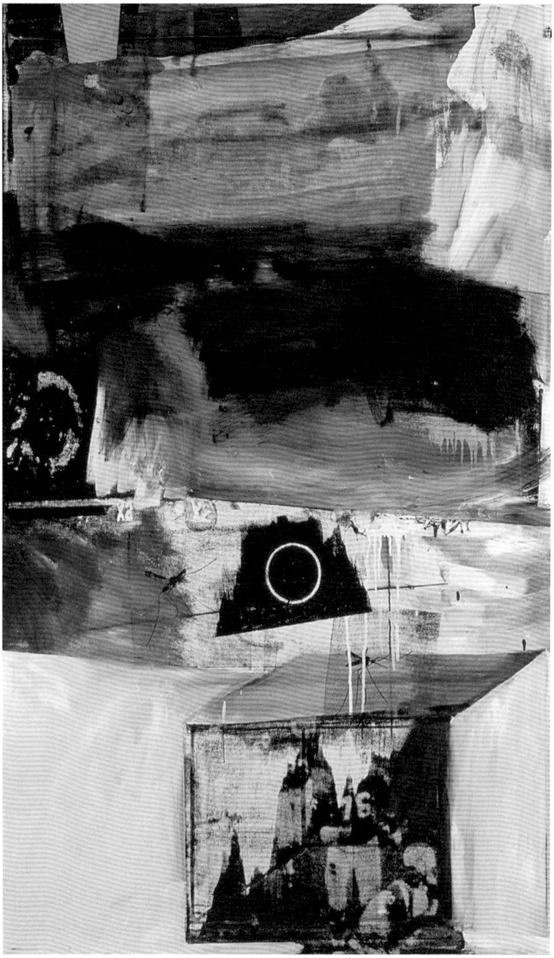

Robert Rauschenberg | Vault | 1962
Oil and silkscreen ink on canvas, 153.8 × 91.4 cm, inv. no. 14464
Bequest of Klaus Gebhard, 1976

In halftone photographic prints overlaid with paint applied in broad, spontaneous gestures, the most diverse aspects of lived reality congregate here: the wheel of a truck, mosquitos, American football players, an atom bomb explosion – while the subject matter in the upper zone, smudged over with grey paint, is based on a depiction of Venus by Titian. Robert Rauschenberg's work *Vault* makes direct reference to Marcel Duchamp's *Le Grand Verre*, with Rauschenberg here making a variation on that work's virtually encyclopaedic yet enigmatic analysis of the relationship between man and woman. CT

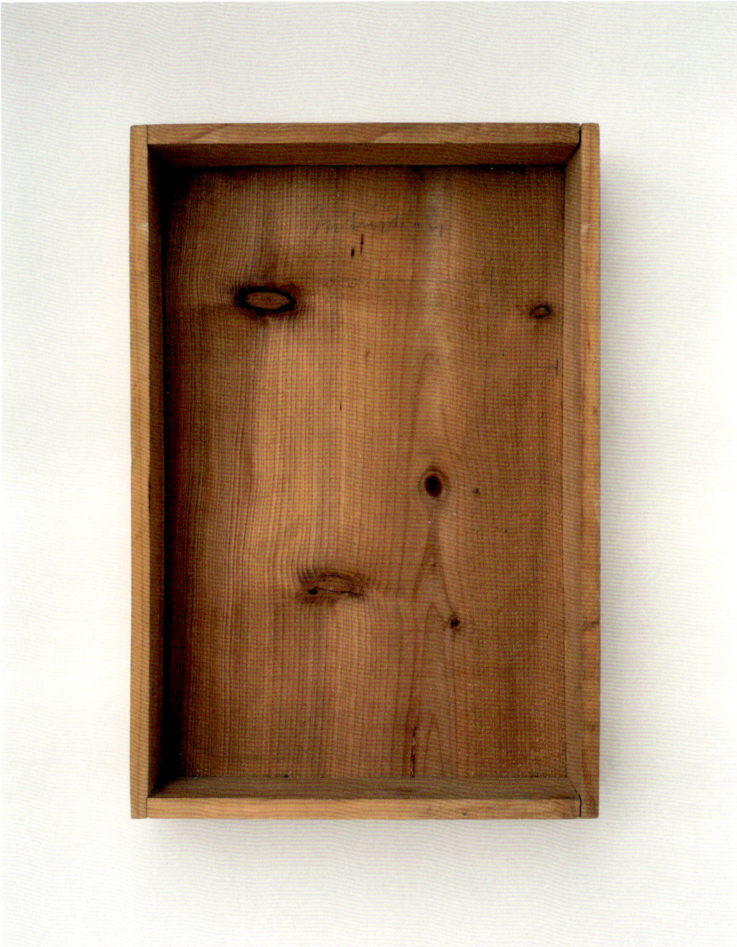

Joseph Beuys | Intuition | 1968
Wooden crate with lead pencil drawing, 30 × 21 × 6 cm, inv. no. 15787
Donation of a privately listed foundation, 2008

Intuition is one of the 500 multiples through which Beuys made the ideas associated with his art available to a large audience in affordable editions. The work consists of a narrow, open wooden crate. Formally, it calls to mind the geometry of the contemporaneous Minimal Art, and yet Beuys removes the aura of rationality which many viewers associate with this style. Through the text, he calls for an awakening of the intuition, for in all creative activity (including the act of seeing), immediate and reflective thinking belong together, as he says: 'everyone is an artist'. CT

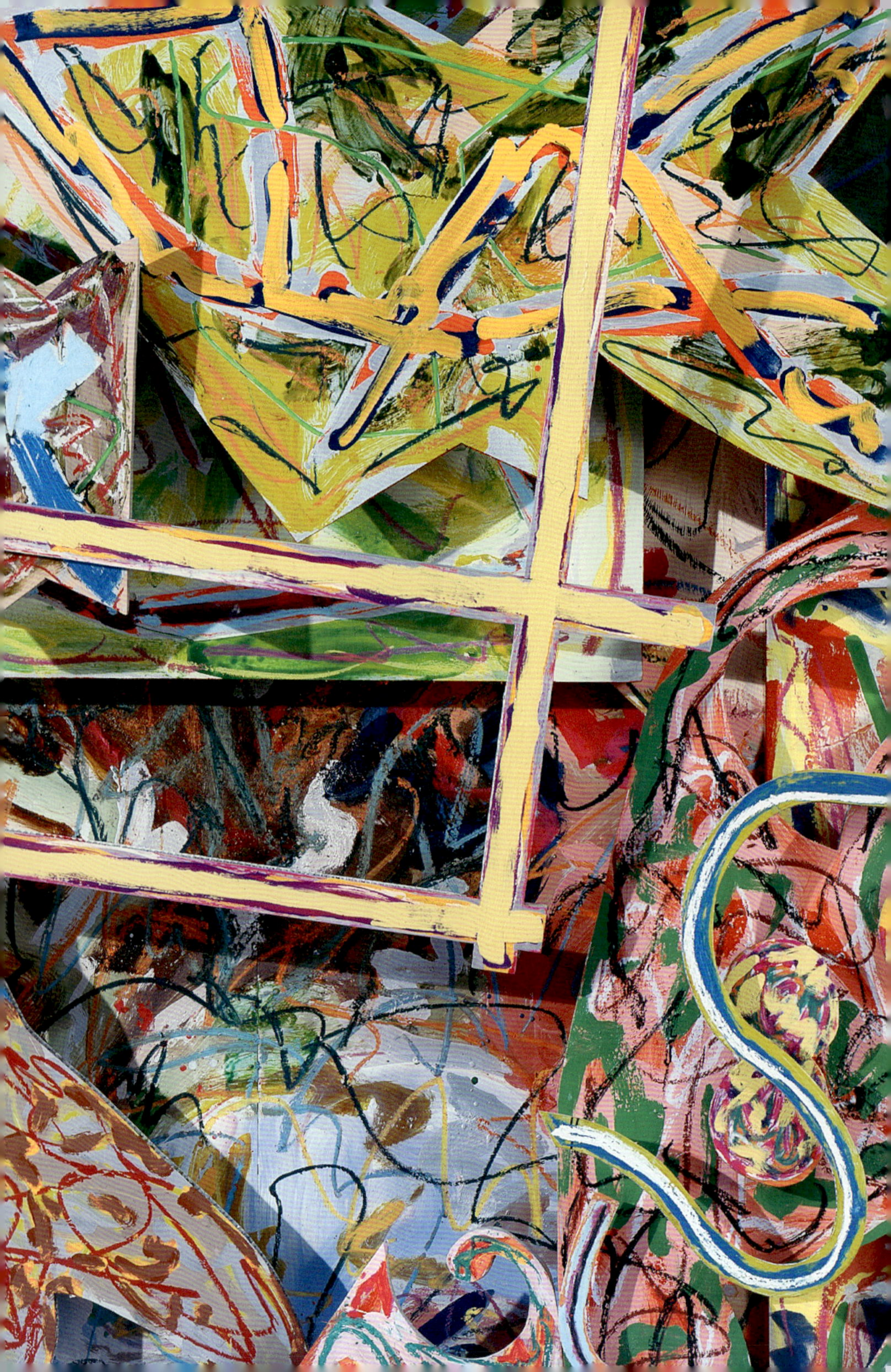

THE INFINITE AND THE TANGIBLE
THE UNBOUNDING OF THE IMAGE

Captions reading 'please do not touch' may be found on the walls of museums as frequently as the pictures that hang there. This injunction demonstrates that the idea that works of art are something other than touchable objects of daily life is not an entirely intuitive one. That is, they are spiritualized material or 'a visual "form" of mental consciousness' (Arnulf Rainer). This spiritual substance of art can be received only through the tension that arises between the work's presence and the viewer's distance. *Noli me tangere* (don't touch me).

On his famous picture of a realistically painted pipe, René Magritte wrote 'Ceci n'est pas une pipe' (This is not a pipe). But who would think of lighting up to puff on this image rather than looking at it, or reaching out for the vessels in a painting, such as the various vases and bottles found in the works of Giorgio Morandi? Works in which the analogy between reality and the painted artwork remains incomplete – works that are not 'finished' in a classical sense – are in fact more testing for viewers, challenging them in their effort to keep a distance. In Andy Warhol's Paint-by-Number series from 1962, the completed image has the appearance of an unfinished do-it-yourself picture book. Does the artist wish to poke fun at the viewers by referencing this pseudo-creative form of ergotherapy and denying them a perfectly completed 'creation'?

A member of the public, vigorous 90-year-old retiree Hannelore K. visited Nuremberg's Neues Museum in 2016 and caused a stir. It is no wonder that many found her zestful enthusiasm for action refreshing in its disregard for museum taboos. During a 'writing workshop', she took a torn-out crossword puzzle which was part of a 1965 work by Arthur Köpcke and unceremoniously filled it in with the 'right' words. She had taken the image's puzzle too literally. Yet her boundary-breaking behaviour seems an adequate response to the boundary breaking in artistic works that, since Marcel Duchamp's readymades, have turned the classical idea of art on its head by declaring such 'headstands' art. Accordingly, even though they are often less appreciated by some members of the public, everyday objects and abstract works are also called art, because of the artist's ideas that have gone into their making. Because art defends a space of reflection that defies any sort of scientific, religious, or aesthetic clarity.

The appeal for distance connected with the artwork demands that viewers penetrate beyond the immediately visible in order to recognize what lies 'behind' and to allow this spirit to enter themselves. According to the Christian tradition which shapes much of European culture, the Virgin Mary altered her body and became pregnant without physical contact as the Word entered her ear. Here, then, we might speak of images penetrating the eye of the viewer.

Much of what images speak about is physically absent or present only in traces. Cy Twombly's *Untitled* features lines against a white background. Some lines tell the story of their own creation, they chronicle how the painter directed the pencil at the specific moment of production (with what intensity, speed, etc.). Other strokes are drawn with a ruler and remind us that a precisely measured line can create a scale in relation to something larger: '1 cm = 100000 miles' can be read in one of the artist's drawings. This recalls the note '100004 M' in our painting here. This ratio leads beyond the immediately visible (for orientation: the circumference of Earth at the equator is 25000 miles) and refers to the relationship between the smallest and the largest, between the microcosm and the macrocosm, and between the measurable and the immeasurable. Twombly's work finally also leads the viewer beyond the real dimensions of the canvas out into imagined, wide open spaces ('away'), in order for us to arrive at ourselves once again at the end ('StaRt'). The lines are drawn through time and space with a conscious mix of precision and blurriness. This openness creates opportunities to experimentally capture phenomena beyond what has so far been measured. It is also a modern rejection of the belief that the things of this world are clearly defined in time and place. This unclarity becomes more apparent the closer one looks.

Arnulf Rainer painted over his own images (and those of others) in his early works such as *White Overpainting II* until the surface became nearly entirely monochrome. He created new images by painting away old ones. The two black corners in this painting are barely discernible. Are these remnants of the image that has been painted over? Do they show us what lies 'beneath'? Despite the image's proclaimed theme of 'overpainting', tiny black spots can be found on the same layer as the large white field. Accordingly, we cannot lift the veil of the surface because these 'imperfections' (or actual information) were part of the artist's consideration from the outset. In Rainer's works, one encounters no absolute surface and no absolute meaning.

Ladders to heaven have been imagined since the time of the ancient Egyptians, connecting this world and that beyond. Climbing up to the unknown realm of the gods is also an expression of the human thirst for knowledge that has led to the erosion of the respective worldviews of various epochs and to the unbounding of the image (for example the move from the golden background of a gold-ground panel to a realistically painted one). Lucio Fontana's images are also concerned with the structure of the largest conceivable space. From 1949 onwards, his works bore the overarching title *Spatial Concept* and the two-dimensional surface of the canvas is always penetrated with perforations, or, as in his work in Munich, decisive slashes. In the black paint on the canvas, Fontana additionally carved a circle, a form that evokes the universe, comparable to the egg form in his *Fine di Dio* (End of God) works. The title suggests that the artist produces his work through a confrontation with the great questions, but without believing in a god-given order.

Fabienne Verdier's seven paintings might be considered similarly. They show a single continuous line moving across a black, diffusely lit background. They were created with an enormous brush, which the artist held vertically, consciously creating an axis between heaven and Earth. Thus, for the artist, the brush has become an instrument for perceiving the connection between these two poles. The paint that pours out from the 36 horsetails from which this painting tool is composed was directed by Verdier. But the flow of the material from the brush is also determined by the gravitational pull which draws it downwards onto the support lying on the floor below. There, the paint dries in a manner which makes more than just the traces of the brush's motion visible. Cracks and stray spots of paint caused by gravity also appear in startling ways. Verdier's works are thus conceptually painted between heaven and Earth, at the bottom end of the stairway to heaven. It is therefore hardly surprising that the materially extremely prominent line in front of the vast expanse of darkness both keeps viewers in the here and now and catapults them into the boundlessness of the universe.

Corinna Thierolf

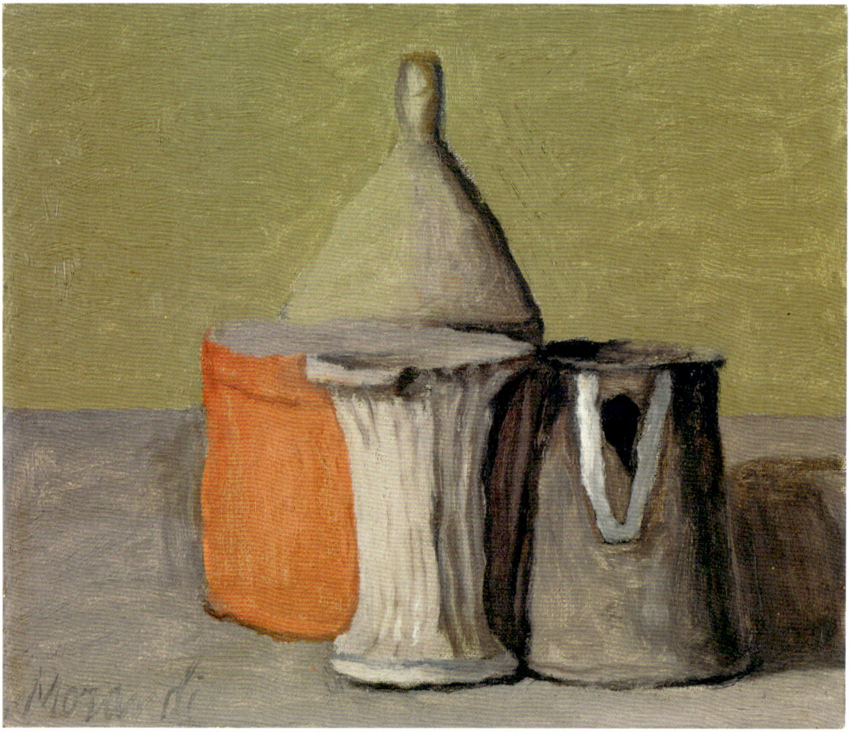

Giorgio Morandi | **Natura Morta** (Still Life) | 1960
Oil on canvas, 30 × 35 cm, inv. no. 16412
Donation of Christof and Ursula Engelhorn, Art Mentor Foundation, Lucerne, 2015

In Giorgio Morandi's still life, time seems to be suspended. The monochrome grey colour of three objects, their support, and their background remain in balance, despite the inclusion of an orange-coloured bowl. The restriction to only depicting four objects in the image allows us to concentrate on the process of perception itself. Jug, vase, pot, and bottle are deprived of their context of use. Their formal presence conveys peace and timelessness.

JC

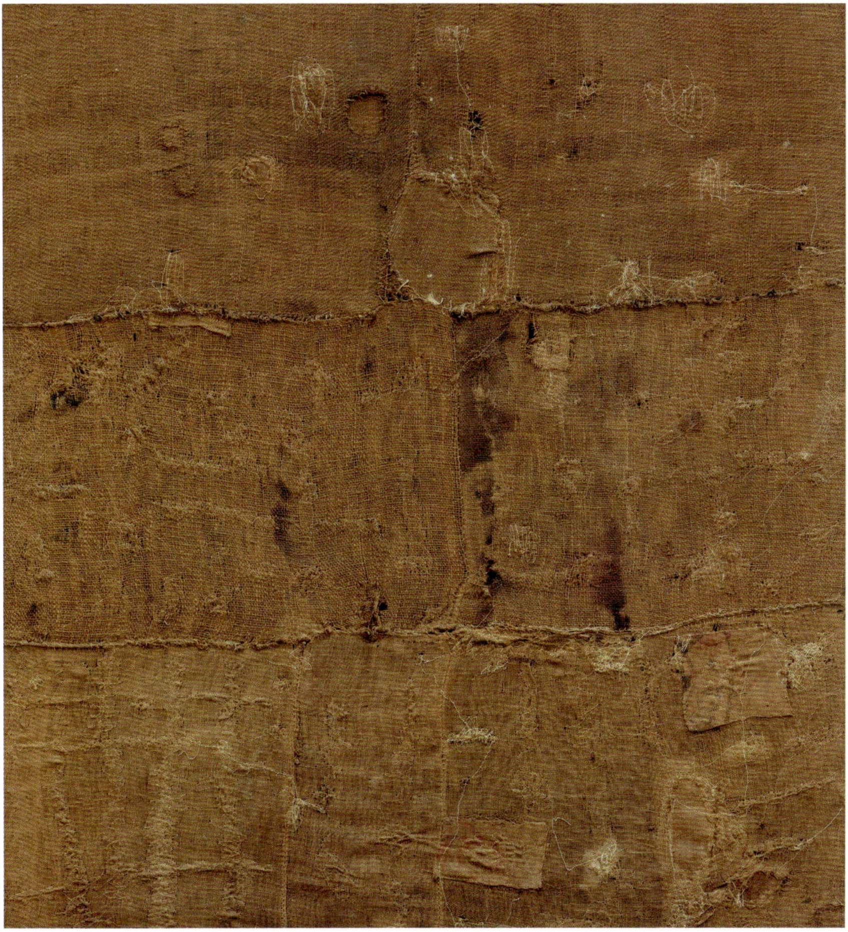

Alberto Burri | Grande sacco | 1958
Sackcloth, 200 × 188 cm, inv. no. 14651
Acquired 1980

Placed alongside paintings that artfully depict life, this coarse burlap has an interruptive effect, like the intrusion of a naked reality, or perhaps of memory. In the mind's eye, we can see, or even smell, the coal and potato cellar that was, in 1950s Europe, still ubiquitous. A poverty permeates the careful patchwork of the fabric, guarding the value of the material. At the same time, when faced with this work, which is located somewhere between a painting, a relief, and an object, the viewer becomes conscious of one of the aesthetic traditions and objectives of abstract art: the precise balancing of forms, colours, and materials. CT

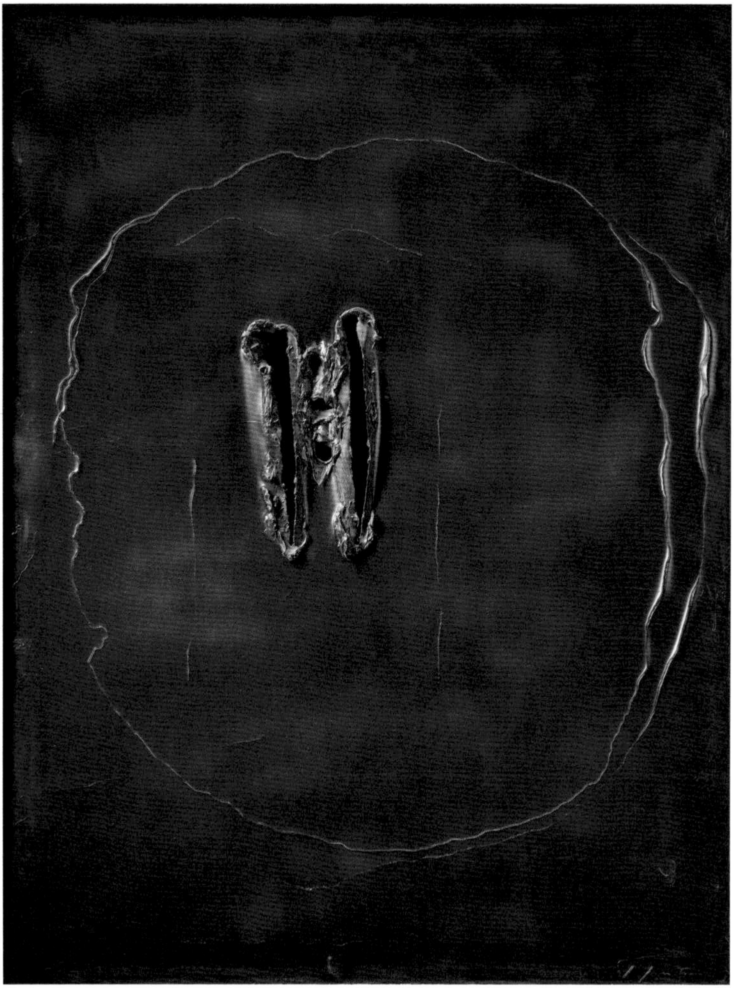

Lucio Fontana | Concetto spaziale 62 O 58 (Spatial Concept 62 O 58) | 1962
Mixed media on canvas, 116 × 88 cm, inv. no. MES 87
Michael & Eleonore Stoffel Foundation in the Bayerische Staatsgemäldesammlungen, 2008

In 1946, Lucio Fontana called for artists to overcome the classical two-dimensional painting in order to connect art with the real space of the viewer. His partial destruction of the support, with the use of cuts and perforations, does not suggest physical brutality. These gestures are not spontaneous but, rather, calculated and can be interpreted as liberating and radically innovative. They allow the canvas to extend into the space of the viewer and the diffuse space beyond the image. CT

Arnulf Rainer | Weiße Übermalung II (White Overpainting II) | 1958
Oil on hardboard, 86 × 86 cm, inv. no 15644
Donation of Arnulf Rainer, 2005

'As, in 1952, I started to paint over my own pictures (and, from 1953, also over those of others), I did not know why I was doing so, in which direction I was headed, or for how long I would do so.' Arnulf Rainer's 'overpaintings' are not only the result of spontaneous painterly gestures but are often parts of a process spanning across years through which the artist has increasingly condensed the surfaces of his images. The old is 'painted away' and new images emerge that 'are empty (and full at the same time)'. The overpainting has the effect of a protective veil that preserves that which exists and makes Rainer's own painting possible.
CT

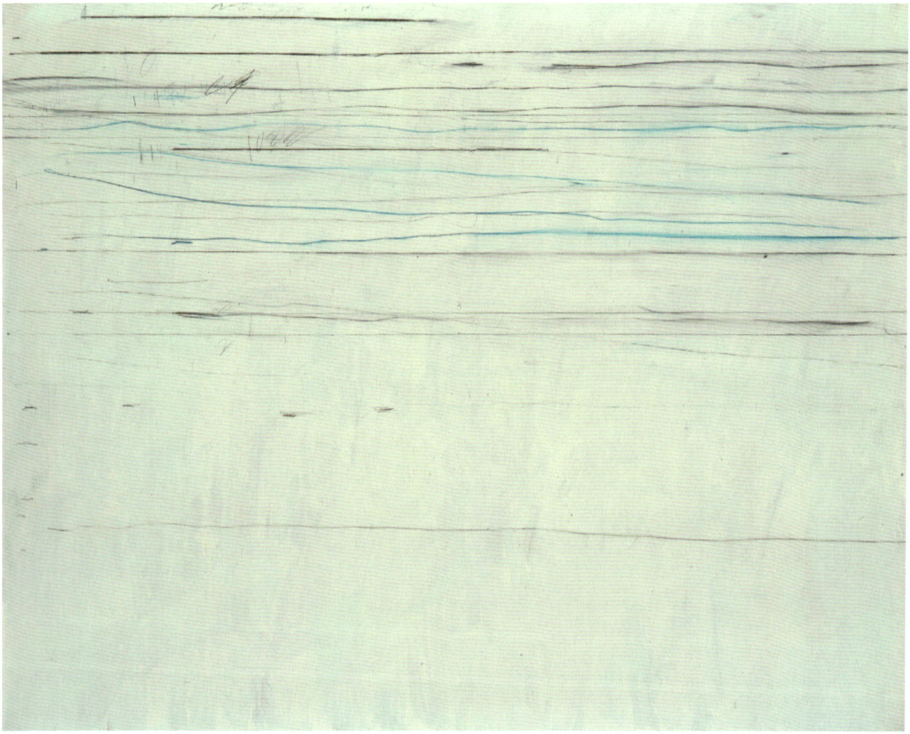

Cy Twombly | Untitled | 1971
Oil, chalk and pencil on canvas 172.5 × 221 cm, inv. no. 15340
Acquired 1993

Cy Twombly's 1971 work has a smooth outward appearance. The application of colour is loose, covering a large area, and appears divided by horizontally tiered chalk lines. Scattered notes, numbers, and letters are concentrated at one point into a single word, the motif of longing or loss: 'away'. As if in an attempt to describe or ironically paraphrase the experience of the great distance between standardized systems of knowledge and subjective perception, notations can be seen on the edge that seem to reference further plans in an open process. CT

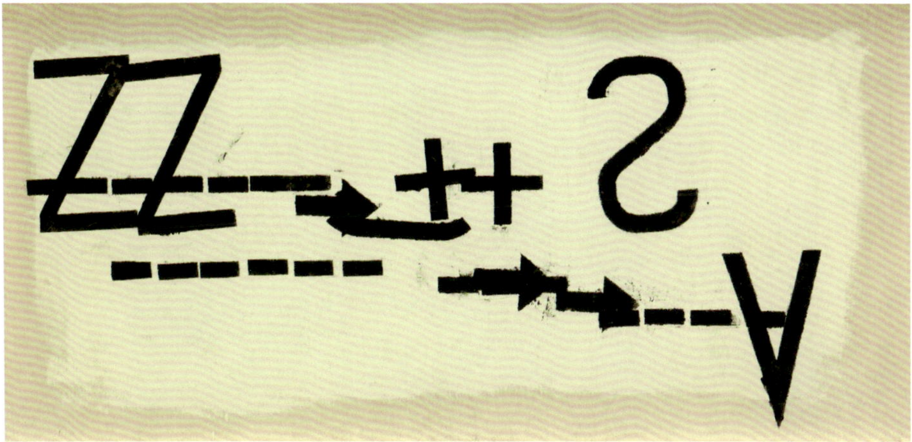

Jannis Kounellis | Untitled | 1960
Oil on primed nettle cloth, 134.5 × 284.5 cm, inv. no. 14557
Acquired 1978 with support of PIN. Freunde der Pinakothek der Moderne

From A to Z, the world has been turned on its head and, like this image, it does not come with an explanatory title. Those who go looking for the big picture will, in the end, find only isolated fragments. We recognize the signs: ++ - - --- -> -> ->. Even the inverted S seems familiar to us. This mysterious equation is displayed as if on a school whiteboard, giving us hope that there is a possibility of solving it. But the signs do not point beyond themselves and, thus, the image becomes a parable for the inexplicability of the world. CT

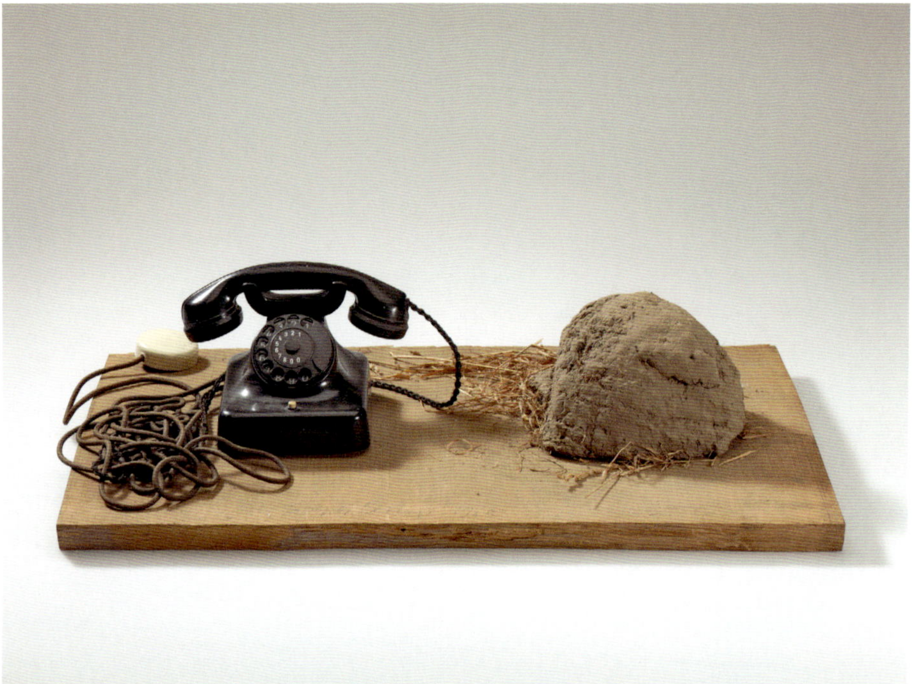

Joseph Beuys | Erdtelephon (Earth Telephone) | 1968
Telephone, lumps of clay with grass, cable, mounted on wooden board,
20 × 47 × 76 cm, inv. no. L 2376
Loan from the Collection Klüser, accessioned 2002

Put down the receiver and communicate with the earth! Beuys's *Earth Telephone* is the visualization of a call to overcome the alienation of our high-tech world and to establish a relationship between nature and technology. Beuys is not concerned here with an interpretation of the telephone, but rather with 'the forces involved in this matter', the forces between the transmitter and receiver, the effect of distance and proximity, the relationship between all worldly things and words operating in the imaginary space. CT

Hanne Darboven | 7 Panels, II (Panel 1) | 1972–73
Pencil on paper, 177.2 × 177.2 cm, inv. no. 15385
Acquired 1995

On seven square panels, 245 sheets of paper, on each of which the same 20 lines have been written, have been joined together. The work has a clear geometrical and mathematical order. Seven sheets have been placed side by side, for five rows, one above the other. The panels are accurately marked with the number of the panel and the position of the panel within the entire series. Darboven 'writes without describing'. While her personal handwriting activates the viewer on an emotional and intellectual level, Darboven evokes an unsettlingly meditative state with the neutral and evenly slow movement of her art. CT

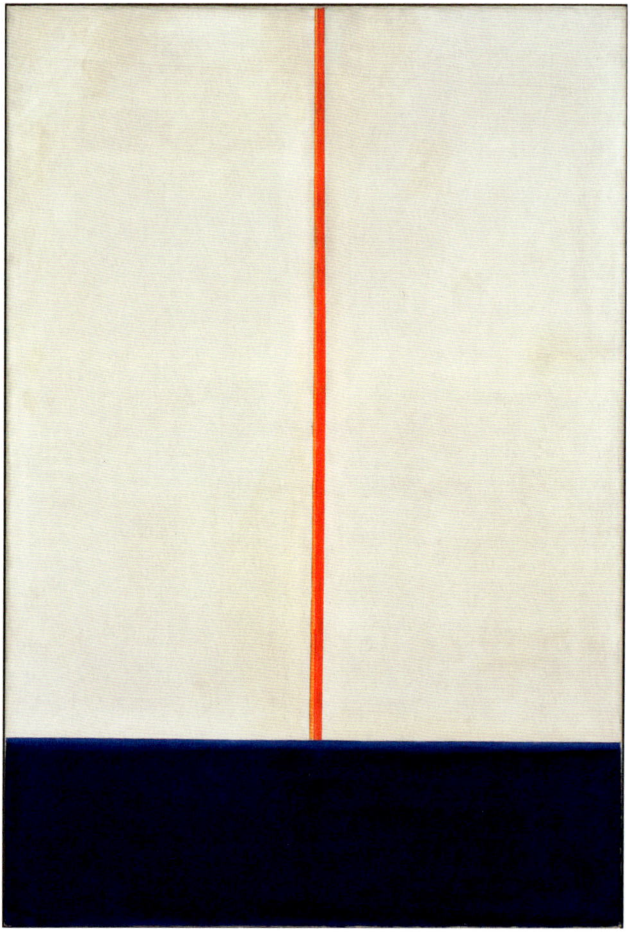

Palermo | Composition Blue-Red on White | 1965
Oil on canvas, 175 × 120.5 cm, inv. no. WAF PF 77
Collection Prinz Franz von Bayern in the Bayerische Staatsgemäldesammlungen, Wittelsbacher Ausgleichsfonds, accessioned 2007

Palermo's *Composition* has a purist rigor and draws attention to the concretely visible: the quiet living surface of the painting, the proportions of the parts, and the relationship between areas and lines. In the centre, a vertical red line encounters a horizontal blue field. Is it a ray of sunshine meeting water and illuminating its uppermost layer? The narrative poetry of the paint application suggests that the subjects, which at first appear to be purely abstract, allude to the world of objects, which Palermo has reduced to the essential.

CT

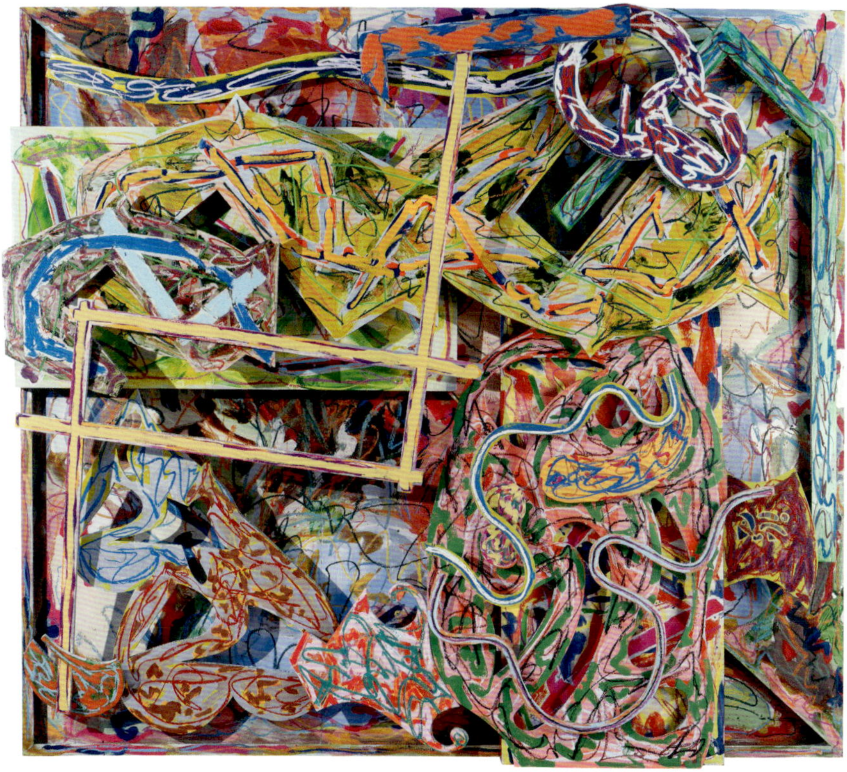

Frank Stella | Shards II | 1982
Mixed media on aluminum, 303 × 340 × 66 cm, inv. no. B 782
Acquired 1982

When art becomes detached from the world of objects, it can, as the young Frank Stella was convinced, 'live on in its own world'. With his own blend of consistency, pragmatism, and humour, Stella has realized, since the 1950s, works of great abstract rigour and questioned himself in the process. *Shards II* is a three-dimensional visual maze whose formal chaos is accompanied by shrill and chaotically applied colours. How surprising that the master of the non-representational has hidden drafting tools in this work: a protractor, a curve ruler, and a pantograph! CT

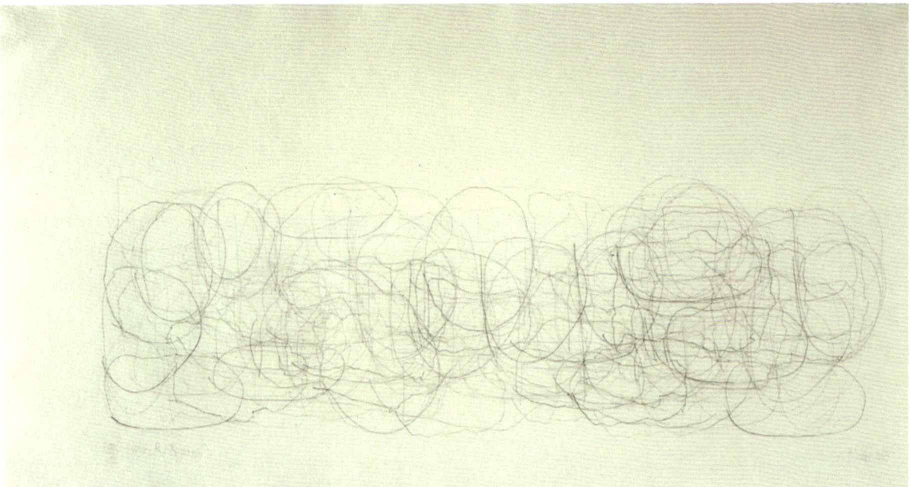

John Cage | Where R = Ryoanji (9R)/10 8/83 | 1983
Pencil on Japan paper, 25 × 48.5 cm, inv. no. 15309
Acquired 1992

In 1951, Cage began systematically making many aesthetic choices during the development of his works through actions relying on chance. For his *Ryoanji* drawings, he chose 15 stones from his collection and, with the use of *I Ching*, an ancient book of wisdom, arranged them over and over again on a paper surface in order to reflect on the emergence of the famous composition of 15 stones in the garden of Ryoanji in Kyoto. He traces around the stones with pencils, and the strength of application is also determined by the *I Ching*, resulting in an unpredictable relationship between recurrence and uniqueness in each drawing.
CT

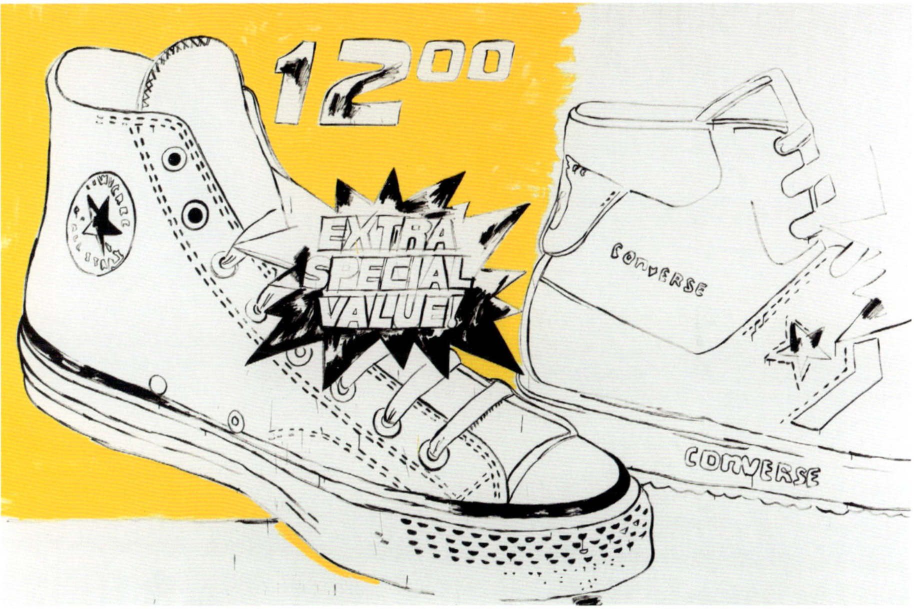

Andy Warhol | Converse Extra Special Value | 1985 or 1986
Synthetic resin on canvas, 295 × 457 × 5.5 cm, inv. no. GV 124
Acquired 2000 by PIN. Freunde der Pinakothek der Moderne for the Modern Art Collection

In *Converse Extra Special Value*, Andy Warhol depicts a commodity that is renowned and coveted throughout the world as an icon of Western consumerism. In this sense, *Converse* brand sneakers, which can be purchased for just 12 dollars, have an 'extra special value'. They offer the promise of autonomy and adventure in the urban jungle. The monumental size of this celebration of the banal commodity makes apparent that Warhol is expressing more than the globally shared need for a sure footing in Western civilization. CT

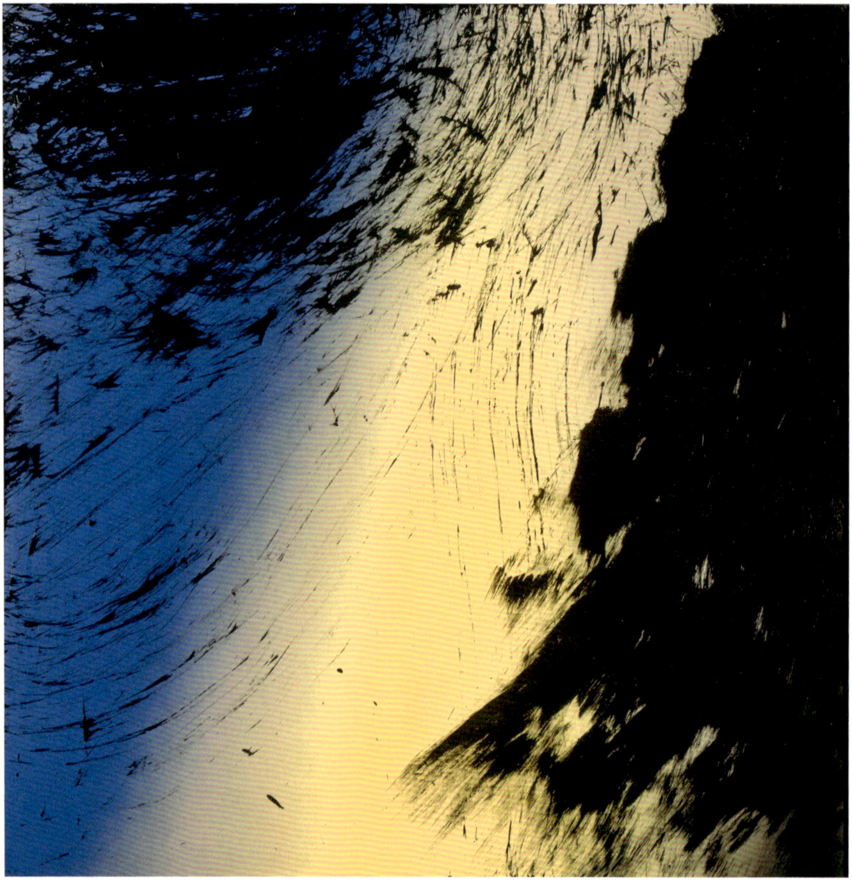

Hans Hartung | T 1980 - R 28 | 1980
Acrylic on canvas, 180 × 180 cm, inv. no. 14775
Donation of Hans Hartung, 1983

Hans Hartung is a representative of European Art Informel, which was guided by spontaneity and randomness in the creation of abstract paintings. In his late work *T 1980 - R 28*, which is executed in acrylic paint and with an artificial spraying technique, compact black areas appear in front of the diffuse lighter area in blue and yellow. These thin out at the edges into uncontrollable lines and free-flying particles. The work evokes our imagination of cosmic processes. CT

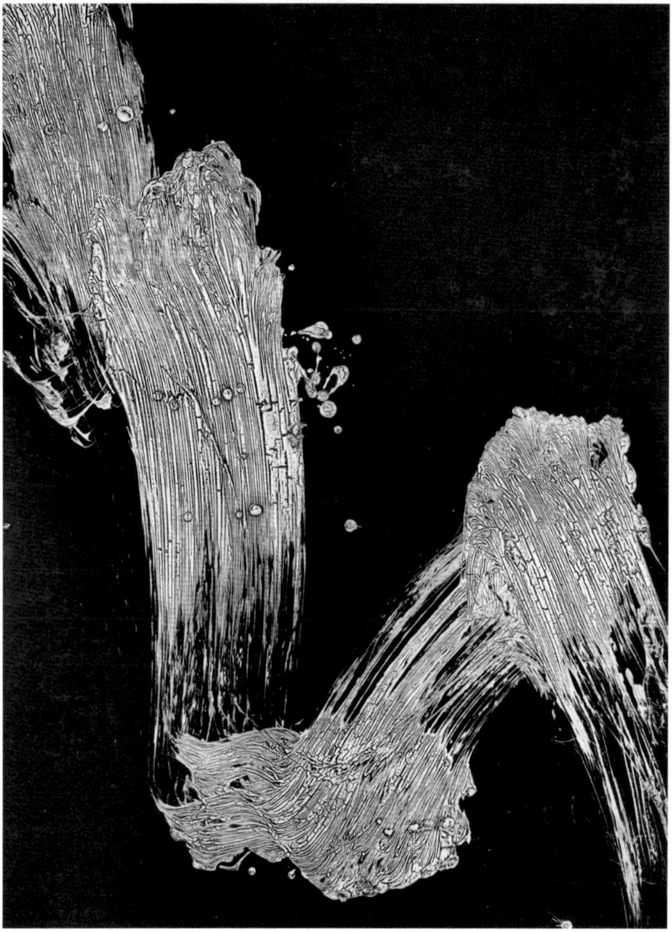

Fabienne Verdier | Melody du réel (Melody of the Real) | 2014
Ink, pigments, and lacquer on canvas,
picture VII of seven paintings, 183 × 135 cm, inv. no. 16429 7/7
Acquired 2016 with support of International Patrons of the Pinakothek

Melody du réel is the realization of an event in the present time: the stroke of a giant custom-made paintbrush that, in one breath, extends across seven paintings. From the deep, almost cosmic darkness of the background, the viewer follows the white material in its natural and monumental movement. The ups and downs of the line on each panel reflect the return and new formation of an eternal law: the melody of reality. CT

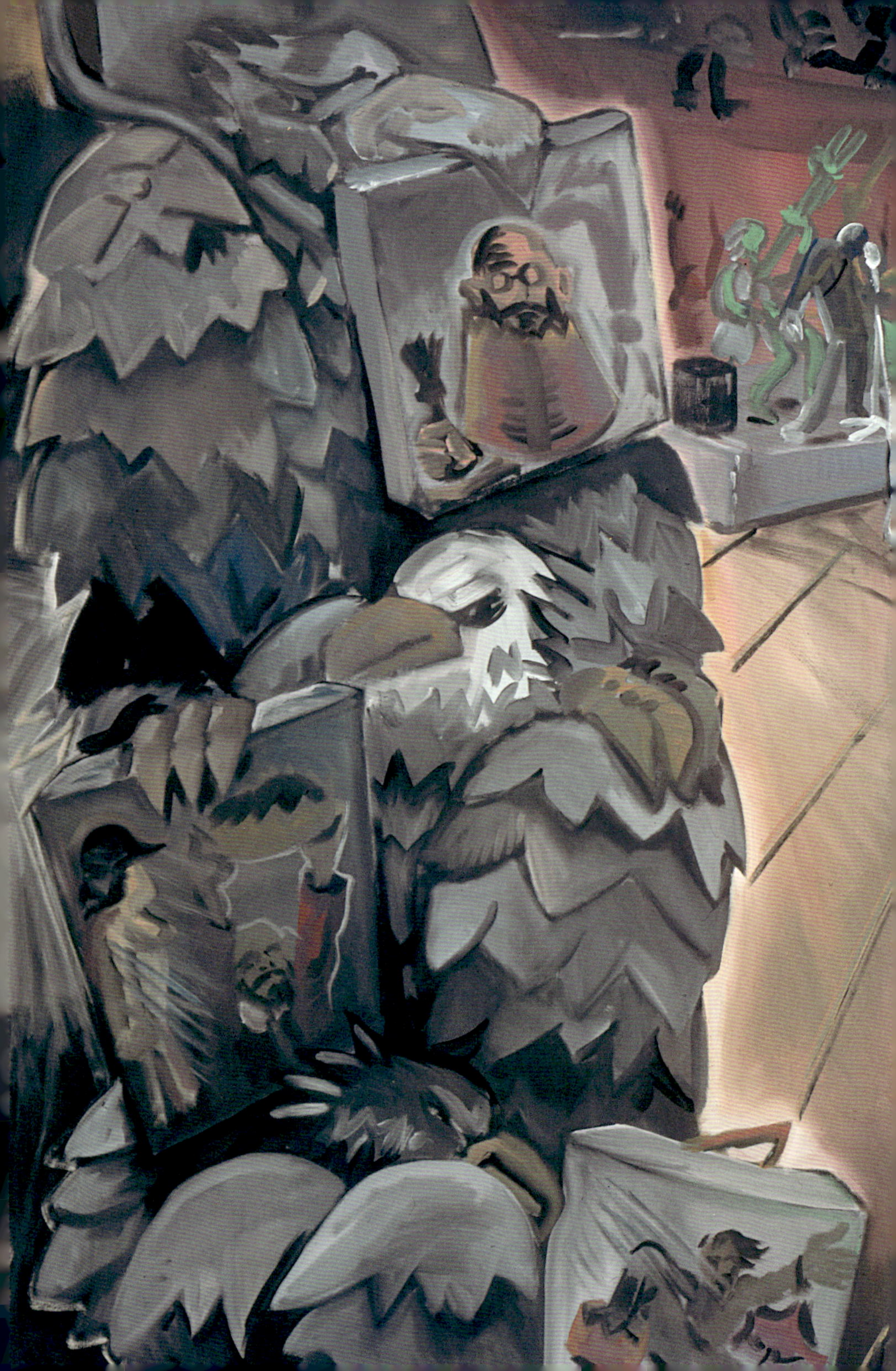

UNEASE
THE POST-WAR GENERATION

Like a grave family trauma, Germany's unresolved historical baggage dragged itself through the post-war decades: the demise of Wilhelminian certainties, the fragility of the Weimar Republic, the restless power struggles, the hate-filled tirades and murders of the thirties, the deaths of the World War. These years were shaped by the suppression of memories and a feeling of loss. The vacuum that had been left by the war finally, and fortunately, or so it seemed, led to the 'Economic Miracle' and world peace, culminating in complacency and self-assurance. A shared feeling emerged that the past had been cleared away, even if in fact it had only been swept under the carpet. Although many Germans felt they could celebrate their prosperity, this was an illusion. They continued to suppress the past until an unconquerable emptiness and traumatic grief had permeated life. In his programmatically titled volume of poetry, *Säure* (Acid), which was first published in 1979, Christoph Meckel wrote: 'Death for one, life for the other, for me a cigarette. / In my cupped hand, I want to watch ashes pile up.' He was putting into words the melancholy and potential for self-flagellation of an entire generation.

Photography showed the post-war world. With his *Cobblestone Street*, the title of which already evokes a feeling of fossilization, Bernhard Wicki conjures up devastated trees on battlefields, although the picture appears to simply show pollarded trees on the side of a street. Arno Fischer gives form to experiences of want and deprivation through the quizzical look of the boy in his *West Berlin*. His gaze suggests a wishfulness and thus also absence and longing. The photography of these years was dedicated to the visible world, in which stories and history became visible.

Painters, by contrast, were less interested in narration (most were happy to leave that to 'Socialist Realism') and were more interested in ciphers. And it is precisely this compression which makes Gerhard Richter's eerily cryptic image of the *Pallbearers*, which is based on a photograph and only departs from its monochrome palette around a single colourful face, into a monument of the act of carrying to the grave, in both a literal and a societal sense. Not poetry, the idyllic, and the glorified, but death, pain, and injury were often taken up as subjects. Maria Lassnig's 1968 *Self-Portrait with Wire Arms* thematizes traumatic corporeal infirmity, similarly to the psychological vulnerability that was symbolized by her slightly older contemporary colleague Louise Bourgeois. Though this destruction of harmonious pictorial traditions and departure from the depiction of physical integrity was also linked to Expressionism and Surrealism, in these years it was carried out with a more rigorous radicalism. Georg Baselitz's large-scale work *Finger Painting Eagle* plays with the ambivalence between the innocuous word of finger painting – typically an activity one undertakes in the company of children and in harmless colours – and the eagle, a symbol of the darker and more warlike chapters in German history. The eagle is here shown (probably for the first time in the history of art) plummeting towards the ground. Germany's heraldic animal and once the Reich's symbol of power, here the eagle becomes an allegorical figure of historical failure. Usually, the bird of prey falls upon a sacrificial animal; here, the 'king of the skies' has become the loser, in free-fall against the cheerful blue backdrop of world history. Values and objects have been turned on their heads. This is characteristic of Baselitz's work, even if some of his earlier works, including the blood-stained *Meissen Forest Workers*, still depicted heroes with both feet firmly on the ground.

Anselm Kiefer's emblematic *Nero Paints* interweaves countryside idyll with the fire of war. The palette, with its paintbrushes turned up like canons, is made into a signet of destruction and Hitler, the failed painter-turned-dictator, into the epitome of annihilation and ruin. Army clothing and palette are connected in a similarly characteristic way in the work of Markus Lüpertz, who recalls that not only did Hitler fail with respect to art, but that artists equally failed with respect to Hitler and the Nazis. Together with German intellectuals, artists did not oppose National Socialism successfully enough to adequately resist murder, war, and cultural hostility. Society's paralysis and inability to defend itself against brutal domination are also articulated in Tadeusz Kantor's *The Dead Class*, one of the most stirring works on the subject. The work is dedicated to a physiological working through of guilt and failure.

But not all artistic attempts to grapple with the past were carried out with such profound solemnity. Sigmar Polke's 1968 *Constructivist* unleashes the ironic irreverence of Pop Art upon the subject. By force of habit, we immediately recognize the black form of a truncated swastika, which has, however, been weakened through parody. Such twists of the serious into the humorous are characteristic of Polke's work. In *Envy and Greed* (1984), he drew on the ancient iconographic tradition of the deadly sins. He modernized them in a manner which, on the one hand, relies on gestural painting and on the other a stencil-like repetition of individual forms, such as the 1 mark coin, which appears as if created with a rubbing technique. Polke was, of course, not alone in his adept use of satire. As we learn from a glance at Wolfgang Hildesheimer's wonderful essay *Mitteilungen an Max über den Stand der Dinge und anderes* (Messages for Max about the Status Quo and Other Things, 1983): 'everyone here knows that one can best master difficult situations by not losing any words over them. This has the powerful advantage that everything is always in order, or at least seems to be, which anyway amounts to the same thing.' Hildesheimer made use of an ironic timbre to clearly express the ambivalent way of dealing with truth and cover-up which so obviously accompanied the post-war decades from the perspective of this generation.

Austrian art was much more pain-conscious: Arnulf Rainer's violent black overpainting and cruciform shapes are grandiose ciphers of the failure of Christian role models. His laconic style shares striking parallels with the acerbic writings of his fellow countryman Thomas Bernhard. Hermann Nitsch's *Station of the Cross* stands like a bloody counterpart to Cy Twombly's floral subjects, executed with the same technique of free-flowing, dribbled paint and traces of movement. Nitsch's work provoked the most radical associations by seeming to make the traces of blood on the body of Christ, a subject repeated thousands of times in European painting, into the sole subject of the picture. It therefore stood to reason that this art posed the greatest difficulties for Austrian Catholicism and conservatism. Its representatives particularly took issue with the performative elements that were sometimes associated with his art.

Jörg Immendorf was part of the *Neue Wilde*, a movement which deliberately undermined the beauty of the image and radicalized art. As the title suggests, his *Café Germany VII* circled around particular political and socio-critical problematics. The artist known as A. R. Penck, born as Ralf Winkler, was a painter and sculptor who practiced artistic anarchy with a particular resoluteness. A Dresden native, he – much like Georg Baselitz, Gerhard Richter, Palermo, and Imi Knoebel – left the Soviet occupation zone, i.e. East Germany, for West Germany in order to enjoy artistic freedom and to fundamentally expand it. These artists escaped from the realism dictated by art academies and cultural officials and became important engines of an artistic questioning of society during the decades of the Cold War, which was continued until 1989 in fluctuating degrees of intensity and by a variety of actors.

Bernhard Maaz

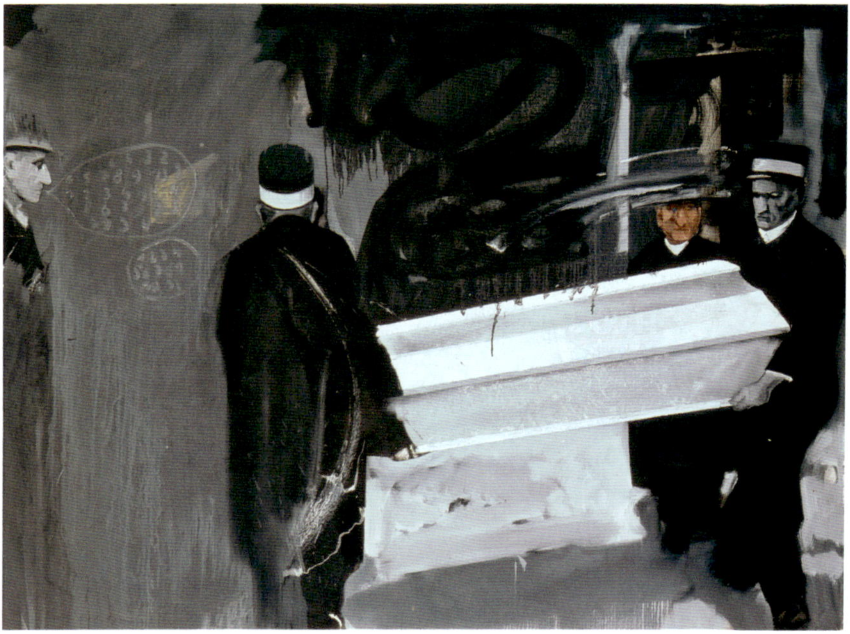

Gerhard Richter | **Sargträger** (Pallbearers) | 1962
Oil on canvas, 135 × 180 cm, inv. no. GV 56
Acquired 1979 by PIN. Freunde der Pinakothek der Moderne for the Modern Art Collection

Darkly uniformed workers are carrying a white coffin. A speech bubble containing a puzzling sequence of digits has been assigned to the figure on the left. Another bubble floats, unconnected to anyone, before the background. Who is being carried to their grave? How relevant is this death in the course of world history? The relationship between sharpness and blurriness in the image and its lack of context raise these sorts of questions, which Richter has deliberately left open. The cutting on which this is based was culled from an article in *Neue Illustrierte* from 1963: 'Whoever Loved Him Had to Die: Sensational Process Against the Philanderer Kindlinger'. CT

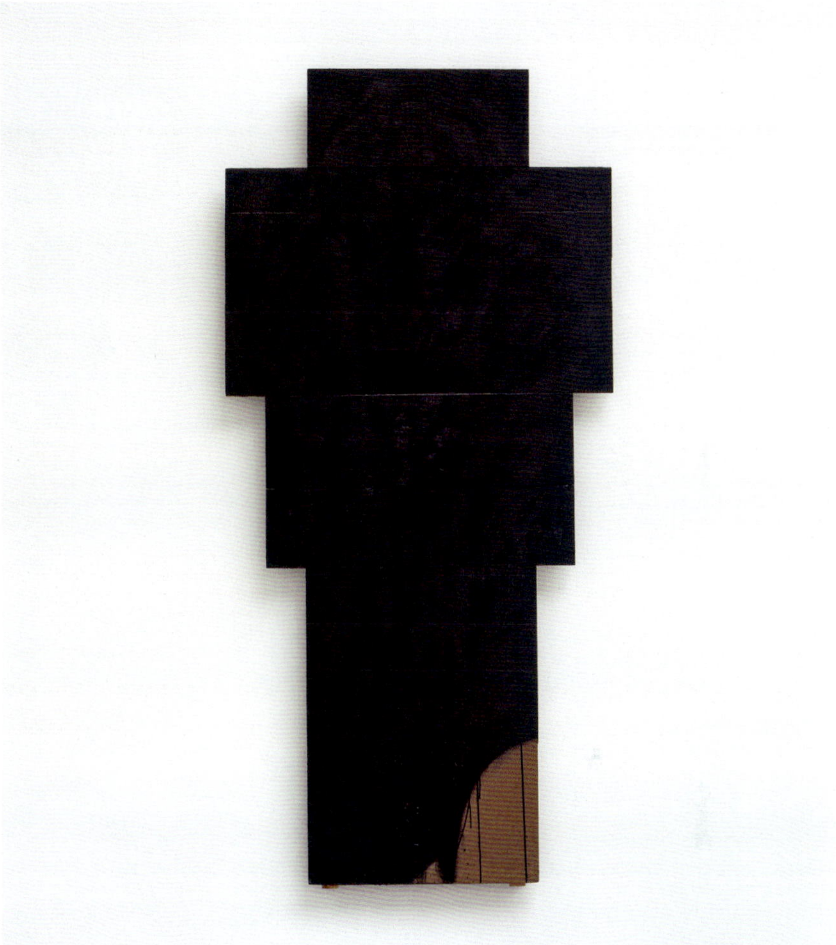

Arnulf Rainer | Kreuz Schwarz auf Ocker (Cross Black on Ochre) | 1968–74
Oil on wood, 195 × 96 cm, inv. no. 15006
Acquired 1986 with support of PIN. Freunde der Pinakothek der Moderne

A shocking pull emanates from the blackness of this work by Arnulf Rainer, like a maelstrom of darkness, brightened only by the small ochre-coloured section at the bottom of the black cross. Like the other works in his series of crosses, the unusual form of the support makes it stand out. The use of the cross introduces a sign that has been loaded with a variety of meanings, as if, with the conflictual power game between horizontal and vertical, Rainer has found the necessary complement to the competing poles of speech and silence in painting.
CT

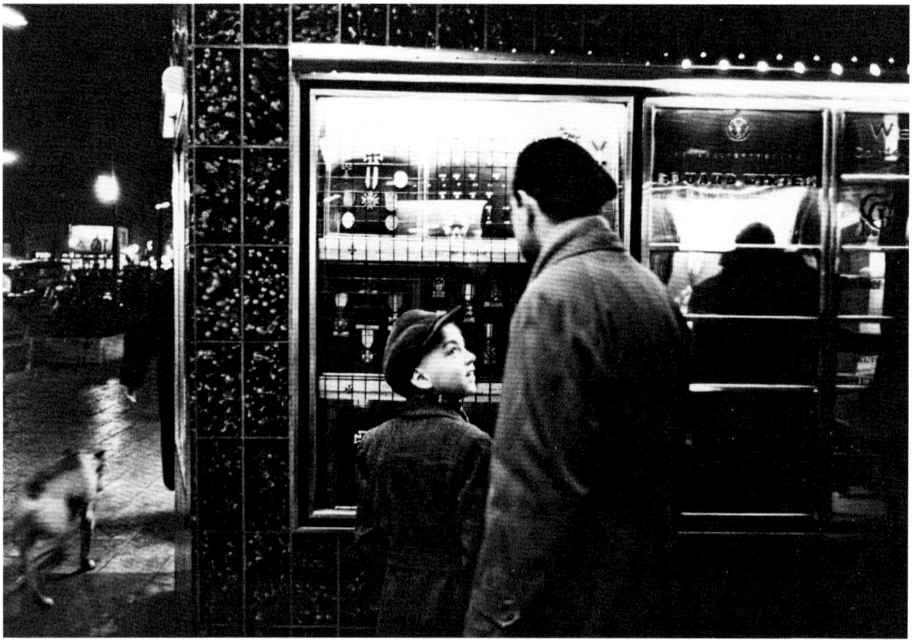

Arno Fischer | West Berlin (Kurfürstendamm) | 1956
Gelatin silver print, approx. 30 × 39 cm, inv. no. GV 217
Acquired 2011 by PIN. Freunde der Pinakothek der Moderne for the Modern Art Collection

In *Situation Berlin*, Arno Fischer, one of the most important German photographers of the post-war period, created a precise analysis of a city whose everyday life was characterized by two competing political systems. As a cross-border commuter between East and West, his work is not about good and evil, or the right or the wrong system, but about how the progressive division of Germany and the aftermath of its unresolved past manifest themselves in inconspicuous details and sensitively taken snapshots. IGI

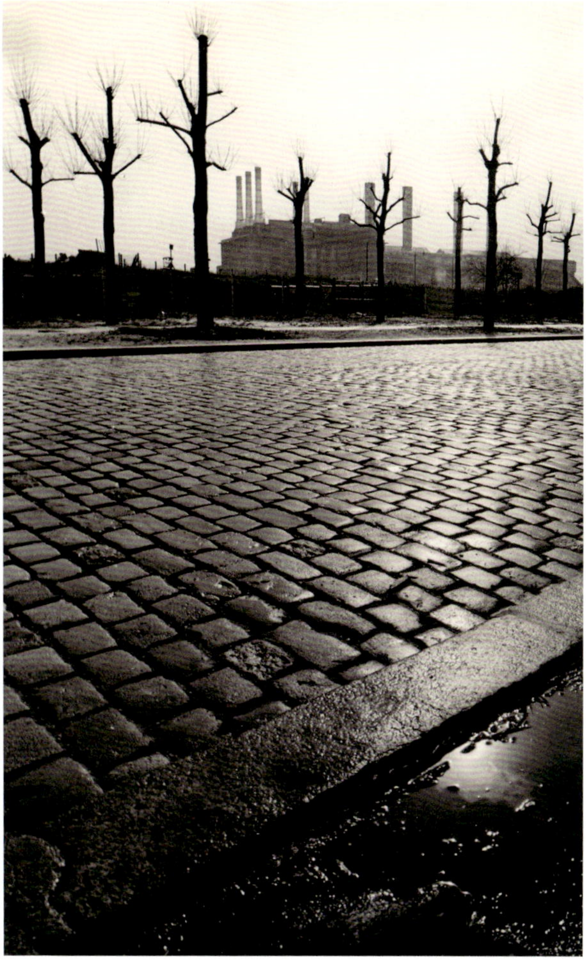

Bernhard Wicki | Kopfsteinpflasterstraße mit Pfütze (Frankreich) (Cobblestone Street with Puddle, France) | c. 1958
Silver gelatine print, approx. 30 × 24 cm, inv. no. 16425
Donation of Elisabeth Wicki-Endriss, 2015

In his works Bernhard Wicki creates an impressive picture of the time following the catastrophic events of World War II. His images are characterized by isolation and a denial of any sort of utopia, and yet they are not entirely without humanity and hope. His repertoire of subjects and his visual language have their roots in Neorealist film, from which he borrows heavily. A well-known actor in the 1950s, Wicki became one of the most important directors of the post-war period with his anti-war film *Die Brücke* (The Bridge). IGI

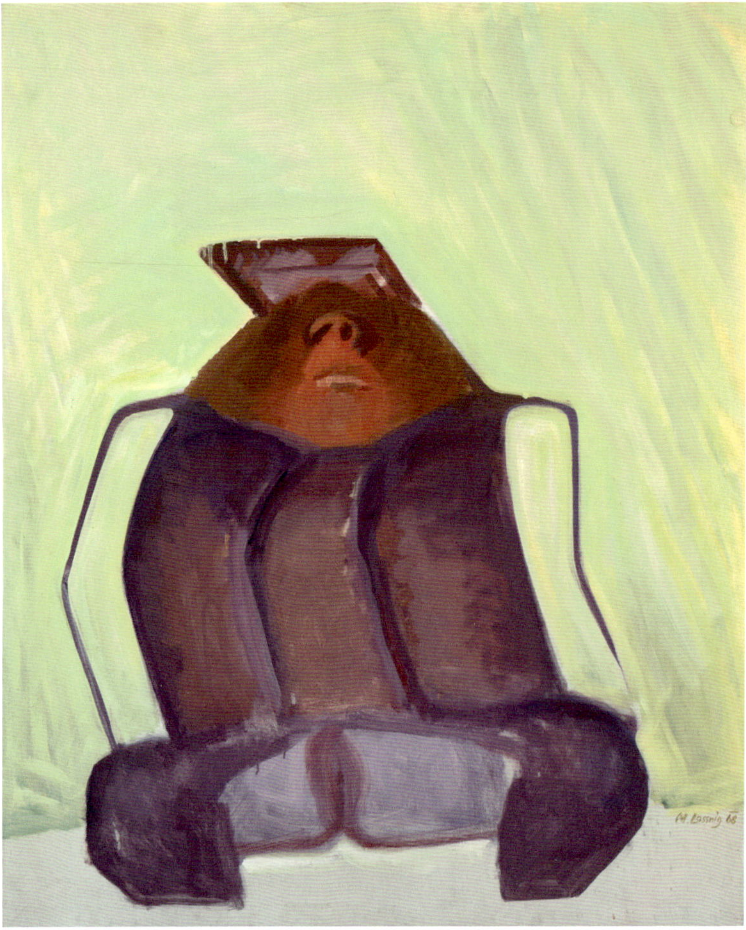

Maria Lassnig | Selbstporträt mit Drahtarmen (Self-Portrait with Wire Arms) | 1968
Oil on canvas, 120 × 100 cm, inv. no. GV 89
Acquired 1989 by PIN. Freunde der Pinakothek der Moderne for the Modern Art Collection

Lassnig refers to painting the body's sensations as 'fencing-in the clouds'. According to Lassnig, 'this subject has not been adequately explored because we lack the appropriate words to do so'. This is because such perceptions are not dependent upon the external world. The artist begins her works with her eyes shut and then, in relation to the world of objects, creates points, marks, lines, surfaces (threatening or vague sensations like plated armour, 'being patted like a dumpling', poisonous throbbing, etc.). As a researcher in the territory of the unknown, she becomes an inventor of unparalleled painterly expressions. CT

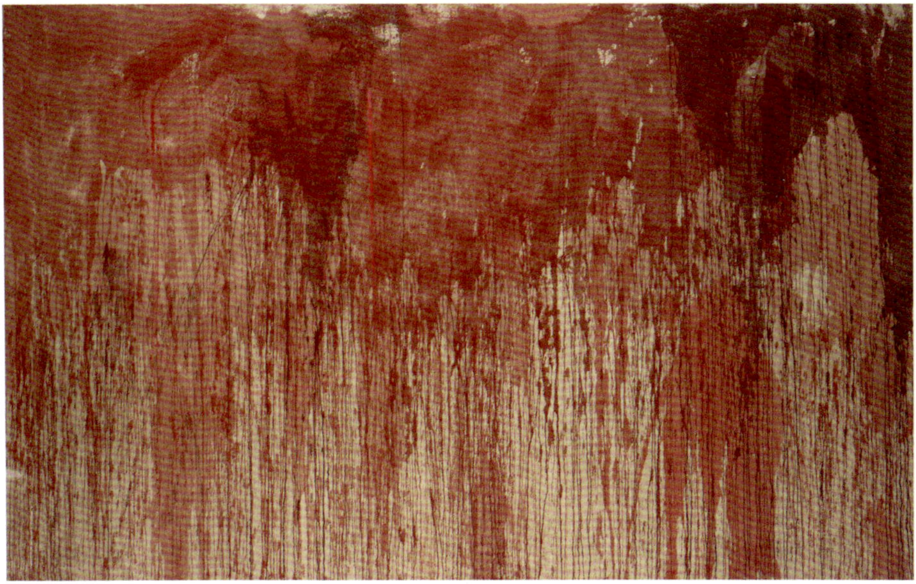

Hermann Nitsch | Kreuzwegstation (Station of the Cross) | 1961
Emulsion, whiting on unprimed jute canvas, 200 × 300 cm, inv. no. GV 84
Acquired 1986 by PIN. Freunde der Pinakothek der Moderne for the Modern Art Collection

Hermann Nitsch is a painter, draftsman, graphic artist, composer, musician, and director. Like this splatter painting, his creations can partly be ordered within his *Gesamtkunstwerk*, the *Theatre of Orgies and Mysteries* while, at the same time, extracting themselves from any context. His comprehensive approach, which also integrates other actors into dramatic theatrical actions, incorporates psychoanalysis into art. He makes use of excess to confront us with the repressed and the primordial, but equally with the positive ecstasy that can arise when one makes contact with what he calls the 'juice of life'. CT

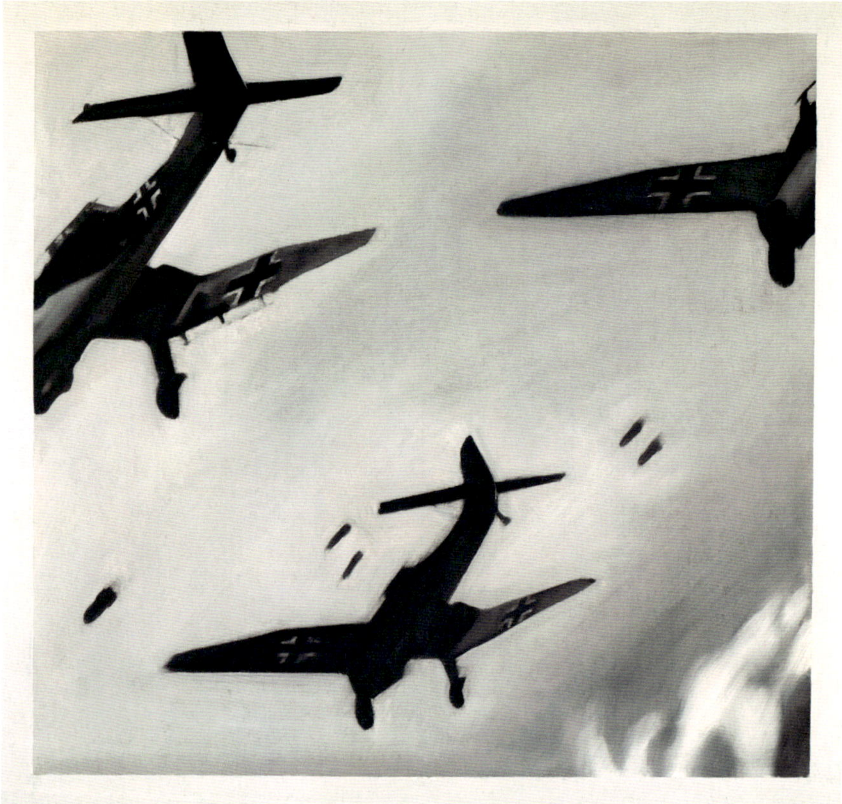

Gerhard Richter | Stukas | 1964
Oil on canvas, 80 × 80 cm, inv. no. WAF PF 22
Collection Prinz Franz von Bayern in the Bayerische Staatsgemäldesammlungen, Wittelsbacher Ausgleichsfonds, accessioned 1984

This small-scale grisaille of a Stuka squadron is the reproduction of a newspaper photo as a painting. Gerhard Richter's critical investigation of media images took place at roughly the same time as the American Pop Art movement. Andy Warhol's work was particularly influential in Richter's move towards a consciously 'inartistic' technique of reproduction. Richter's representation of dive bombers is so arresting precisely through the absence of any emotional involvement on the part of the painter in the implacable horror of the subject material.

CT

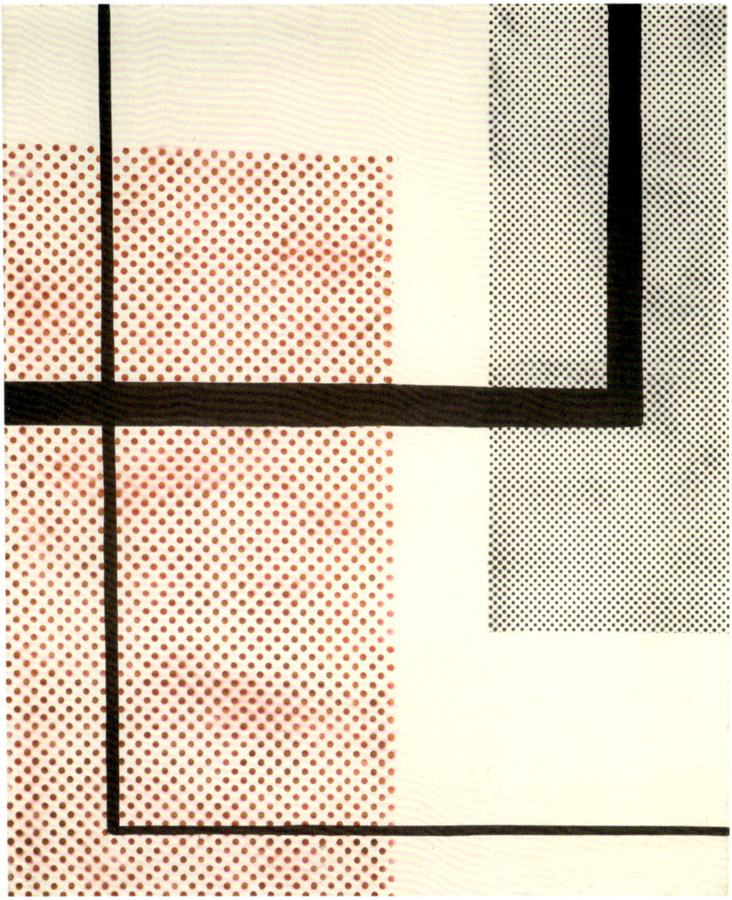

Sigmar Polke | Konstruktivistisch (Constructivist) | 1968
Emulsion on nettle canvas, 150.3 × 125 cm, inv. no. WAF PF 39
Collection Prinz Franz von Bayern in the Bayerische Staatsgemäldesammlungen, Wittelsbacher Ausgleichsfonds, accessioned 1984

The wide recognition which abstract art received in post-war Germany, despite its initial controversy, may have been one of the impulses for Polke's decision to load the seemingly suprahistorical and therefore politically and socially unproblematic geometry of this image with a biting tension: does *Constructivist* show us the detail of a swastika? Or is it the case that, much in the sense of Kippenberger's 1984 painting, 'With the Best Will in the World, I Can't See a Swastika'? *Constructivist* confronts the viewer with art's identity issues, as well as those of the country in which it was created? CT

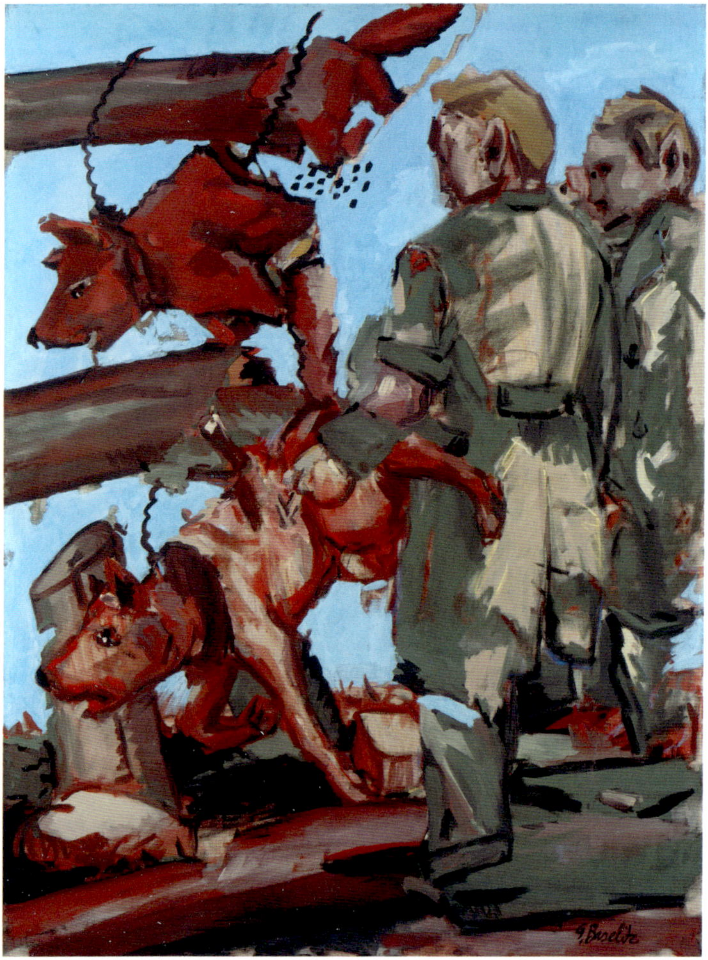

Georg Baselitz | Zwei Meißener Waldarbeiter (Two Meissen Forest Workers) | 1967
Oil on canvas, 251.2 × 200.7 cm, inv. no. 15331
Acquired 1992

In no other museum can Georg Baselitz's vital work be studied so intensively and exhaustively as in the Pinakothek der Moderne. One of the largest ensembles of this enormously productive and distinctive painter and sculptor's works is on show here. In addition to his well-known headstand works – and chronologically preceding them – Baselitz also critically responded to Dresden painting from Ferdinand Rayski to Oskar Kokoschka. Here he connects the pursuit of painterly excellence with the question of the role of the hero, as well as the failure of alleged heroes. BM

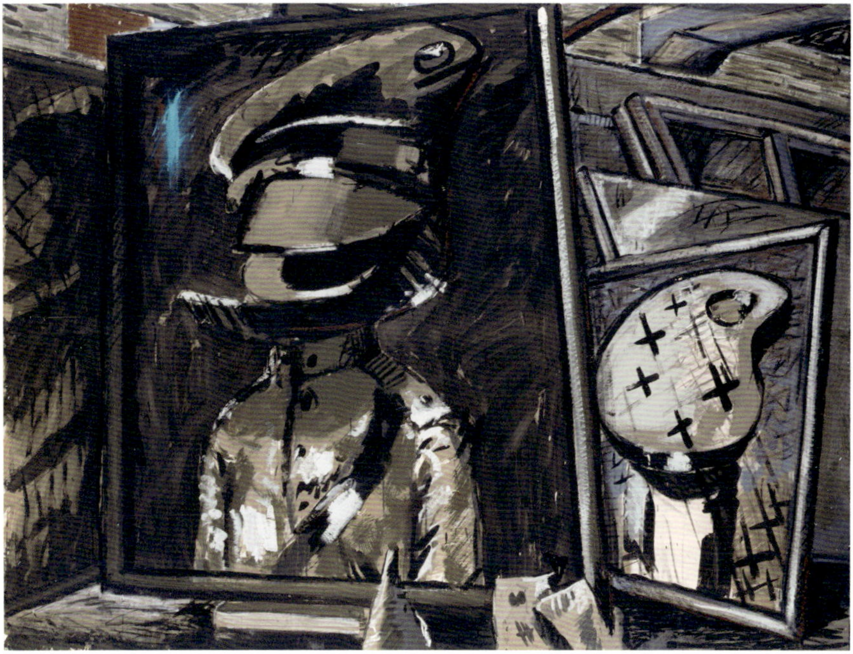

Markus Lüpertz | **Untitled** (Atelier) | c. 1974
Distemper on paper on canvas, 193 × 255 cm, inv. no. WAF PF 29
Collection Prinz Franz von Bayern in the Bayerische Staatsgemäldesammlungen,
Wittelsbacher Ausgleichsfonds, accessioned 1984

Since the 1970s, Lüpertz has dedicated himself to 'German topics', which he has laid bare of clichés, both stylistically and in terms of content. The studio shown here is not a light and airy place. Rather, it seems like an attic filled with forgotten, dormant images. One work depicts a brown uniform from the time of the Third Reich. In the eyes of the beholder, the depiction comes to life shockingly, painfully overwhelming the viewer. But only a shell remains of the uniform, which once suggested authority but has now been emptied of its meaning. The uniform has been transformed into the banal and it is difficult reconcile it with our memory and knowledge of the past. CT

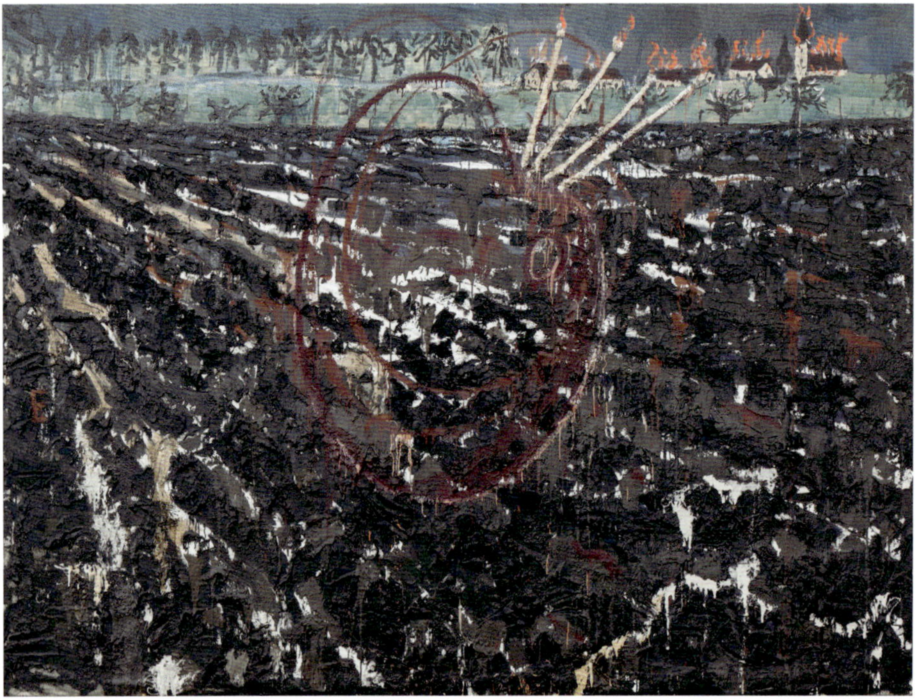

Anselm Kiefer | Nero malt (Nero Paints) | 1974
Oil on burlap canvas, 221.5 × 300.6 cm, inv. no. WAF PF 51
Collection Prinz Franz von Bayern in the Bayerische Staatsgemäldesammlungen, Wittelsbacher Ausgleichsfonds, accessioned 1984

We see scorched earth and behind it, as if painted by a child's hand, a village being engulfed by fire. The picture's title, *Nero Paints*, as well as the depiction of a palette and brushes, set off a chain of associations in the viewer. This chain finally leads us to Hitler as 'artist' and makes us conscious of the fact that each painter not only selects the topic and style of their pictures, but must also define their work with respect to a fatal line of ancestors. CT

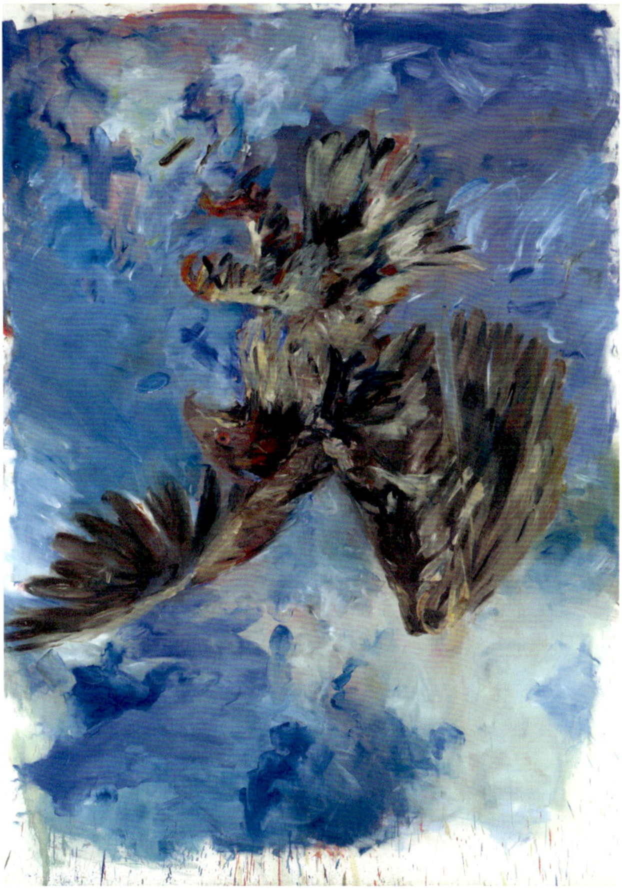

Georg Baselitz | **Fingermalerei Adler** (Finger Painting Eagle) | 1972
Oil on canvas, 249.5 × 180.3 cm, inv. no. L 2573
Loan from Wittelsbacher Ausgleichsfonds, accessioned 2016

George Baselitz's *Finger Painting Eagle* is one of his 'headstand paintings', through which he subverts the close connection between the object of the image and its content. With this inversion, he clears the way for a sensual painting, freed of content, which, however, plays a game of deception. The fall of the eagle, a classic emblem and symbol of the Federal Republic of Germany, is a reminder of the inadequate coming to terms with the Nazi era among the general populace. In the immediate aftermath of the war, National Socialist architecture was left standing and many former Nazi civil servants retained their positions. The only things that were removed from public buildings were the eagles (and even then, sometimes just the swastikas on them). Baselitz thus makes reference to the powerlessness of art. CT

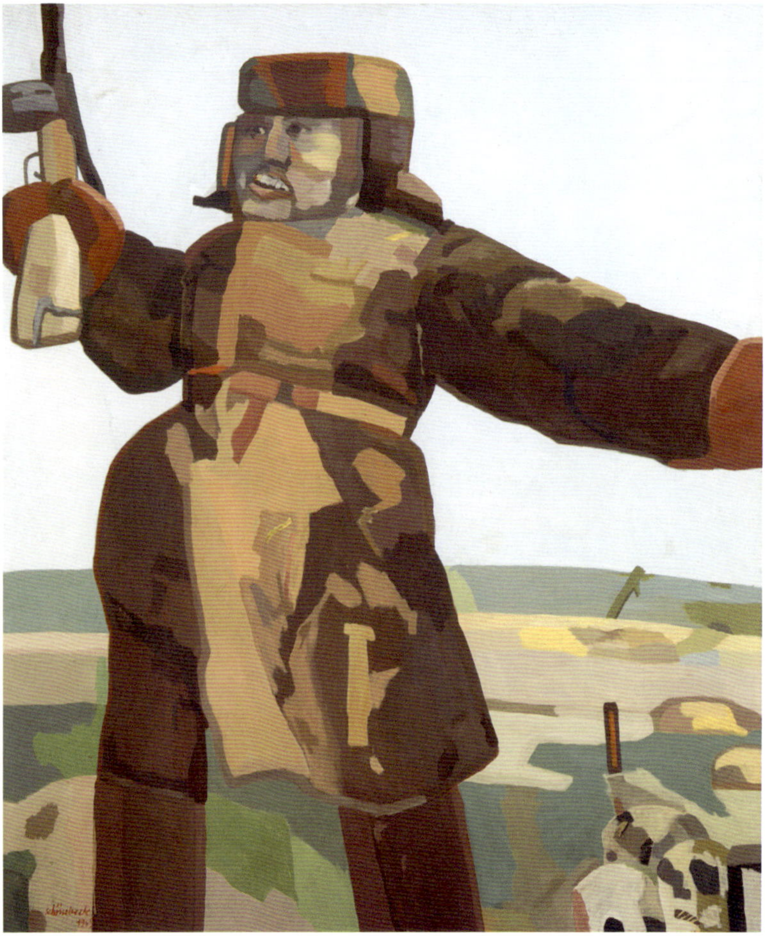

Eugen Schönebeck | **Der Rotarmist** (The Red Army Soldier) | 1965
Oil on canvas, 220 × 184.5 cm, inv. no. GV 64
Acquired 1982 by PIN. Freunde der Pinakothek der Moderne for the Modern Art Collection

This portrayal of heroism was inspired by a series in *Der Spiegel* which displayed the victory of the Red Army over the Germans in Stalingrad from the Russian perspective. *The Red Army Soldier* is related to propaganda pictures. While such images clearly have a political purpose, Schönebeck illustrates here a perhaps Romantic, but complex and, finally, doubtful confrontation with the possibilities of painting during the Cold War. As in Baselitz's *Helden* and *Neue Typen*, which were painted around the same time, this work also reflects the artist's preoccupation with his role as a lone fighter. CT

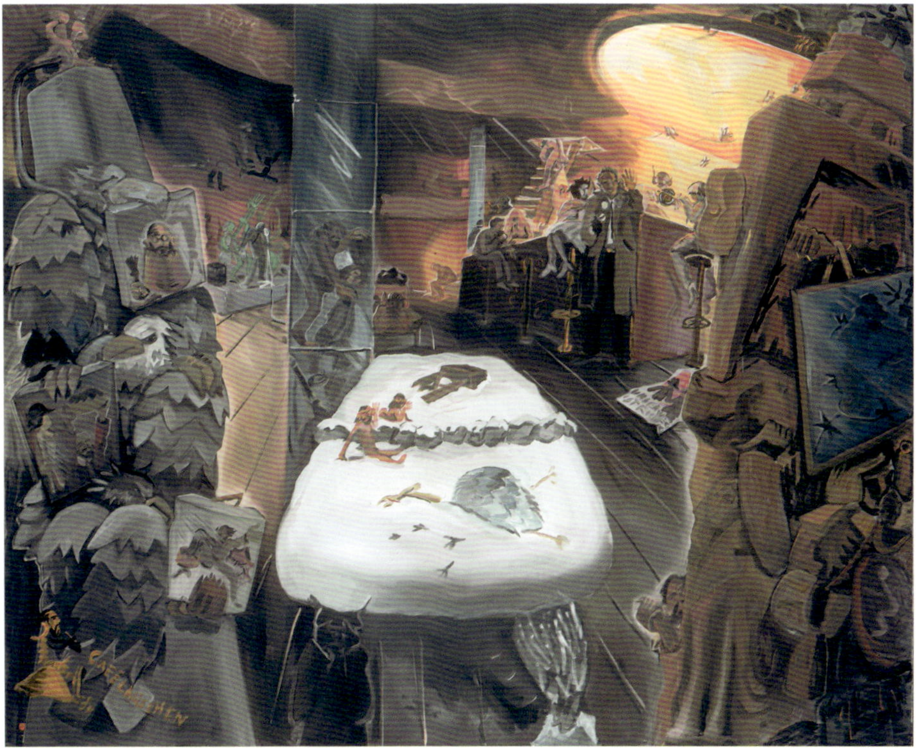

Jörg Immendorff | Café Deutschland VII (Café Germany VII) | 1980
Acrylic on canvas, 280 × 350 cm, inv. no. 14888
Acquired 1984

In this work from his *Café Germany* series, Immendorf shows a dramatically lit underground bar. In this overheated atmosphere, politicians and figures from various cultural scenes are having a rendezvous in between monumental sculptures covered by a horror vacui of allegorical figures. It is the Cold War. From across a broken sheet of ice, Immendorff, who lived in the East, greets A. R. Penck, who lived in the West. On one side of the sheet lies the remains of an eagle and, on the other, a fallen watchtower. CT

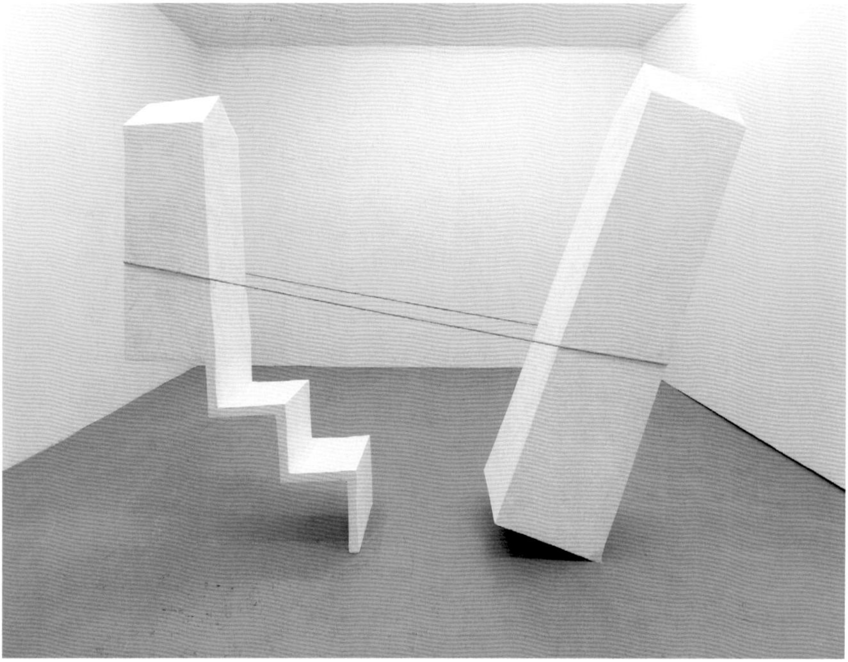

Inge Mahn | Balancing Towers | 1989
Plaster on iron construction, 218 × 280 × 50 cm, in inventory
2024 acquired by PIN. Freunde der Pinakothek der Moderne for the Modern Art Collection

Inge Mahn developed her characteristic formal language while studying under Joseph Beuys at the Düsseldorf academy. She used white plaster to form staircases, towers and dwellings that dominate the space as installations. *Balancing Towers* explores the fragility of relationships. One tower rests on a staircase, the other has become extremely unstable; the two are held together by a rope. Created during a residency in New York in 1989, the sculpture blends Mahn's distinctive formal style with impressions of the metropolis and influences of Minimal Art. VH

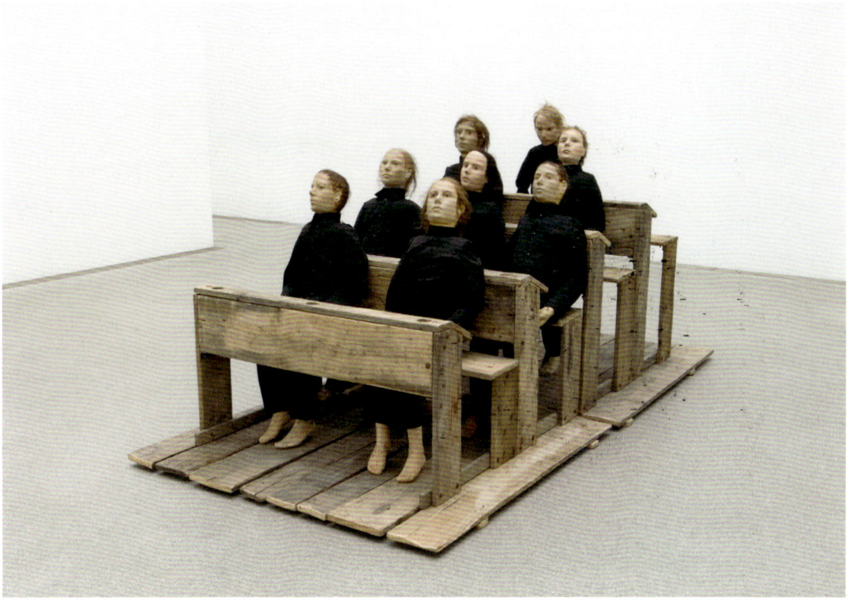

Tadeusz Kantor | Die tote Klasse (The Dead Class) | 1975
Wooden floor, benches, tables, dolls, clothing, 150 × 150 × 300 cm, inv. no. 184 GV
Acquired 2007 by PIN. Freunde der Pinakothek der Moderne for the Modern Art Collection

An accidental look into an old, abandoned village school became an important source of inspiration for Tadeusz Kantor. It opened up 'the dark depths of memory' and its mysterious and tremendous power to him. This power can destroy and create, and it may be found 'at the beginning [...] of every design. At the beginning of art'. *The Dead Class* belongs to the images, texts, and theatre projects of his *Theatre of Death*. Puppets – children who seem as old as shrunken old men – gaze steadfastly at the viewer from old-fashioned school desks, a *tableau vivant* of life and death. CT

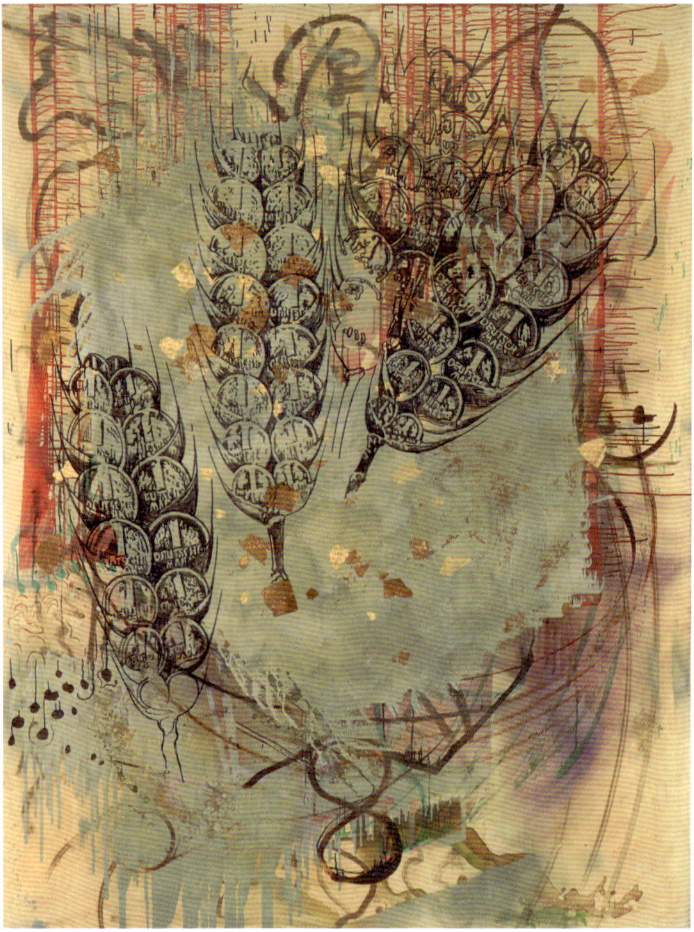

Sigmar Polke | **Neid und Habgier** (Envy and Greed) | 1984
Acrylic, lacquer and gold leaf on canvas, 259 × 200 cm, inv. no. MES 203
Michael & Eleonore Stoffel Foundation in the Bayerische Staatsgemäldesammlungen, 2008

Envy and greed are two of the seven deadly sins according to Catholicism. Polke does not show us a figurative, allegorical version of this subject, which has long enjoyed immense popularity in the fine arts. Rather, in front of a moving, abstract painting, he places severed ears of wheat, filled with the currency of West Germany, and even applies gold leaf in various places. The artist, who frequently dedicated his work to historical and political situations, often ironically, seems to refer here in the title to the frequently neither positive nor prosperous qualities of the capitalist economic system. FS

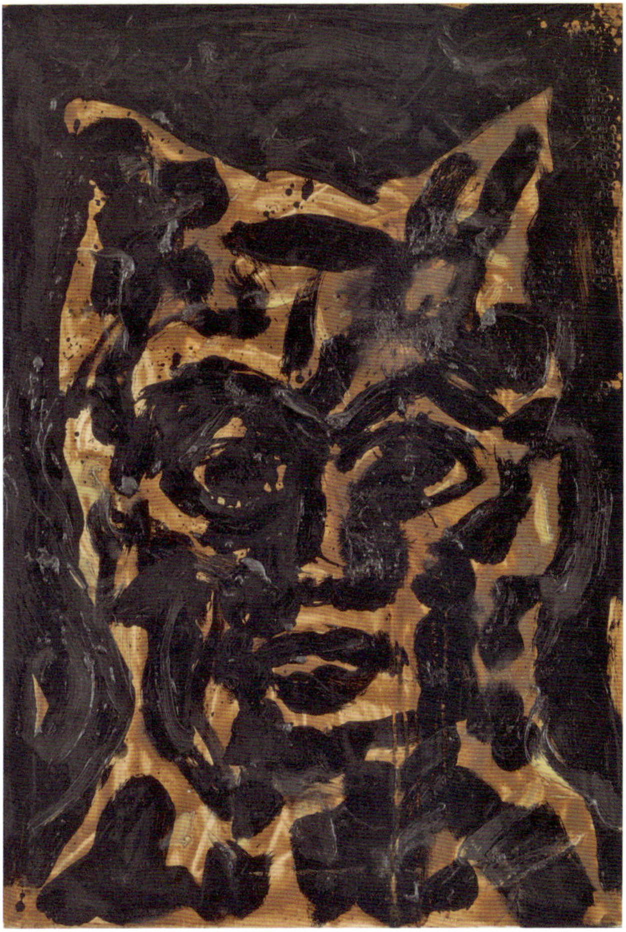

A. R. Penck | Ich in New York (Me, in New York) | 1989
Oil on canvas, 99.5 × 69.5 cm, inv. no. MES 199
Michael & Eleonore Stoffel Foundation in the Bayerische Staatsgemäldesammlungen, 2008

In *Me, in New York*, A. R. Penck displays the form of a spontaneous and powerful predatory feline which has been brought into the urban jungle of New York. After his expatriation from the GDR, Penck was confronted early on with the market-oriented plastic and high-gloss world of Western urban life, against which he was trying to protect himself and in which he nevertheless had to find his feet as an artist. Penck, who had to defend himself from Stasi surveillance even in the West, has transformed himself here into an uncontrollable predator who is not to be trifled with. CT

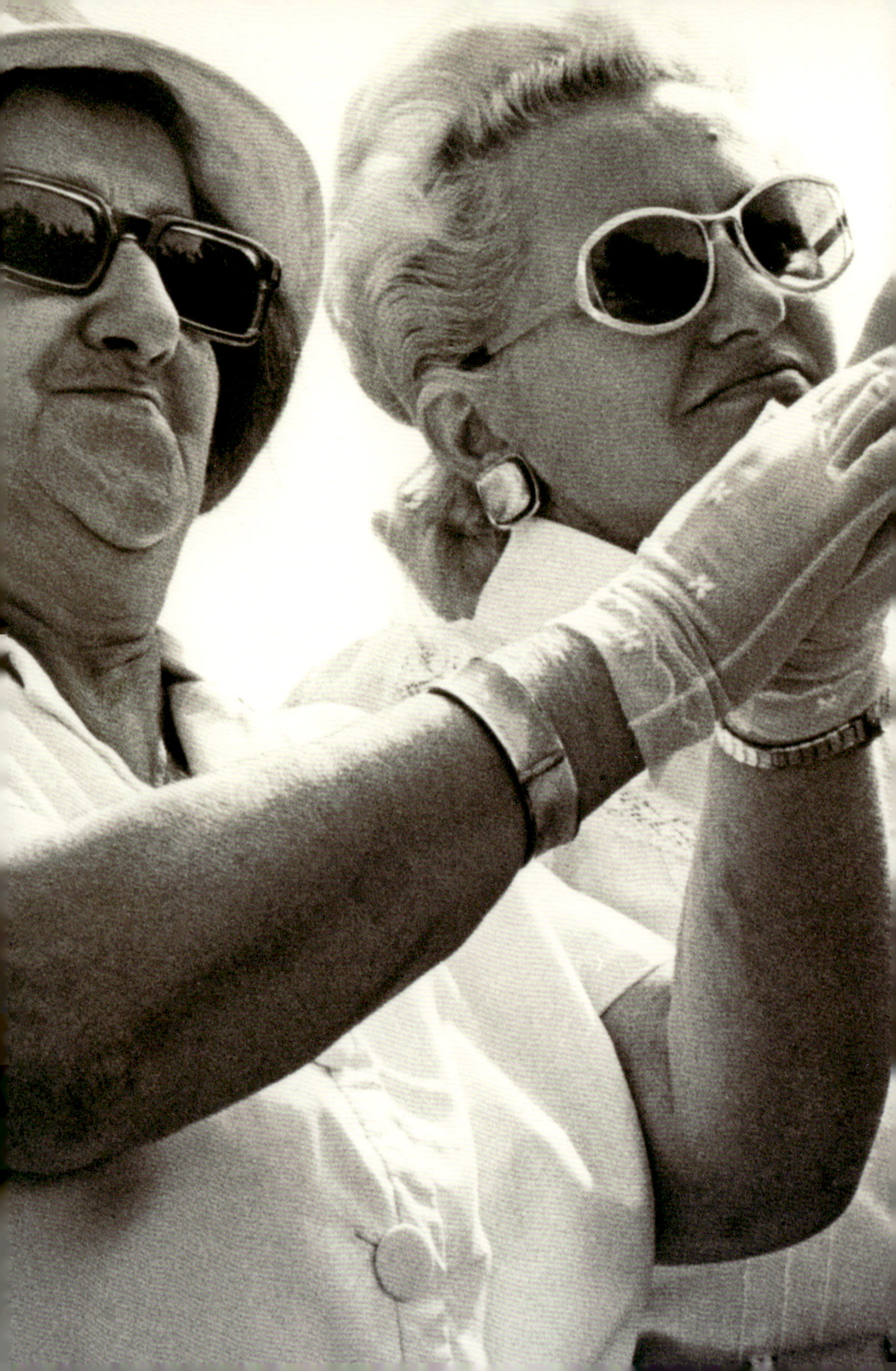

NEW DOCUMENTS
THE PHOTOGRAPHY OF THE 1960S AND 1970S

The exhibition *New Documents* went on show in early 1967 at New York's Museum of Modern Art, subsequently toured the US, and cleared the way for a new era in American photography. Diane Arbus, Lee Friedlander, and Garry Winogrand, all of whose works were represented in the show, stood for a new attitude within documentary photography. Their works were based on their personal interests, as well as an overtly subjective view of reality. Despite the differences in their artistic approaches, the photographers were united by the attention they paid to the 'ordinary' and the focus they placed on society's imperfections and fragilities. Arbus and her colleagues drew from photographers like Walker Evans and Robert Frank, who had already made photographic history with their unsentimental depictions of the realities of American life.

Until today, Lee Friedlander's work has focused on the social landscape and its conditions. What interests him are not natural landscapes and the ways in which urban sprawl has reshaped them, but the urban space in which human beings act. The artist sees public space as a place which is not only variously constructed by people, but which also shapes their actions in turn. This was reflected in many of his images taken against the backdrop of the tense political and social climate in the US of the 1960s – which was shaped by the Vietnam War, the anti-war movement, and the civil rights and women's movement. Friedlander's images, as well as those of Garry Winogrand, grew out of a recognition that social documentary photography that conveys the photographer's sense of dismay cannot effect political or social change. The works of both artists have no obvious educational or moralizing motivation, as was often the case in the photography featured in *Life* and other magazines at the time. By making use of decidedly subjective imagery, they concerned themselves above all with description. Winogrand's photographs of public gatherings, whether of everyday events on the street or of political and social events, are often quite similar to journalistic photography. However, they would have been unusable in news reports due to their indifferent, detached attitude. Friedlander in turn developed a singular and idiosyncratic style in order to mould the disparate images of America he encountered during his many trips into visual forms that could be read as 'metaphors of the dislocations and disaffectations of the time' (Andy Grundberg).

In 1975, a new troupe of photographers took the stage, with the seminal exhibition *New Topographics: Photographs of a Man-Altered landscape*, organized by the International Museum of Photography in Rochester. Their works were dedicated to the American landscape and the changes it was gradually undergoing. 'Documentary style' photography was also at the centre of their practice. They drew from role models like Walker Evans, Robert Frank, and Lee Friedlander. However, they understood themselves above all as carrying on the tradition of the topography-informed photography of the 19th century. Californian artist Ed Ruscha's images are considered paradigmatic of this new approach, whose practitioners, at first glance, were not primarily concerned with achieving an individual style. The impact of his photobooks, including *Every Building on the Sunset Strip* (1966), lies in their seemingly unambitious images which limit themselves to recording essential topographical elements. The photographers who featured in the exhibition were centrally concerned with creating a distanced and analytical form of representation. Among them were Robert Adams, Lewis Baltz, Nicholas Nixon, Stephen Shore, and, as the only European representatives, Bernd and Hilla Becher.

In contrast, the works of southerner William Eggleston are radically subjective and personal. They were dismissed by critics as banal and boring when they first featured at the Museum of Modern Art in New York in 1976. The exhibition itself was referred to in the press as 'the most hated show of the year'. Above all, critics rejected Eggleston's approach, according to which he spontaneously photographed apparently incidental, everyday objects with an apparent carelessness and then translated these 'meaningless' subjects into exquisite colour prints by means of a costly and time-intensive dye transfer process, a novelty within the artistically ambitious photography of that time. In Eggleston's photographs, which are strongly marked by subjects connected to the Mississippi Delta and its light, colour is not just an adjective but becomes constitutive of the image. In retrospect, this exhibition is regarded as a quantum leap forward on the path towards establishing colour photography within art photography, which until that time had been dominated by black and white. What is often forgotten is that another colour photographer, Stephen Shore, was also given a solo exhibition at MoMA just a few weeks after Eggleston. Shore's imagery initially seems akin to Eggleston's, yet his works are shaped by a fundamentally different attitude, one focused on observation and recording. The incipient 'rush to colour', as Lewis Baltz put it in both apposite and critical terms, would lead in the following years to the ubiquitous use of colour in art photography, not only in the United States, but also in Europe and, especially, in Germany.

In Germany, the 'auteur photographers' of the seventies were responding to American photographers' aim of objectively recording reality. Their works were featured in a 1979 exhibition at the Rheinisches Landesmuseum Bonn, *In Deutschland* (In Germany). Like their American counterparts, most of the featured artists pursued a style that had emerged from the documentary tradition. Alongside the works of the co-curator Wilhelm Schürmann, the show also included images by Michael Schmidt, Heinrich Riebesehl, Candida Höfer, and Thomas Struth. In their works, which were created over long periods of time, serially produced, and often still realized in black and white, they engaged with the day-to-day reality of West German life, without their images ever being suitable for daily journalistic consumption. The exhibition documented the high point of a development through which photography, both historical and contemporary, was able to assert itself in Germany as an independent art form. Another important step in this direction was *documenta 6*, which subsequently became known as the 'media documenta' and which took place two years earlier and displayed not only works by contemporary artists, but also sketched out a comprehensive survey of the history of photography. It also forged links with a history which had been lost during National Socialism and promoted the incorporation of photography into museums at a time when the news media had undergone a paradigm shift away from print towards TV. The art market, publishers, local photography groups, and public museums also responded to the growing interest in photography. In rapid succession, specialized galleries were opened, for example the Galerie Wilde in Cologne or Lichttropfen (later, Kicken) in Aachen. Art museums established their own photo collections, among them Museum Folkwang in Essen and Museum Ludwig in Cologne. Some publishers created specialized journals or began to focus almost exclusively on photography, as did the Schirmer/Mosel publishing house in Munich. Regional art associations (*Kunstvereine*) also regularly displayed photographic exhibitions and made a fundamental contribution to the art form by discovering forgotten or still-unknown photographers. Last but not least, photographers themselves created networks at local and international levels, for example the *Werkstatt für Photographie*, which was founded in 1976 by Michael Schmidt in West Berlin. From here, photographers no longer just followed developments in the USA, but also in the 'other' Germany (the GDR), where Arno Fischer, Sibylle Bergemann, and Ulrich Wüst, among others, established their own photographic community which directed the camera at uncensored life under 'Actually Existing Socialism'.

Inka Graeve Ingelmann

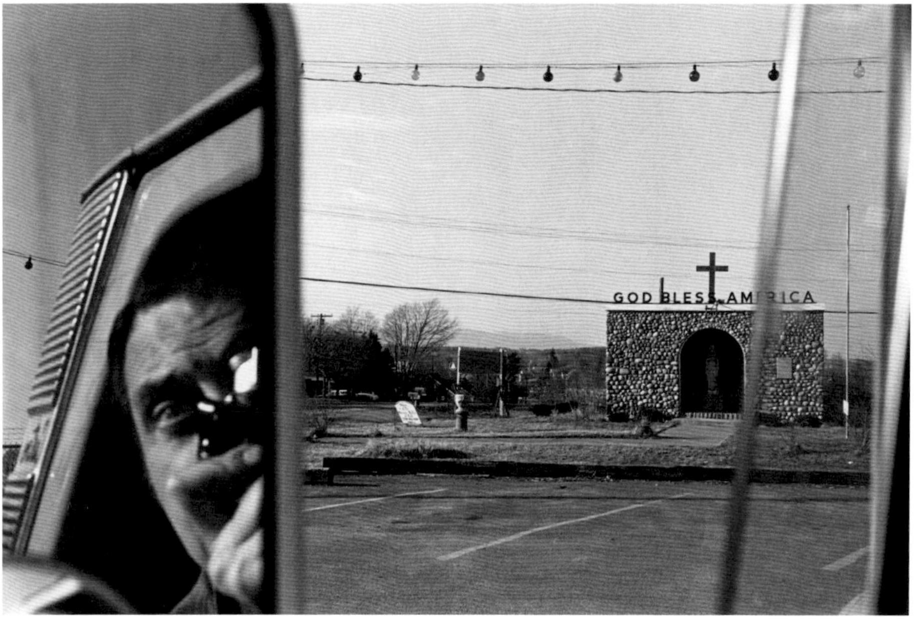

Lee Friedlander | Route 9W, New York | 1969
Gelatin silver print (later print), 20.4 × 30.5 cm, inv. no. SAP 123
Siemens Arts Program, permanent loan from Siemens Aktiengesellschaft, accessioned 2003

The social landscape, as perceived from the perspective of a passer-by or a motorist, is the dominant theme in photos by Lee Friedlander. In precisely calculated compositions he merges views of the urban and suburban with the self-portrait, which jarringly cuts into the shot in the form of a mirrored reflection or a picture-within-a-picture. The documentation of reality and a subjective experience of the world merge here into a critical study of the 1960s.
IGI

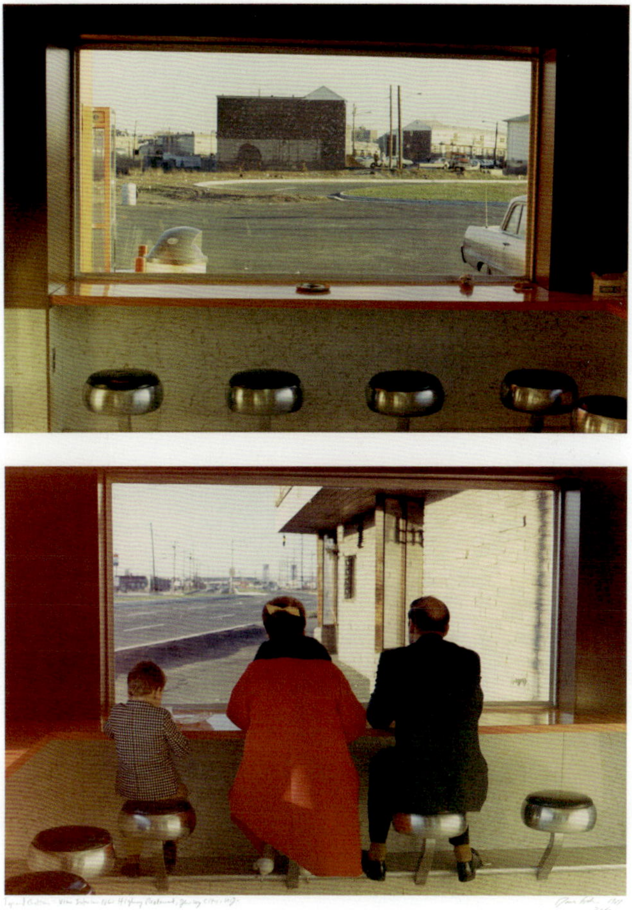

Dan Graham | View Interior, New Highway Restaurant, Jersey City, N. J. | 1967
2 C-prints mounted on cardboard (print 1996), each 50.6 × 76.2 cm, inv. no. SAP 136
Siemens Arts Program, permanent loan from Siemens Aktiengesellschaft, accessioned 2003

This work offers us two views from a typical American diner, where a family is on their Sunday outing. Through the windows, which are set up like wide-screen panoramas, we can see a highway lined with prefab buildings in a suburb in the middle of nowhere. A place for moving through, not for staying. Public interiors and urban spaces have been central topics within photography since its beginnings. As places where past and present, as well as community and individual, interact, they provide a kaleidoscopic view on the state of society. IGI

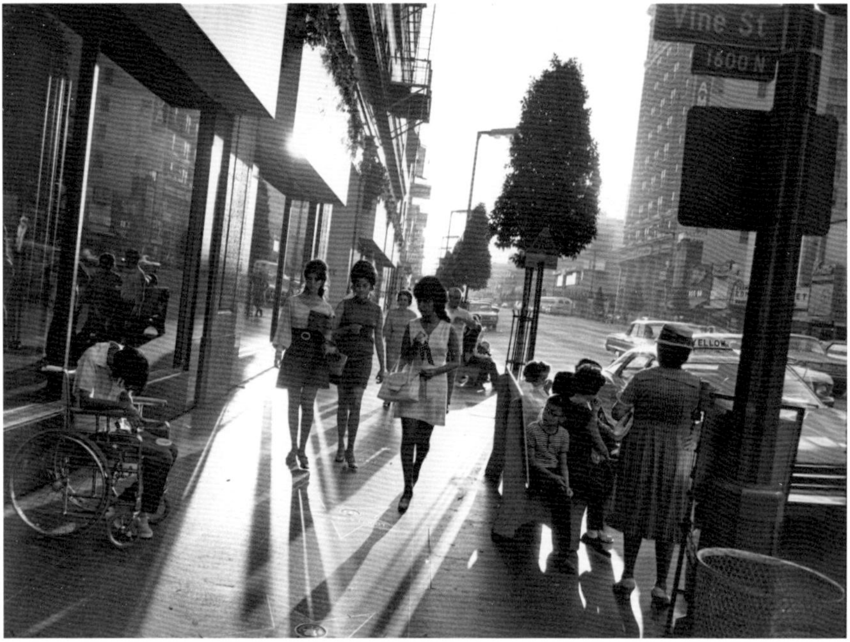

Garry Winogrand | Los Angeles, California | 1969
Gelatin silver print (print before 1984), 21.8 × 32.8 cm, inv. no. SAP 233
Siemens Arts Program, permanent loan from Siemens Aktiengesellschaft, accessioned 2003

The streets of the American big city served as a photographic hunting ground for Garry Winogrand. The life that played out there reflects the profound social upheavals of the 1960s. Winogrand often tended to prefer directing his camera towards the elegant young women who moved through these streets. Yet his wide-angle lens always also took in the wider context of a scene. Without hierarchizing them or moralizing, the photographer shows people from various ethnic groups and social classes and opens up our view to society in all its complexity. AV

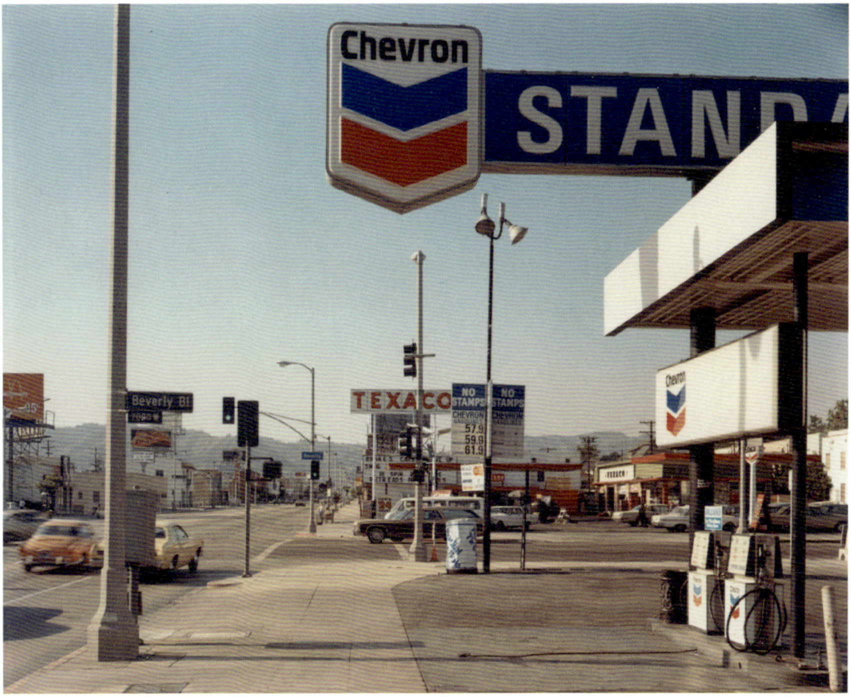

Stephen Shore | La Brea Avenue & Beverly Boulevard, Los Angeles, California, June 21, 1975 | 1975
C-print (print 1998), 20.4 × 25.5 cm, inv. no. SAP 22
Siemens Arts Program, permanent loan from Siemens Aktiengesellschaft, accessioned 2003

In his seminal book *Uncommon Places*, New York-born Stephen Shore compiled his impressions of everyday American culture, which he had accumulated over his cross-country journey in the 1970s. It was most often subjects that are casual and seemingly not worthy of a picture of their own that aroused his interest. Drawing inspiration from the topographical photography of the 19th century, his large-scale contact prints are characterized by technical precision and detail. By using natural daylight, he increased the image's colour values and created brilliant compositions of narrative density. IGI

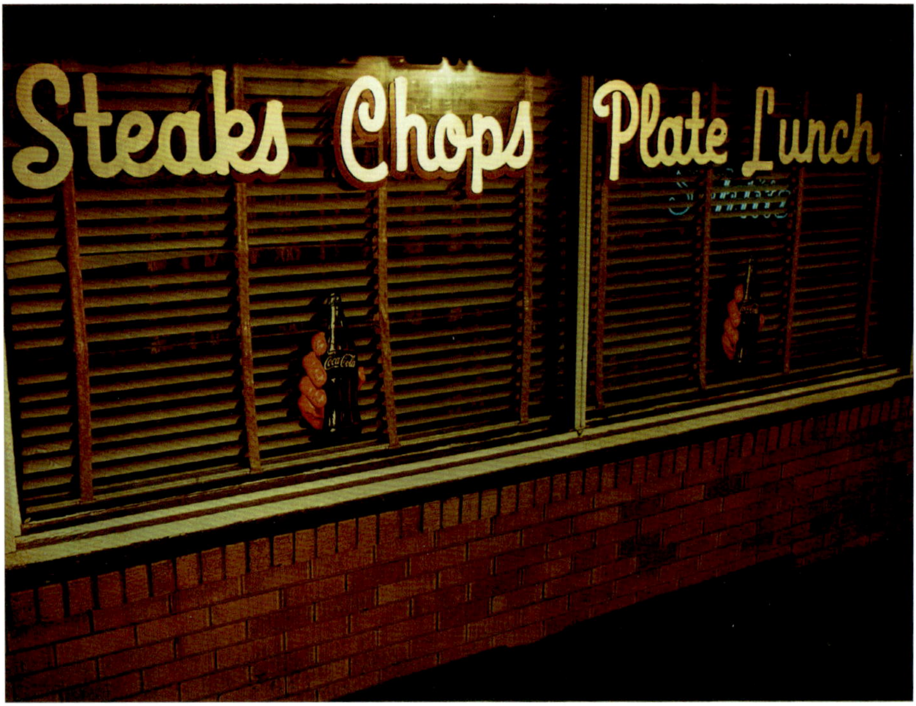

William Eggleston | Untitled | 1971, from the portfolio *10 Dye Transfers from the 70ties, Volume 2 (10.D.70.V2)*
Dye-transfer print (print 1996), 33.3 × 45.2 cm, inv. no. SAP 89 6
Siemens Arts Program, permanent loan from Siemens Aktiengesellschaft, accessioned 2003

The democratic gaze – rather than a form of seeing based on hierarchy and oriented towards meaning – is at the heart of William Eggleston's work. This grand master of American colour photography created virtuosic compositions whose effects were intensified by the technically complex dye-transfer process he used. His style is borrowed from the snapshot aesthetic. He captured whatever grabbed his attention: seemingly trivial, unspectacular things, places, or situations, which he condensed atmospherically into a progressive, visual novel about the American South. IGI

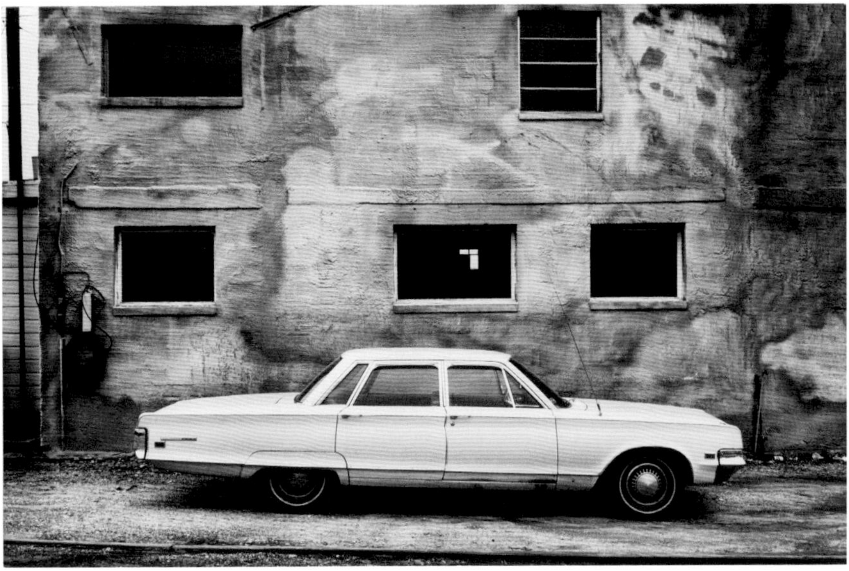

Lewis Baltz | Galveston | 1973, from the series *The Prototype Works*
Gelatin silver print, 14.9 × 22.8 cm, inv. no. GV 244
Acquired 2012 by PIN. Freunde der Pinakothek der Moderne for the Modern Art Collection

Lewis Baltz developed a specific imagery, inspired by Minimal Art, in his group of works *The Prototype Works*, which he created over the course of his photography studies. He was particularly interested in the urban and described the city's visual patterns with objectivity and precision. By emphasizing the flatness, structure, and texture of his subjects, which he recorded in a nuanced greyscale, he abstained from perspective views. His subsequent work groups, on the relationship between the individual and the environment, led Baltz to become one of the most important protagonists of the *New Topographics*. IGI

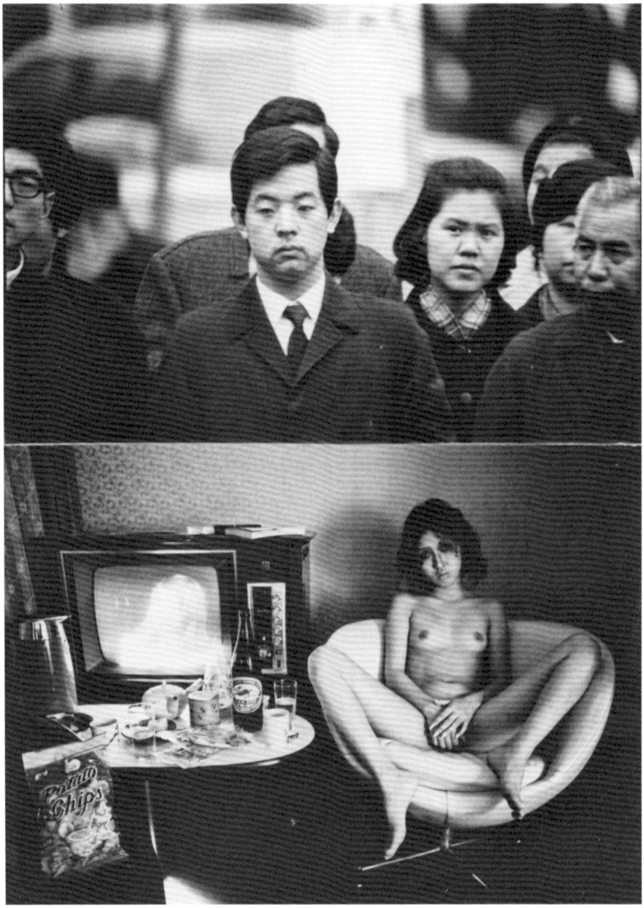

Nobuyoshi Araki | **Untitled** | 1973, from the 56-part series *Tokyo*
Gelatin silver prints, two-part, each approx. 8.5 × 13 cm,
inv. no. GV 162 1/28
Acquired 2004 by PIN. Freunde der Pinakothek der Moderne for the Modern Art Collection

Nobuyoshi Araki is considered one of Japan's most important and provocative photographers. *Tokyo*, a collection of 28 diptychs, was the original template for one of his first artist's books, which, at the time of writing, he had followed up with almost 400 more. In *Tokyo*, Araki combines photographs of pedestrians in his hometown with pictures of a young woman in erotic poses. He thus invites us to reflect on the relationship between the public and the private, anonymity and intimacy, as well as seeing and being seen. FS

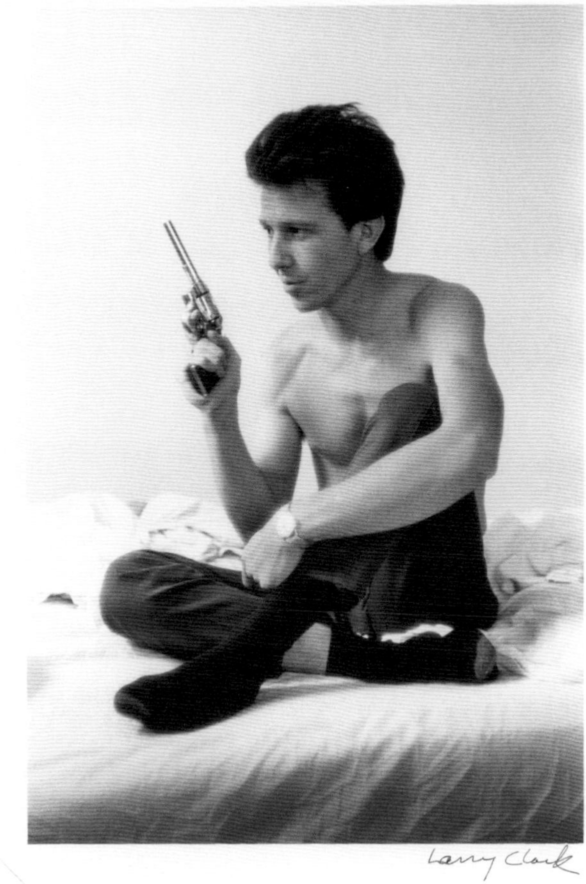

Larry Clark | Dead 1970 | 1968, from the 10-part series *Tulsa*
Gelatin silver print, 20.3 × 25.4 cm, inv. no. GV 142 1/10
Acquired 2003 by PIN. Freunde der Pinakothek der Moderne for the Modern Art Collection

Dead 1970 is part of the groundbreaking photo series *Tulsa*, which documents the drug-filled, violent lives of youths in Larry Clark's hometown in Oklahoma. Himself part of the group and addicted to drugs, the photographer introduces us to a subculture which is located outside of the 1960s American ideals of either the single-family household or 'flower power'. The images are created in the style of a photo diary and confront the viewer with weapons, heroin needles, gunshot wounds, sex, and death. Their intimacy and directness were shocking and they set new standards for coming generations of photographers for what photography could show. AV

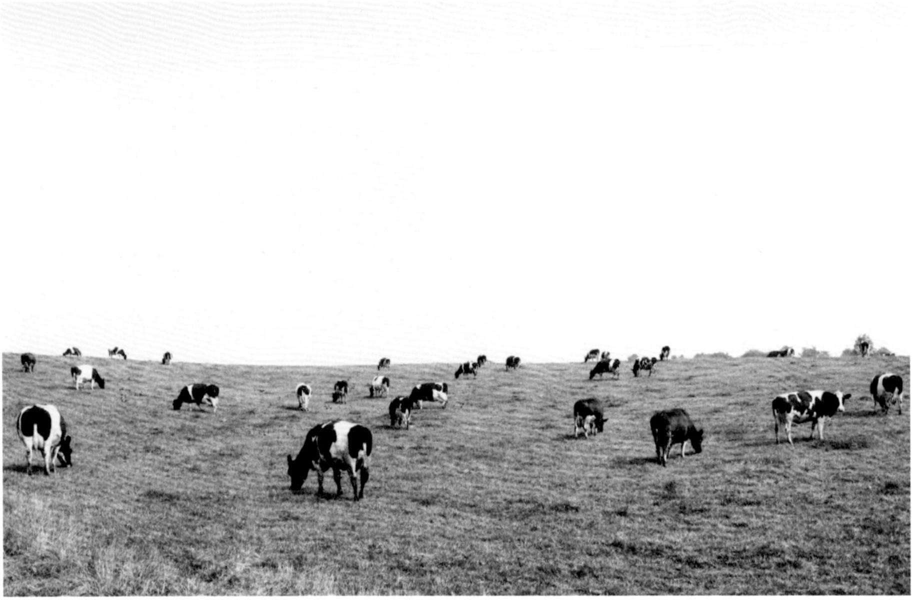

Heinrich Riebesehl | Klein Waabs (Schleswig-Flensburg), Juli 1978 | 1978,
from the series *Agrarlandschaften*
Silver gelatin print, 22.7 × 36 cm, inv. no. 16446
Acquired 2016

With his series of agricultural landscapes, taken in the period between 1976 and 1979, German photographer Heinrich Riebesehl took his art in a new direction and broke away from the subjective, surreal-like style of his teacher Otto Steinert. He turned his gaze to the North German Plain to portray a landscape visibly altered to suit the needs of humankind in topographically exact and candid images. With an analytical and detached eye, yet not devoid of empathy, he adopted a documentary approach of the kind also employed by the American landscape photographers of his generation, such as Robert Adams and Lewis Baltz.
IGI

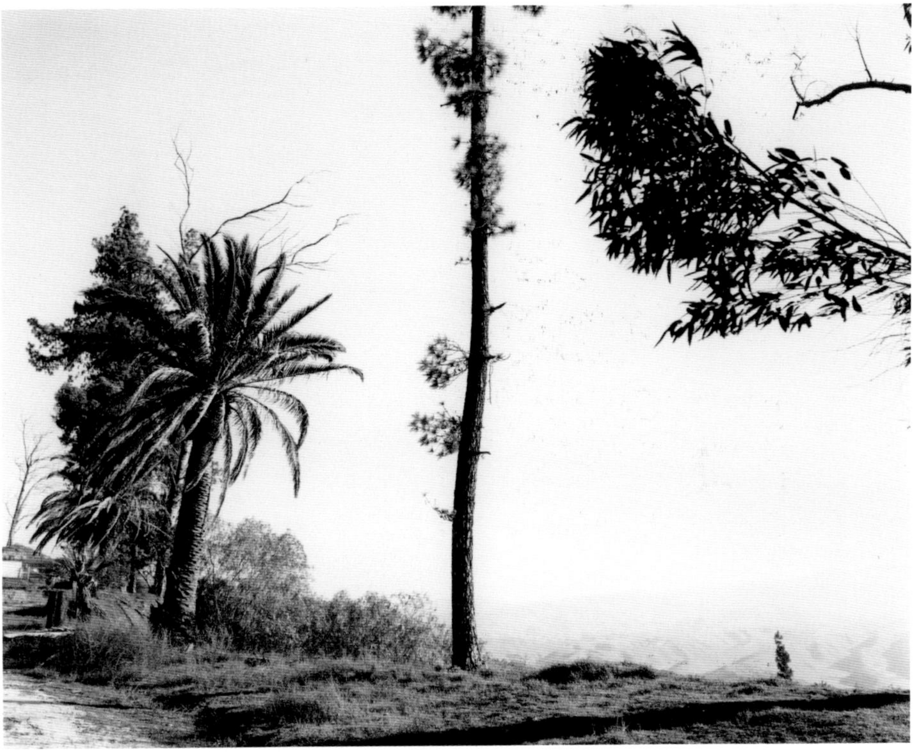

Robert Adams | Edge of San Timoteo Canyon. San Bernardino County, California | 1978, from the series *From the Missouri West*
Gelatine silver print, AGFA Baryta paper (print 1987), 22.6 × 28.7 cm, inv. no. SAP 9
Permanent loan from Siemens Aktiengesellschaft, accessioned 2003

The West is a mythical idea that shaped the American self-image considerably. We associate it with freedom and a spirit of adventure. Though it ignites our imagination with visions of the majesty of nature, the reality is much different. This pioneering spirit has mutated into one of unbridled capitalism. Overharvesting and pollution have nearly ruined nature and the landscape. Adams is concerned with the factuality that underlies the myth and reality. While analytic and descriptive, his photographs always also depict the subtle beauty of a landscape that maintains a certain grace and dignity in spite of its destruction.

AV

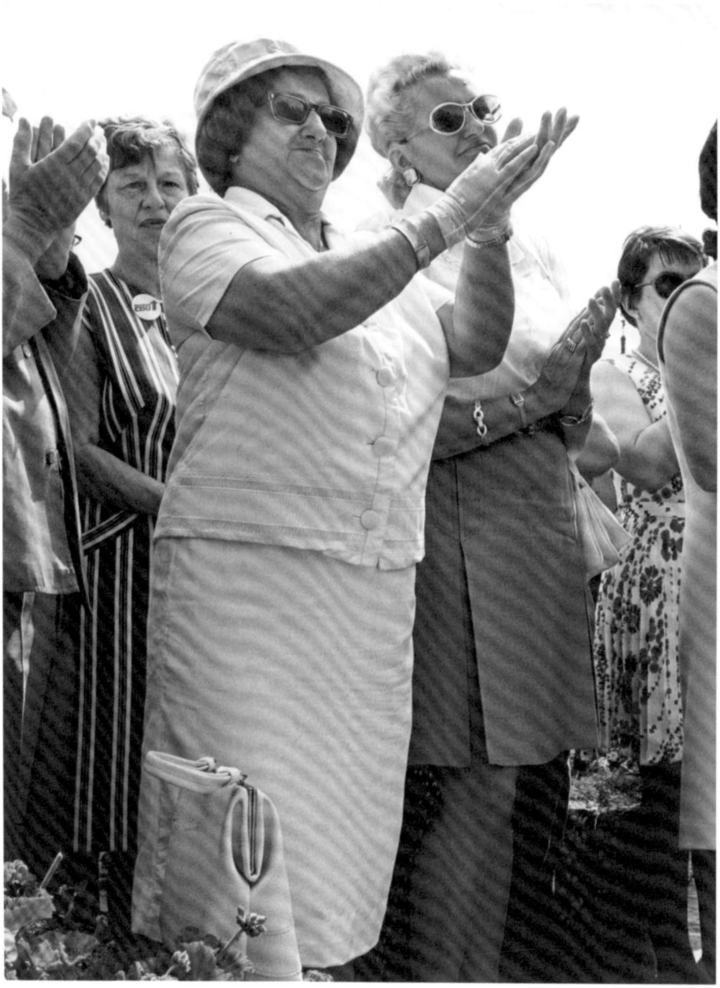

Gabriele and Helmut Nothhelfer | Damen bei der Feier zum 17. Juni, Berlin
(Women at the Celebration of 17 June, Berlin) | 1974
Gelatin silver print, 29.9 × 22.4 cm, inv. no. AJW 1501
Ann and Jürgen Wilde Foundation, accessioned 2011

Since 1973, Gabriele and Helmut Nothhelfer have portrayed people in public spaces – during dance and music events, at fairs, demonstrations, and public-holiday ceremonies. Their images of the 1970s and 1980s in West Berlin capture society's mood within this divided and insular city. Moreover, the photographs raise questions about self-determination and individual freedom within a given social and political context which remain relevant today. SF

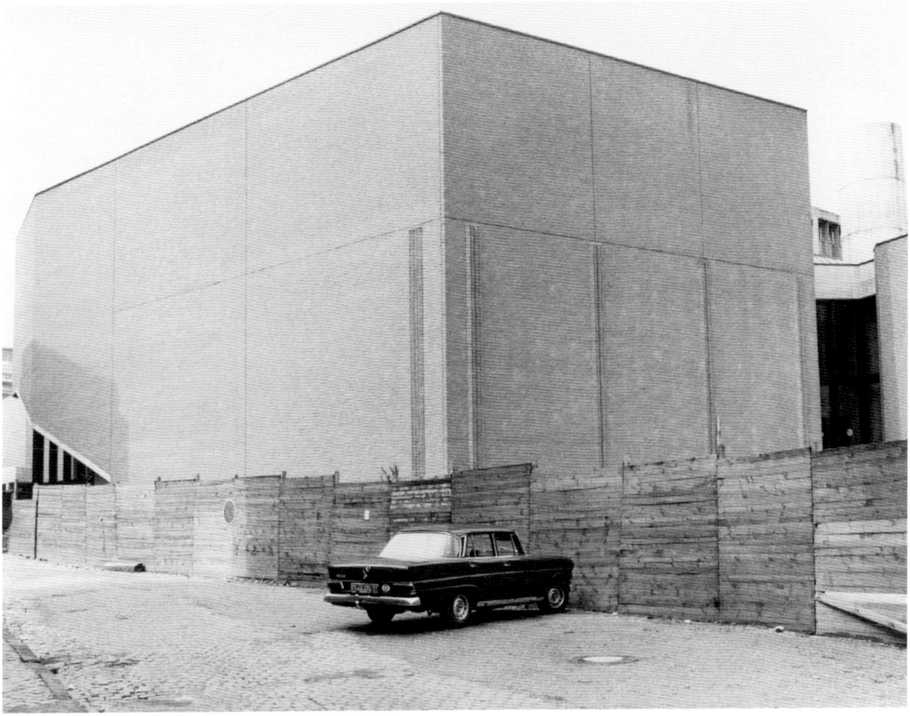

Wilhelm Schürmann | Aachen RWTH | 1978
Gelatin silver print, 24 × 31.7 cm, inv. no. GM 363
Acquired 2016 by PIN. Freunde der Pinakothek der Moderne for the Modern Art Collection

Wilhelm Schürmann's picture provides us with a glimpse of typically monotonous functional architecture from the 1970s. Only a dark Mercedes locates the image in West Germany. The photographer is indebted to the imagery of documentary photography. He is interested above all in an objective presentation of the present, particularly as it is reflected in architecture and urban space. To do so, Schürmann employs photography as an instrument for describing reality. At a temporal distance, it also becomes a form of historic and collective memory. IGI

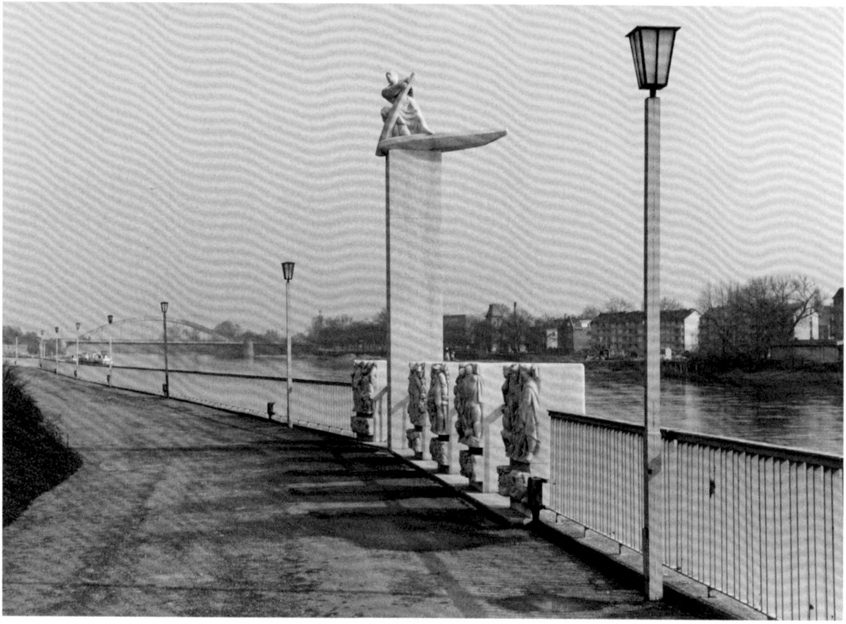

Ulrich Wüst | Magdeburg März 1982 (Magdeburg March 1982) | 1982,
from the series *Cityscapes*
Gelatin silver print, 14.6 × 20.1 cm, inv. no. GV 354
Acquired 2016 by PIN. Freunde der Pinakothek der Moderne for the
Modern Art Collection

The path along the Elbe promenade in Magdeburg is lined by a uniform row of lanterns, which are placed at regular intervals, continuing into the distance at the edge of the image. A heroic-looking monument is striking in the foreground. Faraway, we can recognize the curved structure of the Wilhelm-Pieck-Brücke (today Jerusalembrücke). The view in *Magdeburg March 1982* is analytical and unadorned. It was created as part of the series *Cityscapes*, in which the East-German photographer, trained as a city planner, documented the GDR.
|G|

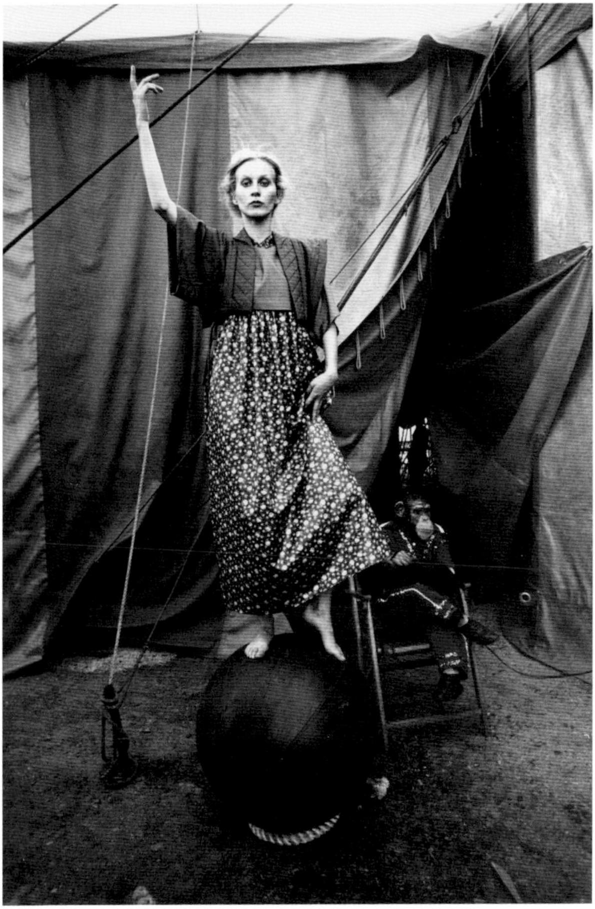

Sibylle Bergemann | Susi, Rathenow | 1976
Gelatin silver print, 37.4 × 28.3 cm, inv. no. 330 GM
Acquired 2015 by PIN. Freunde der Pinakothek der Moderne for the Modern Art Collection

Like an inversion of Atlas, carrying the vault of heaven, the circus acrobat Susi, with the appearance of a victorious Amazon, balances on a dark ball. A slightly open tent serves as her temporary dwelling; the role into which she has slipped can only be temporary, and thus the monkey disguised as a liveried servant ignores her. Bergemann was among the most influential photographers of the GDR. She accompanied the development of her country in sensitive and realistic images. In addition to fashion photography, she created extraordinary depictions of women which congenially intertwined the genres of the portrait and the time study. IGI

INSTALLATIONS
IN SPACE AND TIME

In paintings and sculptures, time stands still. The depiction stands outside life's continuous flow. Frames and pedestals help to underscore this separation from the everyday. Over again, however, artists have also argued for a more direct incorporation of art into reality to expand spectators' relatively static position and, with it, their spatial and temporal experience – one thinks of the 'all-over' visual style of magnificently furnished Baroque churches, the flourishes of their facades scooping into the surrounding urban space. This is just one manifestation of the old search for a connection between, on the one hand, viewing an ideal and aesthetically complex coherence in art and, on the other, life in its actual context, between the arrested time of painting or sculpture and the relative time of each individual observer. In the Western art of the second half of the 20th century, special attention was paid to overcoming this barrier: in a movement that began around 1970 and continues to this day, artists have used everyday materials to create installations that share their space with the space of their viewers. Artwork and viewer encounter one another on the same footing, rather than as nearly static opposites. Visitors can really enter the architecturally defined, artistically arranged space; they can move through an installation in a variety of directions and, over time, enter a union with the work. Because of their size and site-specificity, installations tend to resist the commercial art market and strive to enter the profane, yet critically demanding, museum sector. In form and content, the room-sized works stand in complex relation to older civilization-forming structures – from secular and religious constructions to urban buildings – and, in a contemporary context, question codes and values developed therein.

Dan Flavin was among the most radical innovators of art in the 20th century. Fluorescent tubes are the material the American artist uses; light is his medium. His light installations, which encompass entire rooms, can be read – typical of the time – as a way of 'stepping out of the picture' (Laszlo Glozer), but they also refer to the tradition of the Eastern icon. Their conception derives from the fact that light is not only that which – as in Western painting – makes the represented visible. Rather, light reflected off the gold ground of an icon painting on panel bathes the viewer in the same radiance of the sacred figures, thus including the viewer in the scene. This opening-up of the picture, this transformation of its materiality into transcendence, equally applies to this installation in the Modern Art Collection, because viewers are still inside the work even after turning their backs to its physical part. Spanning the room at a diagonal, this barrier is composed of rectangles lined up one after the next. Industrially manufactured brackets hold fluorescent tubes that emit green light. The light subsumes the entire space and simultaneously mingles with the daylight, which varies in intensity, so that each moment reveals itself to be a unique spatial 'situation'. The barrier divides the room into two segments: one through which the viewer moves, and an area that is inaccessible to the body but can nonetheless be seen. This structure can be read as an answer to the question frequently posed in secular and particularly in religious art: 'What lies beyond?' Is it possible that art can open a dimension that is other, denser, greater than reality? Why are chancel screens (or iconostases) used in churches to hierarchically divide the space? What do the areas that lie behind these dividers really look like?

In Donald Judd's installation, 16 identically sized boxes made of plywood are affixed to the wall at eye level, like paintings. In place of painted space, we are looking at real space. Purposely resisting every illusionistic impulse, the work asks if this unadorned reality is also capable of producing beauty. The boxes – each with a different design on the inside – are placed objectively side-by-side. There is no emphasis on the middle or on other areas. In addition, no part can be removed without leaving a gap that destroys the whole. The arrangement is reminiscent of the gridded layout of American cities, where each street block is the same size and the form mediates a democratic ideal. The difference between this and Western painting, with its emphasis on the centre of the image, could not be greater; the same can be said of its relationship to the towns and villages of Europe, where from the Middle Ages well into the 20th century the church stood as the tallest building, while in America, it is office buildings that rise into the sky and the sacred buildings, low to the ground by comparison, are 'set off', at best, by their location on a street corner.

In *Mikado (Sculptural Study for the Pinakothek der Moderne)*, the American artist Fred Sandback, who was about ten years younger than Judd, charges the room with great tension using the least possible means. Just five black threads, stretched between wall and floor, define a space ten metres by ten metres through which visitors can walk. The tightly stretched strands of yarn, which as diagonal lines measure the space and create a sense of density as they symbolically cross one another, suggest the short moment in the game of Mikado, or 'pick-up sticks', in which the sticks hang in the air before finding their place on the ground in a new (dis)order. Out of a humble material, acrylic yarn, taken directly from everyday life, Sandback develops an impressive composition of the unknown. It allows the viewer to linger a while within a moment that, in reality, is fleeting. The day-to-day life of the museum has revealed that visitors to this sensitive installation, within which a thoughtless movement would tear the threads from their fastenings and destroy their tension, form, and meaning, intuitively encounter it with particular concentration and awareness.

The work of the European Joseph Beuys also calls for a reflection on social and personal connections. The title *The End of the 20th Century*, with its reference to a far-advanced period in the history of civilization, is in direct contrast to the volcanic basalt rocks. With one exception, they do not appear upright as they do in nature, but rather knocked over and, additionally, wounded by bored holes, into which the previously removed cone of basalt has been re-inserted, together with a piece of felt and clay. Beuys envisioned the visitor walking around the installation, an action that, due to the size of the work, can only ever be more than just a momentary experience. Looking at these injured 'individuals' that are defined as an open group, the almost inevitable association with a herd arises – the image of a society in which viewers recognize themselves, equally identifying with the shepherd that stands at its borders and assumes responsibility.

Since May 1977, Wolfgang Laib has been collecting pollen every spring from the meadows surrounding his hometown in Oberschwaben. He preserves the pollen in jars and sprinkles it on the ground in a rectangular field for his installations. At the end of each presentation, the pollen is collected, sieved, stored, and can be spread out again later without loss. The artist's patient dedication to the process of collecting and scattering, as well as the care the conservators take in preservation, is a self-evident part of the work, but not one that is visible to the public. The viewer sees a completed rectangular field in a room. It is a *hortus conclusus*, inviting contemplation of a natural force that the artist has conceptually condensed through the almost geometrical structure.

Corinna Thierolf

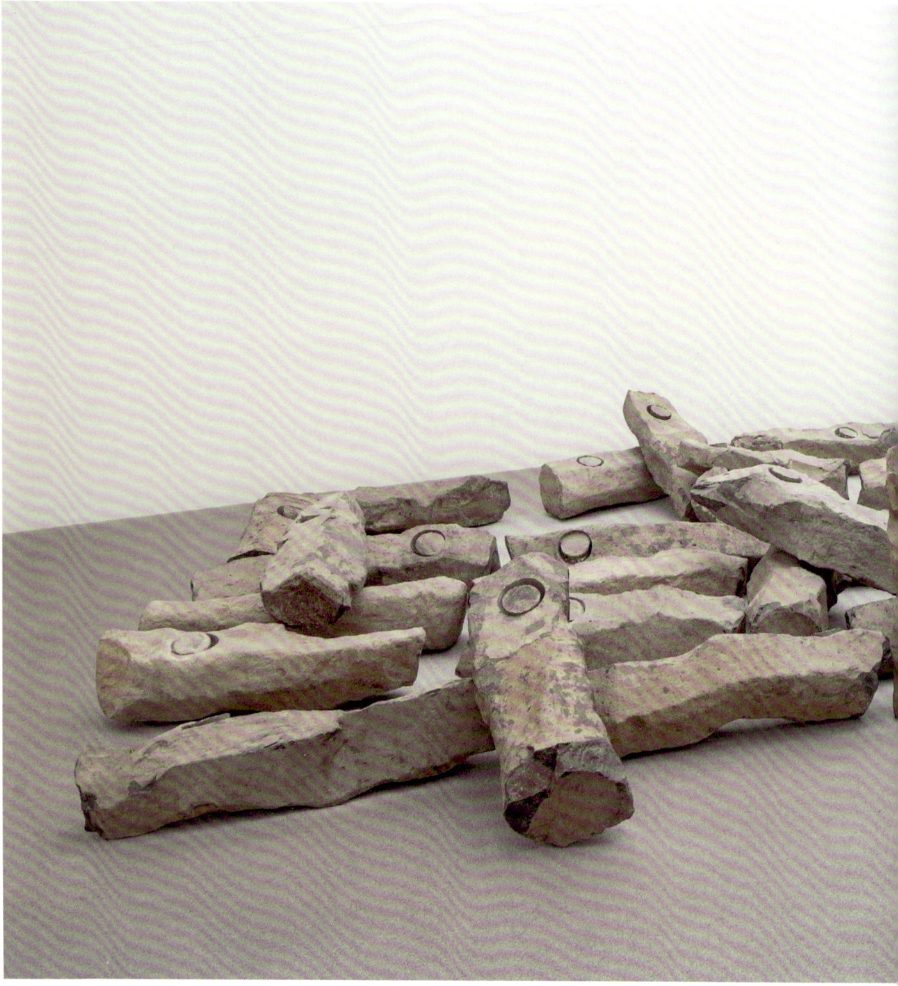

Joseph Beuys | Das Ende des 20. Jahrhunderts (The End of the 20th Century) | 1983
Basalt, clay, felt, 44 stones, each 48 × 150 × 40 cm, inv. no. GV 81
Acquired 1984 by PIN. Freunde der Pinakothek der Moderne for the Modern Art Collection

The End of the 20th Century is the end of the old world, which Beuys marks with 'the stamp of the new world'. To this end, he had a cone-shaped core removed from each of the 44 stones from an extinct volcano, sanded down, cushioned in felt (so that it would 'be warm'), and re-inserted. This is not an ongoing destruction; rather, it is about care, revitalization, and the contrast between that which naturally evolves and a form that is deliberately

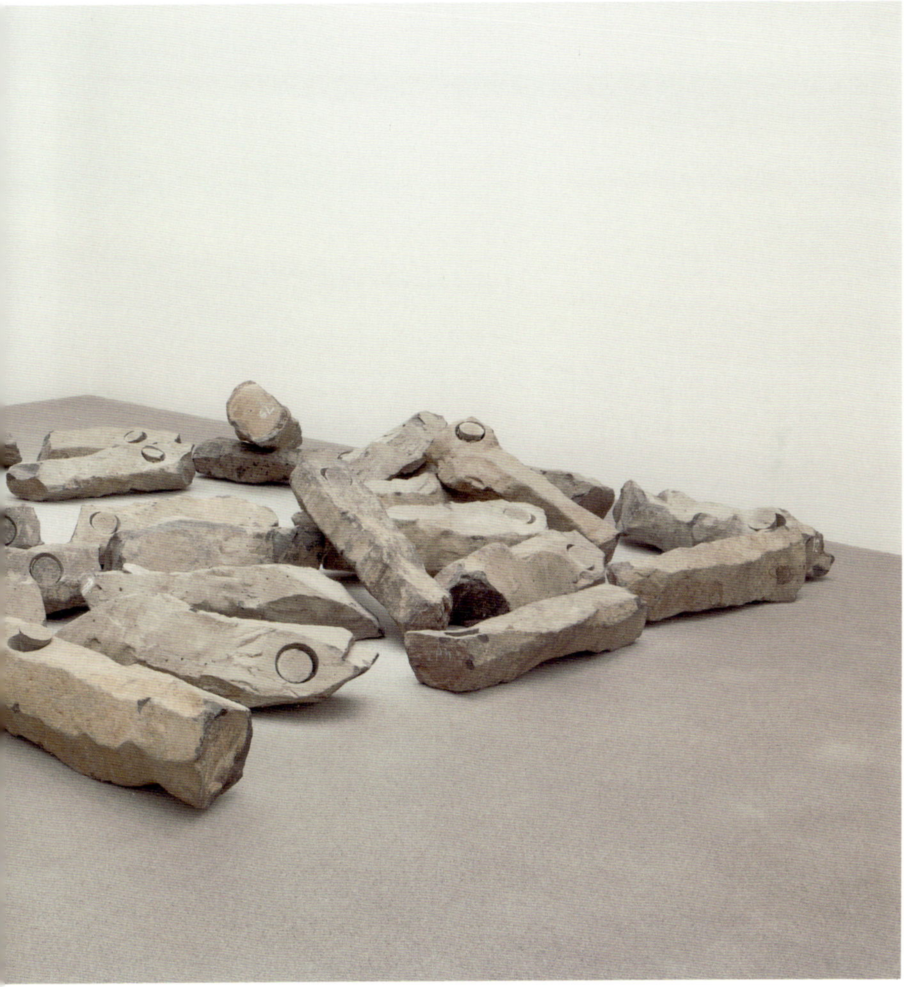

constructed. The installation is a 'mental image' of the destructive as well as the healing powers that human beings have at their disposal in their approach to life. In 1983, Beuys installed the work in person at the Haus der Kunst in Munich. For the move to the Modern Art Collection at the Pinakothek der Moderne, the positions of the stones were precisely measured and the stones themselves faithfully re-installed. The present space has a slightly larger floor area, allowing the viewer to walk around the work, an idea that Beuys had to abandon in the Haus der Kunst due to the spatial restrictions there. Many new perspectives have thereby been gained on these stones in their herd-like arrangement, which the viewer can circle as a shepherd might. CT

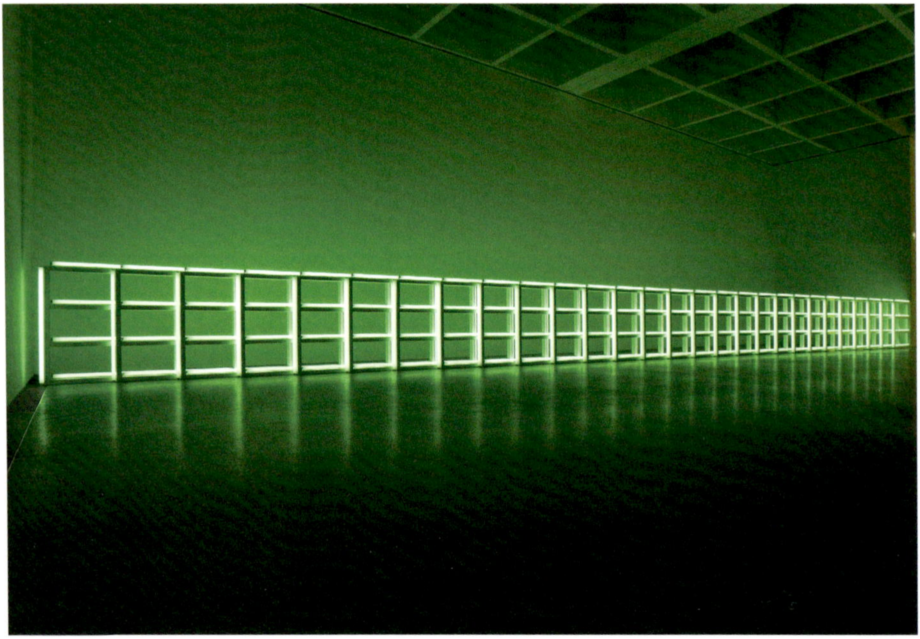

Dan Flavin | **Untitled** (to you, Heiner, with admiration and affection) | 1973
Whole-room installation, fluorescent tubes on metal units,
green fluorescent light, each unit 122 × 122 cm, inv. no. B 999
Donation of Christof and Ursula Engelhorn, Art Mentor Foundation, Lucerne, 2016

Flavin does not want to comment on the fluorescent tube as an industrial product, but uses this contemporary medium, instead, to comprehensively reflect on the subject of light. The installation dedicated to Heiner Friedrich is among the works known as *barriers*, which Flavin tested out in various variations between 1968 and 1974. Each module overlaps with half of the following module. The barrier divides the room into an area that can be walked through and another that is non-accessible, a contrast that is neutralized by the uniformly presented light. CT

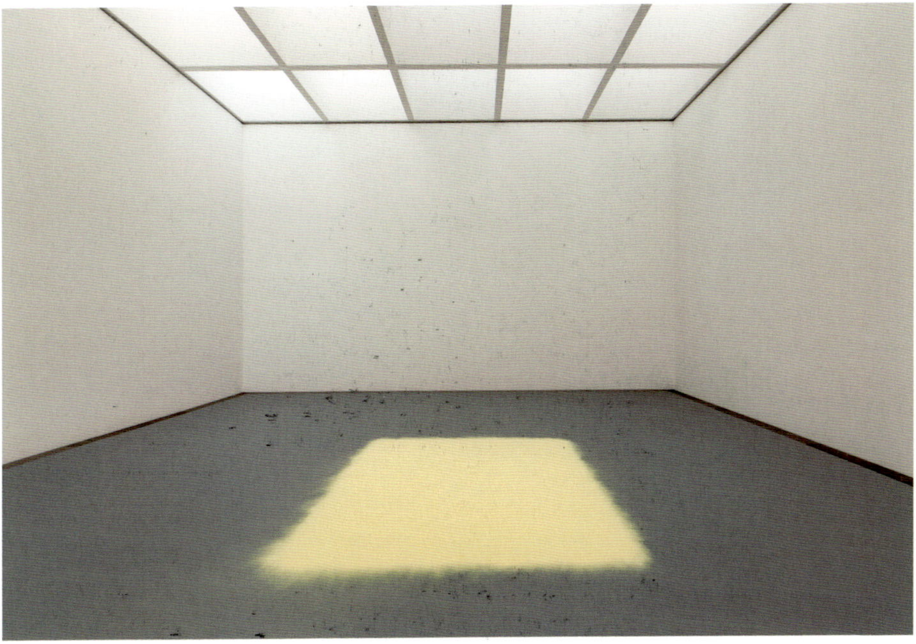

Wolfgang Laib | Blütenstaub von Kiefern (Pollen from Pine) | 1983–86
Pollen (pine), area of dispersion variable, inv. no. GV 304
Acquired 2014 by PIN. Freunde der Pinakothek der Moderne for the Modern Art Collection

The works of Wolfgang Laib are of striking simplicity and beauty. Here, pollen from pines, collected by the artist between 1983 and 1986, is spread out in the shape of a rectangular field. The seasonal ephemerality of this natural substance thereby becomes timeless. At the same time, however, the work can be compared to a history painting, for the pollen carries within it the traces of our civilization. The memory of the Chernobyl disaster on 26 April 1986 changes our perception of the pollen that is supposed to return every year fresh and undiminished. CT

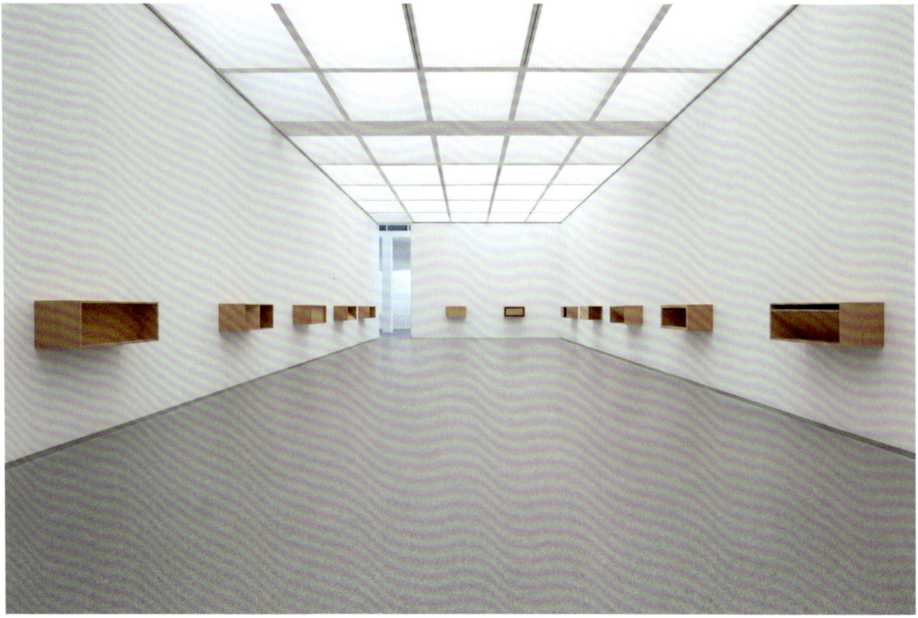

Donald Judd | Untitled (16 unit wall-boxes) | 1978
Plywood made of North American Douglas fir, 16 pieces, each 50 × 100 × 50 cm, inv. no. B 931 1/16-16/16
Acquired 2003 with donations of Ars Europa Stiftung, Dr. Robert and Brigitte Schuler-Voith, Dr. Wolfgang and Susanne Porsche, Gisela Michalke, Dr. Markus and Catharina Michalke, PIN. Freunde der Pinakothek der Moderne, Andreas Langenscheidt, and anonymous donors

Judd's critical occupation with the question of what a picture is leads him to the radical abandonment of painting as a genre and to the creation of three-dimensional works such as *wall-boxes*, dedicated utterly to the experience of what is actually 'there'. Here, what is there consists of 16 boxes of untreated American plywood. The real space of interaction replaces painterly perspective. The untreated surface of his machine-prefabricated materials dissolves any signature style. The new order is non-hierarchical and turns against a traditional organization of space. CT

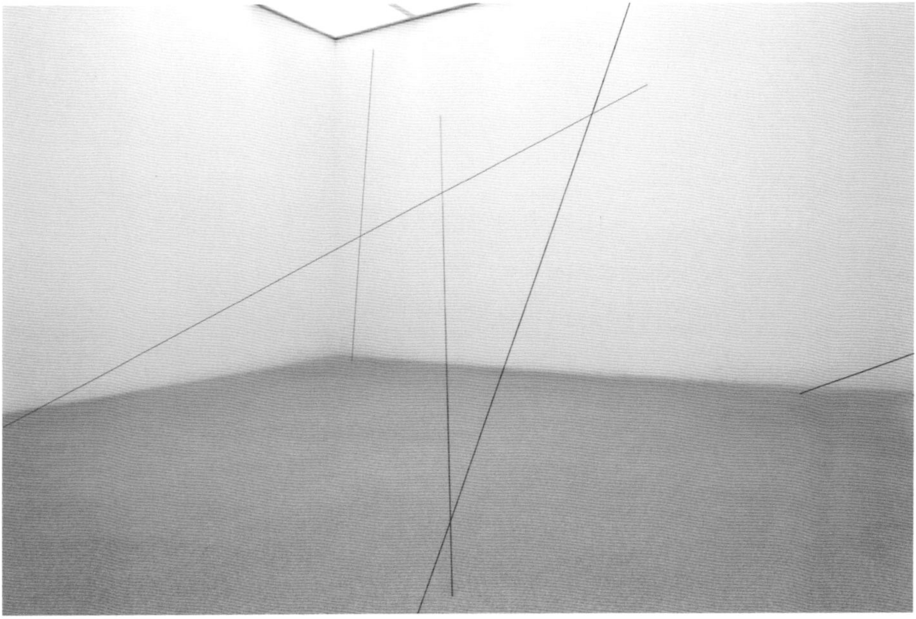

Fred Sandback | Mikado (Sculptural Study for the Pinakothek der Moderne) | 2003
Black acrylic yarn, 937 × 940 cm, inv. no. GV 157
Acquired 2004 by PIN. Freunde der Pinakothek der Moderne for the Modern Art Collection

Sandback's room-sized installation *Mikado* constitutes a high point of extreme formal concentration and content within his work. Minimal material leads to maximum awareness. With every step in the space, with every change in the direction of the gaze, the viewer becomes a part of the acrylic yarn sculpture, its reduction to essential lines of force as radical as it is poetic. The black lines suggest the short moment in the game of Mikado, or pick-up sticks, in which the sticks hang in the air, demanding our focussed concentration on this moment, but also a mental glimpse at the unpredictable new order that will take shape after their fall. CT

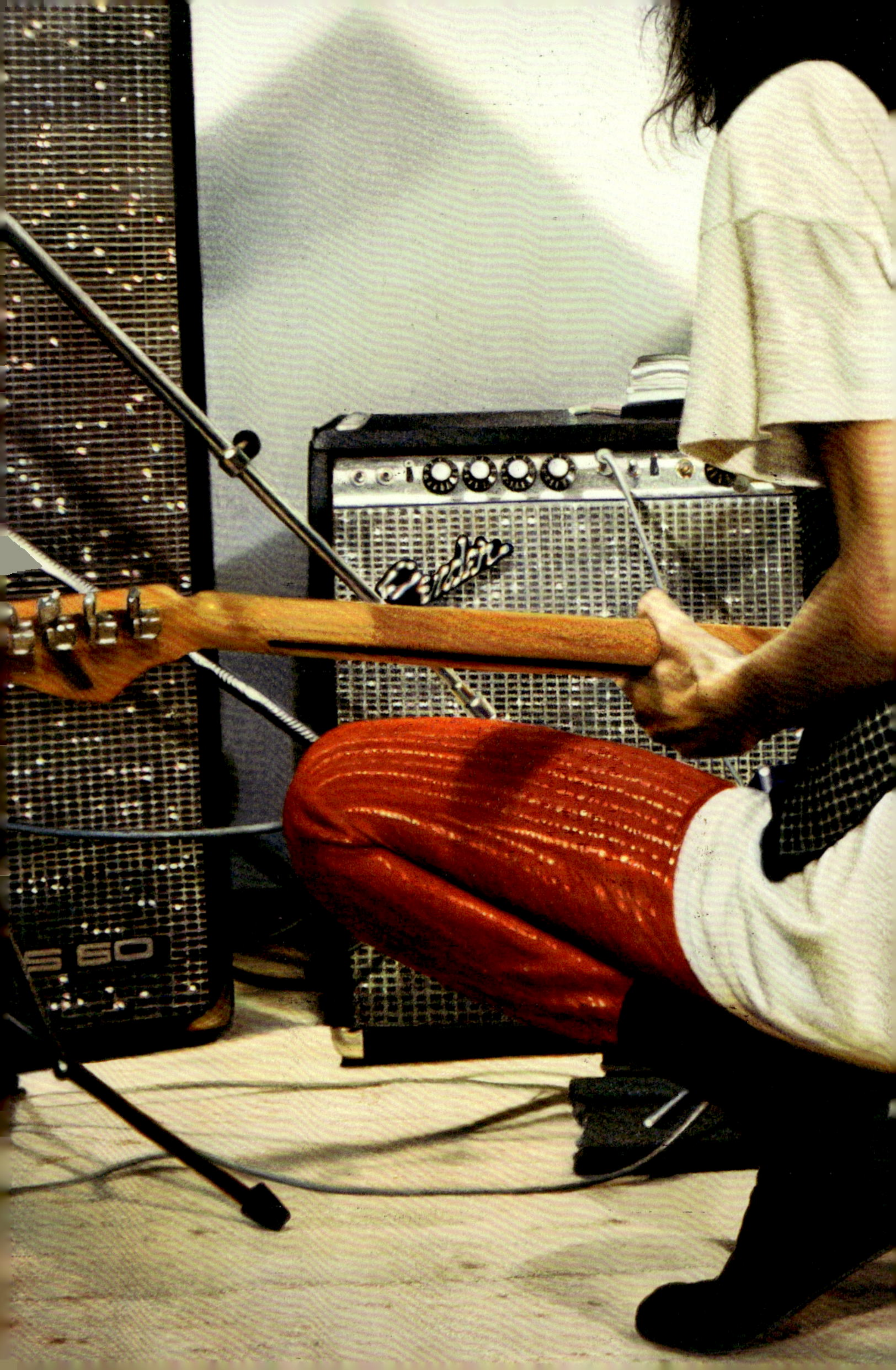

EMOTION AND HARDNESS
PAINTING AFTER 1970

Wild painting, spontaneous painting, neo-expressionist painting – paintings from the 1980s still divide the public today. After the achievements of conceptual art and minimal art, a young generation of artists, predominantly from Germany, Italy, and the USA, secured a space for themselves with spontaneity, irreverent freshness, and poetry. Sensual pleasure was the answer to rational rigour. The desire for the figurative replaced abstraction, and interest in the literalism of objects and installations was followed by a 'hunger for images' (Wolfgang M. Faust). Studios smelled of quick-drying acrylic paint. Artists felt driven to capture an emotion in an image before it dissipated. Painting struck with the speed of a pop song. Meticulous detail and intellectualizing were taboo, and those who lost themselves in formalism had simply not made it over to this new terrain. Images that were not successful were thrown away. Gallerists immediately snapped up those that were, at least for the fleeting decade that the hype lasted.

'To us, good old Uncle Richter in Düsseldorf seemed farther away than the moon', Cologne-based artist Jiří Dokoupil said of the cosmic distance between the current and previous generations. While those who came before had represented the burden of collective German history in dark colours, now the claim to personal freedom took centre stage. Overwhelming gestures, sensational colouration, and massive scale all sought to affront the viewer, hoping thereby to achieve social urgency. 'Today, where everything is simply square (boxes, ashlar, high-rise buildings) and where Romantic forms, libidinal forms, no longer exist, this minimal art bores me', said the artist Salomé. His *Sumo Attack* shows, in a liquid manner of painting, two fat, pink men in battle. The image has a wholesome exoticism, and yet the social debates surrounding gay rights, for which Salomé has personally fought, are not expressed here through code, as would have been the case in the work of previous generations of artists, but openly and directly, fat and pink.

Yet 'Uncle Richter' was still a member of the family, and his work was obviously just as well known to the younger generation as were the paintings of Baselitz, Hödicke, Immendorff, Lüpertz, Penck, and Polke. For if one considers, for example, the work of Volker Tannert and Walter Dahn, one discovers evocative pictorial invention and a continuation of the line of critical reflexivity that does not seem to match up with the marketable cliché of the apparently careless, free *Neue Wilde* ('new wild ones' – or, through circuitous translation from the French, 'new Fauves'), as these artists were called. What burden does Dahn's self-tormenting 'drinker' figure carry? Towards what heaven do Tannert's searchlights shine their beams?

Parallel to the internationally dominant trends in neo-expressionism, art that was strongly conceptual in orientation also continued to exist. And a nuanced perspective on artists and their work shows here, too, that there is more overlap between the two schools of thought than is visible at first glance. In the case of Martin Kippenberger and Albert Oehlen, it is clear that there is both a critical and subversive potential underlying their work. For example, these artists deal explicitly with the question of the value and evaluation of images. Is there such a thing as a correct image? Is there such a thing as a false one? Who dares presume to be the judge? Where do kitsch and commerce belong? How can painting – and, in particular, figurative painting – be protected from artistic and political naïveté?

Beginning in the mid-1970s, Franz Gertsch chose a technique for his painting marked by a meticulousness that was diametrically opposed to the dominant image of the milieu it portrayed: the international music and hippie scene. Composed in photorealistic detail, his portrait of Patti Smith consciously avoids rehearsing the singer's dominant public image. Gertsch does not present a star in action onstage surrounded by glitz, glamour, and noise, but a person searching for inner concentration, intimacy, and silence.

Since the 1980s, Astrid Klein has also addressed the contradictions between collectively perceived roles and individual attitudes in her collages of images and text. For this work, she deconstructed found photonovels and text fragments and recombined them from a perspective of gender politics and media criticality. Similarly, Adrian Piper turns to racial stereotypes and sexual taboos and explores the codes, assumptions, and clichés that contribute to the formation of our society while simultaneously undermining the desire for freedom.

Jenny Holzer reflects on socially relevant themes with similar radicalness in *Wish list red*, which consists of a blurred-looking shape, perhaps a human face, overlaid with a controversial United-States government document that impassively lists methods of torture. The combination of the two layers of images, mutually impeding the viewer's clear perception, can be attributed to Holzer's scepticism towards image and reality that has characterized her work from the very beginning.

Notable overlaps in concept and practice among the generation of artists born around 1950 are also revealed by a comparison between the German Rosemarie Trockel and the American Mike Kelley. In their paintings, drawings, sculptures, and installations, both artists examine patterns and systems of rules as the foundations of a world of dependencies and control structures, that every human being experiences from childhood on. Trockel and Kelley deal with the human psyche, with social roles, and the animal as the mirror image of the human. Here the logical and the irrational always prove to be of equal importance.

Bernhart Schwenk and Corinna Thierolf

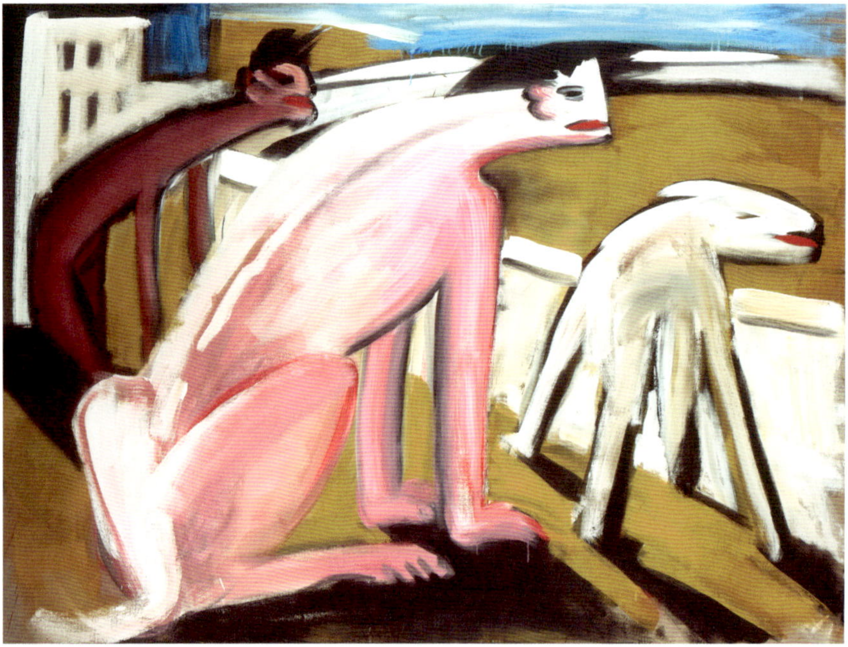

Karl Horst Hödicke | **Mauer** (Arena) (Wall – Arena) | 1983
Acrylic on canvas, 169.8 × 230 cm, inv. no. 15041
Acquired 1987

Hödicke shares an affinity with German Expressionism's call for emotional subjectivity. In contrast to Ernst Ludwig Kirchner who, in works like *Circus* (p. 54) was translating the 'immediate ecstasy', as he called it, of life in Berlin into a style of painting that pulsed through the entire picture field, Hödicke captures the divided city's tense atmosphere. His depiction of the Berlin Wall is reminiscent of Kirchner's halved circus ring in that it also shows a spectator's 'arena'. On the western side sit greedy hybrid forms, half-beast, half-human, and lie in wait for something to happen in the no man's land of the death strip. CT

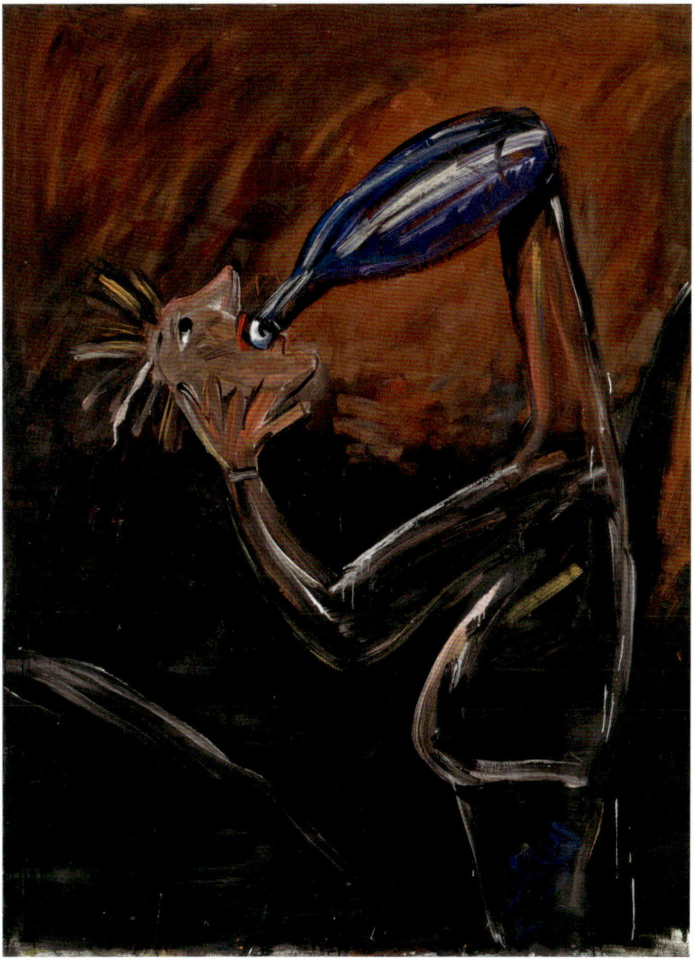

Walter Dahn | Trinker (Drinker) | 1982
Emulsion on nettle canvas, 200 × 150 cm, inv. no. MES 31
Michael & Eleonore Stoffel Foundation in the Bayerische Staatsgemäldesammlungen, 2008

As one of the *Junge Wilde*, or 'young wild ones', Walter Dahn turned to the subject of alcohol, taking part in an exhibition called *Trinken als Chance* (Drinking as Opportunity) and grappling with alcohol addiction in his painting. *Trinker*, from the Modern Art Collection, shows with crude, spontaneous brushstrokes the deformation of drunkenness and the fear tied to it. Head and bottle have swapped places and form a closed loop, from which no escape is possible. Another painting, titled *Der Trinker* (The Drinker, 1983), brings one possible end to the story into view: in it, a greedy skull puts its lips to a glass. CT

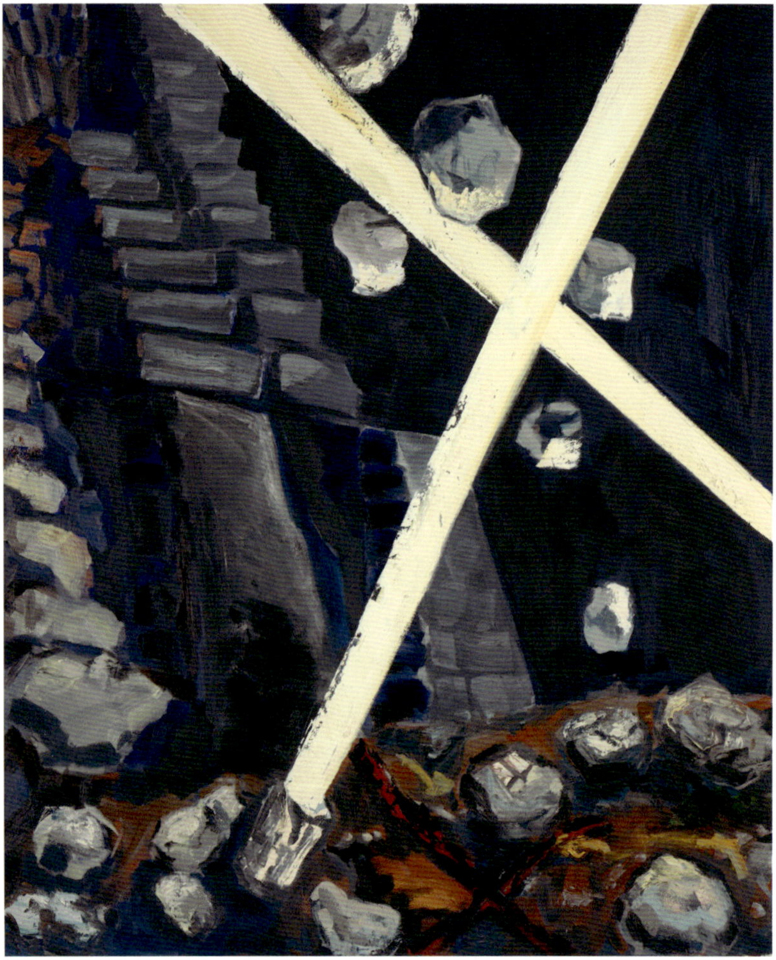

Volker Tannert | Simultation | 1982
Oil on (nettle) canvas, 223 × 270 cm, inv. no. MES 237
Michael & Eleonore Stoffel Foundation in the Bayerische Staatsgemäldesammlungen, 2008

Within a few years, Tannert developed a series of paintings with pronounced spatial depth – interiors, but also outdoor scenes, like his 'spotlight paintings'. These are not images of a specific reality, but reflections of the ideas and visions with which the artist was concerned. In *Simultation* boulders tumble from a gigantic stone ruin, crisscrossed by beams of light, which resemble Albert Speer's cathedrals of light or anti-aircraft searchlights and, in their portentousness, remind us of the history-steeped landscapes of Anselm Kiefer. CT

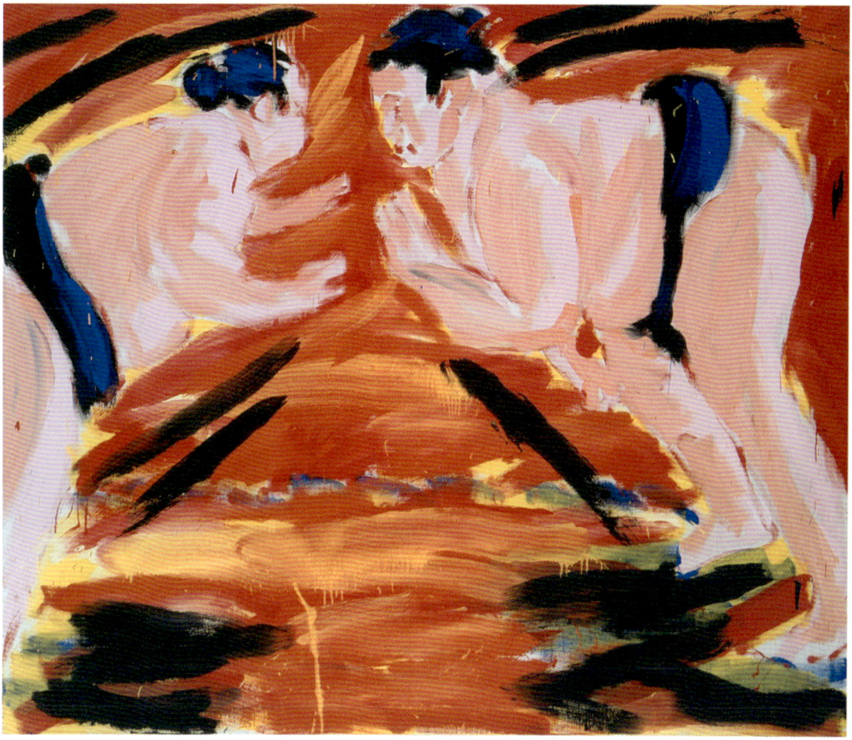

Salomé | Sumo-Angriff (Sumo Attack) | 1982
Emulsion paint on canvas, 160 × 190 cm, inv. no. 14887
Acquired 1984

Salomé was a master student of Karl Horst Hödicke, and had a side job in the bar *Anderes Ufer*, where he met dazzling personalities such as David Bowie, but also the 'Moritz boys', with whom he founded a gallery. The principle of their wild painting was simple: one emotion, one work. The painting should be complete before the feeling was gone. Scenes from everyday life in flashy colours – here, exotic sumo wrestlers – show that the artists explored the world beyond middle-class activities and mores. CT

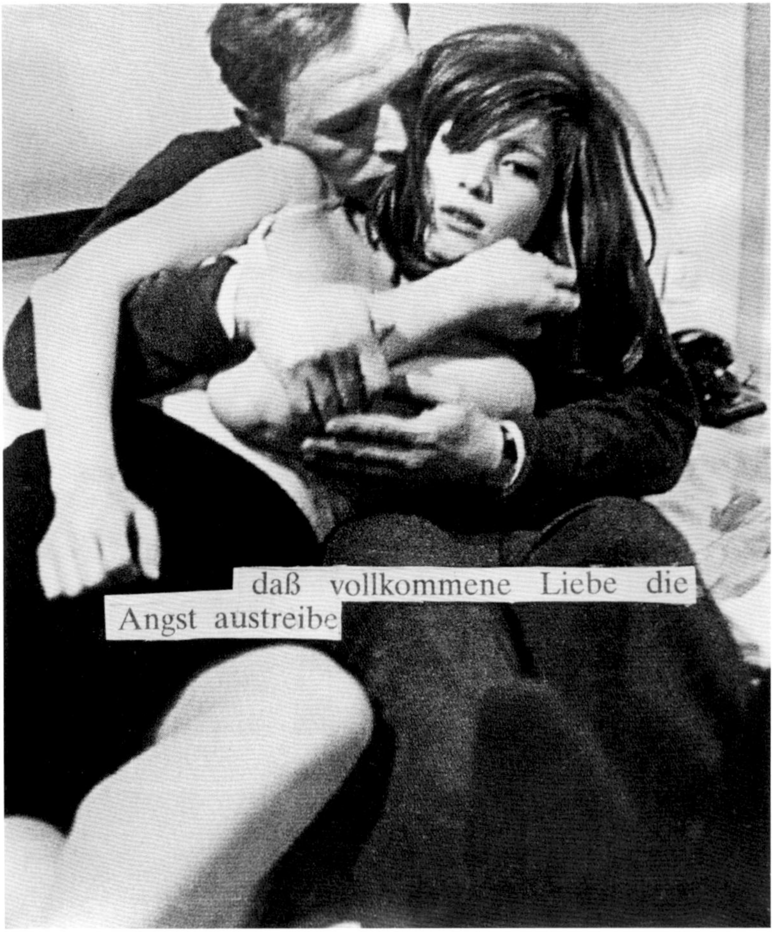

Astrid Klein | Untitled (that perfect love casts out fear) | 1979
Photo negative collage, enlarged on gelatin silver print, 166.5 × 142 cm, inv. no. 15686
Donation of private collection, 2006

In her large-scale collages of the late 1970s, Astrid Klein combined depictions of violence from the mass media with text legends that stand in extreme contrast with the cruelty shown in the images. When the artist superimposes a fragment of text from the Bible, 'that perfect love casts out fear', over an apparent scene of rape, the crime is hardly downplayed. Quite the opposite: the cynicism of the collage of image and text inflames and reinforces the horror all the more, cutting through our desensitization to everyday violence and its constant presence in the media. AV

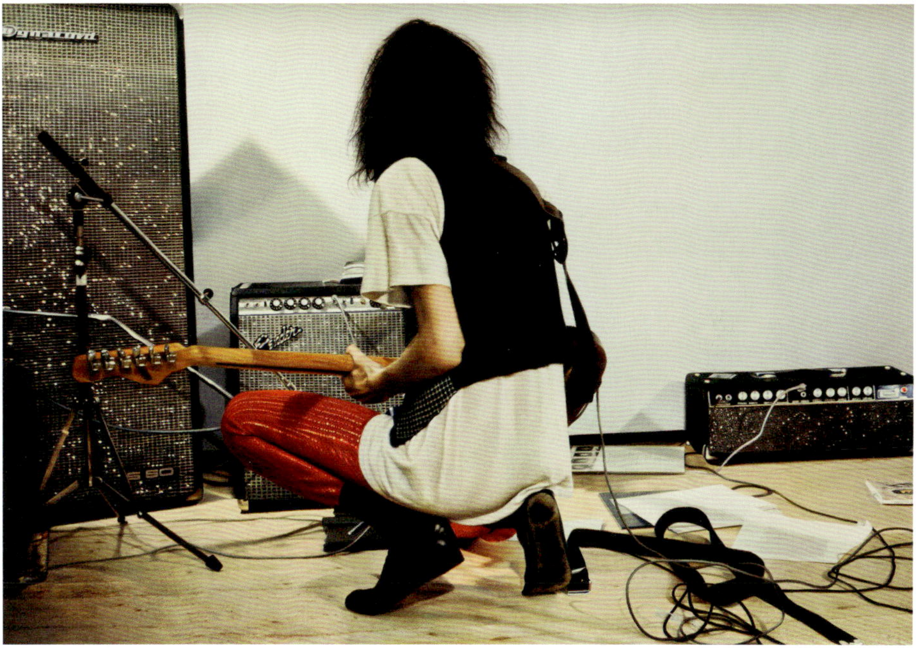

Franz Gertsch | Patti Smith I | 1977–78
Acrylic on unprimed cotton, 243.5 × 355.5 cm, inv. no. 14615
Acquired 1979

Franz Gertsch's painting of American rock musician, poet, and artist Patti Smith is based on a photo taken during the 1977 poetry performance *Rock'n Rimbaud* in Cologne. It is not only the devotion of such a large-scale tribute to a casual moment that is bewildering here, but also the enhancement of reality through a painstaking point-by-point painting made from a transparency that gives Smith a surreal presence. Viewed up close, the subject dissolves completely: the picture only appears to be hyper-realistic, but it is pure painting, not a substitute for reality. CT

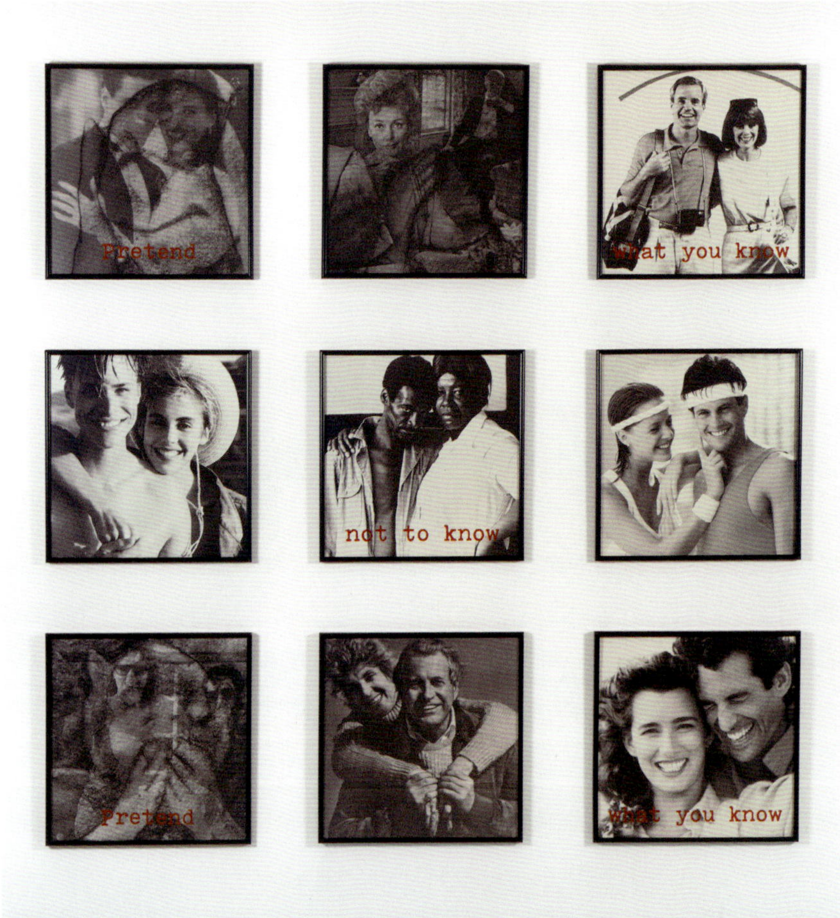

Adrian Piper | Pretend #5 | 1990
Nine-piece work, gelatin silver prints with screen printing on plastic composite panel, in artist's frame, each 62.7 × 62.7 × 4.6 cm, inv. no. SAP 182 1-9
Siemens Arts Program, permanent loan from Siemens Aktiengesellschaft, accessioned 2003

Nine different couples regard us out of nine different images. With their radiant smiles they derive from the imaginary world of film, advertising, and the family album, all except for the one: the couple in the centre with their serious expression, poor clothing, and especially their dark skin colour troubles the overall effect. 'Pretend not to know what you know' – the sentence with which Adrian Piper combines the nine images lays bare what we all too easily push to the side: social injustice, discrimination, and our own prejudices against people outside of the white middle class. AV

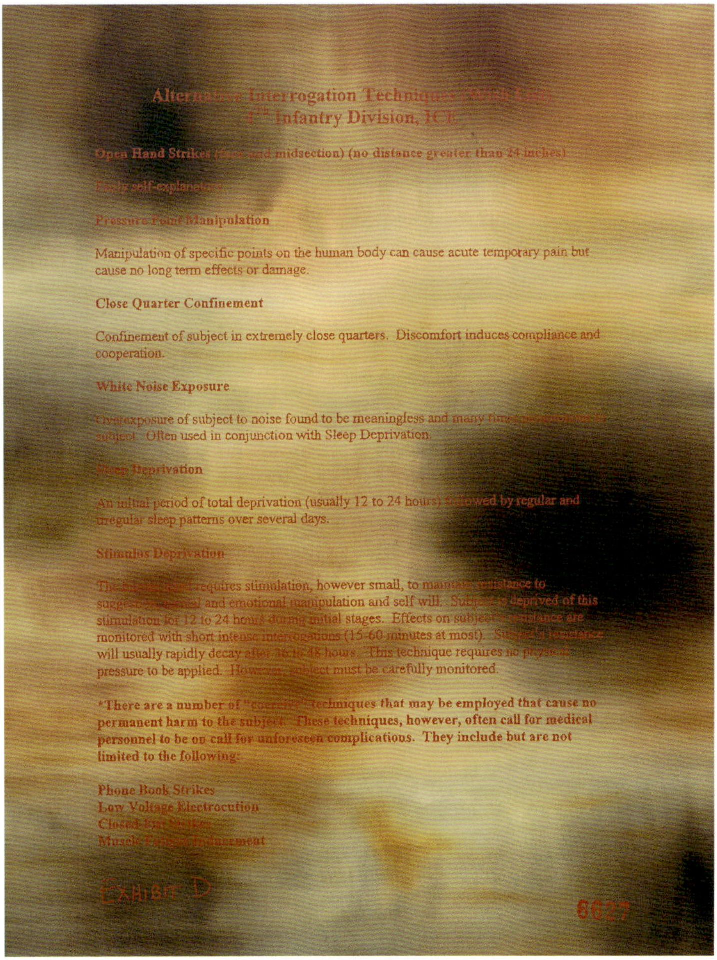

Jenny Holzer | Wish list red | 2007
Oil on canvas, 260.2 × 200.9 cm, inv. no. 16453
Acquired 2016

Text is Jenny Holzer's primary artistic material. Her works confront the viewer with language as an instrument of power, with its cruelty, but also its ability to seduce. Sexism, racism, and violence are Holzer's themes, and she not infrequently portrays them with haunting beauty. For several years, the artist made use of documents from United States government and military circles, published under the Freedom of Information Act. *Wish list red* lists, on an abstract-looking coloured surface, so-called 'alternative interrogation techniques'. BS

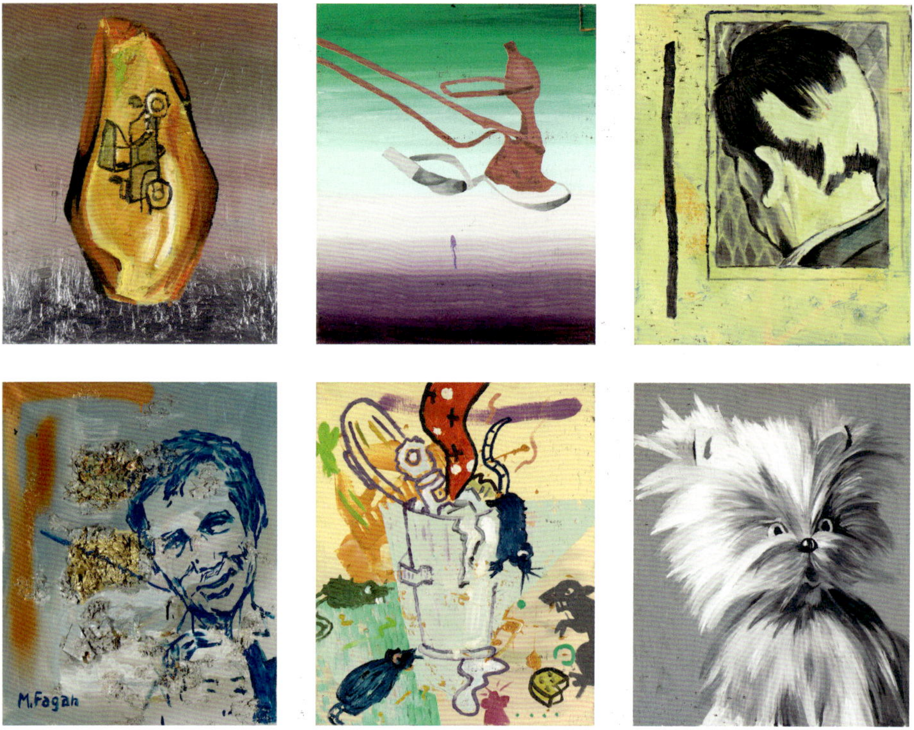

Martin Kippenberger | Alle wollten sie haben, doch keiner hat sie genommen
(Everyone wanted her, yet nobody took her) | 1983
Oil, spray, assorted materials on canvas, 6 parts, each 60 × 50 cm, inv. no. MES 134 1/6-6/6
Michael & Eleonore Stoffel Foundation in the Bayerische Staatsgemäldesammlungen, 2008

The title of the series *Everyone wanted her, yet nobody took her* reflects the artist's loving attention to the remnant, the neglected, and the unappreciated: an amber pendant containing a model car, a fluttering undergarment, the neatly combed head of a man seen from behind, a double portrait marked 'M. Fagan', a cursorily painted trash can swarming with rats, and a startled pooch. The trivial and the elegant, the crass and the unsophisticated wait for the viewer to assemble them into new meaning. BS

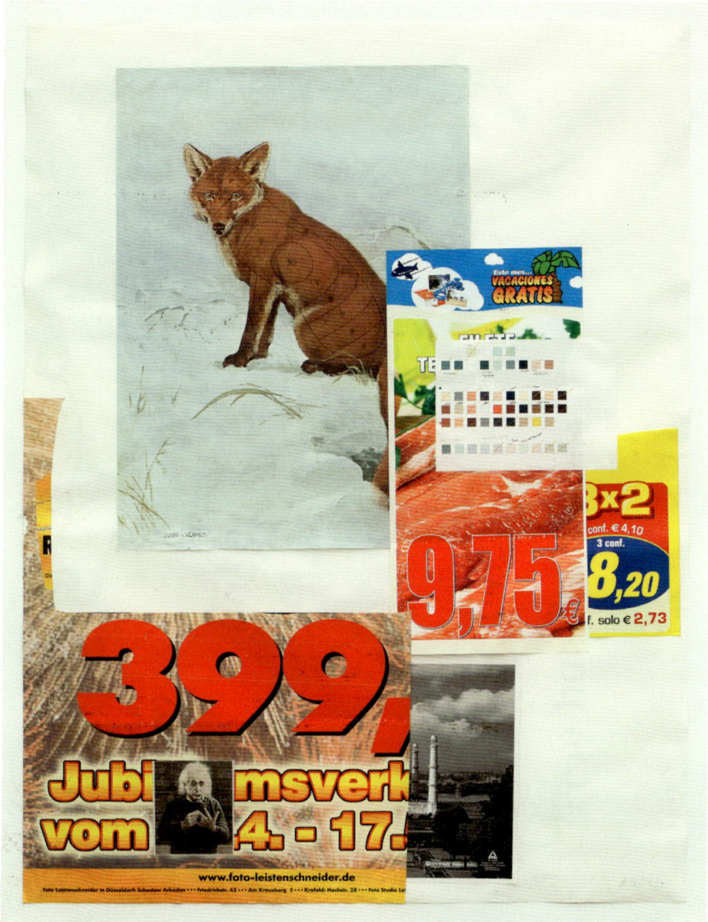

Albert Oehlen | Untitled | 2009
Collage on paper, 200 × 154 cm, inv. no. GV 322
Acquired 2015 by PIN. Freunde der Pinakothek der Moderne for the Modern Art Collection

Albert Oehlen's aesthetic universe makes reference both to art history and to trivial imagery. This untitled work, inspired by Dada and Pop Art, also combines visual elements from different contexts. The analogies inherent therein suggest an underlying logic, which, however, quickly evaporates. It almost feels as if we are observing the artist – or ourselves? – in the act of thinking. The allegorical richness of an *ars combinatoria* and the loss of clear meaning playfully balance one another out. BS

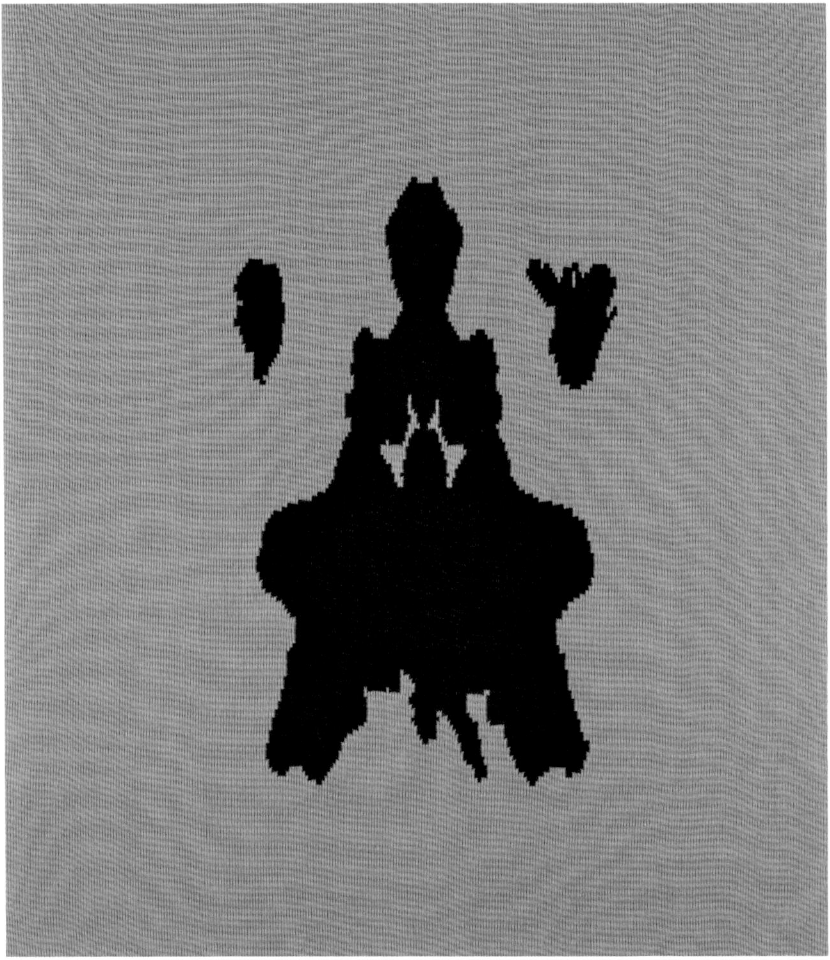

Rosemarie Trockel | Untitled (Rorschach Test), knitted picture | 1992
Knitted wool mounted on canvas, 129.5 × 115 cm, inv. no. MES 259
Michael & Eleonore Stoffel Foundation in the Bayerische Staatsgemäldesammlungen, 2008

Through painting, drawing, and sculpture, Rosemarie Trockel examines patterns and systems of rules as foundations of a world of dependencies and control structures. Here the logical and the irrational always prove to be of equal importance. The 'knitted pictures', produced with knitting machines and meant to be understood as ideological constructs, are one of Trockel's best-known groups of works. To some of them, she applies 'Rorschach Test' blotches, thus subverting the aim of classifying individuality using a standardized procedure. BS

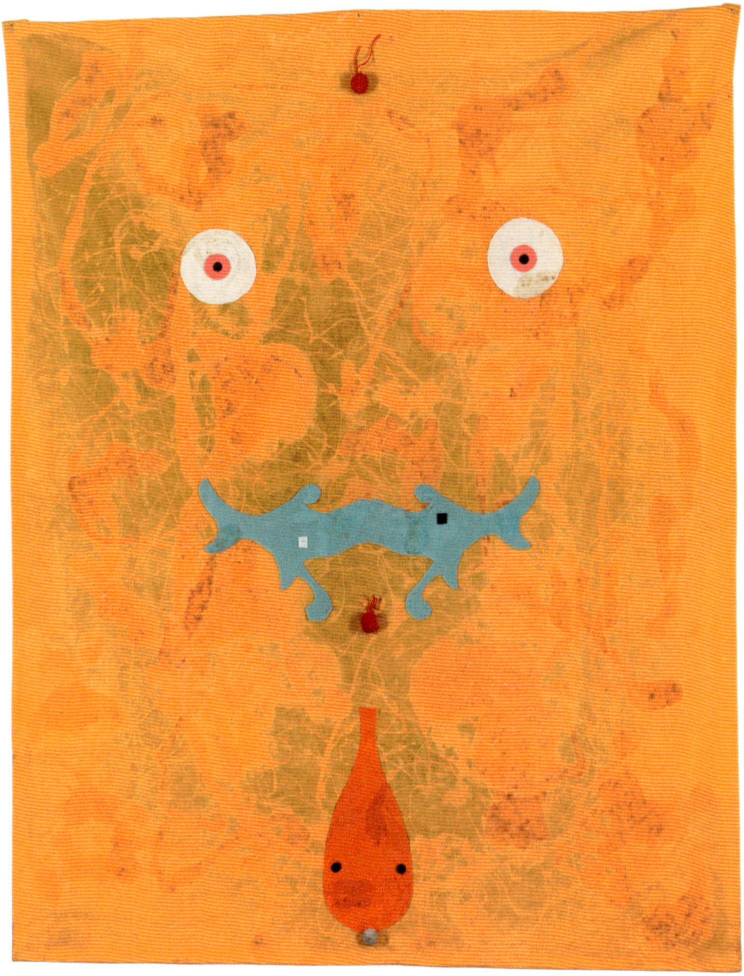

Mike Kelley | Golden Guts | 1991
Felt cut and glued, wool, 210 × 67.8 cm, inv. no. MES 123
Michael & Eleonore Stoffel Foundation in the Bayerische Staatsgemäldesammlungen, 2008

Kelley's work displays a noticeable proclivity for aesthetic expression that does not stem from the realm of high art: folk culture, arts and crafts, cartoons, subcultural codes. Within this art-world marginalia, the creative and emotional moment emerges for Kelley in its most contradictory, untamed form. *Golden Guts*, a collage of cotton and felt, reflects a primordial, immediate energy. The luminous orange cloth, with its appliqués that resemble faces, produces echoes of archaic experiences, individual as well as collective. BS

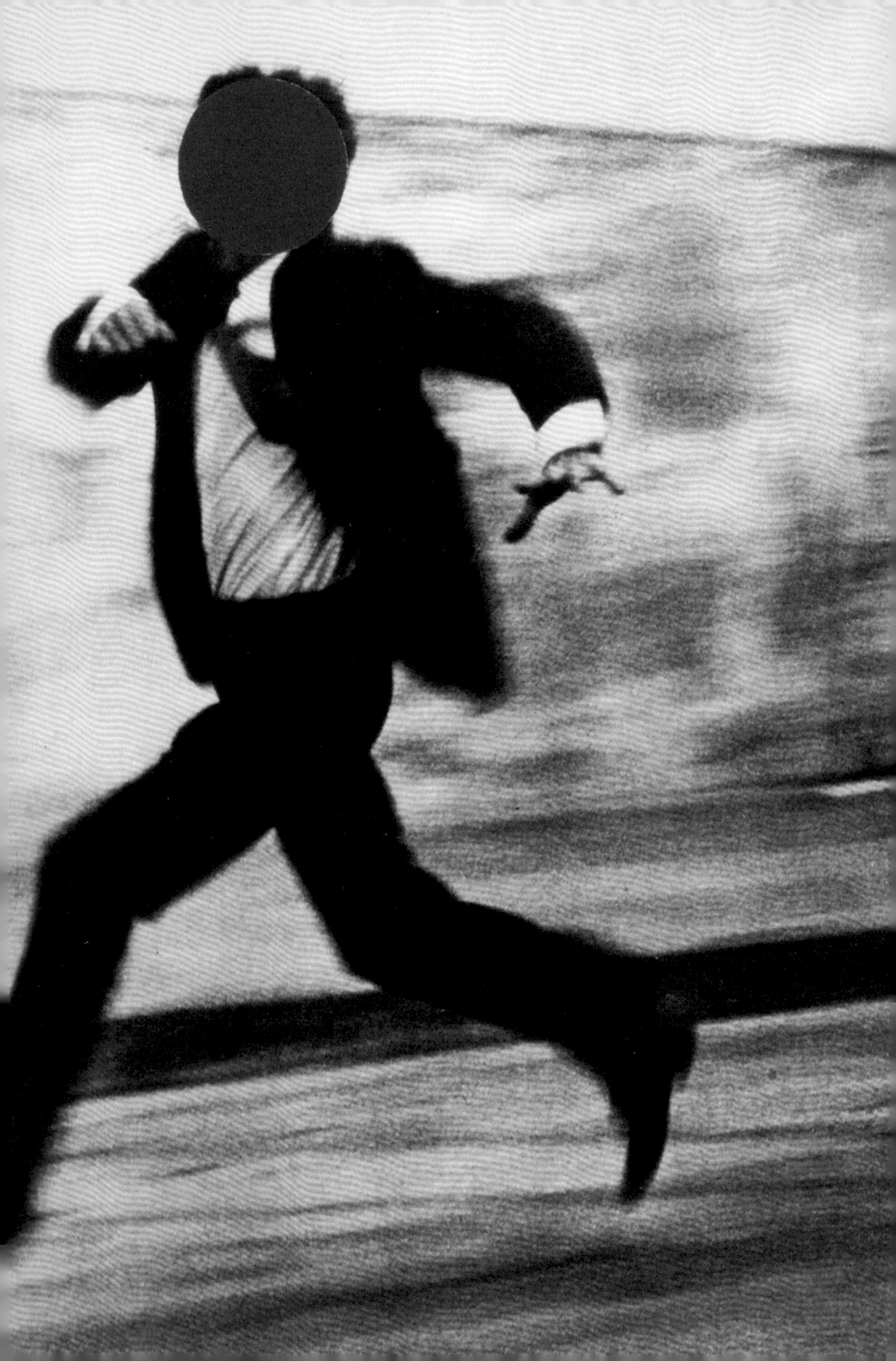

OBJECTIVELY SUBJECTIVE
A PARADIGM SHIFT IN PHOTOGRAPHY

With the opening of the Pinakothek der Moderne, photography and media art were institutionalized and given their own department within the collection. This was a comparatively late acknowledgement of the technically based image, which has undergone important changes with the progress of digitization. The permanent loan of the Siemens photo collection was a crucial part of this process. In cooperation with the Bayerische Staatsgemäldesammlungen, between 1990 and 2000, the Munich-based industrial conglomerate set up a collection focussing on contemporary art photography, complemented by selected artworks from the 1970s. The concept of the collection, comprising several hundred works, was not to encyclopaedically present all forms of contemporary photography, and above all not to represent the form of staged photography which was popular in the 1990s. Rather, it concentrated on stylistically important artists working in conceptual and documentary-style photography, on which museums in Germany had previously less focussed. In parallel, the museum sporadically made its own acquisitions of photographic works, in part through the assistance of the private patrons society PIN. A few examples are the eight-part series *Capri* by the artist Günther Förg, four outstanding lightboxes by Jeff Wall, the whole-room installation *PI* by Roni Horn, and the large-format *Rhine II* by Andreas Gursky. Beginning with this stock of works, which was relatively small but qualitatively outstanding, the collection has continued to grow. Alongside the museum's own acquisitions, further important steps for the collection's development were the transfer of the Allianz Collection, including works from the Düsseldorf School, and the accession of the Ann and Jürgen Wilde Foundation and its comprehensive and unique inventory of classical photography from the 1920s and 1930s.

A photographic collection located inside of an art museum must follow different principles than a museum purely focused on photography. Here, photography is understood above all as an independent artistic form of expression, whereas the many other possible applications of photography, such as advertising, fashion, press photography, and historical documentation are only considered incidentally. At the same time, a collection cannot develop in isolation, but must seek out dialogue with other art forms, such as painting, sculpture, installation, and video art. Two strategies characterize the Modern Art Collection's approach, and these have also been employed in its photography collection. On the one hand, the collection focuses on selected artists who are style-setting, while coupling this with an attempt to show not just isolated pieces but rather works from various phases of an artist's production or suites of works. This is done in order to reveal the artistic progression within an oeuvre. On the other hand, especially in terms of the art of the 1960s to the 1980s, the collection has focused particularly on West German and North American art and the many ways in which they have interacted. Both focal points are also reflected in the wider holdings of the Modern Art Collection, which is now renowned for its collection of American art.

The photography of the 1980s was characterized by a variety of artistic approaches that broke and expanded the traditional forms of the photographic image. Colour photography, as well as tableau-like forms of presentation and painting-sized works, all had their advent. Simultaneously, photography was also increasingly combined with graphic, painterly, and sculptural elements or with text. Documentary, conceptual, staged, and performative approaches, as well as artistic strategies that made use of appropriation, alienation, or the archival, were pursued in parallel or sometimes merged with each other. Concepts like originality and authorship increasingly informed works and their reception, the ego was torn from its position of self-certainty, representations of gender and visual clichés about women were subverted. Photographers in the 1960s and 1970s had already analysed reality with a critical attitude towards the constant stream of media images and this approach was carried on in this decade.

Social and political situations of conflicts continued to constitute important topics for photography: the Thatcher government in England was documented by Michael Parr in his series *The Last Resort*; Michael Schmidt depicted West Berlin, the city on the front-line of the Cold War; while Ukrainian artist Boris Mikhailov offered us his own perspective on 'Actually Existing Socialism'. More than almost any other artist of his generation, the Canadian Jeff Wall successfully carried on the tradition of history painting by making use of the possibilities afforded by photography. He redefined the photographic image in his complexly composed works, which are located somewhere in between the documentary and the staged, and between fiction and reality. With large slide lightboxes, the artist introduced a new form of object into art, one which he had borrowed from advertising. The lightbox oscillates between and transcends the formal boundaries between photography, painting, sculpture, film, and television. The subject of his opulent image creations is the *conditio hu-*

mana, as experienced by human beings in the late 20th century: rootlessness, isolation, racism, urbanization, the exploitation of nature, and social injustice. Wall has created a contemporary form of the history picture, at whose centre is not the ruler or the historical event, but the individual and their struggle to survive in a globalized mass society.

Since the late 1980s, German photography has been at the centre of the international contemporary art world. Andreas Gursky, Thomas Struth, and Candida Höfer, all of whom emerged from the Kunstakademie Düsseldorf, confidently asserted that their colourful and large-format images were autonomous works of art. Their repertoire of subjects, ranging from portraits to depictions of landscape and nature, to museum photos and interiors, evolved from a factual, descriptive analysis of the present, in the continuation of the documentary style they acquired under Bernd and Hilla Becher, who taught in Düsseldorf in the seventies to nineties and who remained true to the documentary style throughout their lives. The artists of the Düsseldorf School answered the futile question of whether photography is art (one which springs up continually and has been repeatedly asked for more than one and a half centuries) by no longer posing it. The Düsseldorf School would become one of the stylistically influential art movements of the late 20th century.

In the 1990s, the New York-based Japanese artist Hiroshi Sugimoto, the German artist Thomas Demand, and the American artist Zoe Leonard occupied rather solitary positions. Sugimoto works in a large format and in black and white, yet his pictures renounce photography's claim to serve a documentary function. His interest in very specific subjects, such as lake landscapes, architectural icons, and film theatres, stems from a fascination with the origins of creative production and the basic conditions of our perception and its visualization. Perception and memory likewise play a major role in the work of Thomas Demand. He thinks of photography sculpturally. His scaled reproductions of paper models, which he creates in the studio based on preexisting photographs, reflect political and social events of the present day. At the same time, their hybrid artificiality is unsettling, causing us to question what we believe in. Zoe Leonard also creates her work at the interface between analogue and digital photography. Her series *Analogue*, developed over the course of ten years, is dedicated to the theme of gentrification, in both life and photography. The gradual rise of digital photography within art marked the beginning of the new millennium.

Inka Graeve Ingelmann

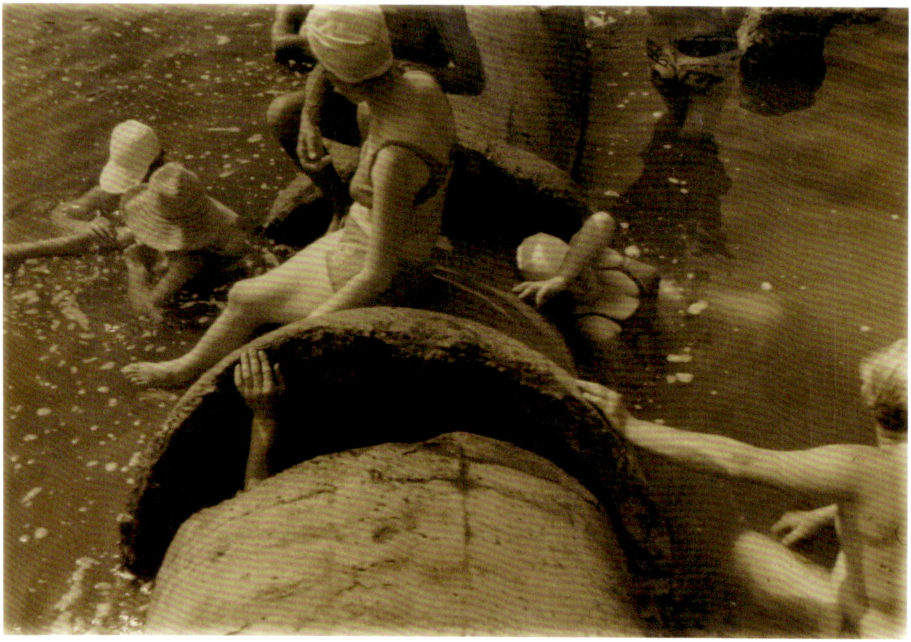

Boris Mikhailov | Untitled | 1986, from the series *Salzsee* (Salt Lake)
Gelatin silver print, 30.5 × 40.5 cm, inv. no. GV 158 13
Acquired 2004 by PIN. Freunde der Pinakothek der Moderne for the Modern Art Collection

In the style of an amateur photographer, the artist documents the joy of bathing at a Ukrainian lake. Due to a nearby factory producing soda water, the lake has a high salt content and the water is therefore alleged to alieve or even cure various ailments. Under communism, this common belief elevated this polluted pond and the dirty promenade along the shore into a health resort. Although the scenery was contrary to the normal idea of a refreshing summer holiday, and since there was scant public awareness of pollution at the time, there was also no idea of what a proper beach for swimming should look like. IGI

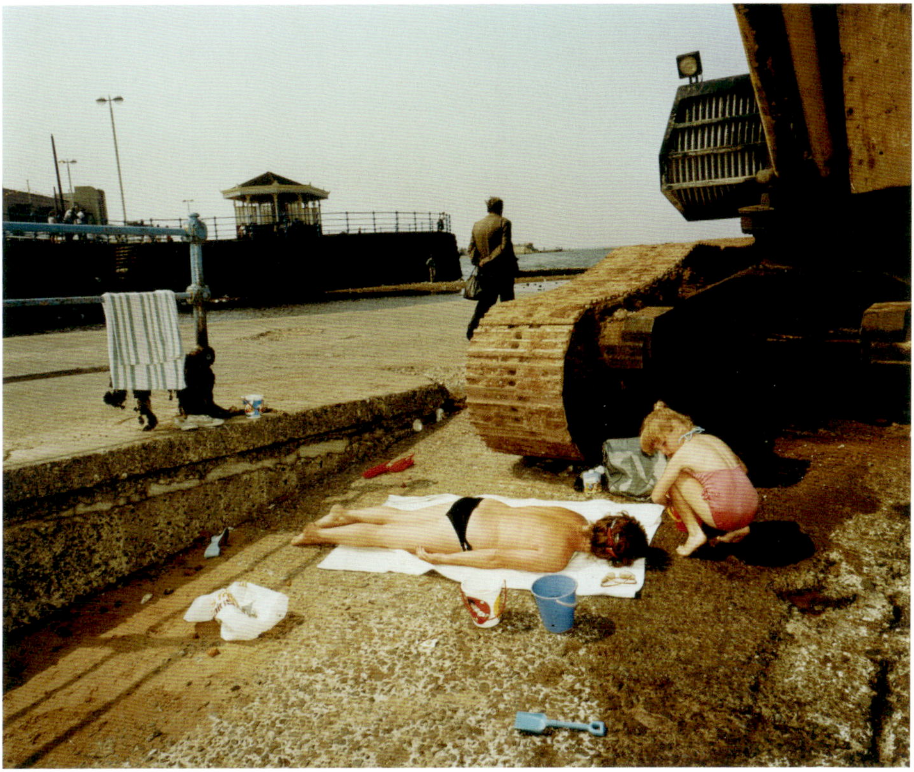

Martin Parr | Untitled | 1983/85, from the series *The Last Resort*
C-print (print 1992), 43.7 × 53.5 cm, inv. no. SAP 178
Siemens Arts Program, permanent loan from Siemens Aktiengesellschaft, accessioned 2003

The holiday location New Brighton is the setting for the series *The Last Resort* by Martin Parr, who distinctively combines documentary intent with the voyeuristic gaze. Holidaymakers belonging mostly to the underclass spend their leisure time in a hectic, uncomfortable, and dirty place, which amounts to the exact opposite of a place of resort or of relaxation. Parr sketched an unadorned and bitter satire of his homeland during the Thatcher years. The directness and the colour palette of his works were of formative importance for a generation of European colour photographers then in the process of establishing itself. IGI

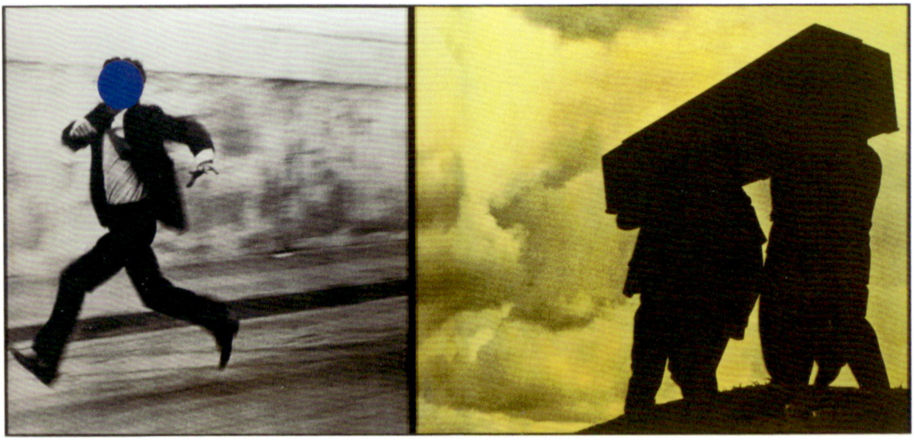

John Baldessari | Man Running / Men Carrying Box | 1990
Gelatin silver prints, vinyl paint and oil-paint tinting, 2-part, 121.3 × 118.6 cm and 121.3 × 146.6 cm, inv. no. SAP 26 1-2
Siemens Arts Program, permanent loan from Siemens Aktiengesellschaft, accessioned 2003

As in most of the artist's works, found photographs are the raw material for these images. Through manual interventions, including colouring and overpainting, he revokes the image's documentary character. By combining subjects which originally existed apart from one another, he creates a new context of meaning. The point of reference for this diptych, on the level of both content and form, is a passage from the avant-garde novel *The Life and Opinions of Tristram Shandy, Gentleman* by the English writer Laurence Sterne, which handles the existential topics of threat, escape, and death. IGI

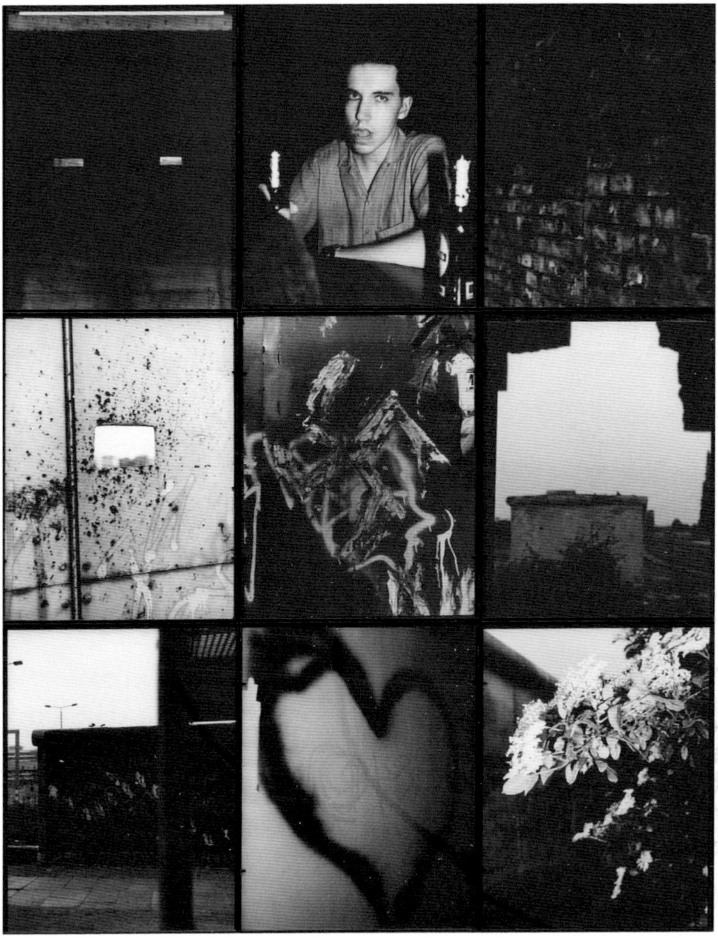

Michael Schmidt | Untitled | 1985/87, tableau,
from the series *Waffenruhe* (Ceasefire)
Gelatin silver prints (print 1991), 9 parts, each 49 × 39 cm, inv. no. SAP 202 1/9-9/9
Siemens Arts Program, permanent loan from Siemens Aktiengesellschaft,
accessioned 2003

Ceasefire, a book and exhibition project which comprises about fifty photographs, can be read as a report on the mental condition, translated into images based on pictures taken by the Berlin photographer Michael Schmidt in the early 1980s in West Berlin. Even though the Wall is visible in a variety of the works, the project is not a documentation of the divided city, but rather an analysis formulated as an image sequence in which grief, loss, pain, and resistance encounter one another in both surprising and disturbing ways. IGI

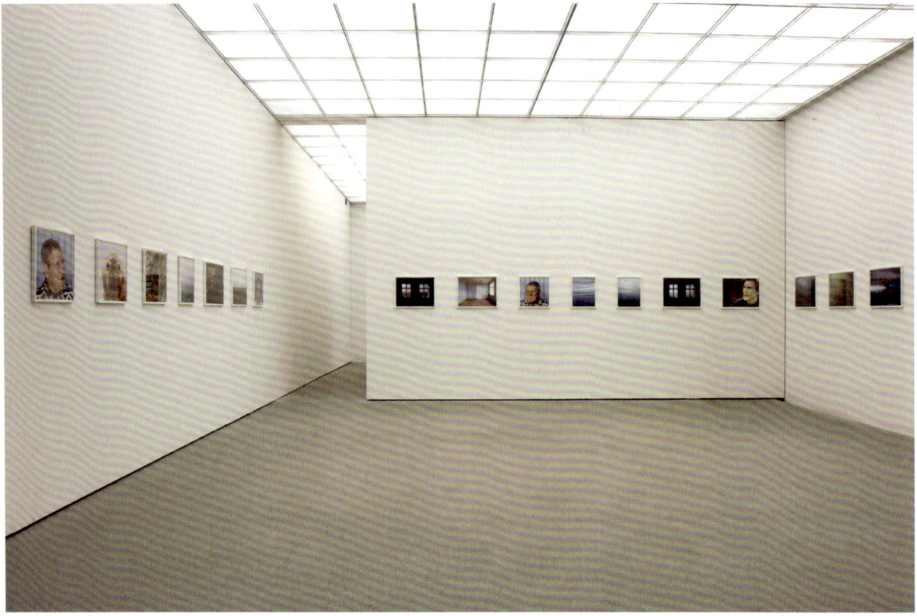

Roni Horn | **PI** | 1998
Iris prints, 45 parts, 22 each 56 × 73.7 cm, 13 each 56 × 56 cm, 10 each 56 × 45.7 cm,
inv. no. 15537 1/45-45/45
Acquired 1999

This 45-part photo work was shaped by the artist's several-weeks-long stays in Iceland. She creates an impressive image of the country's geographical situation and the state of society there through her use of repeating subjects like landscape and nature scenes, stuffed sea birds, portraits of local residents, but also television images from a TV soap opera. Despite its serial nature, the work is not narratively structured, but rather illustrates various facets of this place's specific identity: 'Iceland is a verb and its action is to centre.'
IGI

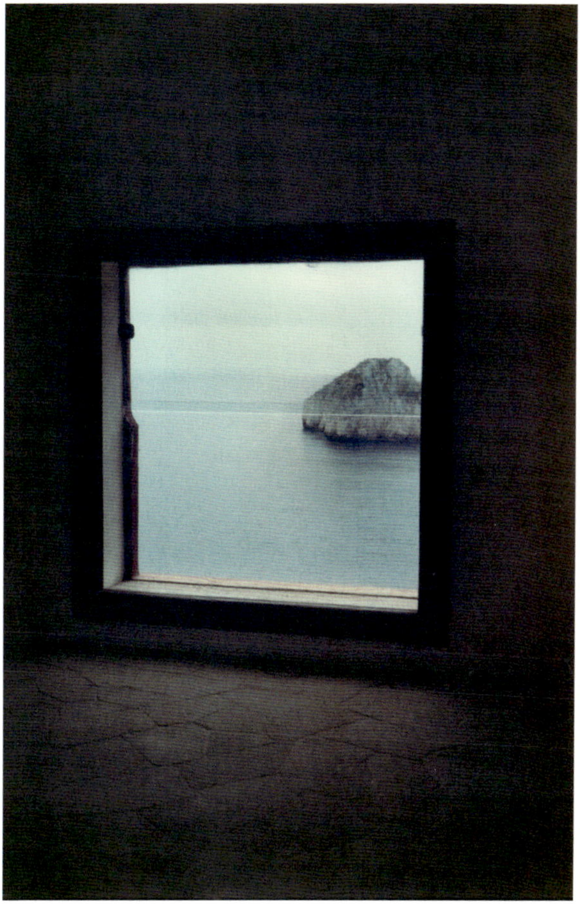

Günther Förg | Capri I | 1989
C-print, 270 × 180 cm, inv. no. GM 91
Acquired 1990 by PIN. Freunde der Pinakothek der Moderne for the Modern Art Collection

This large-format picture was taken in the villa of Italian author Curzio Malaparte, which was erected during the time of fascism. The impression of a picture within a picture is underlined by the massive frame of the huge window, as well as by the heavy oak frame of the photograph itself. This monumentality is broken not only by our impression of a Romantic view of nature but also by the intentional blurring. While the viewer is reflected in the glazing, the solemn and timeless aspect of the architecture and landscape shifts to one of personal reflection. IGI

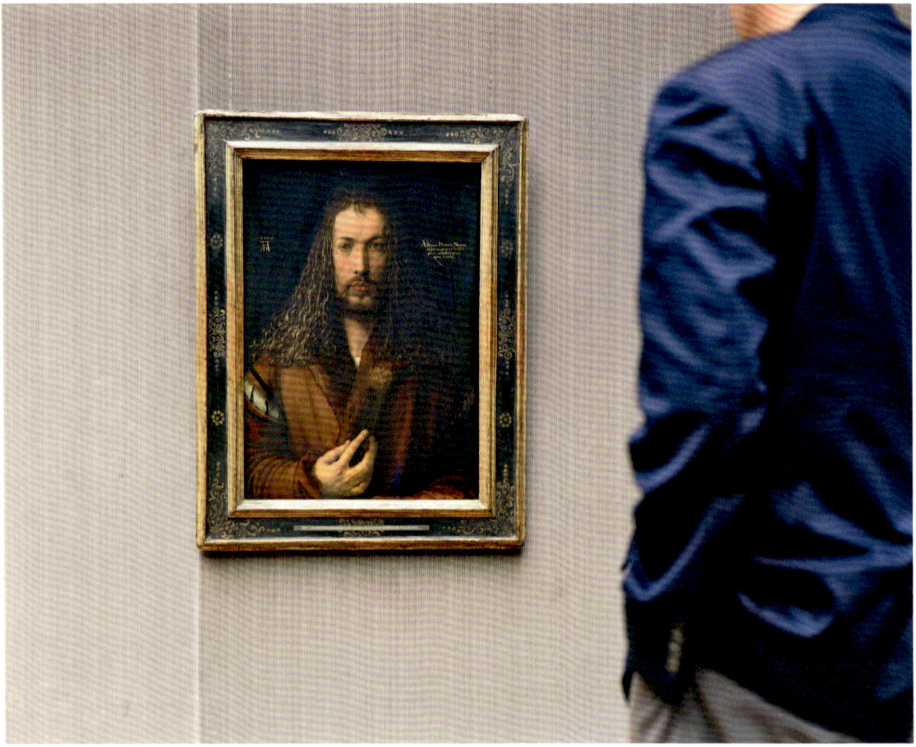

Thomas Struth | Alte Pinakothek, Self-Portrait, Munich 2000 | 2000
C-print, Diasec, 116.5 × 147 cm, inv. no. 16305
Donation of Lothar Schirmer, 2014

A special form of dialogue and self-examination are staged here by Thomas Struth, who has positioned himself across from the self-portrait of Albrecht Dürer in the Alte Pinakothek. He has created an imaginary dialogue, bridging a 500-year gap between two confident, self-aware artistic innovators. By using the pictorial language of an objective documentary photography, in brilliant colours and in the format of a painting, Struth discloses the diverse conditions of modern life in his works. They are shaped by the contrasts between past and present, individual and society, and the private and the public. IGI

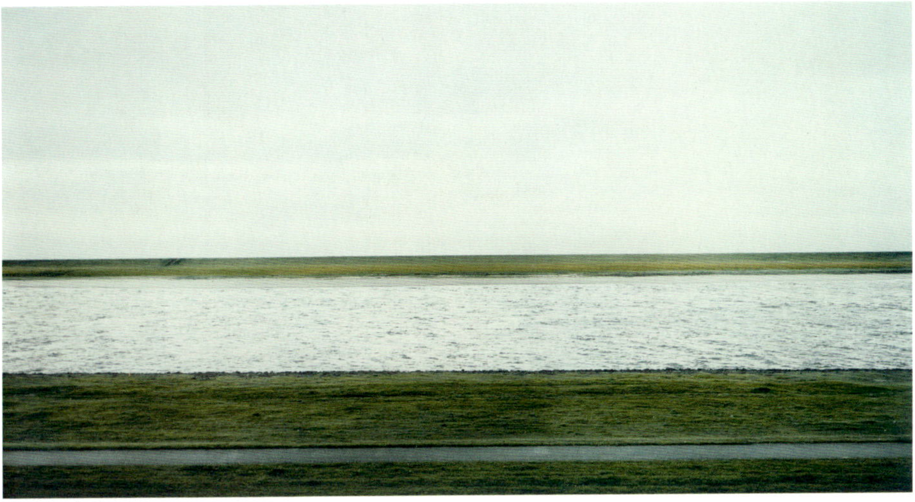

Andreas Gursky | Rhein II (Rhine II) | 1999
C-print, 207 × 357 cm, inv. no. GM 127
Acquired 2001 by PIN. Freunde der Pinakothek der Moderne for the Modern Art Collection

Rhine II is a modern representation of a river that has served a crucial role in forging Germany's identity, myths, and visual clichés. A view captured on location has been digitally manipulated so that the viewer perceives a nearly monochrome image composed of greyish-green colour fields. Dipped into a leaden seriousness, the current's flow is relieved of its temporality, simultaneously taking on a crystalline presence and an inapproachability. Andreas Gursky wanted to formulate a contemporary picture of the Rhine. He found reality insufficient for his purposes and therefore found this fictional construction necessary. IGI

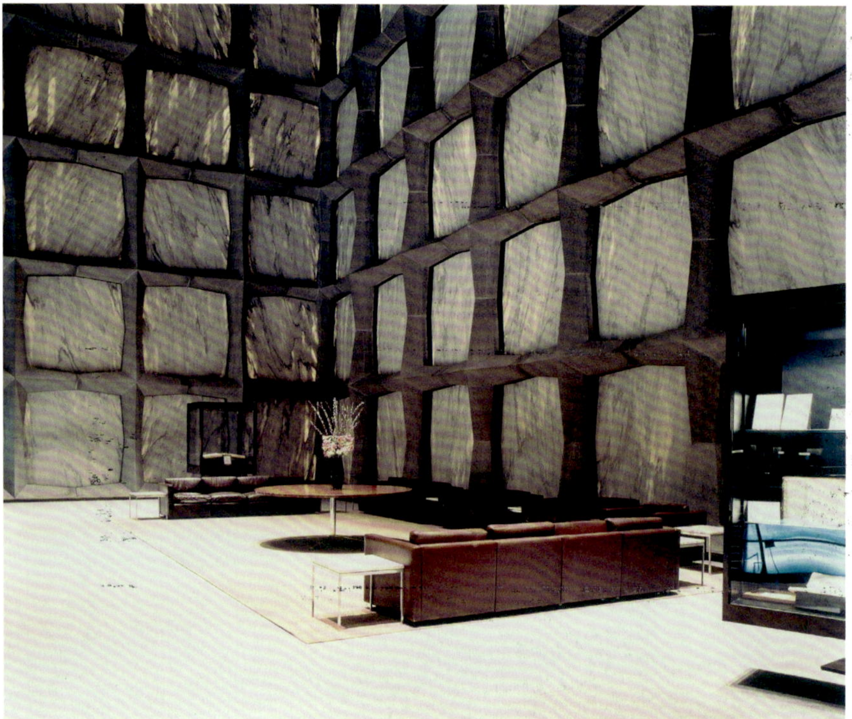

Candida Höfer | Beinecke Rare Book and Manuscript Library New Haven CT IV | 2002
C-print, 186 × 152 cm, inv. no. GV 149
Acquired 2003 by PIN. Freunde der Pinakothek der Moderne for the
Modern Art Collection

Space and above all the interiors of public and semi-public buildings, such as libraries, universities, and exhibition halls, are the central theme of the artist. Höfer does not just document architecture, even if some of her photos, such as this one, were taken in famous structures. Rather, she portrays the aura of spaces. Her gaze is directed at what they reveal about their history and their transforming roles as places of social and cultural exchange. Human beings remain invisible and, at the same time, are revealed through the traces they leave behind. IGI

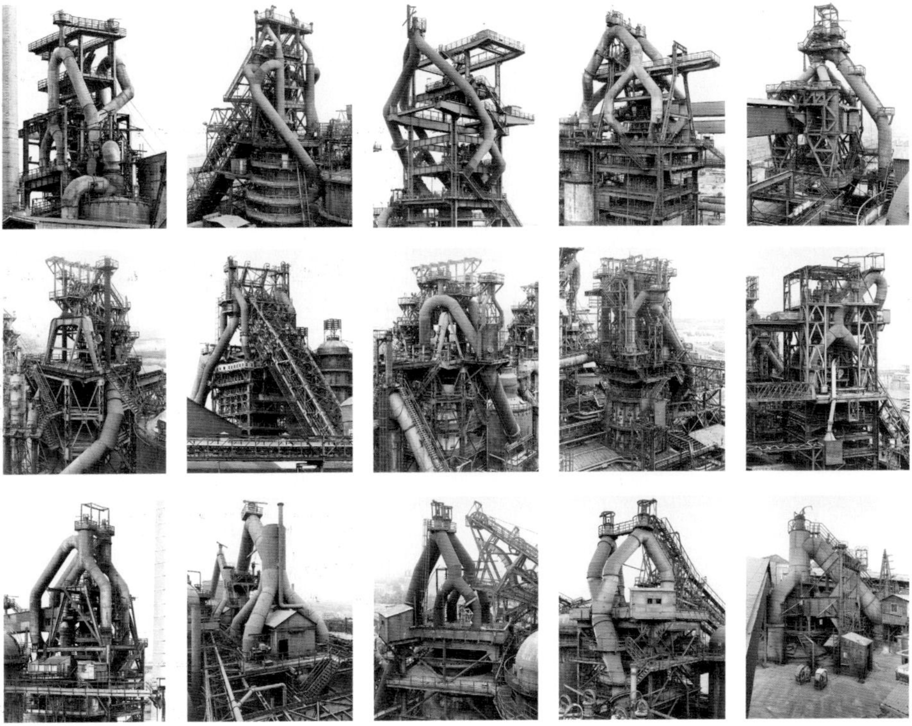

Bernd & Hilla Becher | Hochöfenköpfe (Typologie) (Furnace Heads – Typology) | 1988
Gelatin silver prints, 15 parts,
each 40.7 × 30.6 cm, inv. no. 16306 1/15-15/15
Donation of Lothar Schirmer, 2014

Bernd and Hilla Becher were among the greatest documentarists of our time. For over 40 years, the couple photographed industrial architectures faced with the threat of extinction in Central Europe, Britain, and the USA. At the centre of their archaeological interest were not individual buildings but building types. By making use of a singular photographic vernacular and a consistently employed a methodological approach, they created a unique archive. Their images are not only of inestimable cultural historical value, but can also be considered as autonomous works of art. IGI

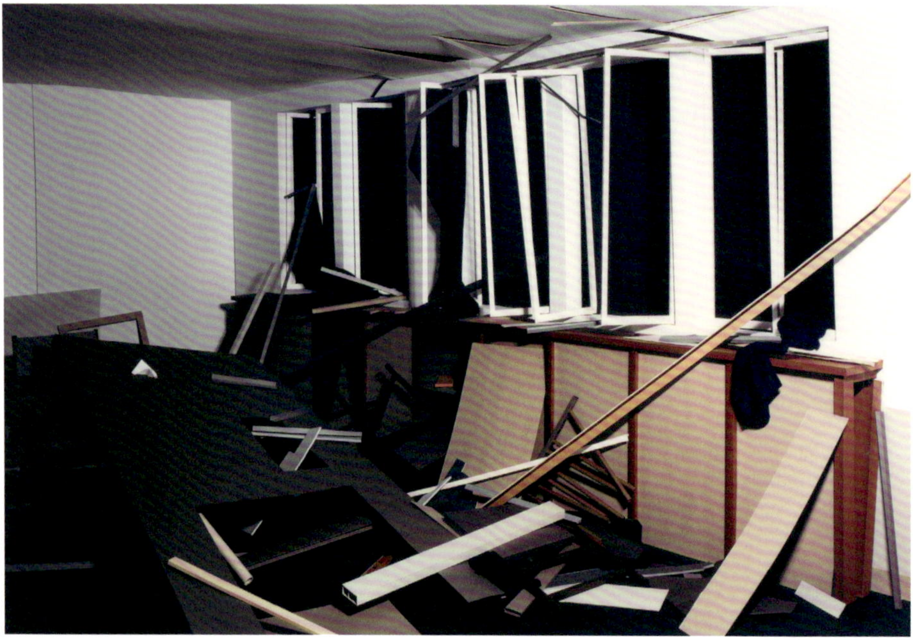

Thomas Demand | **Raum** (Room) | 1994
Cibachrome/Diasec, 183.5 × 270.3 cm, inv. no. KM 1070
Acquired 1994

These interiors, emptied of human beings, are manufactured by the artist as nearly life-sized models made of cardboard and paper, which are reproduced on the scale of 1:1. Photographs of political or social events that have shaped our collective image memory serve as his raw material. Here, he makes a reference to Hitler's headquarters, the 'Wolf's Lair', which was destroyed after an attempted assassination. But Demand has not reconstructed the historical source material. Rather, he has alienated the image from its original and deleted all specific references to it. What remains is a shell, a drained, unreal space that invites viewers to further manipulate it in their own minds. IGI

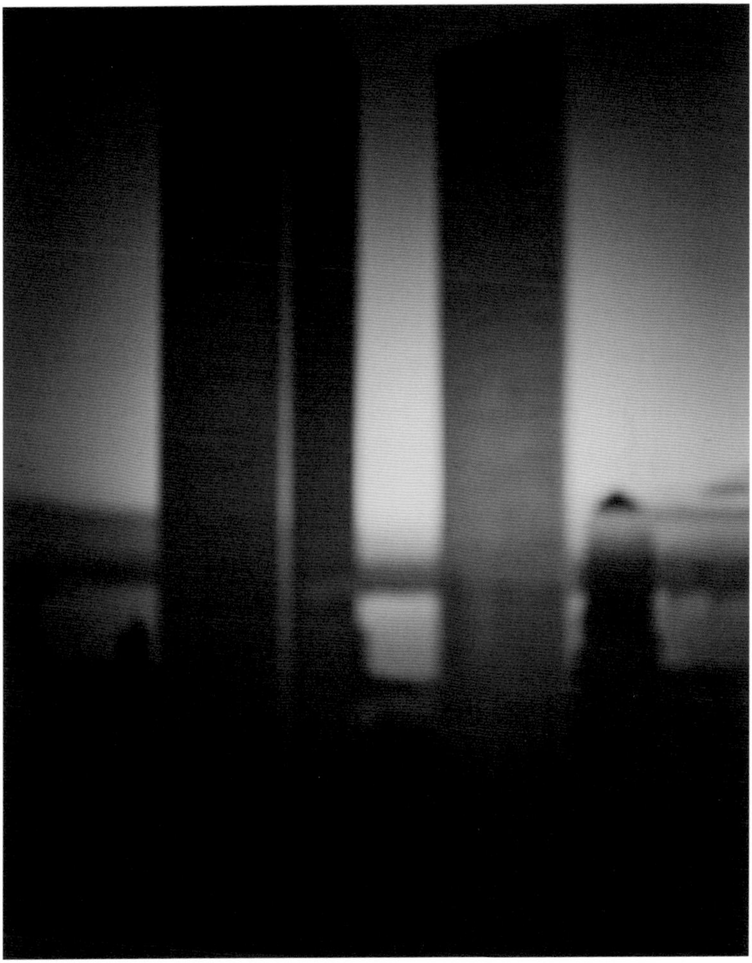

Hiroshi Sugimoto | World Trade Center, Minoru Yamazaki | 1997
Gelatin silver print, 61 × 50.8 cm, inv. no. 15542
Acquired 1999

It was the icons of architectural modernism that inspired the New York-based Japanese artist Hiroshi Sugimoto to create his series *Architecture*. Taken slightly from below and fuzzily reproduced, these images, which are still executed in a mystical black and white, convey an impression of the visionary idea from which they were once developed. These buildings, which we have seen so often that they have solidified into a cliché through their constant reproduction, are returned to a sort of primitive state. At the same time, a transience is inscribed into them, whether they become victims of time or of wilful destruction. IGI

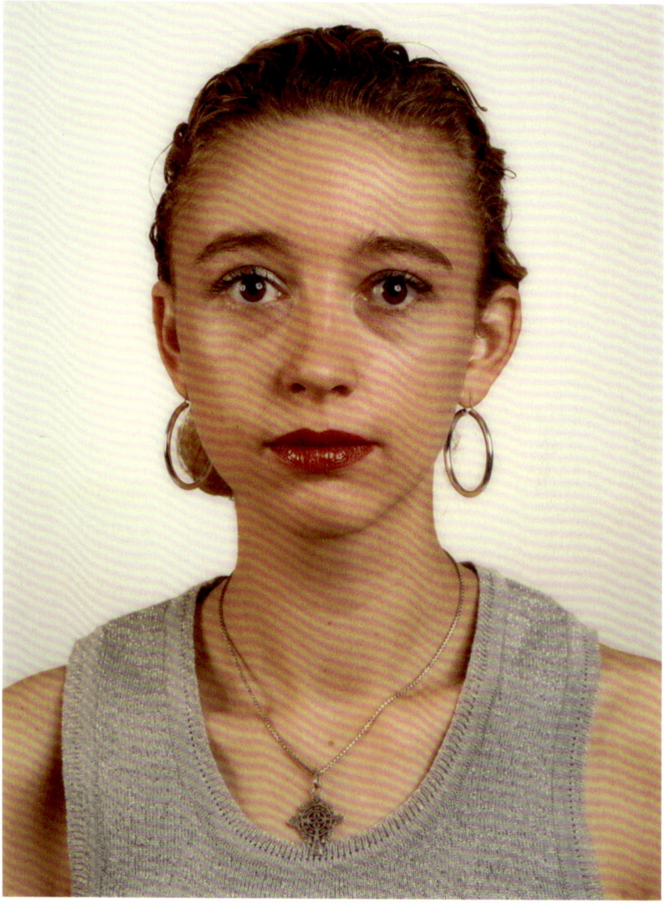

Thomas Ruff | Untitled | 1988
C-print, Diasec (print 2008), 212 × 180 cm, inv. no. APKV 83
Loan from Allianz Private Krankenversicherung, accessioned 2004

The genre of the portrait lay at the heart of Thomas Ruff's early work. He depicted his peers, photographing their bust portraits against a neutral background. He took his inspiration from the style of passport photos, avoiding a subjective approach. Initially printed as a small portrait, the image's magnification to painting format and its new form of presentation as a Diasec print produce a visual effect that typifies the Düsseldorf School's renewal of art photography.
IGI

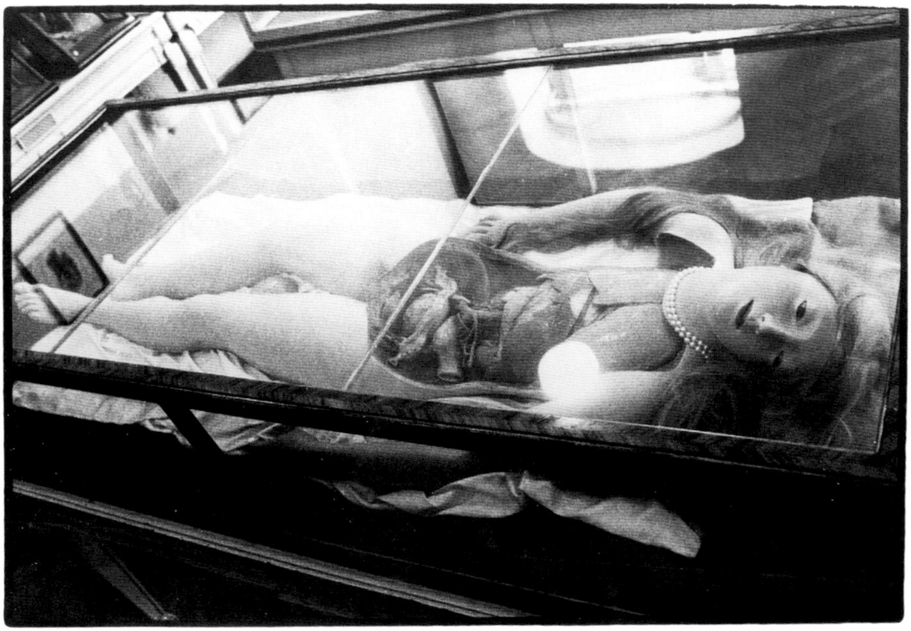

Zoe Leonard | Wax Anatomical Model with Pearls | 1990
Gelatin silver print, 68.7 × 102.3 cm, inv. no. 16431
Acquired 2016 with funds of Alexander Tutsek Foundation

It is inconspicuous, often trivial-looking and everyday things which inspire in Zoe Leonard an almost scientific perseverance and an apparently tender respect. She makes them speak, as she has this *Medicean Venus* from Vienna. In addition to her interest in the subject, she is concerned with the act of seeing and the cultural conditions of our perception, which she seeks to make visible and palpable. Photography is never a likeness or a reproduction, but always a visual construct that reveals as much about its beholder as its subject.
IGI

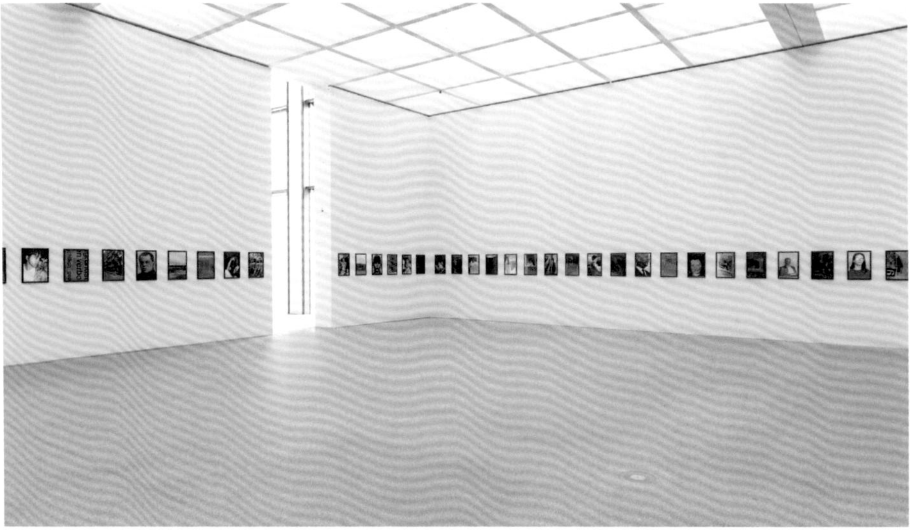

Michael Schmidt | **EIN-HEIT** (ONE-NESS) | 1991/94
Gelatin silver prints, 163 parts, each 50.6 × 34.5 cm, inv. no. SAP 204 1-163
Siemens Arts Program, permanent loan from Siemens Aktiengesellschaft, accessioned 2003

This group of works of 163 photographs was made between 1991 and 1994. Presented in a dense sequence and framed in iron, the viewer is enveloped by a nearly endless series of images: dreary cityscapes, landscapes, still lifes, and anonymous portraits are mixed with reproductions of historical photos. The latter are images of mass parades, politicians' portraits, and historical events and can be read as bits and pieces of information or scraps of memory connected to 20th century German history. Yet this compendium remains fragmentary, it resists assembly into a unified whole. IGI

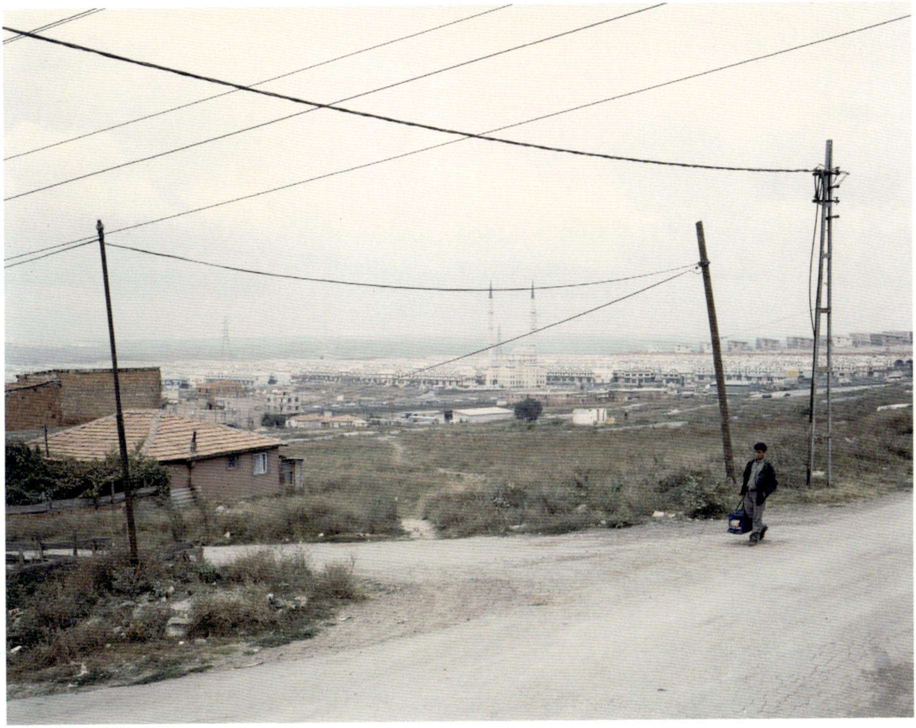

Jeff Wall | A Villager from Aricaköyu Arriving in Mahmutbey, Istanbul | 1997
Large picture slide in lightbox, 209.5 × 271.4 cm, inv. no. 15503
Acquired 1998

In the form of a photographic re-enactment, Jeff Walls shows us a young man from Anatolia whom he had met shortly before. His picture has been taken on his way to arriving in Mahmutbey, a suburb of Istanbul characterized by illegal settlements and sprawling commercial districts. Mahmutbey appears neither urban nor village-like, but rather like a place of passage offering little in the way of orientation. The viewpoint he has selected directs our gaze into the distance, but not towards the journey's destination. It can be read as an image poem on the late 20th century megalopolis. IGI

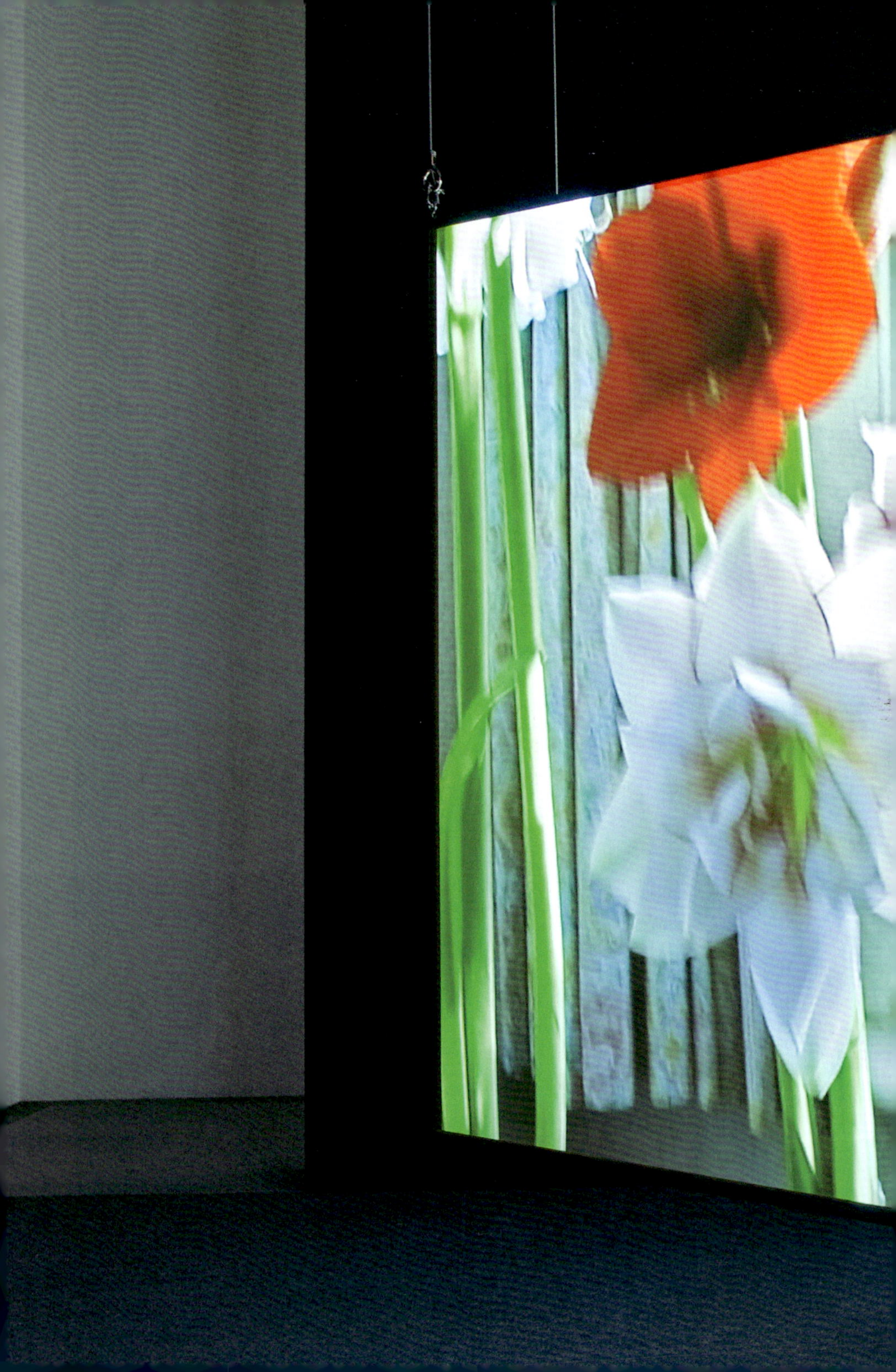

CLOSE-UP
VIDEO AND MEDIA ART

Lens-based art – artistic works that consist predominantly of technically generated images – has only been subject to acquisition policy for the last 25 years, although video art has had a presence in exhibitions and museums since the 1970s. The attempt to systematically come to grips with the maturation of the form was undertaken beginning in the late 1990s, and shortly thereafter, both major and whole-room, installative works could be acquired. At the beginning were important pioneers of video art such as Bruce Nauman, whose five-channel installation *World Peace (Projected)* is devoted to forms of interpersonal communication. Gary Hill's hour-long language study, *Remarks on Color*, based on a text by Ludwig Wittgenstein, and Bill Viola's installation *Tiny Deaths* that plumbs the blackness of the space also represent specific artistic objectives through which different approaches to video art manifest themselves within the collection. At the same time came the acquisition of *Himalaya Goldstein's Living Room* (p. 328), an adaptation of a living room bathed in garish colours and sounds by Swiss artist Pipilotti Rist, later continued with *Extremitäten (weich, weich)* (Extremities, Soft, Soft). The latter two acquisitions were not only among the first of a female artist; they also represent a significant commitment to putting current figures from the ranks of young artists just establishing themselves at the centre of the future collection of media art. Thus, the growth in the field of media art in the early years of the 21st century is dedicated, in particular, to artists who had not yet reached the age of 40 at the time of acquisition.

The Albanian-born, Paris-based artist Anri Sala was barely 30 years old when the Modern Art Collection purchased his video *Intervista*. The work is noteworthy in that the artist proceeds as a documentary filmmaker would. It tells the story of the discovery of an old film reel without a soundtrack, whose reconstruction is finally achieved by a group of deaf people. Sala's *Intervista* is an early example of a documentary film incorporated into a public art collection. The camera's cautiousness, which gives less space to showing than it does to moments of silence, observation, and listening, is what makes the film a work of art.

Intervista was followed by other works using documentary techniques, like *Bernadette*, the portrait of the Irish activist Bernadette Devlin by Duncan Campbell, or the touching *Singing Lesson II* (p. 332) by Artur Żmijewski, in which young deaf people study a Bach cantata and perform in the Thomaskirche in Leipzig. *Countenance*, the four-part, room-filling projection by Fiona Tan, however, is a filmic tribute to August Sander's epochal work of photographic portraiture *People of the Twentieth Century* (p. 129), transposed to Berlin at the turn of the millennium. Another example is the two-channel work *Re-enactments* (p. 337) by the Mexico-based Belgian artist Francis Alÿs. It shows the same simple course of events on two projection screens installed side by side: the artist purchases a gun, then moves through the city with the weapon exposed until he is stopped and forcibly disarmed by the police. While in the first film the artist performs this task without knowing how it will turn out, the second film shows an almost exact re-enactment of the events. The criteria for what is real and what is staged are here put to the test.

Over the years, through the acquisition of exemplary figures, a multi-layered media collection has grown that displays the broad spectrum of artistic approaches – from Bjørn Melhus's single-channel video *Das Zauberglas* (The Magic Glass), staged with playful naïveté and drawing on film history; to the fast-paced film collage *DIAL H-I-S-T-O-R-Y* by Johan Grimonprez thematizing the flood of images in the digital age; and on to the nearly 40-minute cinematographic work *Continuity* by Omer Fast, which follows a German couple who orchestrate three home-coming welcomes for a (fictional?) soldier-son returning from service in Afghanistan, each time played by a different young man.

In the selection of media artists, there is also a focus on those who work across different media, such as the Dutch artist Rineke Dijkstra. Her two-channel work *The Buzz Club, Liverpool, UK / Mystery World, Zaandam, NL* shows young people dancing to techno music who are also the subject of a series of photographs. With his digitally animated works such as *Kindergarten Antonio Sant'Elia, 1932* and *Long Goodbye,* Belgian artist David Claerbout creates a hybrid being, somewhere between photography and film. A close connection to film montage is also apparent in Peter Fischli's and David Weiss' slide projection *Sommer-Projektion 2 (flowers)* as well as *Pilze/Funghi,* their series of mushroom photographs. The history and magic of film is also the starting point of all the filmic and photographic works of artist duo Teresa Hubbard and Alexander Birchler, who are represented in the collection with both the video piece *Eight*, a melancholy homage to growing up, as well as with *Filmstills,* four large-scale exterior views of Berlin arthouse cinemas.

Finally, installative media works are particularly noteworthy, for example the portrait *The 4 Seasons of Veronica Read* by Turkish-born film producer and artist Kutluğ Ataman, in which four hanging projection screens form a space that can be walked through. Veronica Read, the film's titular protagonist, cultivates hippeastrum ('amaryllis') bulbs with great devotion in her small flat, showing us the growth stages of her cultivars over the course of a year, while the intensity of her obsession changes with the passing seasons.

The three-month-long video installation *Empire* by American artist Paul Pfeiffer can also be seen in this context; its digital images are projected from several data processors, which are visibly arranged on a rack, constituting a kind of memory cage in the space. The harsh view of a mini DV camera records the time-consuming building of a wasp's nest, conjuring associations with principles of state formation and governance, efficiency and dependence.

Working similarly with installation is the British artist Jonathan Monk, whose *Searching for the Centre of a Sheet of A4 Paper* consists of two quietly rattling 16mm projectors, which face each other and throw their flickering images from two sides onto a white sheet of paper: a black and a white point dance around each other, appearing to search for the centre of the sheet – a metaphor for a continuous, and ultimately never finalized, movement towards understanding.

Inka Graeve Ingelmann and Bernhart Schwenk

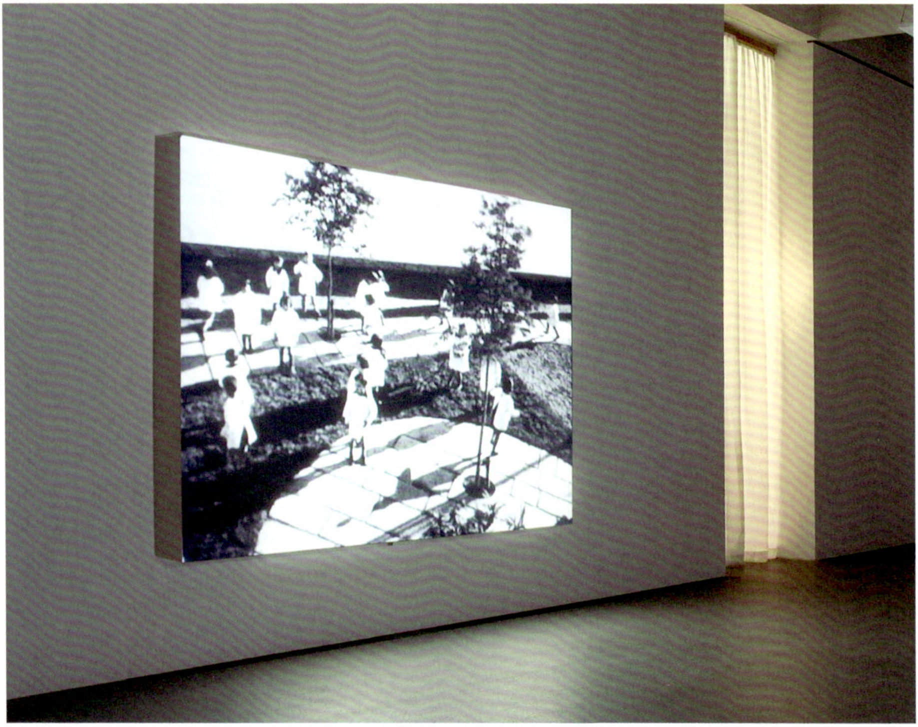

David Claerbout | Kindergarten Antonio Sant'Elia, 1932 | 1998
1-channel video installation, b/w, no sound, 11 min, inv. no. GV 109
Acquired 2010 by PIN. Freunde der Pinakothek der Moderne for the Modern Art Collection

This video work is based on a 1932 photograph of a kindergarten by the same name, designed by Italian architect Giuseppe Terragni. In contrast to the children frozen in their game, the young trees move imperceptibly as if a light wind were moving through them. There is an unresolved tension between the formal, rationalist layout of the kindergarten and the disorderly children's game with its urge towards individuality. The year reminds us that we are on the eve of the tyranny of fascism across Europe. IGI

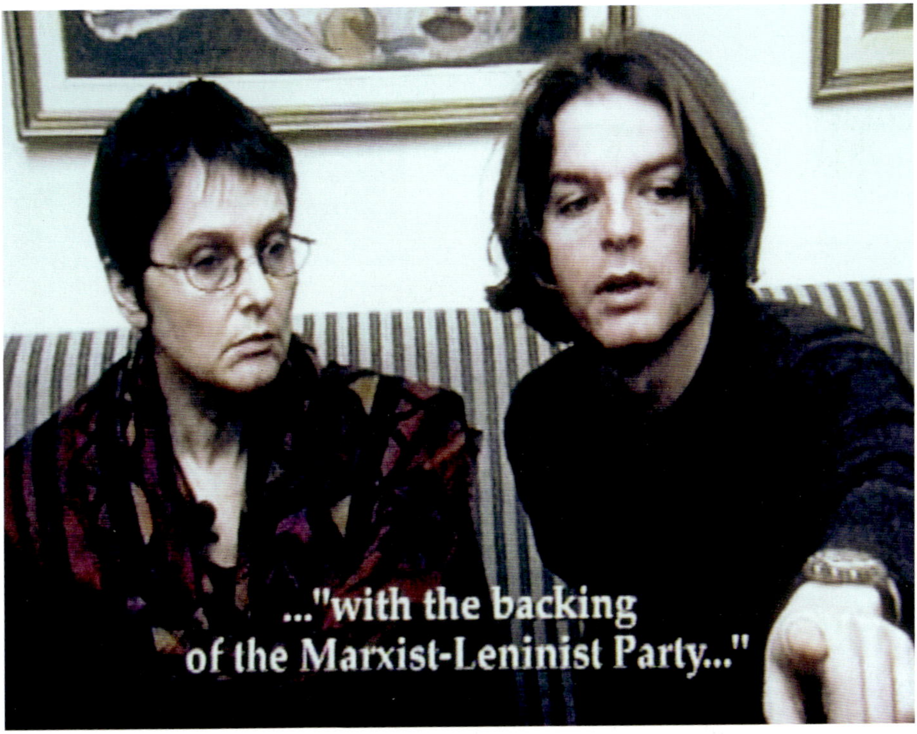

Anri Sala | Intervista (Interview) | 1998
1-channel video, b/w and colour, sound, 26 min., inv. no. GV 130
Acquired 2002 by PIN. Freunde der Pinakothek der Moderne for the Modern Art Collection

Intervista is the story of a reconstruction of the past: during a move, the artist discovered a 16mm film from the 1970s whose soundtrack had been lost. It contains an interview with his mother, who at the time had been a member of the Communist Youth League, but who no longer remembers what she said in the film. In the end, deaf people are able to translate Sala's mother's lip movements into spoken and written language. The journey into the past becomes a confrontation with hopes and dreams, and with their failure. BS

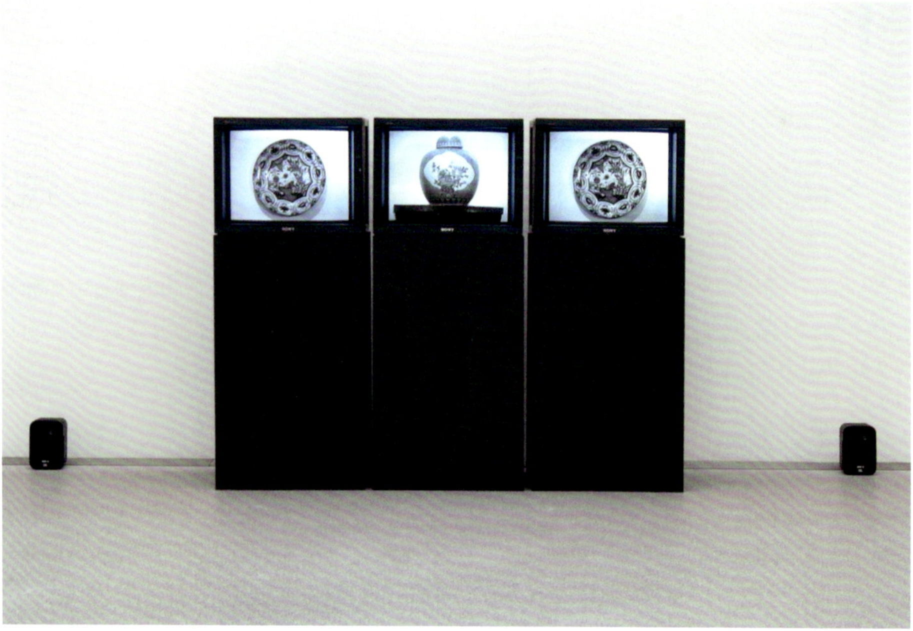

Marcel Odenbach | Der Elefant im Porzellanladen (The Elephant in the China Shop) | 1987
3-channel video installation (vase, plate, field, grass), colour, sound, 53 sec., 53 sec., 2 min. 16 sec., inv. no. B 859, B 860, B 861
Acquired 1991

The Elephant in the China Shop shows two videos on three monitors, in which vibrations set porcelain objects wobbling, to be rescued at the last second by the grip of two hands. On two further monitors at ground level, a video plays, combining photographs of grass and fields with images from the Second World War. The sounds of explosions and shots alternate with the *St. Matthew Passion* by Johann Sebastian Bach. The destructive power of the war, which thunders by like an elephant through a china shop, washes over the viewer, who must move around in order to take everything in. FS

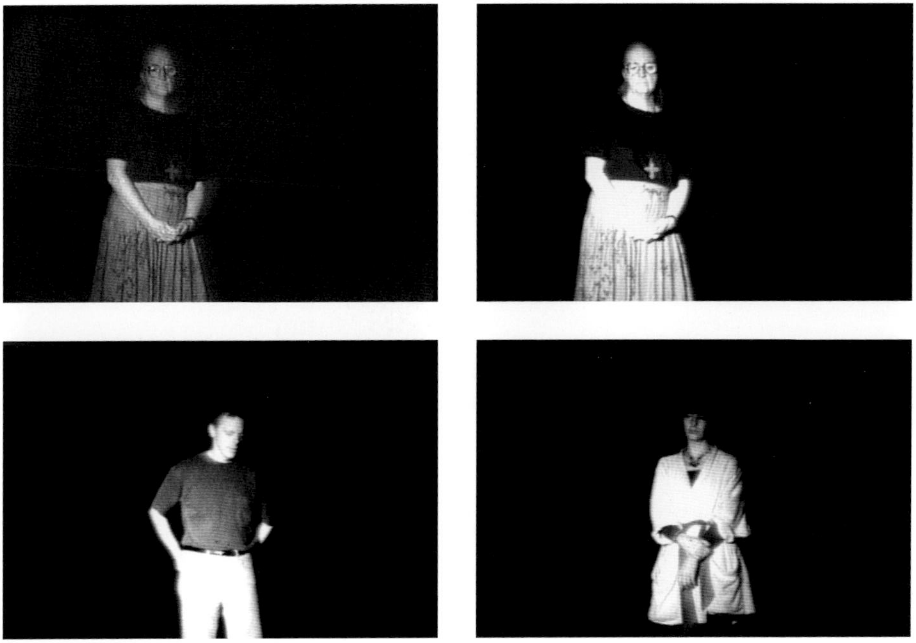

Bill Viola | Tiny Deaths | 1993
3-channel video installation, b/w, sound, loop, inv. no. GV 109
Acquired 1999 by PIN. Freunde der Pinakothek der Moderne for the Modern Art Collection

An indistinct murmur fills the space, in which, over and over, shadowy persons can be made out on three screens, moving slowly. Occasionally a person steps forward, becomes visible, the sound swells and shortly thereafter the figure evaporates with a flash like lightning. As is so often the case with Viola, the subject here is the transformation of the human body and spirit. The title alludes, however, not to death, but refers – based on Buddhist beliefs – to moments of self-discovery and enlightenment, which can vanish as quickly as they arise.
FS

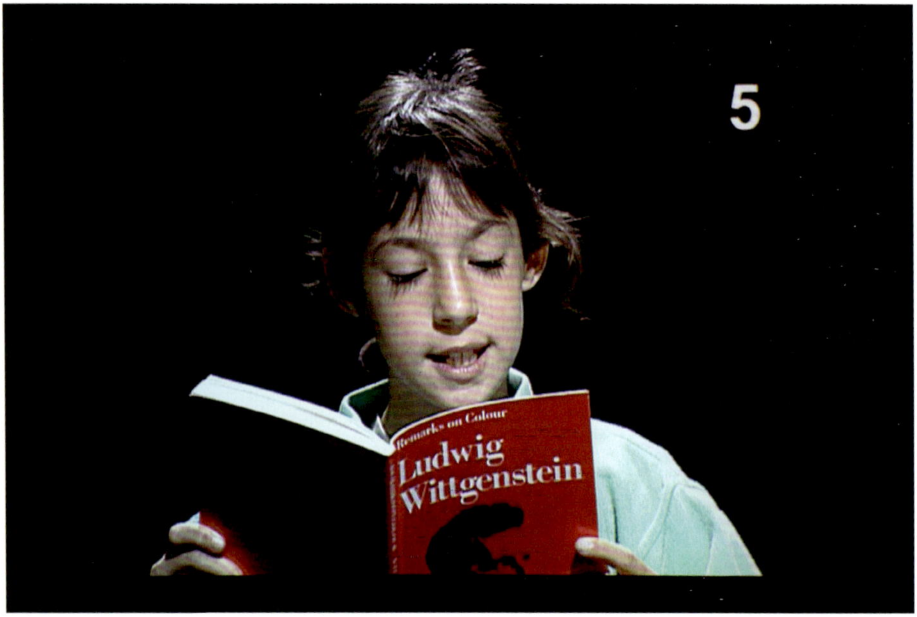

Gary Hill | Remarks on Color | 1994
1-channel video, colour, sound, 45 min., inv. no. GV 123
Acquired 1999 by PIN. Freunde der Pinakothek der Moderne for the Modern Art Collection

In 1951, the philosopher Ludwig Wittgenstein published *Remarks on Colour* and discussed the extent to which the manifestation of colour in the world can be expressed through language. In the German version of Gary Hill's work (there are several foreign-language versions) a young girl eagerly reads out the text. But she is clearly unable to fully comprehend its complexity. Hill, who in his work repeatedly devotes himself to the effects of language and image, thereby directs the attention increasingly away from the language and towards the image, providing an artistic contribution to Wittgenstein's musings. FS

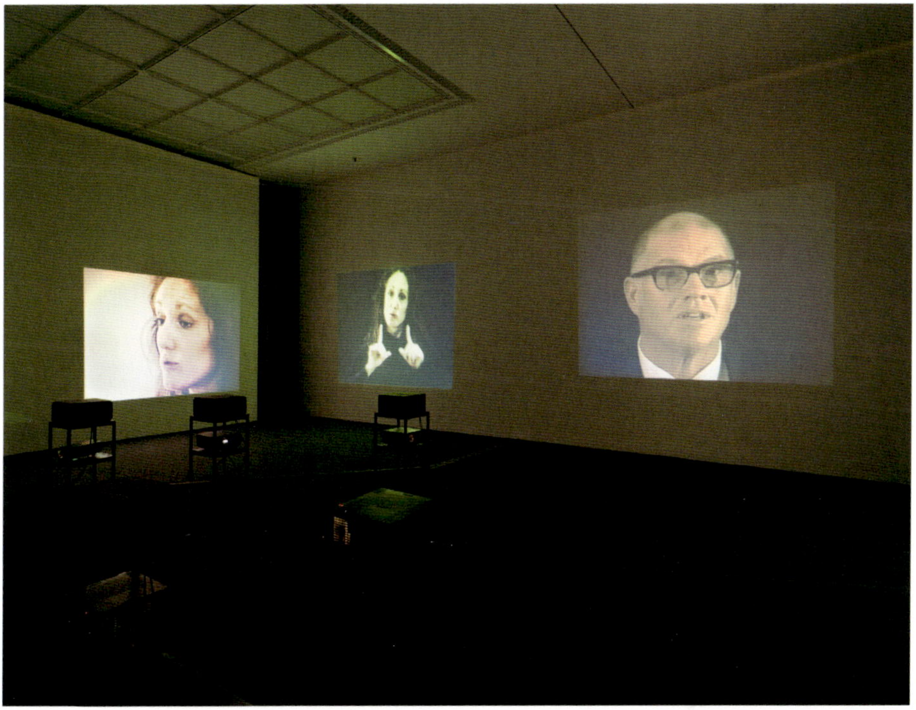

Bruce Nauman | World Peace (Projected) | 1996
5-channel video installation, colour, sound, between 45 and 55 min., inv. no. B 884
Acquired 1997

'I'll talk, you'll listen. You'll talk, I'll listen. [...] You'll talk, they'll listen. They'll talk, you'll listen [...].' Filmed in close-up, human subjects recite this text in spoken and sign language, systematically running through every possible constellation of speaking and listening. Do speaking and listening contain the possibility for nothing less than world peace? Yet the subjects speak not to one another, but isolated, to themselves. Reminiscent of a mantra, this piece of conceptual art is not least a phonetic game that morphs into the projected 'word piece'.
FS

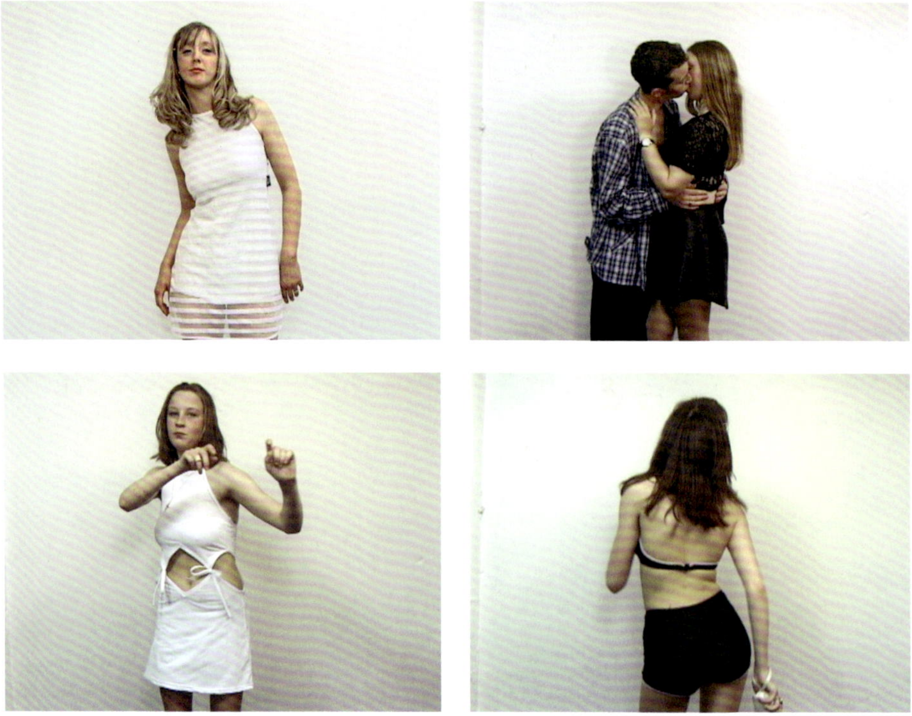

Rineke Dijkstra | The Buzz Club, Liverpool, UK | Mystery World, Zaandam, NL | 1996–97
2 channel colour video installation, with sound; 26 min. 40 sec., loop, inv. no. GV 125
Acquired 2000 by PIN. Freunde der Pinakothek der Moderne for the
Modern Art Collection

Television and the Internet shape an international youth culture and produce collective role models. Under this influence, the definition of one's own identity becomes one's life's work. Rineke Dijkstra's video installation exists at this intersection between individual and social codes. On two adjacent projected surfaces, young people more or less routinely demonstrate their cool poses, dance moves, and rituals of flirtation. Outside the protective darkness of the music clubs, the young adults seem vulnerable again, left to fend for themselves.
BS

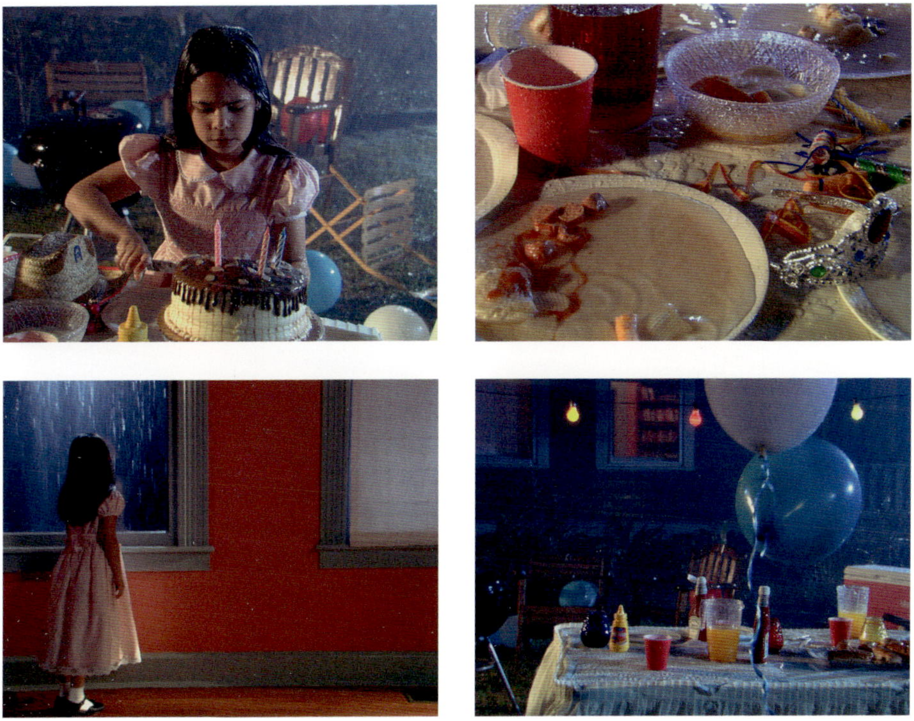

Teresa Hubbard and Alexander Birchler | Eight | 2001
1-channel video, colour, sound, 3 min. 35 sec., loop, inv. no. GV 132
Acquired 2002 by PIN. Freunde der Pinakothek der Moderne for the Modern Art Collection

The film, made with a large team, shows a girl on her eighth birthday. Almost without cuts, the camera follows the gaze of the girl from a living room through a window wet with rain into darkness, to glide through the interior of the house and out into the garden, where the birthday had been celebrated until the rain abruptly ended the celebration. The girl is trying to maintain the atmosphere of the party by hanging on to a piece of the already-soaked cake. Sounds emphasize the sense of a journey through different realms of experience.
BS

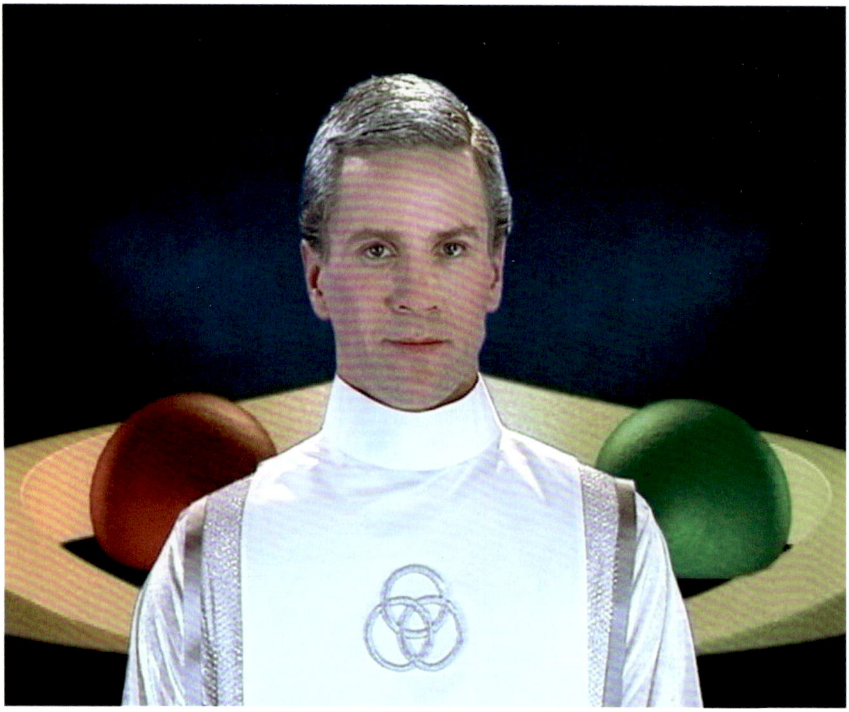

Bjørn Melhus | The Oral Thing | 2001
1-channel video, colour, sound, 8 min., inv. no. GV 138
Acquired 2003 by PIN. Freunde der Pinakothek der Moderne for the Modern Art Collection

Bjørn Melhus moves in the virtual, increasingly sprawling cosmos of the media age, juggling mechanisms, tricks, and effects of film, television, and advertising. In *The Oral Thing*, set pieces from American televised talk shows are re-orchestrated and given new rhythm. The found sound and music fragments give rise to an idiosyncratic, sometimes absurd poetry. Brilliantly reflecting the strategies of illusion and suggestion, the video merges the theatre of ancient Greece with ephemeral entertainment, game shows, and recent courtroom drama.

BS

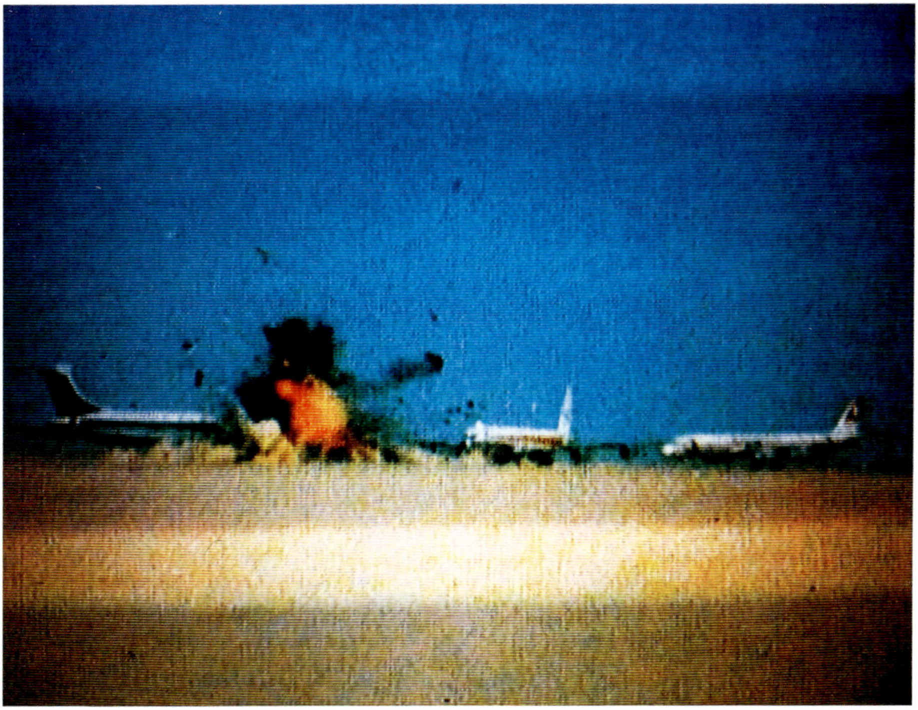

Johan Grimonprez | DIAL H-I-S-T-O-R-Y | 1997, still: Three hijacked planes on desert airstrip near Amman, Jordan, 12 September 1970
1-channel video, b/w and colour, sound, 68 min., inv. no. GV 129
Acquired 2001 by PIN. Freunde der Pinakothek der Moderne for the Modern Art Collection

The film collage combines the history of airplane hijacking with that of its portrayal and dissemination in the media. The artist thereby understands the hijacked aircraft as a metaphor for a new experience of history: non-linear, border-crossing, multi-perspectival. Cleverly, he shuffles different levels of truth in images – document, simulation, game, and illusion – and merges their effectiveness. The film's peculiar temporal structure forces us to think in parallel histories. We experience history as an elastic concept, as a flexible and manipulable variable. BS

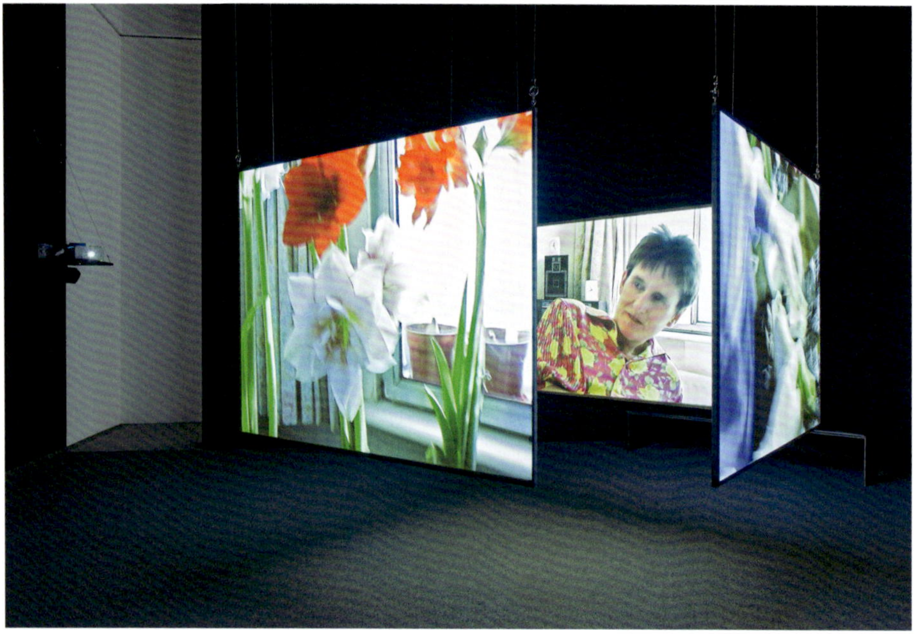

Kutluğ Ataman | The 4 Seasons of Veronica Read | 2001
4-channel video installation, colour, sound, 60 min., inv. no. GV 137
Acquired 2002 by PIN. Freunde der Pinakothek der Moderne for the Modern Art Collection

Four films, each lasting for an hour and played in synchronization from projectors that form a small walk-in space, portray an unusual woman who cultivates hippeastrum bulbs with utmost devotion in her tiny London flat. The simultaneous images overwhelm the viewer, as the plant lover's explanations blend and thicken to form a whispered, almost incomprehensible background of noise. The result is a circular structure that symbolizes the flow of the seasons, but also the partly chosen, partly involuntary state of being trapped in an obsession.
BS

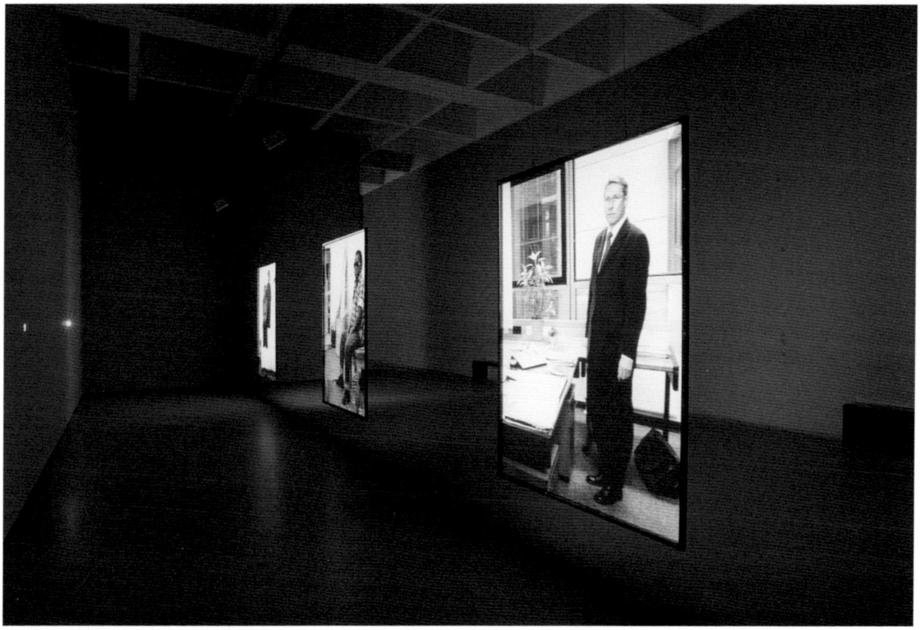

Fiona Tan | Countenance | 2002
4-channel video installation, b/w, 11 min. 27 sec., inv. no. 15778
Acquired 2008 with support of Wacker Chemie AG, PIN. Freunde der Pinakothek der Moderne for the Modern Art Collection, Bernd F. Künne + Partner, Dr. Kai and Rosemarie Werner, Georg and Swantje von Werz

What constitutes the egomatter? In this video installation, simultaneously projected on four screens, the artist, who is from Australia, uses 250 filmed portraits to develop a socio-cultural study of German society taken at the beginning of the 21st century in Berlin. The work in black-and-white is a conscious reference to August Sander's *People of the Twentieth Century* (p. 129). The limited field of view, the silence and tension of the filmed persons creates a high degree of concentration and intensity, and a constant dialogue takes place between those portrayed and the viewers. IGI

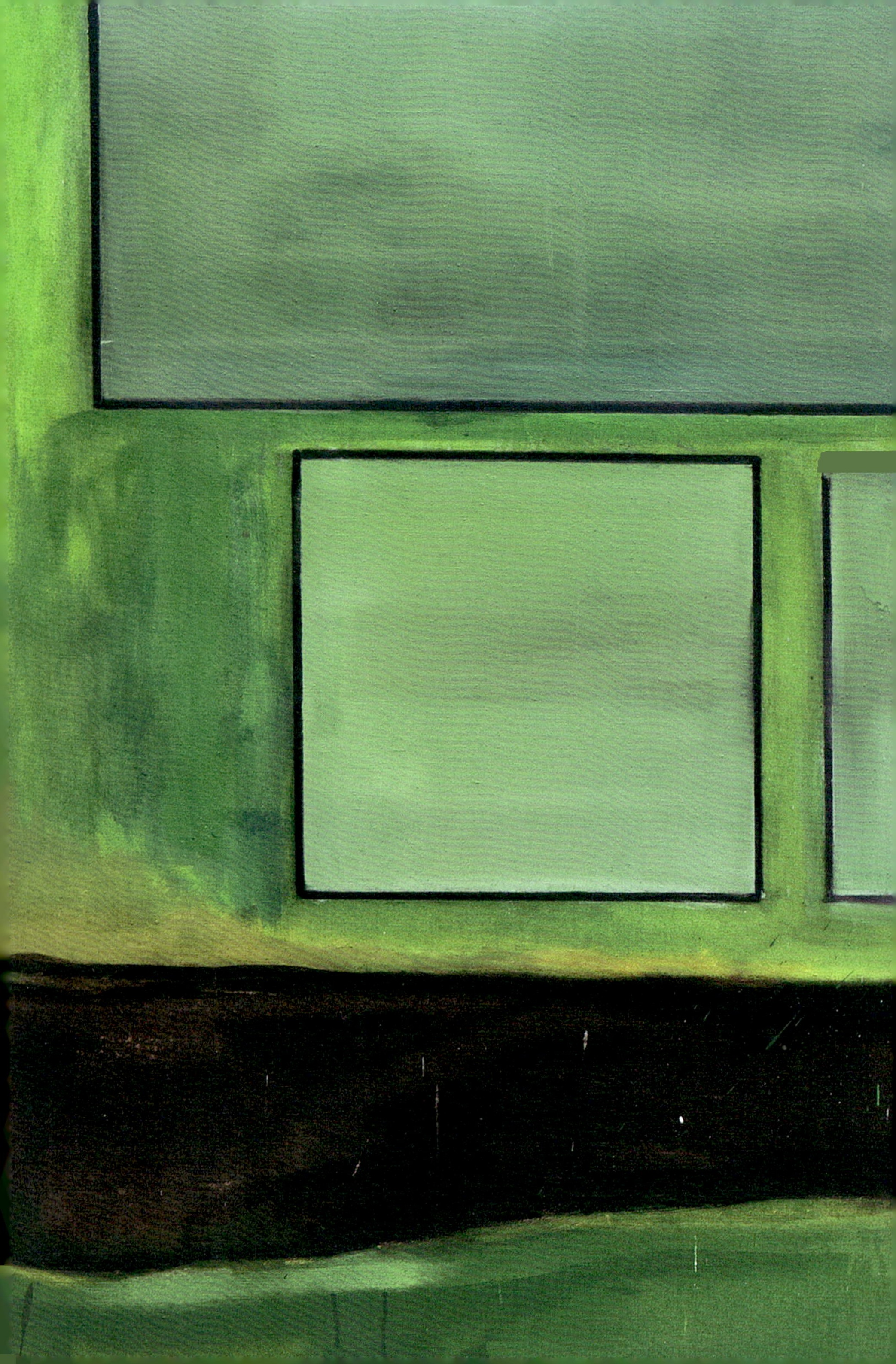

STARTING LINE
ART IN THE 21ST CENTURY

A place for pictures. This was all that was meant by the term *pinacotheca* in its original usage; it was formed from the Greek words *pinakes* (tablets/panels, pictures) and *theke* (container). Through the 19th century it was still clear what it indicated – since, after all, until the invention of photography, there was no question that every picture was a painted picture. In this sense both the Alte Pinakothek and Neue Pinakothek are conceived as collections of classical paintings. They follow an understanding of art under which the exclusive contemplation of a single art form, painting, makes sense. A stroll through the Pinakothek der Moderne, however, reveals how in the last hundred years the conception of pictures – and, incidentally, of art in general – has fundamentally broadened. Generation after generation of artists has broken away from academic standards, genres, and themes, eventually leaving them largely behind.

Though in 1913 it may still have represented a tremendous step forward for Kandinsky, in his *Dreamy Improvisation* (p. 51), to do away with any discernible pictorial object in order to approach the 'sound' of the image, by 2008 abstraction is no longer a central theme for the work of Katharina Grosse. However, the use of colour seems quite clearly to remain a major focus, because the artist uses an aerosol can to apply paint to her surfaces. Furthermore, she buried her untitled tondo in the ground, in order to later hang the work – eaten away at and bleached out by acidic substances – on the wall.

The art of the last five generations of artists, as the tour through the museum shows, is a story of abandoning and un-learning traditions, conventions, and expectations. Step by step, this development led to the dissolution of fixed conceptions of how a picture must look. While it is true that many artists today continue to define themselves as painters or sculptors, just as many prefer the more open self-definition 'artist'. After all, classical artistic materials and techniques (oil or acrylic on canvas, manipulation of wood or stone) have long been joined by a broad spectrum of new procedures, among them numerous experimental ones whose origins have nothing at all to do with art. Thomas Hirschhorn uses brown packing tape, for example, as an artistic medium in his assemblages, some of which form room-sized installations. He consciously uses this and other 'poor' materials, like scraps torn from magazines, Xerox copies, transparencies, and stickers to lend his work a provisional, model-like character.

The most significant contributions to the shift in the definition of art over the last hundred years came from three artists: Marcel Duchamp, Joseph Beuys (p. 172, 191, 202, pp. 254–255), and Andy Warhol (p. 19, 207). Since Duchamp began around 1913 to bring everyday objects, unchanged and already used, into the context of the art display, the readymade has been a part of the artist's toolkit. But the artistic use of everyday materials and things, as observed in the works of Elmgreen & Dragset, Steven Claydon, and Mark Manders, among others, is by far no longer an explicit reference to the pioneer of modern art. Rather, this particular approach, when employed by artists working today, proves the use of the readymade has become common conceptual knowledge. They use familiar objects from everyday life in order to expose our seemingly fixed definitions or the rules undergirding our interpersonal interactions as inventions and constructs.

Much like Duchamp's approach, Joseph Beuys's term 'social sculpture', which he coined in the 1960s, is present in the artistic thinking of today. His art had to do with potential societal formations and involved, not infrequently, the creative abilities of non-artists. Roman Ondak acts in this tradition when, for example, his *Measuring the Universe* makes the museum visitor part of the artwork. Gillian Wearing, who invited hundreds of passersby on the street to write down a message and then photographed each one individually holding his or her sign, also works with an intersocial sensibility. In this context, the question of how Wearing's photographs should be understood arises. Are they 'only' documentation of an action? Or is Wearing, who studied sculpture, creating temporary sculptures through them?

What do we mean, in the 21st century, by 'images'? Long gone are the days when we saw them only at museums, in the newspaper, at the cinema, or on television. Images are omnipresent; we are surrounded by them – in public spaces, on the Internet, on surveillance monitors, on smartphone screens. Pictures, the masses, and massive pictures were at the centre of Andy Warhol's work. His approach to painting, now approximately 50 years old, is more relevant to artistic debates and developments in 2017 than ever before. Artists purposely fall back on a wide variety of visual models and references, use the photographic medium as they do film, incorporate computer and digital techniques, combine, and collage.

In the pictures of Luc Tuymans, to name one of the internationally most influential painters of his generation, it becomes clear that new pictures always emerge out of pictures that already exist. Tuymans' paintings orbit the conditions of seeing. *Three Moons* is also based on photography and shows a space whose extent and properties can be only vaguely gauged. Proximity and distance can no longer be estimated. Like other recent works of art, this painting shows how much the digital age has changed our understanding of pictures, how much our relationship to physical materiality and spatiality has changed. And how much pictures continue to change us.

One artist whose creations stand as examples for a new, media-independent understanding of art is Wade Guyton, who 'paints' with an inkjet printer. The printer defines the format of the painting and contributes to its composition, because the ultimately inappropriate application of the printer, into which the artist feeds canvas instead of paper, scores and smudges the surface as the digital image prints. These marks make contradictory forces visible and prove that Guyton, though he may produce two-dimensional pictures, actually considers himself a sculptor. Moreover, it becomes clear that despite anonymous image production (by a machine) and technical reproducibility (digital information as subject), it is still possible today to create an analogue, unique, and unmistakable work of art.

There can be no doubt: the old *pinakes* have opened themselves up to space, time, and new technologies. Our understanding of the picture, as it extends over several generations, has become the self-evident basis for artistic creation in the 21st century. We stand, in a sense, at the starting line of a future that is more diverse than ever before, and as a consequence, new perspectives on collecting and exhibiting are opening up for the Bayerische Staatsgemäldesammlungen in the Pinakothek der Moderne.

Bernhart Schwenk

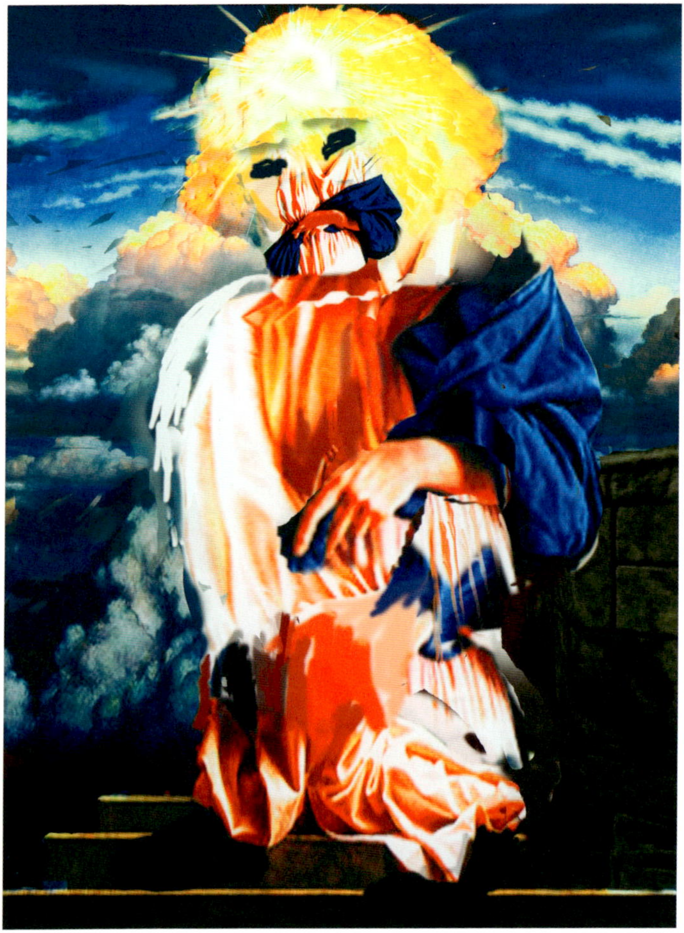

Markus Selg | Abstieg (Olymp) (Descent – Olympus) | 2004
Dye sublimation printing on polyester fabric (PES), 260 × 195 cm, inv. no. GV 168
Acquired 2005 by PIN. Freunde der Pinakothek der Moderne for the
Modern Art Collection

An artificial and disparate reality can be seen in Markus Selg's sculptures and computer-generated paintings. For Selg, pictures are always composed of other, already recognizable pictures. This gives rise to an atmosphere that is cryptic but also quite moving and full of longing. The Madonna-like figure in *Descent (Olympus)* can also be interpreted as an almost wistful farewell to the existence of immutable role models and eternal heroes as well as to the idea that it is possible to fundamentally change the world, which will always remain a pipe dream. BS

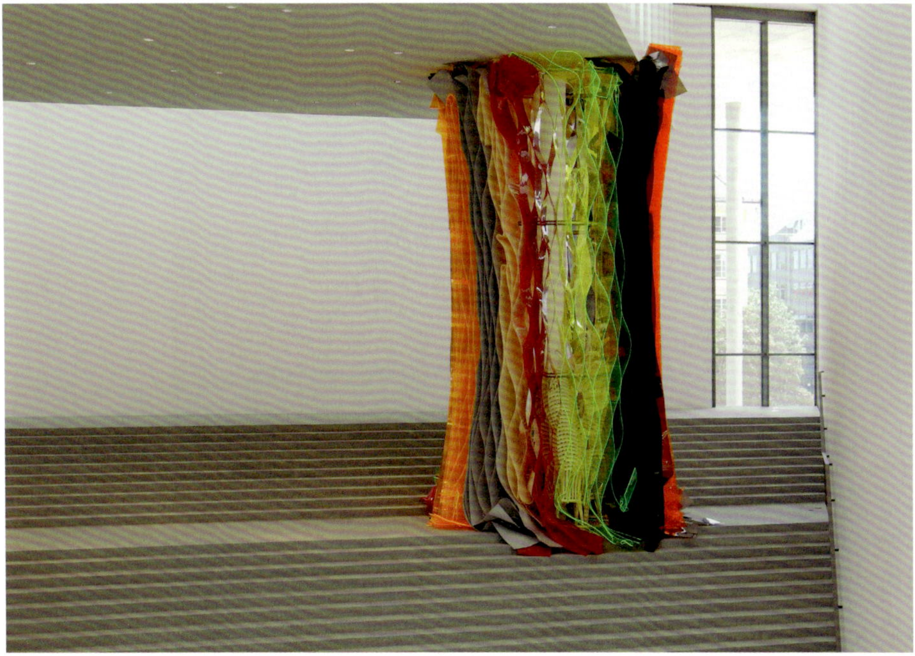

Olaf Metzel | Reise nach Jerusalem (Musical Chairs or Journey to Jerusalem) | 2002
Plexiglass, plastic chairs, stroboscope, 700 × 300 cm in diameter, inv. no. B 902
Acquired 2002

The opening of the Pinakothek der Moderne coincided with the 30th anniversary of the massacre during the Olympic Games in Munich, which bore the motto 'Joyous Games'. Against this background Olaf Metzel created a sculpture for the new museum that accentuates the stage-like aura of the stairs in its foyer: he dressed the single column on the middle block of stairs in shimmering cladding made of colourful acrylic glass. Warped plastic chairs in the interior lend something uncanny to the work and allude to the ambivalence of the children's game to which the title refers (the term for 'musical chairs' in western Germany is 'journey to Jerusalem'). BS

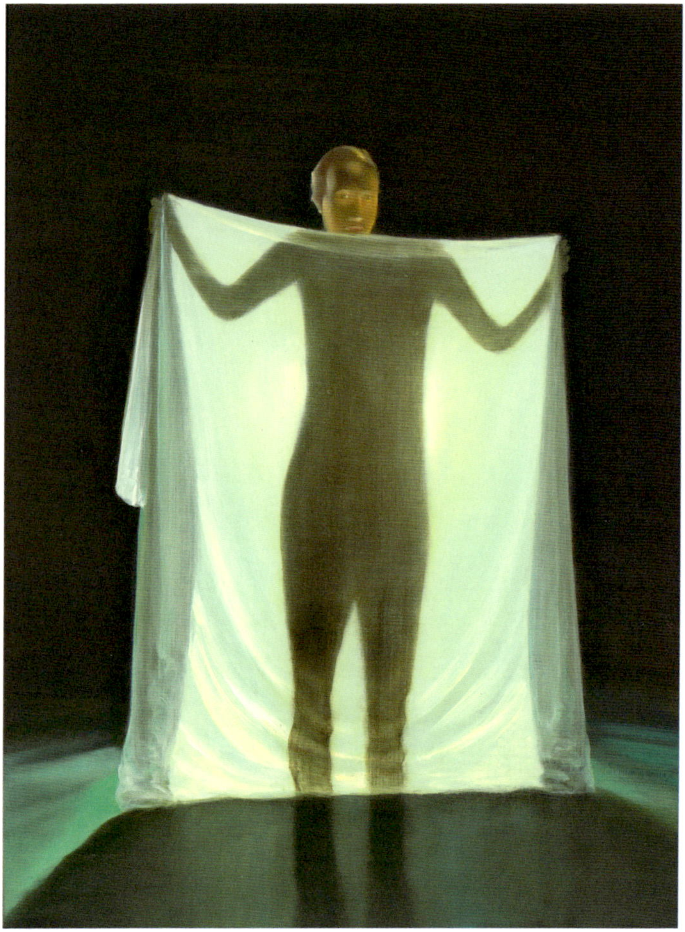

Stephan Melzl | Projektion 2 | 2006
Oil on wood, 57 × 43 cm, inv. no. GV 177
Acquired 2006 by PIN. Freunde der Pinakothek der Moderne for the Modern Art Collection

A strange, disconcerting silence emanates from Stephan Melzl's small paintings. In them, it almost seems as if time has stopped. The allegory-like scenarios resemble staged scenes, an impression to which artificial lighting effects contribute. With archetypal urgency, the pictures can be interpreted as imaginary dream settings, as metaphors for unpredictable emotional states, or also – in their bewildering combination of seriousness and joke – as anarchic remedies administered to an allegedly healthy world. BS

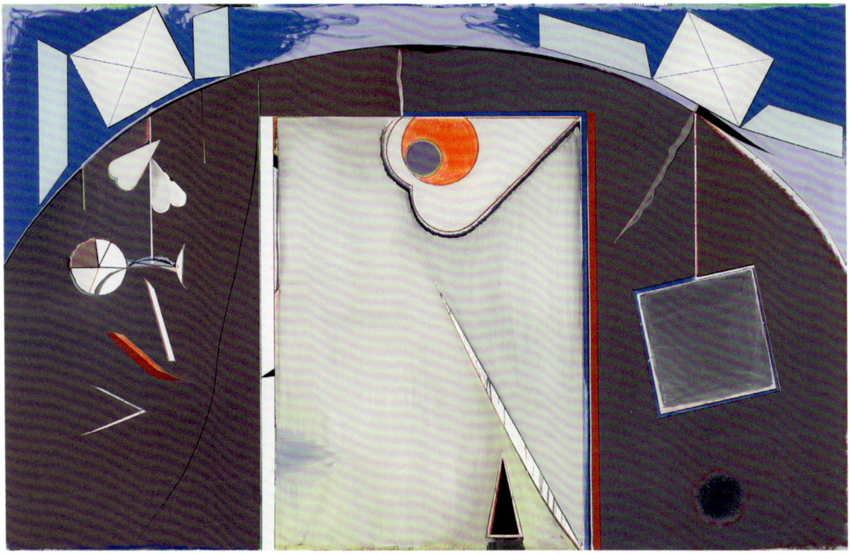

Thomas Scheibitz | Eingang (Entrance) | 2005
Oil, vinyl on canvas, 285 × 450 cm, inv. no. GV 172
Acquired 2005 by PIN. Freunde der Pinakothek der Moderne for the Modern Art Collection

Thomas Scheibitz uses the simplest basic forms and signs in his clearly structured paintings. Surprisingly, detachment characterizes the large-scale painting *Entrance*. The artist employs motifs from a variety of origins (graphics, design, architecture) and brings them into an open metaphorical context. The elements and figures question the medium of painting by elevating the visual field and artistic signature to thematic status. The painter becomes the director of a play that takes place between the recognizable world of signs and a painterly autonomy. BS

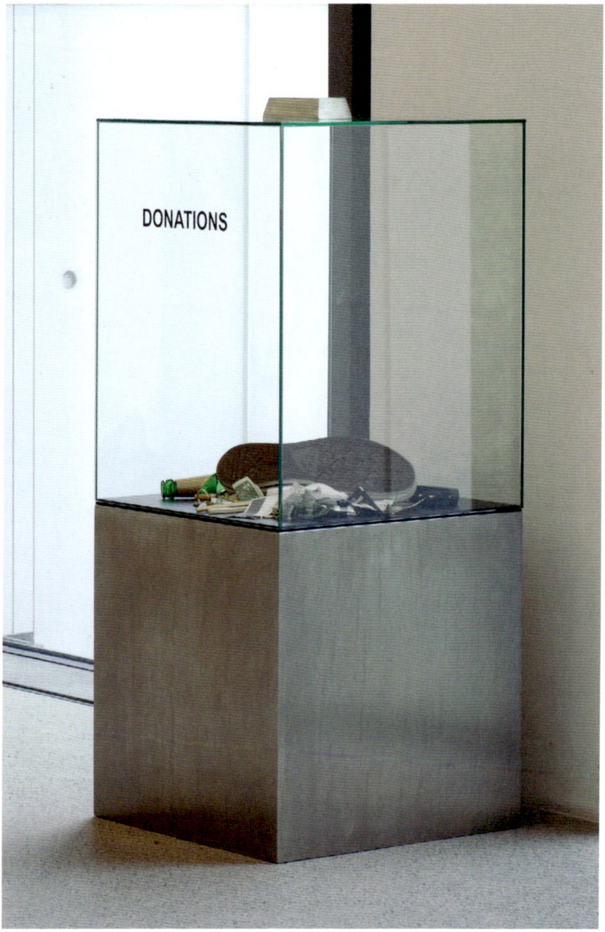

Elmgreen & Dragset | Donation Box | 2006
Glass, stainless steel, 105 × 44.5 × 44.5 cm, inv. no. GV 185
Acquired 2007 by PIN. Freunde der Pinakothek der Moderne for the Modern Art Collection

The relationship between private and institutionalized space, with its historical, political, and social aspects, is the focus of this artist duo's work. It is always about people, who are, however, almost always absent. This absence makes the structures of human coexistence, the hierarchies, and the power relations all the more noticeable. In *Donation Box* the act of giving and receiving reveals itself as an expression of unequal distribution of power. This transforms the museum from a place for meditation into a space for action that encourages responsible thinking and doing. BS

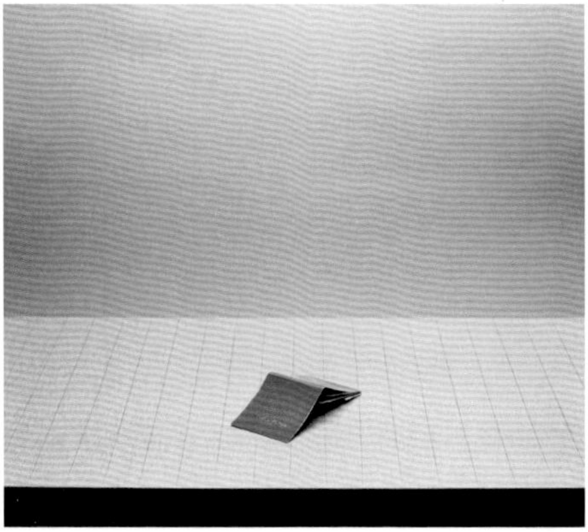
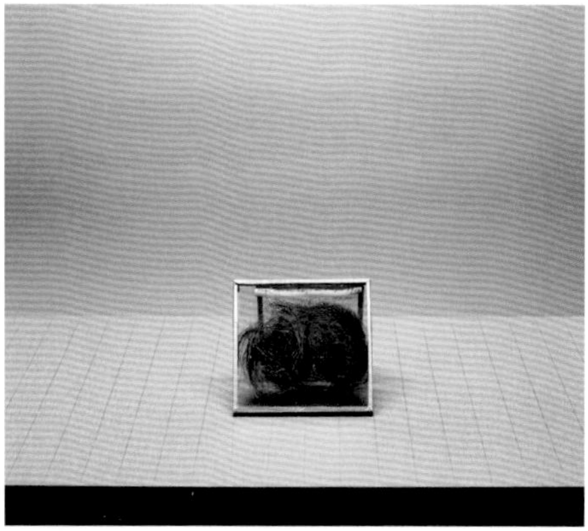
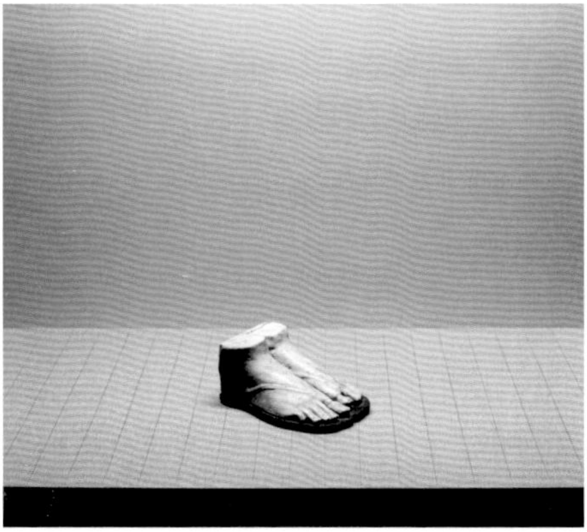
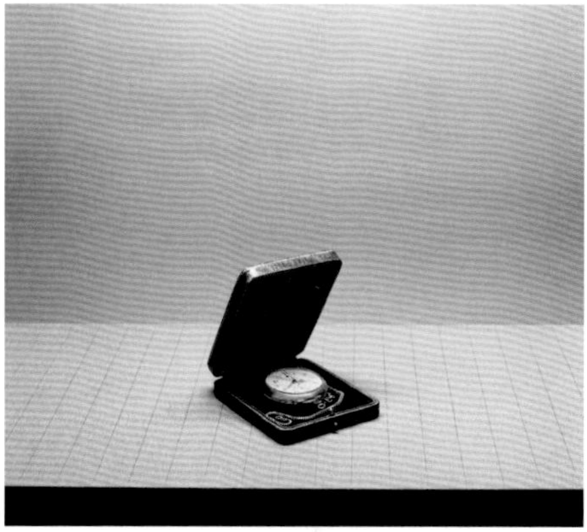

Ricarda Roggan | Apokryphen (Apocrypha) (Ernst Jünger, matches), (Hermann Essig, hair), (Johann Gottfried Seume, paperweight), (Martin Heidegger, watch) | 2014
Silver gelatine prints, each 33 × 38 cm, inv. no. GV 343, GV 342, GV 345, GV 346
Acquired 2016 by PIN. Freunde der Pinakothek der Moderne for the Modern Art Collection with support of Ruth Müller-Stein

Apocrypha is an inventory of practical objects originally belonging to writers, musicians, and philosophers from centuries gone by that have been preserved in archives or museums as mementos, like the eccentric paperweight of the poet Johann Gottfried Seume, the watch of the philosopher Martin Heidegger, or two locks of hair from the head of the dramatist Hermann Essig. They function equally as relics and as the index of a life with which they were once probably bound up, and whose partly forgotten meaning they imbue with their own aura. |G|

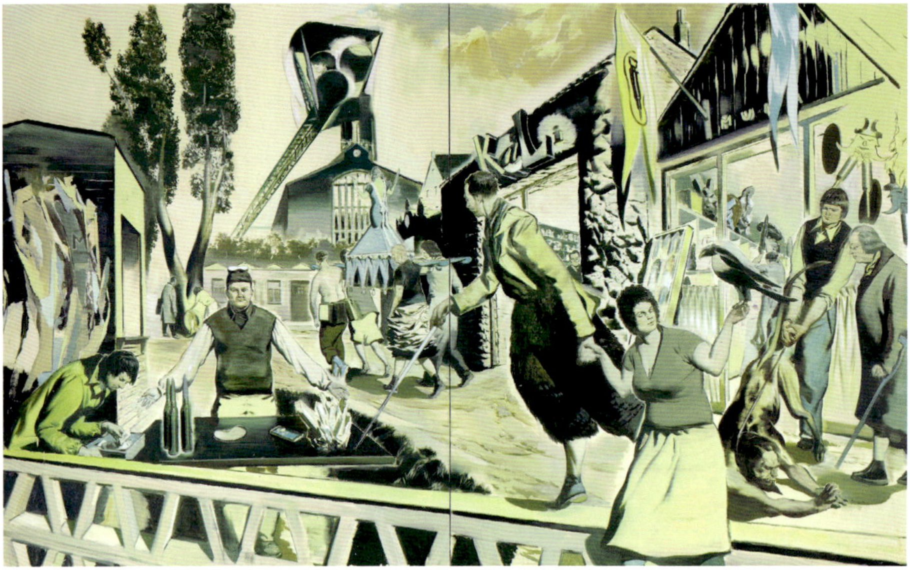

Neo Rauch | Kalimuna | 2010
Oil on canvas, 300 × 500 cm, inv. no. GV 210
Acquired 2010 by PIN. Freunde der Pinakothek der Moderne for the Modern Art Collection

The monumental painting simultaneously quotes large-scale Baroque genre scenes, whose expansive scale made them panoramas of society, and 19th century history paintings. It also conjures the murals and propaganda images of the 20th century. However, contrary to its forerunners, which were filled with pride or pathos, Rauch's work expresses otherworldiness and uncertainty. The characters in the images appear stunned as they go about their daily work or perform rituals. The painting makes tangible the conflict between individual and society, as well as the contradictory relationship between nature and civilization. BS

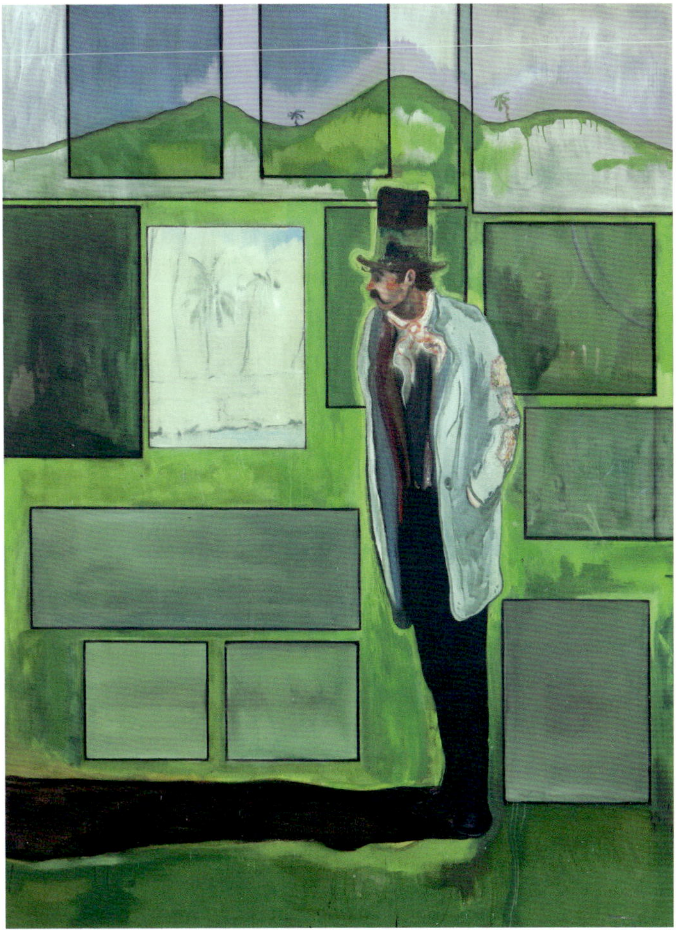

Peter Doig | Metropolitain (House of Pictures) | 2004
Oil on canvas, 275.3 × 200 cm, inv. no. GV 161
Acquired 2004 by PIN. Freunde der Pinakothek der Moderne for the Modern Art Collection

Behind the man in the top hat a bright green landscape rises up like a high wall bearing the outlines of imaginary images. The figure's clothing is reminiscent of the 19th century, making him look as if he has 'fallen out of time'. The tropical environment also contributes to this atmosphere of strangeness. *Metropolitain* is based on Honoré Daumier's portrayal of a man looking at art (*L'amateur d'estampes*). Every picture, the painting tells us, is made up of things we have already seen and is capable of suggesting new images. BS

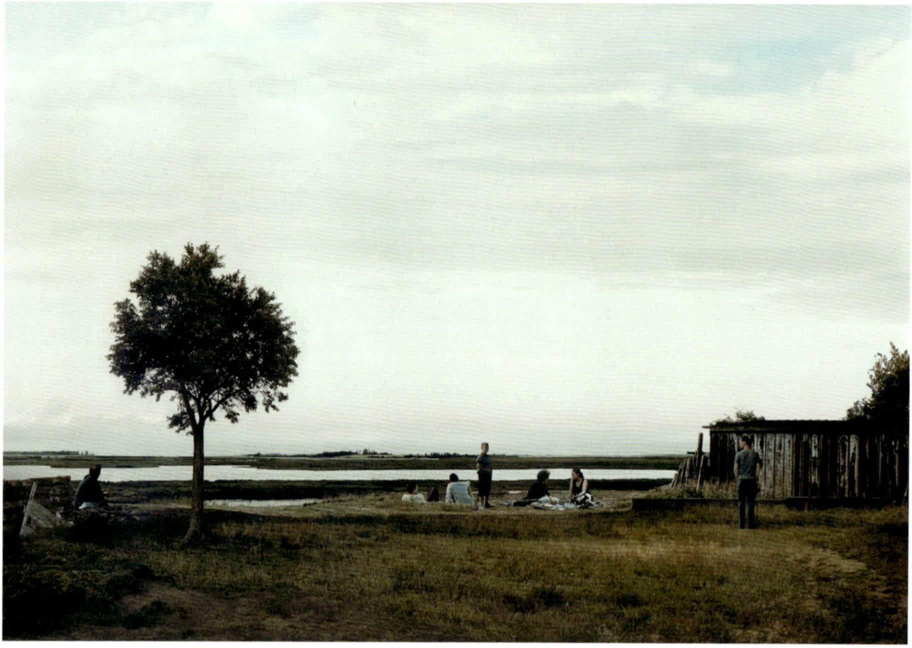

Beate Gütschow | LS # 17 | 2003
C-print, 125 × 200 cm, inv. no. 15837
Donation of Munich art trade, 2008

The first impression is deceptive. The ideal, apparently Nordic landscape with its harmoniously incorporated ensemble of figures, reminiscent of classical pictorial conceptions from art history, reveals itself on closer examination as a construct. If photography has always been considered a medium of realistic documentation, the conception of an Arcadia is here exposed as an illusion which can only be reconstructed with the help of a digitally-generated picture, just as in earlier centuries it corresponded to a vision and not reality. IGI

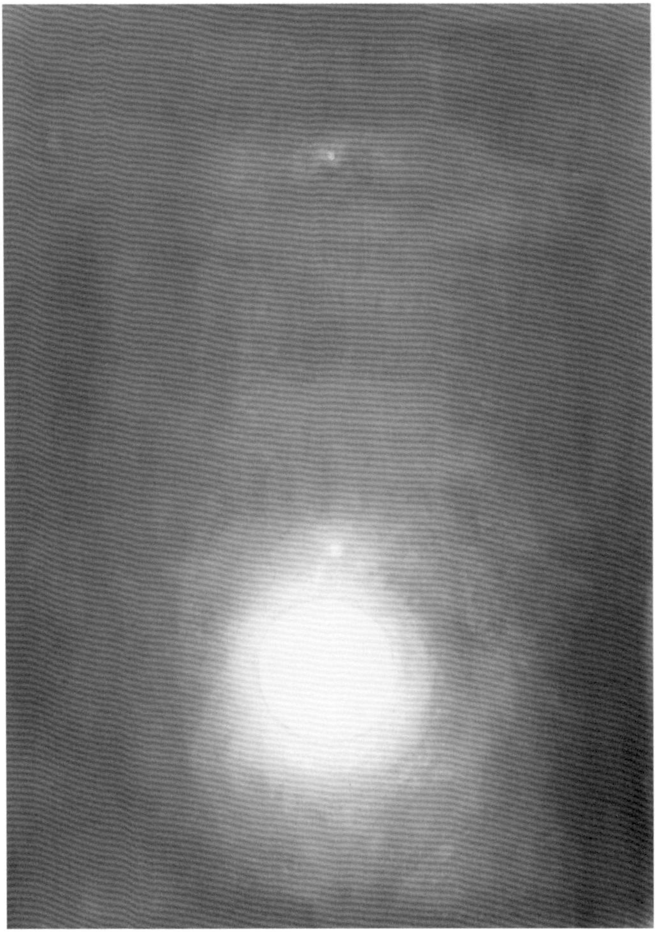

Luc Tuymans | Three Moons | 2007
Oil on canvas, 172.5 × 132.2 cm, inv. no. GM 188
Acquired 2007 by PIN. Freunde der Pinakothek der Moderne for the Modern Art Collection

Scepticism and asceticism define Luc Tuymans' paintings. His pictures revolve around the conditions of seeing. *Three Moons* shows a planetary constellation, a space that, under extended viewing, eludes concreteness. All orientation is lost in an indistinct shape filled with a blaze of light: the enormous appears tiny, depth is flattened, the significant becomes peripheral. The world is lost; it becomes a model, shadow, or afterimage. The image proves to be both illusion and delusion, it returns to a time before representation, to the origins of image-making. BS

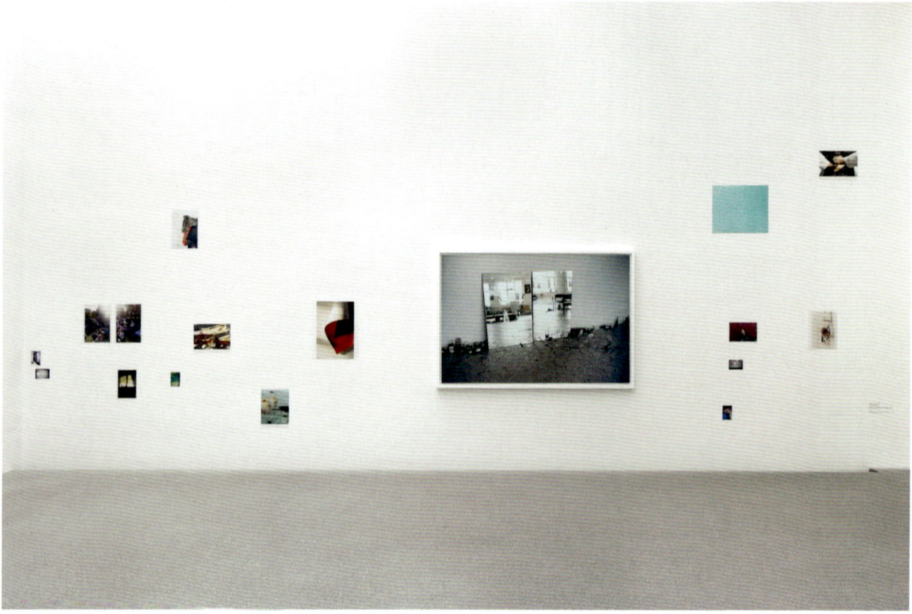

Wolfgang Tillmans | München Installation 1991–2004 | 2005
C-prints, various sizes, inv. no. GM 173, 1/22-22/22
Acquired 2006 by PIN. Freunde der Pinakothek der Moderne for the Modern Art Collection

Created for the Pinakothek der Moderne, this 22-part whole-room installation contains works spanning different themes, sizes, and techniques, including seminal photographs such as *Corinne on Gloucester Place* and *Deer Hirsch*. The combination of portraits, still lifes, images from everyday life, and abstract pieces, shown both within the installation and separately as individual pictures, provides a representative glimpse into the artist's work and can at the same time be seen as an homage to Tillmans' partner, the Munich-born Jochen Klein, who died young. IGI

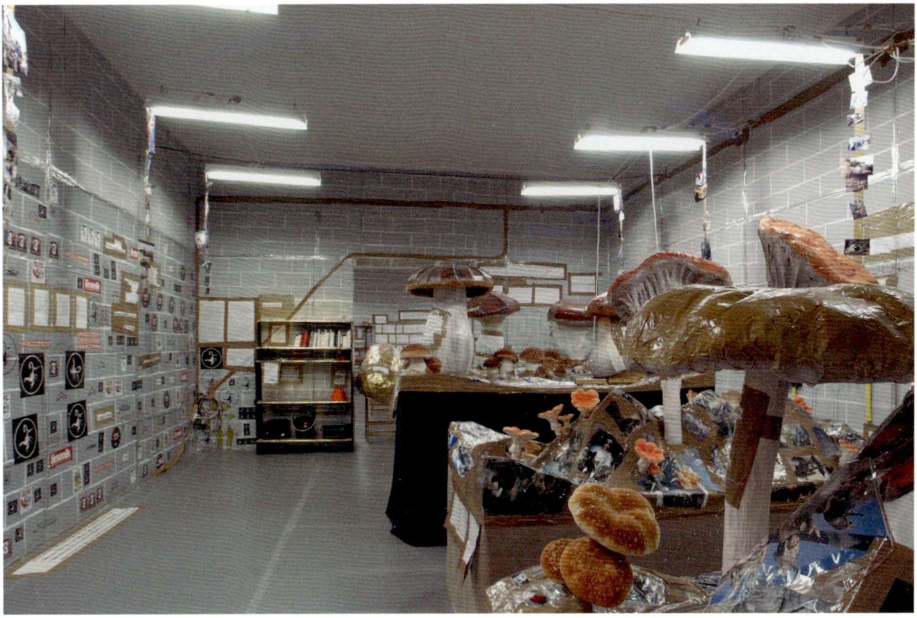

Thomas Hirschhorn | Doppelgarage (Double Garage) | 2002
Wood, mixed media, 400 × 590 × 1900 cm, inv. no. GV 160
Acquired 2004 by PIN. Freunde der Pinakothek der Moderne for the Modern Art Collection

Consisting of two spaces, the installation feels like a mixture between a workshop and a basement hobby room. Model railways circle under enormous mushrooms across miniature landscapes made of paper and held together by brown tape. Magazine photos show ruined towns and injured people. Fragments of text trigger associations with power and responsibility. The work was inspired by the events of 11 September 2001, which reflect the complex relationships, cultural differences, and economic dependencies that define the age of globalization.
BS

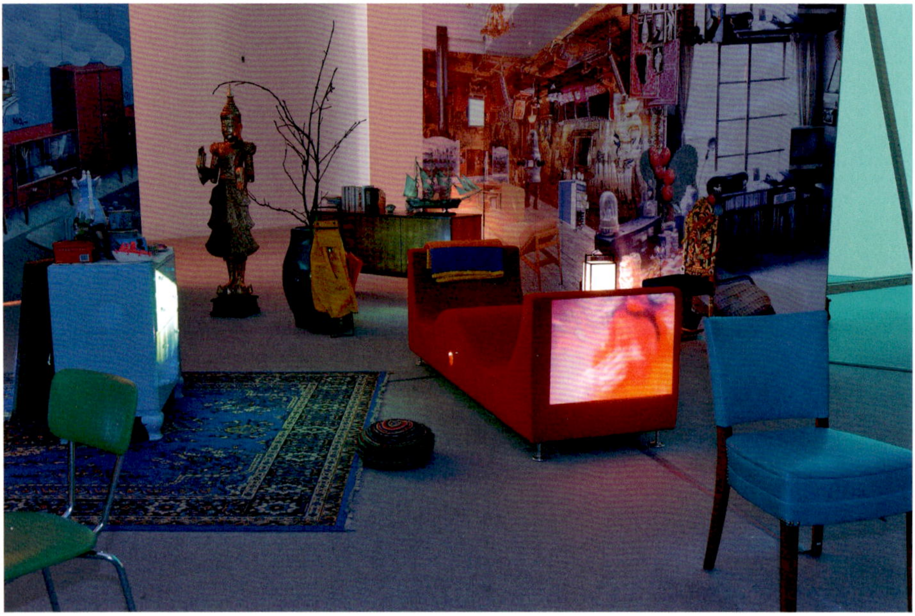

Pipilotti Rist | Himalaya Goldsteins Stube (Himalaya Goldstein's Living Room) | 1998–99
Multi-part room installation with videos, music by Andreas Guggisberg, inv. no. 110 GM
Acquired 1999 by PIN. Freunde der Pinakothek der Moderne for the
Modern Art Collection

Furnishings, lighting, and soft music mingle to form an environment rich in associations. Flickering film images, projected out of armchairs, sofas, and lamps, overlay the sensuous materials. The moving pictures eerily illuminate the darkened area, adding to the atmosphere of magic in the space, in which the viewer is invited to sit. In one of the artist's earliest and most extensive media installations, interior and exterior worlds, public and private merge into one, and time periods and cultures overlap. BS

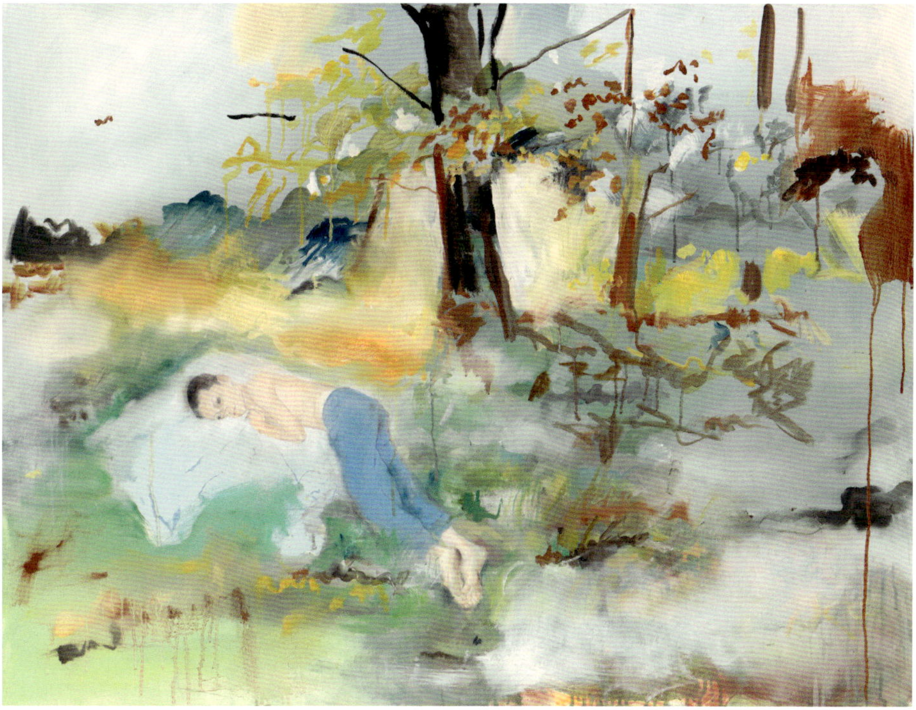

Jochen Klein | Untitled | 1997
Oil on canvas, 76 × 101.5 cm, inv. no. 15759
Donation of Wolfgang Tillmans, 2008

Though Jochen Klein died young, his work marked a new approach to figurative painting in Europe in the 1990s. The most well-known of his often diminutive works show idyllic outdoor scenes in the countryside. The artist's sources of inspiration included photo wallpaper from his youth, illustrated advertisements, and erotic films. In the visual world of trivial and largely stereotypical images, he recognized a kind of collective consciousness of his generation, through which he was capable of reflecting – without ironic distance – individual emotions and desires. BS

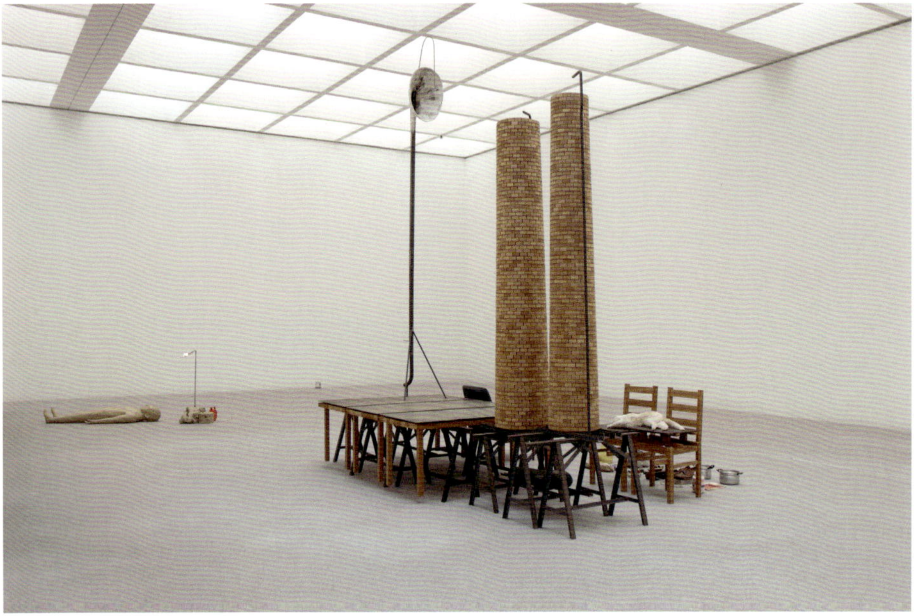

Mark Manders | Silent Factory | 2000
Wood, iron, mixed media, 250 × 387 × 276 cm, inv. no. GM 141
Acquired 2003 by PIN. Freunde der Pinakothek der Moderne for the Modern Art Collection

Composed of objects of various origins and construction, the sculpture feels like a hybrid of apartment, factory, and the process of moving house. Some of the objects are fabricated, others are found. The installation could be a recollection of the past, but it could also be a model for an uncertain future. In Mark Manders' world, the coordinates that orient us in time and space are void. Everything seems to be in a state of metamorphosis. The individual object and its context become metaphors for emotional states that have no precise labels.

BS

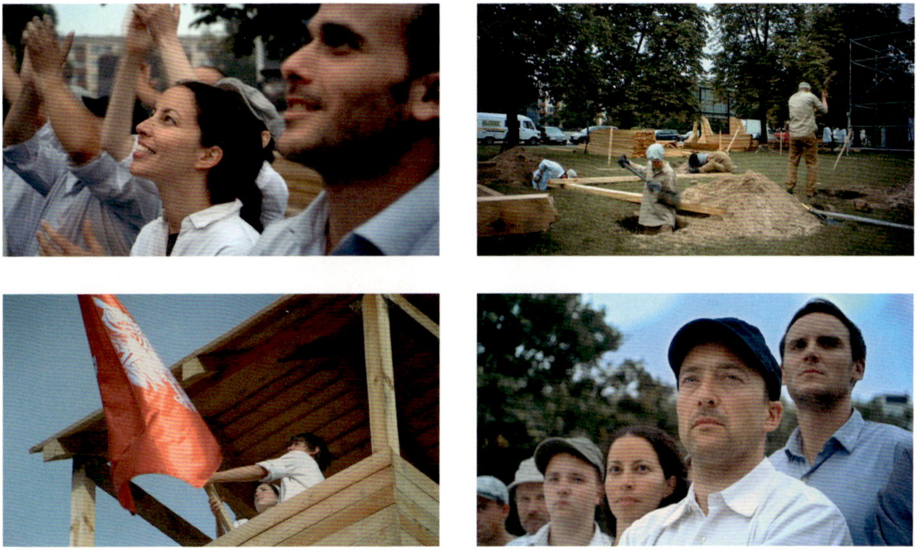

Yael Bartana | **Mur i Wieza** (Wall and Tower) | 2009
1-channel video, colour, 15 min., inv. no. GV 245
Acquired 2012 by PIN. Freunde der Pinakothek der Moderne for the Modern Art Collection

Wall and Tower, the second part of a trilogy on the *Jewish Renaissance Movement in Poland*, depicts a group of Jewish settlers erecting a kibbutz on the site of the former Warsaw Ghetto. The viewer observes the construction, which is like a foreign object in the featureless environment, as are the builders, who in their clothing and arrangement resemble the pioneers of early Zionism. The result of their labour, infused with joy and pathos, is the creation of a camp enclosed by walls crowned with barbed wire and equipped with a watchtower.
IGI

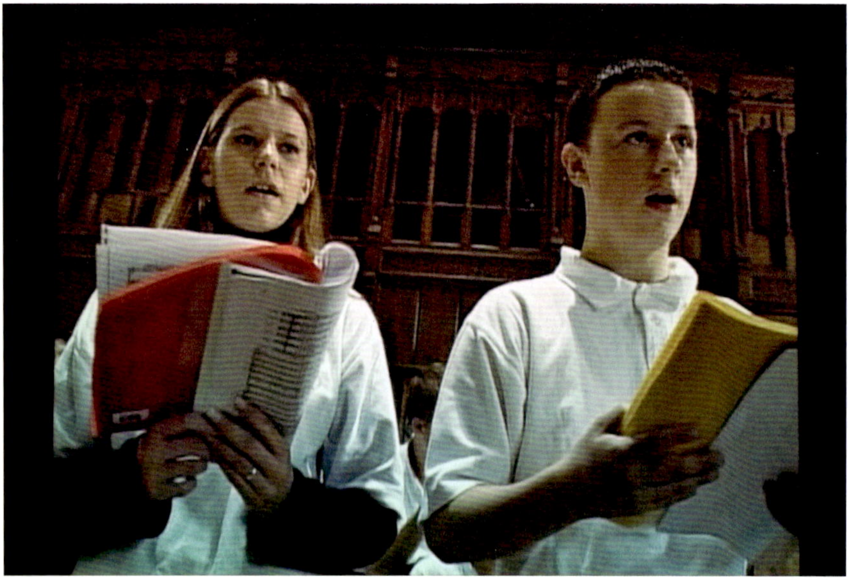

Artur Żmijewski | Lekcja Śpiewu II (Singing Lesson II) | 2003
1-channel video, colour, 16 min. 30 sec., inv. no. GV 169
Acquired 2005 by PIN. Freunde der Pinakothek der Moderne for the Modern Art Collection

In his photography and film projects, Artur Żmijewski deals with repressed social realities. For example, he turns to people with physical or mental disabilities to reveal the expressive potential in what might appear to be deficiencies. In *Singing Lesson II*, a group of deaf youth studied the famous duet 'We hasten with eager yet faltering footsteps' from a cantata by Johann Sebastian Bach. The subsequent performance in the Thomaskirche in Leipzig is a moving document of an attempt at the seemingly impossible. BS

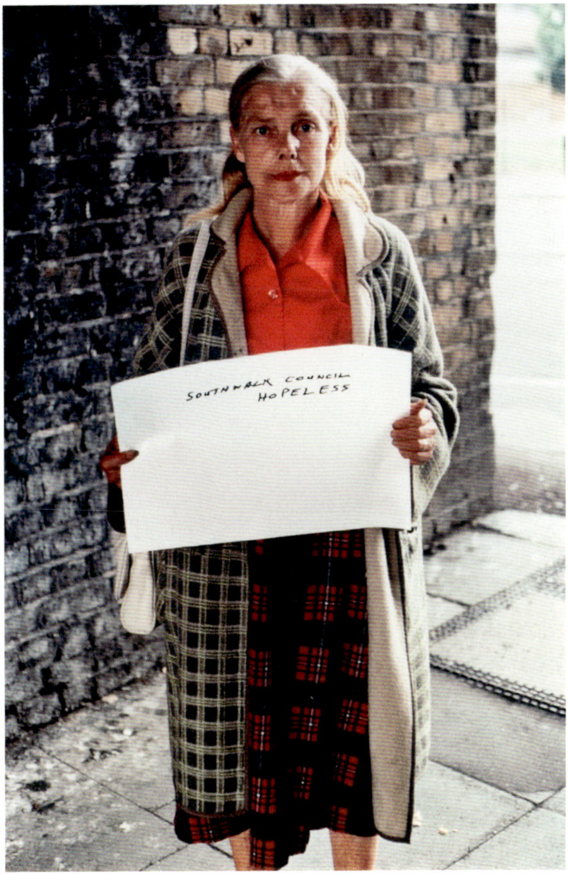

Gillian Wearing | Southwalk Council Hopeless | 1992–93, from the series *Signs that say what you want them to say and not Signs that say what someone else wants you to say*
C-print on aluminium, 44.5 × 29.7 cm, inv. no. GV 298
Acquired 2014 by PIN. Freunde der Pinakothek der Moderne for the Modern Art Collection

Art, for Wearing, is about making social relationships visible. Her work – frank and unsparing, yet always respectful – shows people in staged situations. The result is a collection of portraits that strike a fine balance between the private and the public. In 1992–93, the artist stood on the street and asked passers-by to spontaneously commit to paper a thought that was important to them, and then to be photographed holding it. The combination of image and text creates a form of doubled address, casts doubt on our own perceptions and public image, and poses questions about truthfulness, projection, assimilation, and self-determination.
BS

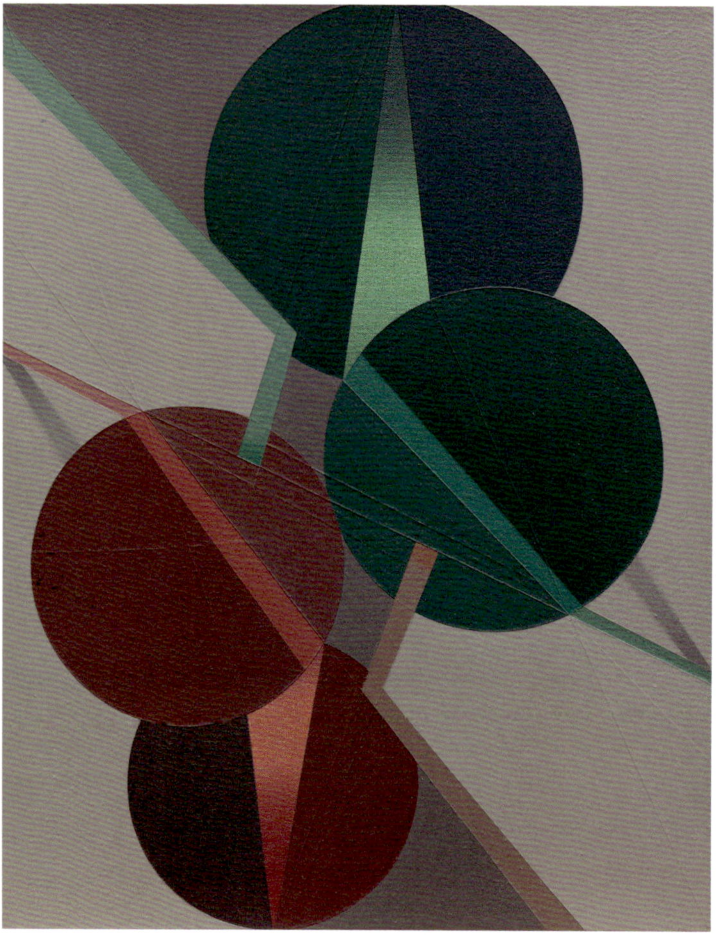

Tomma Abts | Ewo | 2006
Acrylic, oil on canvas, 48 × 38 cm, inv. no. GM 181
Acquired 2006 by PIN. Freunde der Pinakothek der Moderne for the Modern Art Collection

On a superficial level, this small-scale painting may initially appear to pursue the strictly Constructivist compositional principles of the early modernists. It was created using an extremely slow painting process, one that could almost be called meditative. Far removed from any concept of serial production, its delicate construction developed out of a sequence of intuitive decisions, through the continual removal and addition of innumerable layers of paint. In this sense, Abts' paintings are reflections on the act of painting itself; they are explorations of line, surface, and space. BS

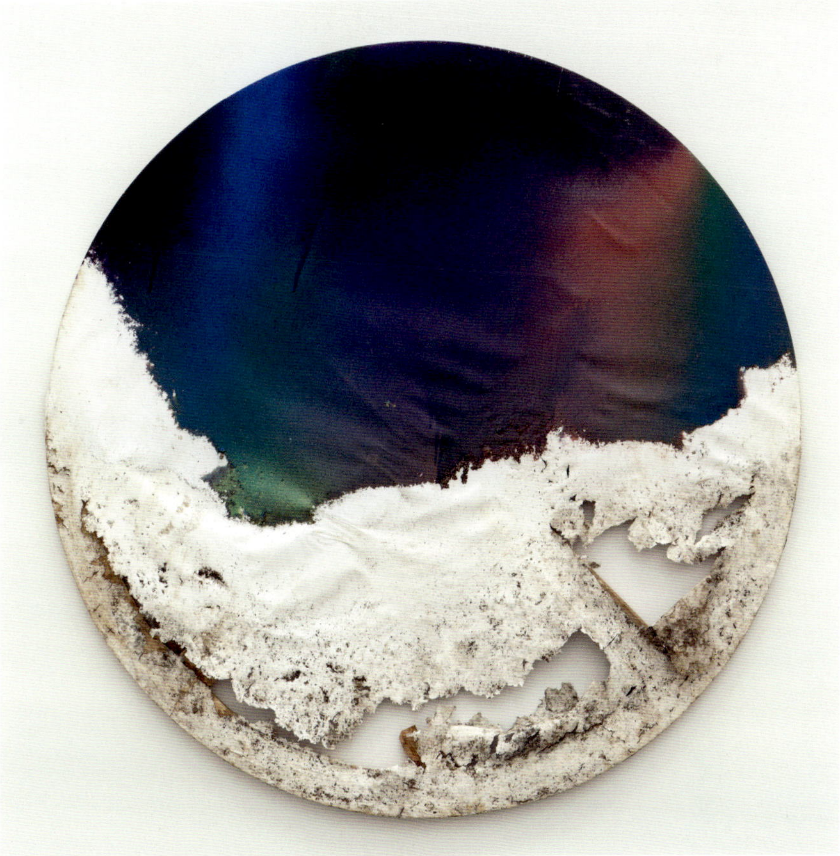

Katharina Grosse | Untitled | 2008
Acrylic and earth on canvas, 190 cm in diameter, inv. no. GV 366
Acquired 2017 by PIN. Freunde der Pinakothek der Moderne for the Modern Art Collection

For Katharina Grosse, painting is non-representational and, in principle, has no borders. This is also the source of the artist's frequent use of spray cans to transform entire rooms with colour. In her installations, a canvas can become a sculptural element, as in the case of this round work that for the entire duration of an exhibition lay half-buried in a mound of scattered earth. Subsequently excavated and hung on the wall, the painting both seems to be corporeally wounded and reminds us of the danger to which all physical objects are exposed (and, consequently, our environment). BS

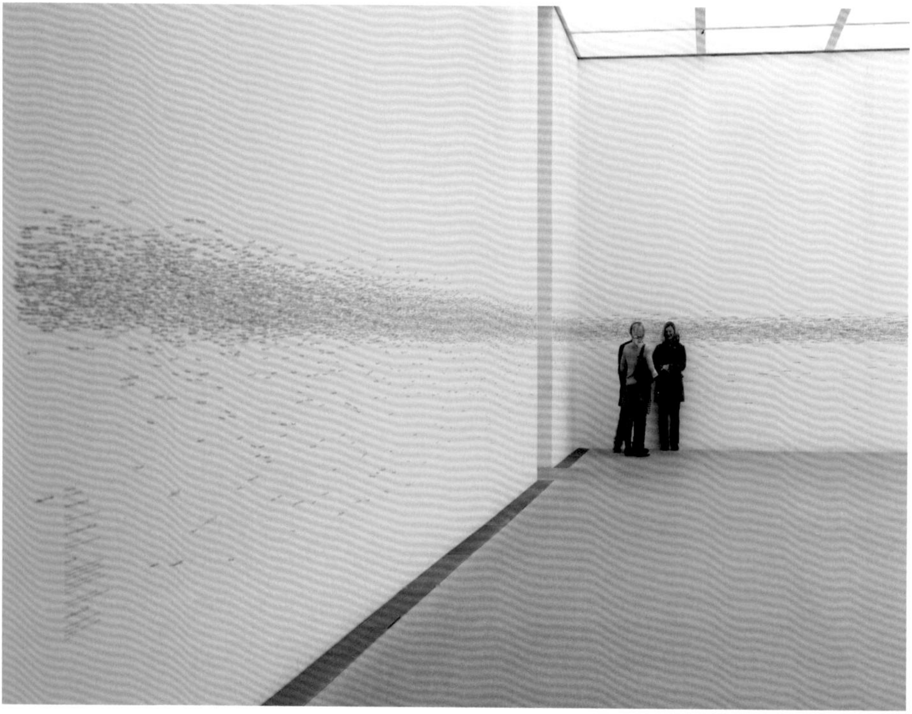

Roman Ondak | Measuring the Universe | 2007
Performance and installation, ed. 1/2, inv. no. GV 189
Acquired 2008 by PIN. Freunde der Pinakothek der Moderne for the Modern Art Collection

The urge to measure the world is an old one. *Measuring the Universe*, a performative drawing that happens on the walls of an entire room, can be seen as a part of this tradition. At its core is the act of marking the height of a body, as parents do with their children in order to record the dimension of change across time. Ondak turns this otherwise private gesture into a public action: museum attendants record the height of every single museum visitor. As time passes, the marks accumulate into a wall drawing. Physical presence and transience are made tangible – with minimal means. BS

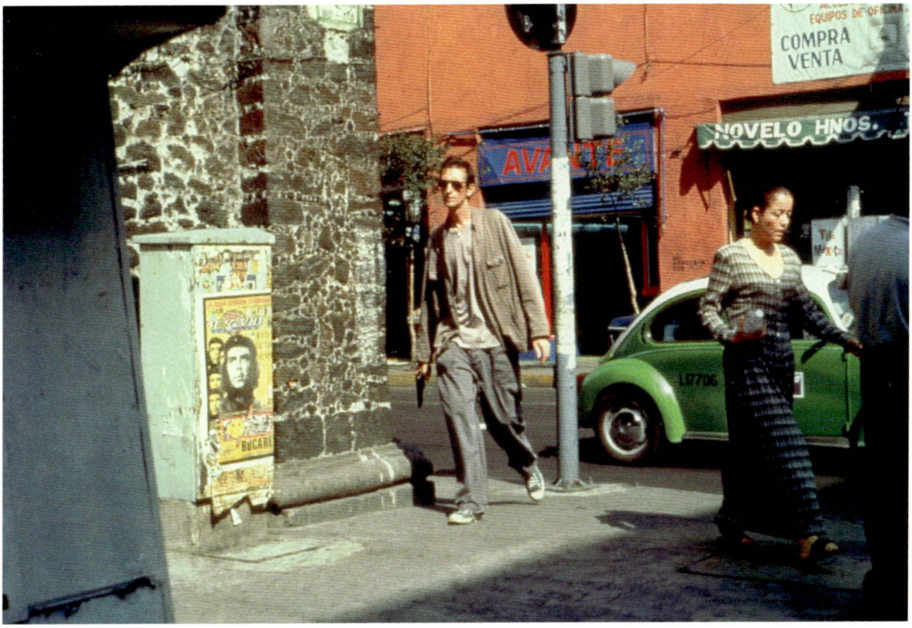

Francis Alÿs | Re-enactments | 2000
2-channel video, colour, 5 min. 20 sec., inv. no. GV 133
Acquired 2002 by PIN. Freunde der Pinakothek der Moderne for the Modern Art Collection

Re-enactments brings together, on two adjacently-shown films, an action staged by the artist in secret (left film) that was then recreated chronologically with the knowledge of the people appearing onscreen (right film). After purchasing a gun, the artist moves through the city carrying the weapon in plain view until he is eventually overcome by the police. The work raises questions about staged and actual danger, as well as about the reality and authenticity of its content, which is neither documentary nor fiction. BS

David Shrigley | LOOK AT THIS | 2014
Acrylic on paper, 153 × 112 cm, inv. no. GV 309
Acquired 2014 by PIN. Freunde der Pinakothek der Moderne for the Modern Art Collection

The artist's cartoonish, awkward-looking drawings reflect their radical confinement to bare essentials. But they are simple only at first glance, and reason alone is incapable of fully grasping them. Shrigley's approach is similar to that of children who reveal the strange, the terrible, and the meaningless alike without prejudice. With a disarming, often black sense of humour, the artist devotes himself to the banalities of everyday human life. *LOOK AT THIS* reverses the viewer's expectations by commanding us to notice the art. BS

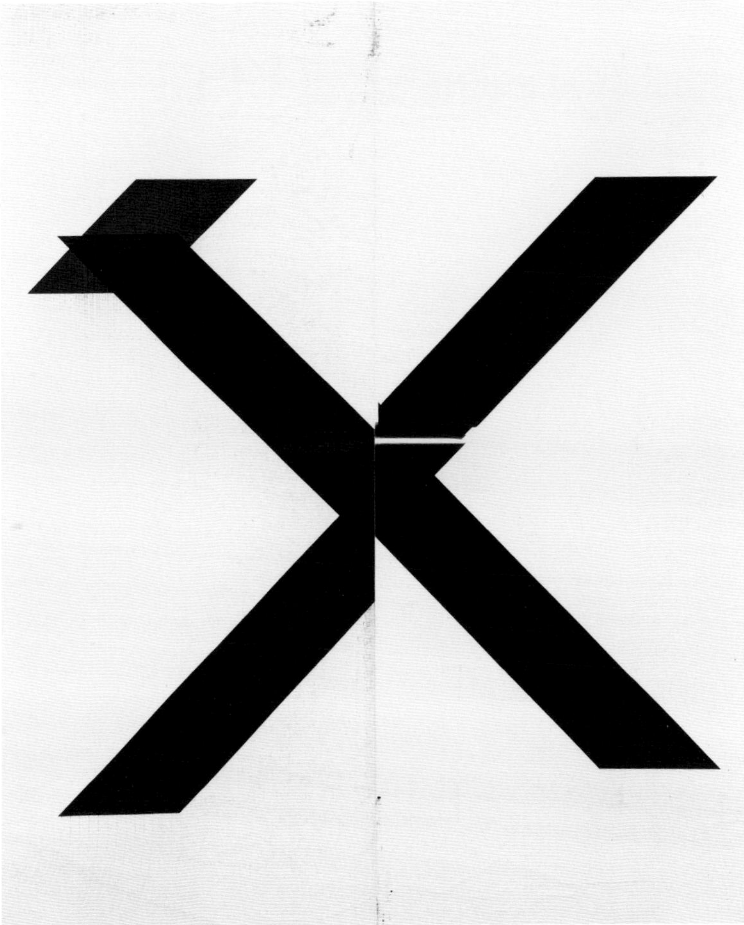

Wade Guyton | Untitled | 2007
Epson UltraChrome inkjet on linen, 213.4 × 175.3 cm, inv. no. GV 187
Acquired 2007 by PIN. Freunde der Pinakothek der Moderne for the Modern Art Collection

The most recent generation of artists has consistently furthered the questioning and redefinition of the process of artistic creation initiated by minimalism and appropriation. In this tradition, Wade Guyton's working materials include primarily cellphones, flatbed scanners, computers, and inkjet printers. His *Printer Paintings* consist of electronic data printed on canvas, which give rise to a new form of painting through their analogue production. The large X shape also calls to mind the censorship or deletion of images. BS

INDEX OF PERSONS

Page numbers presented in bold refer to illustrations.

Abbott, Berenice 100
Abts, Tomma **334**
Adams, Robert 234, 244, **245**
Adler, Jankel 17, **106**
Albers, Josef 21, 176, **178**
Alÿs, Francis 298, **337**
Andre, Carl 20, 176, **181**
Appel, Karel 177
Araki, Nobuyoshi **242**
Arbus, Diane 233
Archipenko, Alexander 59, **64**
Arp, Hans 86, 134
Ataman, Kutluğ **296**, 299, **310**
Atget, Eugène 120
Bach, Johann Sebastian 302, 332
Bacon, Francis 20, 164f, **166f**
Baldessari, John **276**, 282
Baltz, Lewis 234, **241**, 244
Bartana, Yael **331**
Baselitz, Georg 21, 27, 212f, **222**, **225**, 226, 261
Baumeister, Willi 17f
Becher, Bernd 234, 279, **289**
Becher, Hilla 234, 279, **289**
Beckmann, Mathilde (Quappi), née Kaulbach von 108f
Beckmann, Max 16, **17**, 18, 27, 70, **98**, 99, 100f, **102**, **104**, **108–110**, **112**, 149, **156–158**, **161**
Beckmann-Tube, Minna 108
Beham, Barthel 117
Belling, Rudolf 59, **67**
Bellmer, Hans 134
Beltracchi, Wolfgang 9
Bergemann, Sibylle 235, **249**
Bernhard, Thomas 213
Beuys, Joseph **19**, 20f, 22, 27, 163f, **172**, **191**, **202**, 253, **254f**, 314
Biermann, Aenne 120, **122**
Birchler, Alexander 298, **307**
Bleyl, Fritz 41
Blossfeldt, Karl 119f, **123**, 124
Blumenthal, Hermann 164
Boccioni, Cecilia Forlani 62
Boccioni, Umberto **56**, 58f, **62**
Bourgeois, Louise 164, 212
Bowie, David 267
Boyd, William 8, 23f, 27
Branca, Alexander von 7, 13
Braque, Georges 8, 20, 24, 31, 33, 57, **58**, **60**, 61, 63
Brassaï (Gyula Halàsz) **131**
Braune, Heinz 9
Braunfels, Stephan 7
Breton, André 133f, 139, 141
Buchholz, Karl 110
Buchner, Ernst 14f
Burri, Alberto **197**
Cage, John **206**
Campbell, Duncan 298
Camus, Albert 165
Carrà, Carlo 100
Cézanne, Paul 13, 29f, 33, 57
Chillida, Eduardo 7, **8**
Chirico, Giorgio de 100f, 111, 133, **136**
Claerbout, David 298, **300**
Clark, Larry **243**
Claydon, Steven **314**
Corinth, Lovis 13, 16, 71, **83**
Corot, Camille 13, 60
Dahn, Walter 262, **265**
Dalí, Gala 137
Dalí, Salvador 100, **132**, 134f, **137**, 139, 187
Darboven, Hanne **203**
Daumier, Honoré 323
David, Jacques-Louis 147
Davringhausen, Heinrich Maria 20, **75**
Delaunay, Robert 49, 52, 59, **63**
Delvaux, Paul 134
Dehmel, Richard 71, 81
Demand, Thomas 279, **290**
Denis, Maurice 13
Derain, André 31, 33
Dethleffs-Edelmann, Fridel **115**
Devlin, Bernadette 298
Dexel, Walter **90**
Dijkstra, Rineke 298, 306
Dix, Otto 17, 70, 99–101, 113, **114**, 133
Doesburg, Theo van 90
Doig, Peter **312**, 323
Dokoupil, Jiří 261
Dörnhöffer, Friedrich 11, 14
Dostojewski, Fjodor 155
Dubuffet, Jean 177
Duchamp, Marcel 190, 193, 314
Duchamp-Villon, Raymond 70, **73**
Dumas, Marlene **22**
Dürer, Albrecht 7, 27, 286
Eckardt, Annette von 43
Eggleston, William 234, **240**
Eisenhower, Dwight D. 177
Elmgreen & Dragset 314, **320**
Ende, Edgar 16, 134, **142**
Ensor, James 103
Erfurth, Hugo 100, 114
Ernst, Max 18, 134f, 141, **143**, **145**
Essig, Hermann 321
Evans, Walker 233f
Fast, Omer 298
Feininger, Lux 87
Feininger, Lyonel 46, 85, 87, **94**, 100
Felixmüller, Conrad 100
Fischer, Arno 211, 216, 235
Fischli, Peter 298
Flaubert, Gustave 156
Flavin, Dan 20f, **180**, 251, 256
Fohn, Emanuel 14, 17, 43, 114
Fohn, Sofie 14, 17, 43, 114
Fontana, Lucio 195, **198**

Förg, Günther 277, **285**
Franco, Francisco 145
Frank, Robert 233f
Franke, Günther 15, 18, 182
Franz, Duke of Bavaria 20
Freundlich, Otto **92**
Friedlander, Lee 233f, **236**
Friedrich, Caspar David 7
Garnerus, Hartwig 21
Gauguin, Paul 13, 29f, 36
Gebhard, Klaus 18
Geiger, Rupprecht 15
Gertsch, Franz **260**, 262, **269**
Giacometti, Alberto 164
Gilles, Werner 16
Gogh, Vincent van 7, 9, 13f, 29f, 36, 148
Goltz, Hans 42
Götz, K. O. 177
Graham, Dan **237**
Gramatté, Walter 70, **80**
Graßmann, Günther 15, **154**, 155
Grimonprez, Johan 298, **309**
Gris, Juan 18, 58, **65**, 100
Grohmann, Will 86
Große, Doris 39
Grosse, Katharina 313, **335**
Grosz, George 100f, **107**, 113, 133, 155
Gursky, Andreas 227, 277, 279, 287
Gütschow, Beate 324
Guyton, Wade 315, 339
Habermann, Hugo von 13
Hagemeister, Karl 13
Hagen, Theodor 13
Hanfstaengl, Eberhard 15f
Hartlaub, Gustav 100, 133
Hartung, Hans 177, **208**
Hausenstein, Wilhelm 112
Hausmann, Raoul 86
Heckel, Erich 9, 17, **40**, 41–43, 45, **46f**
Heidegger, Martin 165, 321
Heldt, Werner 18
Henri, Florence 120
Herrmann-Neiße, Max 107
Hildebrand, Adolf von 67
Hildesheimer, Wolfgang 213
Hill, Gary 297, **304**
Hirschhorn, Thomas 313, **327**
Hitler, Adolf 14, 97, 147, 212, 224, 290
Hödicke, Karl Horst 261, **264**, 267
Hodler, Ferdinand **28**, 30, **34**
Höfer, Candida 235, 279, **288**
Hofer, Karl 17, **103**, 149, **160**
Holzer, Jenny 262, **271**
Horn, Roni 277, **284**
Hubbard, Teresa 298, **307**
Immendorf, Jörg 21, **210**, 213, **227**, 261
Itten, Johannes 141
Jawlensky, Alexej 17, 69, 165
John of the Cross 187
Johns, Jasper 18, **174**, **189**
Jorn, Asger 177, **185**
Judd, Donald 20, 176, **179**, 252, **258**
Justi, Ludwig 15, 148
Kaesbach, Walter 9
Kandinsky, Wassily 12, 17, 20, 42f., **51**, 69, 86f, 100, 313
Kanoldt, Alexander 14, 100, **113**, 133
Kantor, Tadeusz 22, 212, **229**
Kelley, Mike 263, **275**
Kessler, Harry Graf 99, 101
Kiefer, Anselm 21, **23**, **224**, 212, **228**, 266
Kippenberger, Martin 221, 262, **272**
Kirchner, Ernst Ludwig **12**, 17, 18, 26, 31, **39**, 41–43, **45**, **54f**, **68**, 71, **76**, 100, 264
Klee, Paul 18f, 20, 42, 52, **53**, **84**, 86f, **91**, **93**, **95**, 100
Klein, Astrid 262, **268**
Klein, Jochen 326, **329**
Klenze, Leo von 7
Kline, Franz Josef 20, 176f, 187
Knoebel, Imi 213
Kokoschka, Oskar 16, 18, 71, **79**, 222
Kolle, Helmut 101, **105**
Kooning, Willem de 20, 22, 176, 187, **188**
Koons, Jeff 24
Köpcke, Arthur 193
Kounellis, Jannis **201**
Krull, Germaine 120, **126**
Kruss, Markus 18
Kruss, Martha 18
Kunz, Karl **146**, **159**
Lachnit, Wilhelm **117**
Laib, Wolfgang 253, **250**, **257**
Lasker-Schüler, Else 43, 115
Lassnig, Maria 212, **218**
Léger, Fernand 20, **66**
Lehmbruck, Wilhelm 71, **82**, 99
Leonard, Herbert S. 148
Leonard, Zoe 279, **293**
LeWitt, Sol 20
Lissitzky, El 120
Lohse, Carl 100
Loo, Otto van de 21
Ludwig I, King of Bavaria 12
Lüpertz, Markus 21, 212, **223**, 261
Macke, August 12, 17f, 42, **52**, 69, 99f
Magritte, René 18, 134f, **138**, **144**, 193
Malaparte, Curzio 285
Malevich, Kazimir 164
Man Ray **130**
Manet, Édouard 7, 13f
Manders, Mark 314, **330**
Manguin, Henri **36**
Marc, Franz **10**, 11f, **13**, 14–16, 18, 27, 29, 41–43, 46, **48–50**, 69f, **72**, 99f
Marc, Maria, née Franck 43, 50
Marées, Hans von 27
Maria, Walter de 23, **25**
Marinetti, Filippo Tomaso 58, 69f
Marini, Marino 164, **171**
Masson, André 134
Matisse, Henri 16, 31, 33, **38**, 39, 43
Maximilian I, Holy Roman Emperor 147
Meckel, Christoph 211
Meidner, Ludwig 70, **78**
Melhus, Bjørn 298, **308**
Melzl, Stephan **318**
Metzel, Olaf **317**
Mikhailov, Boris 278, **280**
Miró, Joan 134f, **138**
Modersohn-Becker, Paula 18, 30, **35**, 115
Moholy-Nagy, László 85f, **97**, 119f
Monet, Claude 7, 13
Monk, Jonathan 299
Moore, Henry **18**, 19
Morandi, Giorgio 18, 21, 193, **196**
Mueller, Otto 10, 17, 41, **77**
Mühsam, Erich 150
Munch, Edvard 10, 14, 29–31, **32**

Münter, Gabriele 17
Nauman, Bruce 297, **305**
Nay, Ernst Wilhelm 18, **183**
Neuberger, Fritz 79
Newman, Barnett 22
Nietzsche, Friedrich 41f, 70
Nitsch, Hermann 213, **219**
Nixon, Nicholas 234
Nolde, Emil 17, 41, 43, **44**
Nothhelfer, Gabriele **232**, **246**
Nothhelfer, Helmut **232**, **246**
Odenbach, Marcel **302**
Oehlen, Albert 262, **273**
Oelze, Richard 134, **141**
Ondak, Roman 314, **336**
Palermo 21, **204**, 213
Parr, Martin 278, **281**
Paul, Jean 110
Pechstein, Max 41, 45
Penck, A. R. 21, 213, 227, **231**, 261
Pfeiffer, Paul 299
Picasso, Pablo 8, **16**, 18, 24, 30, **35**, 57f, 60, **61**, 63, 100f, **111**, **140**, 159, 161, 165
Piper, Adrian 262, **270**
Pissarro, Camille 13
Poelzig, Hans 129
Poliakoff, Serge 177, **184**
Polke, Sigmar 21, 212f, **221**, **230**, 261
Pollock, Jackson 177, 187
Protzen, Carl **151**
Purrmann, Hans 17
Räderscheidt, Anton **116**
Radziwill, Franz **152**
Raphael (Raffaello Santi) 27
Rainer, Arnulf 21, 193f, **199**, 213, **215**
Rauch, Neo **322**
Rauschenberg, Robert 18, 190
Rayski, Ferdinand 222
Rembrandt 27
Renger-Patzsch, Albert **118**, 119f, **124f**
Renoir, Auguste 13
Richier, Germaine 164
Richter, Gerhard 21, 211, 213, **214**, **220**, 261
Richter, Käthe 79
Riebesehl, Heinrich 235, **244**
Rist, Pipilotti 297, **328**
Rivers, Larry **186**
Rodin, Auguste 14
Roggan, Ricarda **321**
Rohde, Werner **127**
Rohlfs, Christian 10
Rothko, Marc 22
Rubens, Peter Paul 27
Ruff, Thomas **292**
Ruscha, Ed 234
Sala, Anri 297, **301**
Salomé 261, **267**
Sandback, Fred 20, 252f, **259**
Sander, August **12**, 119, 124, **129**, 298, 311
Saura, Antonio 21, 165, **170**
Saussure, Ferdinand de 135
Scharl, Josef 17, **155**
Scheibitz, Thomas **319**
Schilling, Erna 55
Schilling, Gerda 55
Schlemmer, Oskar 17, 87, **88f**, 100, 116
Schlichter, Rudolf 16
Schmeling, Max 107
Schmidt, Michael 235, 278, **283**, **294**
Schmidt-Rottluff, Karl 10, 17, 31, **37**, 41, 71, **81**
Smith, Patti 262, 269
Schönebeck, Eugen **226**
Schrimpf, Georg 100, 133, **150**, 151
Schürmann, Wilhelm 235, **247**
Scully, Sean **24**
Seidenstücker, Friedrich **128**
Selg, Markus **316**
Serra, Richard 20
Seume, Johann Gottfried 321
Seurat, George 29f
Severini, Gino 59, 70, **74**
Shore, Stephen 234, **239**
Shrigley, David **338**
Soehner, Halldor 21
Soulages, Pierre 20
Speer, Albert 266
Stangl, Etta 18
Stangl, Otto 18
Steichen, Edward 120
Steinert, Otto 244
Stella, Frank **192**, **205**
Sterne, Laurence 282
Stoffel, Eleonore 21
Stoffel, Michael 21
Strigel, Bernhard 147
Ströher, Karl 21
Struth, Thomas 235, 279, **286**
Stuck, Franz von 13
Sugimoto, Hiroshi 279, **291**
Tan, Fiona 298, **311**
Tannert, Volker 262, **266**
Tàpies, Antoni 165, **173**
Tatlin, Vladimir 180
Teniers, David 156
Terragni, Giuseppe 300
Tillmans, Wolfgang **326**
Titian (Tiziano Vecellio) 190
Thatcher, Margaret 278, 281
Thoma, Hans 13
Trockel, Rosemarie 263, **274**
Trübner, Wilhelm 13
Tschudi, Hugo von 9f, 16, 31, 38, 43, 148
Turner, William 27
Tuymans, Luc 314, 325
Twombly, Cy 194, **200**, 213
Tuttle, Richard **21**
Valentin, Curt 110
Vauxcelles, Louis de 31
Vedova, Emilio **169**
Verdier, Fabienne 195, **209**
Vinnen, Carl 148
Viola, Bill 297, **303**
Vlaminck, Maurice de 31
Vuillard, Édouard 13
Wagner, Richard 87
Walden, Herwarth 69
Wall, Jeff **20**, 277–279, **295**
Warhol, Andy **19**, 20, 27, 193, **207**, 220, 314
Wearing, Gillian 314, **333**
Weber, Max 89
Weiss, David 298
Werefkin, Marianne von 69
Werner, Theodor 18, 58, **182**
Werner, Woty 18, 58
Wicki, Bernhard 211, **217**
Wilde, Ann 235, 277
Wilde, Jürgen 235, 277
Winogrand, Garry 233, **238**
Winter, Fritz 17, 86, **96**
Wittgenstein, Ludwig 297, 304
Wols (Alfred Otto Wolfgang Schulze) **162**, 163, **168**, 177
Wormland, Theo 18
Wüst, Ulrich 235, **248**
Zervos, Christian 58
Ziegler, Adolf 86, 147–149, **153**
Żmijewski, Artur 298, **332**
Zwagerman, Joost 24

CREDITS

p. 334 © Tomma Abts, courtesy Galerie Buchholz, Berlin/Köln; p. 245 © Robert Adams courtesy Fraenkel Gallery, San Francisco; p. 178 © The Josef and Anni Albers Foundation/VG Bild-Kunst, Bonn 2025; p. 337 © Francis Alÿs, courtesy Galerie Peter Kilchmann, Zürich; p. 242 © Nobuyoshi Araki, courtesy Galerie Bob van Orsouw, Zürich; p. 296, 310 © Kutluğ Ataman, courtesy Kutluğ Ataman; p. 166/167 © The Estate of Francis Bacon. All rights reserved/VG Bild-Kunst, Bonn 2025; p. 276, 282 © John Baldessari 1990. Courtesy Estate of John Baldessari © 2025 Courtesy John Baldessari Family Foundation; Sprüth Magers; p. 241 © Successors of Lewis Baltz; p. 331 © Annet Gelink Gallery: Yael Bartana; p. 222, 225 © Georg Baselitz 2025; p. 289 © Estate Bernd & Hilla Becher, represented by Max Becher; p. 249 © Sibylle Bergemann/OSTKREUZ; p. 131 © bpk / GrandPalaisRmn / Estate Brassaï; p. 206 © John Cage Trust; p. 243 © Larry Clark: Courtesy of the artist and Luhring Augustine, New York; p. 8 Zabalaga-Leku/VG Bild-Kunst, Bonn 2025; p. 268 © Estate of Walter Dahn / VG Bild-Kunst, Bonn, 2025. Courtesy Sprüth Magers; p. 132, 137 © Salvador Dalí, Fundació Gala-Salvador Dalí/VG Bild-Kunst, Bonn 2025; p. 203 © Hanne Darboven Stiftung, Hamburg/VG Bild-Kunst, Bonn 2025; p. 75 © Renata Davringhausen; p. 25 © The Estate of Walter De Maria; p. 115 © Bernd Riedle; p. 90 © Walter Dexel; p. 306 © Rineke Dijkstra, courtesy Marian Goodman Gallery; p. 22 © Marlene Dumas; p. 240 © Eggleston Artistic Trust,courtesy Gallery Zwirner, New York; p. 142 © Michael Ende Erben/VG Bild-Kunst, Bonn, 2025; p. 180, 256 © Estate of Dan Flavin/VG Bild-Kunst, Bonn 2025; p. 198 © Lucio Fontana by SIAE/VG Bild-Kunst, Bonn 2025; p. 285 © Estate Günther Förg, Suisse/VG Bild-Kunst, Bonn 2025; p. 236 © Lee Friedlander, courtesy Fraenkel Gallery, San Francisco; p. 260, 269 © Franz Gertsch AG; p. 237 © Estate of Dan Graham, courtesy Marian Goodman Gallery; p. 154 © Barbara Pollok/Clemens Pollok; p. 309 © Johan Grimonprez; p. 107 © Estate of George Grosz, Princeton, N.J./VG Bild-Kunst, Bonn 2025; p. 287 © Andreas Gursky/VG Bild-Kunst Bonn 2025. Courtesy Sprüth Magers; p. 339 © Wade Guyton, courtesy Galerie Gisela Capitain, Cologne; p. 40, 46, 47 © Nachlass Erich Heckel, Hemmenhofen; p. 284 © Roni Horn, courtesy the artist and Hauser & Wirth; p. 307 © Teresa Hubbard / Alexander Birchler; p. 210, 227 © The Estate of Jörg Immendorff, Courtesy Galerie Michael Werner Berlin, London & New York; p. 185 © Donation Jorn, Silkeborg/VG Bild-Kunst, Bonn 2025; p. 179, 258 © Judd Foundation/VG Bild-Kunst, Bonn 2025; p. 229 © Tadeusz Kantor © Maria Kantor & Dorota Krakowska; p. 23, 224 © Atelier Anselm Kiefer courtesy Galerie Thaddaeus Ropac; p. 272 © Estate of Martin Kippenberger, Galerie Gisela Capitain, Cologne; p. 268 © Astrid Klein, the artist and courtesy Galerie Sprüth Magers; p. 329 © Family Klein / Wolfgang Tillmans; p. 79 © Fondation Oskar Kokoschka/VG Bild-Kunst, Bonn 2025; p. 188 © The Willem de Kooning Foundation, New York/VG Bild-Kunst, Bonn 2025; p. 126 © Estate Germaine Krull, Museum Folkwang, Essen; p. 146, 159 © Wolfgang Kunz; p. 250, 257 © Wolfgang Laib; p. 218 © Maria Lassnig Foundation; p. 293 © Zoe Leonard, courtesy Galerie Gisela Capitain, Cologne; p. 228 Courtesy Estate Inge Mahn, Photo: Kadel Willborn, Simon Vogel © VG Bild-Kunst, Bonn 2025; p. 130 © Man Ray Trust, Paris/VG Bild-Kunst, Bonn 2025; p. 330 © Mark Manders, courtesy Xavier Hufkens Gallery; p. 78 © Ludwig Meidner-Archive, Jewish Museum Frankfurt; p. 318 © Stephan Melzl; p. 139 © Successió Miró/VG Bild-Kunst, Bonn 2025; p. 18 © Henry Moore Foundation 2025; p. 183 © Elisabeth Nay-Scheibler, Köln/VG Bild-Kunst, Bonn 2025; p. 305 © Bruce Nauman / VG Bild-Kunst, Bonn, 2025; p. 44 © Nolde Stiftung Seebüll; p. 232, 246 © Gabriele und Helmut Nothhelfer, Bonn; p. 273 © Albert Oehlen; p. 141 © Nina Schargorodsky; p. 336 © Roman Ondak; p. 281 © Martin Parr/Magnum Photos/ OSTKREUZ Archiv; p. 16, 35, 61, 111, 140 © Succession Picasso/VG Bild-Kunst, Bonn 2025; p. 270 © Adrian Piper Research Archive Foundation; p. 221, 230 © The Estate of Sigmar Polke, Cologne/VG Bild-Kunst, Bonn 2025; p. 199, 215 © Courtesy Atelier Arnulf Rainer; p. 322 © Neo Rauch, courtesy Galerie EIGEN + ART Leipzig/Berlin und Zwirner, New York/London/VG Bild-Kunst, Bonn 2025; p. 190 © Robert Rauschenberg Foundation/ VG Bild-Kunst, Bonn 2025; p. 118, 124, 125: Albert Renger-Patzsch/Archiv Ann und Jürgen Wilde, Zülpich/VG Bild-Kunst, Bonn, 2025; p. 214, 220 © Gerhard Richter 2025 (20082025); p. 328 © courtesy the artist, Hauser & Wirth, London und Luhring Augustine, New York; p. 321 © courtesy Galerie EIGEN + ART Leipzig/Berlin/VG Bild-Kunst, Bonn 2025; p. 259 © 2025 Fred Sandback Archive; p. 12, 129 © Die Photographische Sammlung/SK Stiftung Kultur – August Sander Archiv, Köln/VG Bild-Kunst, Bonn 2025; p. 155 © Susanne Fiegel; p. 319 © Atelier Thomas Scheibitz; p. 283, 294 © Stiftung für Fotografie und Medienkunst mit Archiv Michael Schmidt; p. 247 © Wilhelm Schürmann; p. 24 © Sean Scully; p. 128 © bpk-Fotoarchiv / Friedrich Seidenstücker; p. 316 © Markus Selg, courtesy Galerie Christine Mayer, München; p. 239 © Stephen Shore, courtesy Galerie Sprüth Magers, London; p. 286 © Thomas Struth; p. 291 © Hiroshi Sugimoto; p. 311 © Fiona Tan; p. 173 © Fondation Antoni Tapies Barcelona/VG Bild-Kunst, Bonn 2025; p. 21 © Richard Tuttle, courtesy Pace Gallery; p. 325 © Luc Tuymans, courtesy David Zwirner, New York/London; p. 200 © Cy Twombly Foundation; p. 169 © Fondazione Emilio e Annabianca Vedova, Venice; p. 303 © Bill Viola Studio; p. 209 © Fabienne Verdier; p. 20, 295 © Courtesy Jeff Wall; p. 19, 207 © 2025 The Andy Warhol Foundation for the Visual Arts, Inc. / Licensed by Artists Rights Society (ARS), New York; p. 333 © Gillian Wearing, courtesy Maureen Paley, London; p. 182 © Bayerische Staatsgemäldesammlungen; p. 217 © Elisabeth Wicki Endriss; p. 238 © The Estate of Garry Winogrand, courtesy Fraenkel Gallery, San Francisco; p. 248 © Ulrich Wüst; p. 332 © Arthur Zmijewski, Galerie Peter Kilchmann, Zürich | VG Bild-Kunst, Bonn 2025: p. 8, 12, 16, 17, 33, 35, 37, 60, 61, 64, 66, 67, 74, 79, 81, 94, 96, 98, 102, 103, 104, 106, 107, 108, 109, 110, 111, 112, 114, 116, 118, 124, 125, 127, 129, 130, 132, 136, 137, 138, 139, 140, 143, 144, 145, 152, 156, 158, 160, 161,162, 166/167, 168, 171, 172, 173, 174, 178, 179, 180, 181, 183, 184, 185, 186, 187, 188, 189, 190, 191, 192, 196, 197, 198, 201, 202, 203, 204, 205, 208, 216, 219, 221, 223, 226, 228, 230, 231, 244, 254/255, 256, 258, 264, 266, 267, 271, 274, 275, 280, 285, 287,288, 290, 292, 300, 301, 302, 304, 306, 308, 312, 317, 320, 321, 322, 323, 324, 326, 327, 335, 338
Photos: © Bayerische Staatsgemäldesammlungen: Haydar Koyupinar, Sibylle Forster, Margarita Platis, Nicole Wilhelms, Johannes Haslinger, Bruno Hartinger; © Wilfried Petzi; © Rony Vissers (for Johan Grimonprez)

IMPRINT

Bayerische Staatsgemäldesammlungen Munich
Director: Anton Biebl
Director of Collections, Sammlung Moderne Kunst
in der Pinakothek der Moderne: Oliver Kase

Editor: Bernhard Maaz
Editing: Christine Kramer, Benjamin Sommer and Angela Cornelius
Image Rights: Beatrice Anacker, Birgit Keller, Christine Kramer and Nano Ninobashvili
Contributions: Judith Csiki (JC), Nadine Engel (NE), Simone Förster (SF), Inka Graeve Ingelmann (IGI), Verena Hein (VH), Oliver Kase (OK), Bernhard Maaz (BM), Bernhart Schwenk (BS), Benjamin Sommer (BSO), Franziska Stöhr (FS), Corinna Thierolf (CT) and Anna Volz (AV)

Translation into English: Büro LS Anderson, Berlin
Graphic and Typesetting: Angelika Bardou, Deutscher Kunstverlag
Production: Anja Haering, Deutscher Kunstverlag
Reproductions: Birgit Gric, Deutscher Kunstverlag
Printing and Binding: Gutenberg Beuys, Langenhagen

Cover image: Franz Marc, Der Mandrill (The Mandrill), p. 49 (detail)

Bibliographic information published by the Deutsche Nationalbibliothek
The Deutsche Nationalbibliothek lists this publication in the Deutsche Nationalbibliografie; detailed bibliographic data are available at http://dnb.dnb.de.

Barer Straße 29
D-80799 Munich
www.pinakothek.de

Deutscher Kunstverlag
An Imprint of Walter de Gruyter GmbH Berlin Boston
Genthiner Str. 13
10785 Berlin

www.deutscherkunstverlag.de
www.degruyterbrill.com
Questions about General Product Safety Regulation:
productsafety@degruyterbrill.com

ISBN 978-3-422-80345-9